D1559044

Liaisons

Liaisons

Philosophy Meets the Cognitive
and Social Sciences

Alvin I. Goldman

A Bradford Book
The MIT Press
Cambridge, Massachusetts
London, England

This book was set in Palatino by Asco Trade Typesetting Ltd., Hong Kong and printed and bound in the United States of America.

Library of Congress Cataloging-in-Publication Data
Goldman, Alvin I., 1938–
  Liaisons : philosophy meets the cognitive and social sciences /
  Alvin I. Goldman.
      p.   cm.
  "A Bradford book."
  Includes bibliographical references and index.
  ISBN 0-262-07135-5
  1. Philosophy and cognitive science. 2. Knowledge, Theory of.
3. Knowledge, Sociology of. 4. Philosophy and social sciences.
I. Title.
B945.G593L52   1991
120—dc20   91-18905
                                                    CIP

Contents

Acknowledgments

1. "Interpretation Psychologized" first appeared in *Mind & Language* 4 (1989), 161–185. Reprinted, with revisions, by permission of the publisher, Basil Blackwell.

2. "Metaphysics, Mind, and Mental Science" first appeared in *Philosophical Topics* 17 (1989), 131–145. Reprinted by permission of *Philosophical Topics*.

3. "Cognition and Modal Metaphysics" appears here for the first time.

4. "A Causal Theory of Knowing" first appeared in *The Journal of Philosophy* 64 (1967), 357–372. Reprinted by permission of *The Journal of Philosophy*.

5. "Discrimination and Perceptual Knowledge" first appeared in *The Journal of Philosophy* 73 (1976), 771–791. Reprinted by permission of *The Journal of Philosophy*.

6. "What Is Justified Belief?" first appeared in George Pappas, ed., *Justification and Knowledge* (1979), published by D. Reidel. Reprinted by permission of Kluwer Academic Publishers.

7. "Strong and Weak Justification" first appeared in *Philosophical Perspectives, 2, Epistemology, 1988* edited by James E. Tomberlin (copyright by Ridgeview Publishing Co., Atascadero, CA). Reprinted by permission of Ridgeview Publishing Company.

8. "Psychology and Philosophical Analysis" first appeared in *Proceedings of the Aristotelian Society* 89 (1989), 195–209. Reprinted by permission of The Aristotelian Society.

9. "Epistemic Folkways and Scientific Epistemology" appears here for the first time.

10. "Foundations of Social Epistemics" first appeared in *Synthese* 73 (1987), 109–144. Reprinted by permission of Kluwer Academic Publishers.

11. "Epistemic Paternalism: Communication Control in Law and Society" first appeared in *The Journal of Philosophy* 88 (1991), 113–131. Reprinted by permission of *The Journal of Philosophy*.

12. "An Economic Model of Scientific Activity and Truth Acquisition" first appeared in *Philosophical Studies* 63 (1991), 31–55. Reprinted by permission of Kluwer Academic Publishers.

13. "Toward a Theory of Social Power" first appeared in *Philosophical Studies* 23 (1972), 221–268. Reprinted by permission of Kluwer Academic Publishers.

14. "On the Measurement of Power" first appeared in *The Journal of Philosophy* 71 (1974), 231–252. Reprinted by permission of *The Journal of Philosophy*.

Introduction

Types of Interfaces between Philosophy and the Cognitive and Social Sciences

In the last twenty-five years philosophers have established increasingly intimate relations with neighboring disciplines. Moral and social philosophers regularly exchange ideas with economists, political theorists, medical practitioners, and lawyers. Philosophers of science confer not only with physicists, biologists, and mathematicians but also with historians and sociologists of science. Philosophers of mind and language have eroded or obliterated old boundary lines and pursue ongoing collaboration with psychologists, linguists, neuroscientists, and artificial intelligencers. In almost all of these fields, new journals have sprung up that publish a burgeoning cross-disciplinary literature.

Do these developments create an identity crisis for philosophy? They certainly make philosophy harder, and often more specialized. Still, they are an occasion for satisfaction rather than anxiety. As healthy responses to genuine intellectual forces, they increase the fertility and excitement of philosophy. They also return philosophy to the position it occupied in its most significant historical periods. The giants of ancient philosophy had no fear of intellectual borders; and philosophical developments of the seventeenth and eighteenth centuries were thoroughly interwoven with the scientific advances and political ideas of their day.

This volume of essays is not a survey of philosophy's interdisciplinary activities. Nor does it purport to be representative of the ways philosophy intersects with the cognitive and social sciences. It is, rather, a partial record of how one philosopher has been driven by the "logic" of philosophical problems toward questions and perspectives that occupy cognitive and social scientists. It tries to chart new paths of disciplinary interchange, not just map the old. Often it is absorbed with the basic rationale and structure for such interchange, acknowledging that detailed developments lie in the future. Many of these essays address two fields of philosophy—epistemology and metaphysics—that were traditionally seen as *purely* philosophical, untainted by messy empirical facts and free of the paradigms and pursuits of empirical science. That is not the scenario I envisage for these fields. Even epistemology and metaphysics, properly conceptualized, would invite contributions from empirical disciplines.

To clarify the lines of disciplinary convergence that guide these essays, it will help to distinguish three types of interfaces between philosophy and the cognitive and social sciences. The philosopher can relate to these sciences as a contributor, a methodological critic, or a consumer. I shall illustrate these relations first for the cognitive sciences and then the social sciences.

Philosophy has *contributed* to cognitive science (often serendipitously rather than deliberately) by the creation of intellectual tools and the identification of agenda-setting topics. Various branches of logic and styles of semantical theory are examples of intellectual tools in widespread use within AI and linguistics. Major topics that originated with philosophy but are now the concern of linguistics and the theory of natural language understanding include predication, reference, quantification, modality, indexicals, presupposition, propositional attitudes, and speech act theory. Another central type of contribution by philosophy concerns the conceptual foundations of cognitive science. Whereas Cartesianism erected barriers to the empirical investigation of the mind, and behaviorism imposed narrow restraints on mental theorizing, the functionalist-computationalist model of mental states developed by Putnam, Fodor, and others provided a friendly conceptual underpinning for cognitivism.

The second role for philosophy is *methodological criticism*. This is a stance philosophers of science take toward any science. What are the legitimate theoretical constructs of the science, they often ask, and what is their ontological status? What are the kinds of research programs in the science, and how do they mesh with programs at higher or lower levels of analysis? In philosophy of cognitive science, these questions have centered on propositional attitude constructs and theories. Are belief and desire appropriate concepts for cognitive science, or should they be eliminated from a mature science of the mind-brain? If they should be retained, should they be construed "realistically" or "instrumentalistically"? Should they be used as full-fledged semantical concepts, or treated merely "syntactically"? Is the symbolic level of theorizing a really fruitful level, or are mental processes best studied at the neurological (or "abstract neurological") level? What are the promises and accomplishments of the connectionist research program in cognitive science?

When philosophers speak of "philosophy and cognitive science", these are the topics that leap most readily to mind. Yet these are not the topics that occupy this volume, even in the chapters that intersect with cognitive science. The present essays are not devoted to methodological critique. The foregoing are questions in the philosophy *of* cognitive science; but that is not part of this book's agenda.

The main mission of these essays (those relating to cognitive science) falls in the third category: the consumer relationship. They try to show

how various branches of philosophy can apply the findings and theories of cognitive science. The emphasis, then, is not on a critical appraisal of results in cognitive science but on the philosophical uses to which such results might be put. Of course, we only want to use results or theories that are true; so an appraisal of their epistemic merits is in order. But these essays mostly focus on a prior question: supposing that cognitive science can discover certain facts about the human mind, how would these facts impinge on this or that philosophical endeavor? Various philosophical problems cannot be properly addressed, I contend, without the help of empirical research in psychology or other cognitive sciences.

Chapter 1 argues for this perspective in the philosophy of mind, more specifically, for the question of how mental states (especially the attitudes) are ascribed to other people. The core question here is, What is our (ordinary) concept of a mental state? Third-person ascription of such states has seemed particularly problematic on some accounts of our mental concepts, and this has led to behaviorist, functionalist, and charity (or rationality) theories, which ostensibly accommodate third-person ascription tolerably well. But are these theories, I ask, psychologically realistic? Do people really use a functionalist concept of mind in attributing mental states to others? Do they really impose rationality requirements in interpreting others? Even philosophers who are otherwise well disposed toward cognitivism have typically addressed these issues purely a priori, without conceptualizing them as empirical questions. But if we conceptualize them as questions about the psychological and linguistic activity of cognizers, then the questions are readily seen as (broadly) empirical in nature.

This does not mean, of course, that empirical psychologists have already investigated precisely these questions in (satisfactory) detail. In fact, I do adduce a few specimens of relevant psychology, including some developmental psychology, where this sort of question has begun to be explored. At this point in time, however, recourse must be taken to thought-experiments, at least as a temporary expedient. It is also crucial to notice that since these questions have been largely neglected by psychologists (until recently), they have not framed many hypotheses for testing. Indeed, it is a principal contribution of philosophy to have formulated and reflected on several such hypotheses. Chapter 1 advances a simulation hypothesis, which resembles the "empathy" or "Verstehen" approach endorsed by numerous philosophers since the eighteenth century. Thus, it exemplifies not only the third but also the first type of interface between philosophy and cognitive science: philosophy acting as contributor to cognitive science.

Chapters 2 and 3 advance a conception of metaphysics in which inputs from cognitive science would play an active role. These essays distinguish two branches of metaphysics: descriptive and prescriptive. Descriptive metaphysics seeks to describe and explain our "folk ontology"—the basic categories and concepts deployed in representing and understanding the world. This task can certainly be viewed as a joint venture between philosophy, psychology, and linguistics. Even prescriptive metaphysics, moreover, can benefit from cognitive science. As we learn how cognitive structure shapes or influences such elements of our ontological scheme as object-unity, color, time, and modality, we find it necessary to reconfigure our naive ontology into a more sophisticated one.

The third topic illustrating the philosophy/cognitive science interface is (individual) epistemology. I have treated this interface at length in *Epistemology and Cognition* (Goldman 1986). The central thesis is that epistemic achievements like knowledge and justified belief critically hinge on the use of suitable psychological processes. Since the repertoire of processes available to the human cognizer can only be disclosed through empirical research, epistemology should work hand-in-hand with cognitive science.

In the present context, 'psychological processes' refers to events that cause beliefs. In the not-so-distant past, causal questions were banned from epistemology. Epistemic status was equated with evidential status, which was thought to arise purely from deductive and inductive relations among propositions. To worry about causes was to commit the 'genetic fallacy'. Chapters 4 and 5 played a role—I like to think a substantial role—in changing people's opinions about this (although, of course, not everyone's opinion has changed). Chapter 6 went on to assign central status to 'cognitive processes', invoking them in the account of 'justification' and not merely of 'knowledge'. Although chapters 4, 5, and 6 provide a rationale for incorporating psychology into epistemology, detailed pursuit of this program occurs in chapters 8 and 9. The latter essays not only emulate *Epistemology and Cognition* in its use of psychology but advance beyond it in applying psychology to study the epistemic *evaluator* as well as the epistemic *agent*.

Let us turn now to the relations between philosophy and social science. The same classification scheme introduced earlier will serve us here as well. Philosophy can either contribute to social science, make methodological assessments of social science, or consume the products of social science. 'Consumption' would include the application of social science's models, paradigms, or research findings to various and sundry philosophical ends.

Philosophers standardly address the social sciences as methodological critics. They debate whether social science should be methodologically akin to natural science or methodologically distinct. What is the proper role of experimentation in social science? Are there distinctive forms of explanation in the human sciences—rational or meaningful explanation—that contrast with nomological explanation? What is the proper theoretical perspective for social science: "holist" or "methodological individualist"?

There is only a little in this volume that addresses these questions, and this appears in chapter 1, not in the main "social" essays of parts III and IV. Chapter 1 gives a modern reconstruction of "empathetic," non-nomic explanation of human action, lending support to one party in the dispute over explanation. (However, it does not *exclude* nomic explanation of human action.) Moreover, this reconstruction of Verstehen has already been fruitfully applied by one economist to economic theory (Bacharach 1989). However, the main "social" parts of this book—parts III and IV—are not concerned with the standard methodological issues in the philosophy of social science.

A second arena of intense interaction among philosophers and social scientists is a wide gamut of normative subjects: political theory, social theory, and moral theory. Not only have philosophers contributed to the distinctively philosophical aspects of these subjects but their work has often contributed to mainstream social science. Major historical examples are Condorcet, Mill, and Marx. On the contemporary scene, influence flows in both directions. Welfare economists pay heed to what social philosophers say about justice, and social philosophers utilize analytical tools created by economists and political scientists. Philosophical applications of game theory, social choice theory, and bargaining theory are legion. The adequacy of market mechanisms and the problem of 'public goods' are additional topics of significant philosophical interest.

Part IV falls into the arena of political theory, although more 'positive' than 'normative' political theory. The two essays in this part develop a theoretical analysis of social power. This is an instance, then, of philosophy *contributing* to social science. Even in these essays, however, there is considerable *consumption* of the social science literature. Earlier investigations of power by political scientists are examined and utilized, and one tool of analysis is borrowed from social choice theory (the notion of a "decisive set").

Part III intersects with social science in developing a relatively new and unorthodox topic: social epistemology. According to my conception of epistemology, one branch of the subject—social epistemics—should study interpersonal practices and social institutions that influence belief formation (chapter 10). This conception agrees with recent historians and sociologists of science in their emphasis on the social dimensions of science. Unlike most of those practitioners, however, I favor normative objectivism, which takes seriously the goals of truth acquisition and error avoidance. Moreover, I do not restrict attention to science. Institutional practices in many social domains, including law, education, advertising, and the media, are potential targets of social-epistemological investigation (chapter 11). The study of these institutional practices cannot, of course, be purely a priori; it will inevitably appeal at certain junctures to empirical findings. Thus, social epistemology must be a joint venture among philosophers and social scientists, just as individual epistemology should be a joint venture among philosophers and cognitive scientists.

Social epistemology can profit not only from the findings of social science about particular institutional arrangements but also from its models and paradigms, especially those of economics. This is best illustrated by chapter 12, which explores an 'invisible hand' approach to truth acquisition in science. Assume that scientists and other professional inquirers are motivated to advance their personal reputations; assume that this motive guides their research. Can this self-interested motivation promote the community's discovery and possession of truth? Chapter 12 shows that under specified circumstances the credit-seeking motive does indeed promote truth possession (though not quite as efficiently, in the class of cases investigated, as "pure," truth-seeking motivation).

The multidisciplinary theme I have just outlined is the central unifying theme of this volume, but not the only one; several themes unify smaller segments of the book. Part II, for example, provides the record of my approach to naturalistic epistemology that has evolved steadily from 1967 to the present. Parts II and III together articulate and illustrate a wider naturalistic conception of epistemology (or epistemics), embracing the social as well as the psychological. An emphasis on truth-linked evaluation pervades almost all of these epistemology papers. Finally, a more recent theme links Chapters 2, 3, and 9. This is the idea that both metaphysics and epistemology should distinguish their descriptive and prescriptive missions. Conflation of descriptive and prescriptive questions creates confusion, whereas systematic differentiation of these questions can promote considerable progress.

Each chapter has its own note of thanks to the individuals who helped me with its ideas or formulation. But only one person, Holly Smith, has given me extensive comments on almost all of the papers. Her invaluable help, both philosophical and stylistic, both critical and constructive, has averted many errors and led to numerous improvements.

Part I
Mind and Metaphysics

Chapter 1
Interpretation Psychologized

A central problem of philosophy of mind is the nature of mental states, or the truth-conditions for the ascription of such states. Especially problematic are the propositional attitudes: beliefs, desires, and so forth. One popular strategy for attacking these problems is to examine the practice of speakers in ascribing these states, especially to others. What principles or procedures guide or underlie the ascriber's activity? In identifying such principles or procedures, one hopes to glean the criteria or satisfaction conditions of the mentalistic predicates (or something like this). Now the ascription of the attitudes involves the assignment of some sort of 'content' or 'meaning' to the mind, which can be seen as a kind of 'interpretation' of the agent or his behavior. (It is also related, on many theories, to the interpretation of the agent's utterances.) Thus, ascription of mental states, especially the attitudes, can be thought of as a matter of interpretation; and the strategy of studying the interpreter, in order to extract the conditions of mentality, or propositional attitudehood, may be called the *interpretation strategy*. I do not assume here that this strategy will or can succeed. Nonetheless, its popularity, if nothing else, makes it worthy of investigation.

The aim of this paper, then, is to study interpretation, specifically, to work toward an account of interpretation that seems descriptively and explanatorily correct. No account of interpretation can be philosophically helpful, I submit, if it is incompatible with a correct account of what people actually do when they interpret others. My question, then, is: how does the (naive) interpreter arrive at his/her judgments about the mental attitudes of others? Philosophers who have addressed this question have not, in my view, been sufficiently psychological, or cognitivist, even those who are otherwise psychologically inclined. I shall defend some proposals about the activity of interpretation that are, I believe, psychologically more realistic than their chief competitors.

In the very posing of my question—how does the interpreter arrive at attributions of propositional attitudes (and other mental states)—I assume that the attributor herself has contentful states, at least beliefs. Since I am not trying to prove (to the skeptic) that there is content, this is not circular or question-begging. I assume as background that the interpreter has beliefs, and I inquire into a distinctive subset of them, viz., beliefs concerning mental states. It is conceivable, of course, that a proper theory of interpretation, together with certain ontological assumptions, would undermine the ontological legitimacy of beliefs. This is a prospect to which we should, in principle, stay alert, though it is not one that will actively concern me here. I shall proceed on the premise that the interpreter has beliefs. Indeed, it is hard to see how to investigate the problem without that assumption.

Since I am prepared to explain the interpreter's activity in terms of contentful states, I am obviously not attempting to give a purely 'naturalistic' theory of interpretation, i.e., a theory that makes no appeal to semantical notions. Interpretation theorists standardly hope to extract naturalistic truth-conditions for the presence of content. I take it to be an open question, however, whether the interpretation strategy can yield such fruit.

I structure the discussion in terms of three types of interpretation theories. Two of these have tended to dominate the field: (1) rationality, or charity, theories, and (2) folk-theory theories. According to the first approach, an attributor A operates on the assumption that the agent in question, S, is rational, i.e., conforms to an ideal or normative model of proper inference and choice. The attributor seeks to assign to S a set of contentful states that fits such a normative model. According to the second approach, the attributor somehow acquires a commonsense or folk psychological theory of the mental, containing nomological generalizations that relate stimulus inputs to certain mental states, mental states to other mental states, and some mental states to behavioral outputs. She then uses this theory to infer, from stimulus inputs and behavioral outputs, what states S is in. The related doctrine of analytical functionalism asserts that our commonsense mentalistic predicates are implicitly *defined* in terms of this commonsense psychological theory.[1] The third approach, which I shall defend, is the simulation theory. This approach has been placed in the field but has not received sustained development, and is not yet sufficiently appreciated.[2]

II

The most widely discussed version of the charity approach is that of Donald Davidson (1980, 1984). Actually, Davidson's approach to interpretation involves three strands. First, there is a compositional postulate for assigning meanings to the agent's whole utterances as a function of the meanings of their parts. Second, there is a charity principle that enjoins the interpreter (ceteris paribus) to assign belief states to the agent so as to maximize (or optimize) the proportion of truths in the agent's belief set.

Third, there is the rationality principle that enjoins the interpreter (ceteris paribus) to assign beliefs and desires so as to maximize the agent's rationality. Another prominent specimen of the rationality approach is that of Daniel Dennett (1971, 1987a). Dennett's 'intentional stance' is a method of attributing intentional states by first postulating ideal rationality on the part of the target system, and then trying to predict and/or explain the system's behavior in terms of such rationality.

I shall say nothing here about Davidson's compositional postulate. But a brief comment on his truthfulness principle is in order before turning to more extended discussion of rationality. Davidson holds that one constraint on interpretation precludes the possibility of ascribing 'massive' or 'preponderant' error (by the interpreter's lights) to the interpretee. In an early essay he writes: 'A theory of interpretation cannot be correct that makes a man assent to very many false sentences: it must generally be the case that a sentence is true when a speaker holds it to be' (Davidson 1984, p. 168). And in a more recent essay he says: 'Once we agree to the general method of interpretation I have sketched, it becomes impossible correctly to hold that anyone could be mostly wrong about how things are' (Davidson 1986, p. 317). These contentions, however, are dubious. Along with Colin McGinn (1977) I have presented examples of possible cases in which it seems natural to ascribe to an agent a set of beliefs that are largely, in fact predominantly, false (Goldman 1986, pp. 175–176). Furthermore, if Davidson were right in this matter, one could dismiss the intelligibility of radical skepticism out of hand; but it seems implausible that principles of interpretation should have this result (see McGinn 1986). There are at least two sorts of context in which an attributor, A, will assign beliefs to an agent, S, which are false by A's lights: first, where S is exposed to misleading evidence, and second, where S uses poor inductive methods such as hasty generalization, or inferential maxims such as 'Believe whatever your cult leader tells you'. These points are stressed by David Lewis in his own theory of interpretation (Lewis 1983a).

Let us turn to the rationality component of Davidson's charity approach, a component common to many writers. For the rationality principle to have substance, there must be some specification of the norms of rationality. While few writers say precisely how these norms are to be chosen or fixed, there seems to be wide agreement that they are derived from a priori models of ideal rationality, models inspired by formal logic, by the calculus of probability, and/or by Bayesian decision theory (or its ilk). Even so, there is room for stronger and weaker norms. Dennett often imputes to the intentional stance the component of deductive closure. Davidson usually illustrates rationality with the weaker norm of logical consistency. Let us test the rationality approach by reference to logical consistency and probabilistic coherence. Do interpreters impose these norms in making interpretations? I shall argue in the negative.

Consider a paradox-of-the-preface example. My friend Hannah has just completed a book manuscript. She says that although she is fully confident of each sentence in her book, taken singly, she is also convinced of her own fallibility, and so believes that at least one of her claims is false. At least this is how she *reports* her beliefs to me. But if these were indeed Hannah's beliefs, she would be guilty of believing each of a logically inconsistent set of propositions. Now if the consistency norm were part of our ordinary interpretation procedure, an interpreter would try, other things equal, to avoid ascribing to Hannah all the beliefs she ostensibly avows. Understood as a description of interpretive practice, the rationality approach 'predicts' that interpreters confronted with Hannah's avowals will try to find a way to assign a slightly different set of beliefs than Hannah seems to endorse. Interpreters will feel some 'pressure', some prima facie reason, to revise their belief imputation to be charitable to Hannah. Of course, as Davidson admits, other constraints on interpretation, e.g., the compositional meaning constraint, might make a revision too costly. So an interpreter might settle for imputing inconsistency after all. But some vector will be exerted to avoid the imputation.

Does this approach accord with the facts? Speaking as one interpreter, I would feel no temptation to avoid ascribing the inconsistent belief set to Hannah. And I submit that other everyday interpreters would similarly feel no such temptation. Admittedly, if Hannah said that she recognized she was being inconsistent, but still believed all these things anyway, many people might feel something is amiss. Recognition of inconsistency can be expected to breed caution. But let us suppose that Hannah shows no sign of recognizing the inconsistency. Surely, an ordinary interpreter would have no qualms in attributing an inconsistent belief set to her.

An analogous example is readily produced for the norm of probabilistic coherence. Suppose my friend Jeremy has just been the subject of a probability experiment by the psychologists Amos Tversky and Daniel Kahneman (1983). In this experiment, Jeremy is given a thumbnail sketch of someone called 'Linda', who is described as having majored in philosophy in college, as having been concerned with issues of social justice, and having participated in an anti-nuclear demonstration. Subjects are then asked to rate the probabilities that Linda is now involved in certain vocations or avocations. Like so many other subjects, Jeremy rates the probability of Linda being both a bank teller and a feminist higher than he rates the probability of Linda being a bank teller. But these comparative probability judgments violate the probability calculus: it is impossible for any conjunctive event A and B to be more probable than either of its conjuncts. So if I accept the coherent probabilities norm of interpretation, my duty is to try to reassign contents so as to avoid the indicated imputations to Jeremy.[3]

Again, as one interpreter, I report feeling no such duty. There seems nothing even prima facie wrong about attributing to Jeremy this set of probability assignments, despite their incoherence. I feel no reason to seek a revised interpretation. So this norm must not in fact play its alleged role in interpretation.[4]

Perhaps the rationality approach should be weakened, so that it no longer imposes ideal rationality as the norm for attitude attribution. Christopher Cherniak (1986, p. 10) suggests that a better rationality condition is that an agent must display minimal deductive ability; he must make *some*, but not necessarily all, of the sound inferences from his belief set. As a condition for attitude attribution, this is certainly an improvement over an ideal deductive requirement. But Cherniak's purely existential requirement is too vague. It cannot yield any definite predictive or explanatory inferences that an interpreter would make about an agent's beliefs.

Another variant of the rationality approach might say that interpreters expect agents to make 'obvious' inferences. But obvious to whom? To the interpreter? What is obvious to one interpreter is not necessarily obvious to another. So the rationality approach could no longer maintain that a single set of rationality principles constrain the ascription of the attitudes. Alternatively, there might be an attempt to derive obviousness from pure logic. But this is unpromising; obviousness is a psychological, not a logical, notion. Perhaps the rationality theorist should abandon any attempt to distill norms of rationality from logic, probability theory, decision theory, and the like. Perhaps the norms should be distilled from actual human practices of inference and choice (see L. J. Cohen 1981 and Pollock 1986).

There are two problems with this approach. Experimental findings strongly suggest that human agents think in ways that contravene widely accepted norms. They often commit the so-called gambler's fallacy; in making choices, they commonly flout the 'sure-thing' principle (as Allais's paradox shows); and when it comes to deductive inference, they display a number of failings.[5] It is doubtful, therefore, whether actual practice can establish norms of rationality. Secondly, it is dubious that the naive interpreter has an accurate reflective grasp of actual practice. But it is precisely the interpretive practice of naive agents that we seek to illuminate.

Assuming that correct norms of rationality can somehow be identified, is it psychologically plausible to suppose that ordinary interpreters appeal to such norms in making (or constraining) their interpretations? Untrained adults are not generally acquainted with abstract principles like maximizing expected utility, or the sure-thing principle, or probabilistic coherence. Furthermore, we should bear in mind that children display interpretive skills quite early, at least by age four, five, or six. It stretches credulity to suppose that such children employ any of the abstract precepts that ratio-nality theorists commonly adduce. Thus, if we seek to extract principles of interpretation from the psychological determinants of ordinary interpretive practice, norms of rationality do not look promising.

It may be replied that although children lack any explicitly formulated concept of rationality, or any articulated principles of reasoning, they do have de facto patterns of reasoning that govern their own cognitive behav-ior. Perhaps they simply apply those same tacit patterns in interpreting others. This indeed strikes me as a plausible hypothesis. But it is, in effect, a statement of the simulation approach that I shall be advocating shortly.

III

I turn next to the folk-theory approach to interpretation. Here again one must wonder whether naive interpreters, including children, really possess the sorts of principles or commonsense nomological generalizations that this approach postulates, and whether such principles are indeed applied in (all) their interpretive practice.

At least three sorts of problems face the theory theory: vagueness, inaccuracy, and non-universality. When philosophers try to formulate the laws, their examples are typically larded with ceteris paribus clauses. This vagueness is a problem because it is hard to see how an interpreter could draw any reasonably definite interpretive conclusion using laws so vague. How could they tell when the ceteris paribus clauses are satisfied? Yet interpreters frequently do manage to make quite definite assignments of desires and beliefs. The second problem, the problem of accuracy, arises as follows. It is important for analytical functionalism that the laws be reason-ably accurate. If the names of mental states work like theoretical terms, especially in the Ramsey-sentence account of theoretical terms, they do not name anything unless the theory (the cluster of laws) in which they appear is more or less *true* (see Lewis 1983b and 1972). It is doubtful, however, that ordinary interpreters do possess laws that are true. Third, the standard version of this approach assumes that a single set of laws or platitudes is shared by all competent users of mentalistic vocabulary. But this universali-ty assumption is very dubious.

As Stephen Schiffer (1987, chap. 2) argues, perceptual input conditions may be in the worst shape on these scores. If people really possess laws that relate perceptual input conditions to perceptual beliefs, there must be some way of filling out a schema like "If there is a red block in front of x and ..., then x will believe that there is a red block in front of x"; and it must be filled out so that it is true and really possessed by all competent speakers. But it is unlikely that this requirement is satisfied. Can *any* ordinary speaker complete this schema so that it yields a truth? (Notice that the gap has to be filled with conditions entailing that x is "well enough" sighted, is not colorblind, is sober and undrugged, etc.). It is doubtful, moreover, that *all* speakers who possess the concept of belief share the *same* perceptual input laws. A blind person, for example, may grasp the concept of belief perfectly well, but not possess the same laws of visual input as sighted people.

The accuracy problem also looms large for internal functional laws, including laws that putatively link certain desires and beliefs with further desires. One of the favorite sorts of platitudes offered by philosophers is something like "If x believes 'p only if q' and x desires p, then x desires q". But the relationship formulated by this 'platitude' simply does not systematically obtain. It ignores the fact that merely dispositional, unactivated desires and beliefs do not have the same inference-inducing powers as activated desires and beliefs (see Goldman 1986, section 10.1, and Goldman 1970, chap. 4). If x's belief in 'p only if q' is stored in memory and fails to get retrieved or activated, it does not influence x's practical reasoning. The problem, of course, is not merely that philosophers neglect these differences, but that it is unlikely that common folk have any firm grasp of these relationships, at least in any "theoretical" fashion.

Perhaps the functionalist will reply that although the 'folk' do have (more or less) true laws in their possession, philosophers have simply failed to articulate those laws correctly. But why, one wonders, should it be so difficult to articulate laws if we appeal to them all the time in our interpretive practice? Admittedly, they may be merely tacit generalizations, and tacit representations are characteristically difficult to reconstruct. A skeptic is entitled to suspect, however, that what goes on when philosophers proffer mentalistic platitudes is not the extraction of pre-existing representations in the minds of the 'folk', but the fresh creation of laws designed to accommodate philosophical preconceptions about the character of 'theoretical' terms.[6]

Still more grounds for doubt center on the problem of acquisition. Recall the point that children seem to display interpretive skills by the age of four, five, or six. If interpretation is indeed guided by laws of folk psychology, the latter must be known (or believed) by this age. Are such children sophisticated enough to represent such principles? And how, exactly, would they acquire them? One possible mode of acquisition is cultural transmission (e.g., being taught them explicitly by their elders). This is clearly out of the question, though, since only philosophers have even tried to articulate the laws, and most children have no exposure to philosophers. Another possible mode of acquisition is private construction. Each child constructs the generalizations for herself, perhaps taking clues from verbal explanations of behavior that she hears. But if this construction is supposed to occur along the lines of familiar modes of scientific theory construction, some anomalous things must take place. For one thing, all children miraculously construct the same nomological principles. This is what the (folk-) theory theory ostensibly implies, since it imputes a single folk psychology to everyone. In normal cases of hypothesis construction, however, different scientists come up with different theories. This is especially natural if they do not communicate their hypotheses, which is what obtains in the present case where the hypotheses are presumed to be tacit and unformulated. It is also surprising that the theory should stay fixed in each cognizer once it is acquired, as functionalism apparently assumes. This too contrasts with normal scientific practice, where theories are commonly amended at least to some degree with the accumulation of new data.

Jerry Fodor, a staunch defender of the theory theory, endorses the hypothesis that the folk theory is *innate* (Fodor 1987, pp. 132–133). He cites three pieces of 'evidence' for this: (1) intentional explanation appears to be a cultural universal; (2) a rudimentary awareness of the mental world is present in toddlers and preschoolers; and (3) there are no (plausible) suggestions about how a child might acquire the apparatus of intentional explanation 'from experience'. I agree with Fodor on these points. Indeed, I have just been stressing how hard it is to swallow the supposition that toddlers and preschoolers acquire functional laws by induction or theory construction. Thus, *if* a grasp of the mental world and intentional explanation involves laws, there is credibility in the hypothesis that these laws are possessed innately. But why accept the antecedent? Fodor simply ignores the possibility that the apparatus of intentional explanation may involve no theory at all. By contrast, I submit that intentional explanation and prediction can be accounted for without positing any large-scale theory or set of functional generalizations. This is what I now proceed to argue, apropos of the attribution of intentional states (and mental states generally) to others. The full story may well feature innate components: perhaps an innate propensity to identify mental categories within oneself (analogous to some innate propensities for individuating material bodies), and an innate propensity to project such categories on others. But it need not feature innate possession of *laws*.

IV

The account I favor may be introduced by reference to a proposal of Richard Grandy (1973). Grandy proposes to replace charity principles with what he calls the 'humanity principle'. This is the constraint imposed on translations that the imputed pattern of relations among beliefs, desires, and the world be as similar to our own as possible. This conforms, says, Grandy, with our actual practice of predicting people's behavior based on our attitudinal attributions. We do not use mathematical decision theory (i.e., expected utility theory) to make predictions; rather, we consider what *we* should do if we had the relevant beliefs and desires. Now I do not think that naive interpreters advert to Grandy's humanity principle as an abstract precept. Rather, they ascribe mental states to others by pretending or imagining themselves to be in the other's shoes, constructing or generating the (further) state that they would then be in, and ascribing that state to the other. In short, we *simulate* the situation of others, and interpret them accordingly. This idea has been explicitly put forward by Robert Gordon (1986; also Gordon 1987, chap. 7), and something like it has been endorsed by Adam Morton (1980).The idea has been a dominant motif in the Verstehen and hermeneutic traditions, and earlier precursors include the eighteenth-century Scottish philosophers.[7]

Several writers on interpretation put forward somewhat analogous views in discussing belief ascriptions. W. V. Quine explains indirect quotation in terms of an 'essentially dramatic act' in which we project ourselves into the speaker's mind (Quine 1960, p. 219). Similarly, drawing on Davidson's paratactic account of indirect discourse, Stephen Stich proposes that when I say 'Andrea believes that lead floats on mercury', I am performing a little skit: I am saying that Andrea is in a belief state content-identical to one that would lead me to assert the sentence which follows the 'that'-clause (Stich 1983, p. 84). However, these writers do not explicitly develop the simulation approach; nor do I mean to endorse the proposed paraphrase of belief-state ascriptions.

The simulation idea has obvious initial attractions. Introspectively, it seems as if we often try to predict others' behavior—or predict their (mental) choices—by imagining ourselves in their shoes and determining what we would choose to do. To use one of Gordon's examples, if we are playing chess, I may try to anticipate your next move by imagining myself in your situation and deciding what I would choose to do. Similarly, if we agree to meet for lunch tomorrow, I (mentally) 'predict' that you will expect me at roughly the appointed time and place. I ascribe this expectation to you because this is the expectation I would form if I were in your (presumed) situation. The simulation procedure can also be used for explanatory, or 'retrodictive', assignment of mental states. (Indeed, this is the more central type of case for the theme of 'interpretation'.) If you make a surprising chess move, I may infer a new strategy on your part, one that might have led me, if I were in your situation, to the observed move. To assure the plausibility of this being your strategy, I would see whether I could simulate both (a) arriving at this strategy from your presumed antecedent states, and (b) choosing the observed move given this strategy. Ascriptions of intent that lie behind observed behavior would, on the simulation theory, commonly take this second, explanatory form.

In all of these examples, my inference to a new state of yours draws on assumptions about your prior mental states. Does this not threaten a regress? How do I get any initial entree into your mental world? Can that be explained by simulation?[8] Yes. The regress presumably stops at perceptual cases, and at basic likings or cravings. From your perceptual situation, I infer that you have certain perceptual experiences or beliefs, the same ones I would have in your situation. I may also assume (pending information to the contrary) that you have the same basic likings that I have: for food, love, warmth, and so on.

Simulation is also relevant in inferring *actions* from mental states, not just mental states from other mental states. For ordinary 'basic' actions, I expect your 'choice' of an action to issue in its production because my own choice would so issue. In more problematic cases, such as uttering a tongue-twister, simulation might lead me to doubt that you will succeed. Morton (1980) points out that 'analysis-by-synthesis' accounts of speech perception invoke a (tacit) simulation of motor activity. According to this approach, in trying to categorize a speaker's acoustic sequence as one or another phonemic string, the perceiver constrains the choice of interpretation by 'running a model' of how his own vocal apparatus might articulate those sounds.

It would be a mistake, of course, to use the simulation procedure too simplistically, without adequate attention to individual differences. If I am a chess novice and you are a master, or vice versa, it would be foolish to assume that your analysis would match mine. To optimize use of the simulation procedure, I must not only imagine myself in possession of your goals and beliefs about the board configuration, but also in possession of your level of chess sophistication. People may not always take such factors into account; and frequently they lack information to make such adjustments accurately. In any case, there is no assumption here that people are always successful or optimal simulators. What I do conjecture is that simulation—whether explicit or implicit—is the fundamental method used for arriving at mental ascriptions to others. (A more complex variant of the simulation theme will be briefly sketched in section V.)

I am not saying, it should be emphasized, that simulation is the *only* method used for interpersonal mental ascriptions, or for the prediction of behavior. Clearly, there are regularities about behavior and individual differences that can be learned purely inductively. If Jones always greets people with a smile whereas Brown greets them with a grunt, their acquaintances can form appropriate expectations without deploying simulation. If people who enter a car in the driver's seat regularly proceed to start it, this is the basis for future expectations that need not appeal to simulation. The suggestion, then, is that simulation is an intensively used heuristic, and one on which interpretation fundamentally rests. Inductive or nomological information is not wholly absent, but it is sparser than the folk-theory approach alleges.

Does the simulation approach accommodate the problems confronting the rational norms approach? Very straightforwardly. The mere fact that the 'preface' belief ('at least one of my claims is false') produces inconsistency does not tempt me to withhold attribution of this belief to Hannah. This is just the belief I too would form, especially if I were unaware of the inconsistency (a similar point is made by Stich 1985). Similarly, the mere fact that Jeremy's probability assignments violate the probability calculus does not make me shrink from attributing them; for I too can feel their intuitive pull.

The merits of the simulation approach are further demonstrated by seeing how easily it handles a number of cases that the rival approaches cannot handle, or can handle only with difficulty. In an experiment by Daniel Kahneman and Amos Tversky (1982), subjects were given the following example:

> Mr. Crane and Mr. Tees were scheduled to leave the airport on different flights, at the same time. They traveled from town in the same limousine, were caught in a traffic jam, and arrived at the airport 30 minutes after the scheduled departure time of their flights. Mr. Crane is told that his flight left on time. Mr. Tees is told that his was delayed, and just left five minutes ago. Who is more upset?

Surely people do not possess a tacit folk psychological *theory* that warrants any particular answer to this question. But 96 percent of the subjects in the experiment said that Mr. Tees would be more upset. How did they severally arrive at the same answer? Clearly, by simulation. They imagined how *they* would feel in Mr. Crane's and Mr. Tees's shoes, and responded accordingly.

More evidence in a similar vein comes from the domain of verbal communication. Verbal communicators commonly make assumptions—often correct—about the contextual information accessible to their audience and likely to be used in the comprehension process. For example, inspired by the landscape, Mary says to Peter, "It's the sort of scene that would have made Marianne Dashwood swoon." This allusion to Austen's *Sense and Sensibility* is based on Mary's expectation that this utterance will act as a prompt, making Peter recall parts of the book that he had previously forgotten, and construct the assumptions needed to understand the allusion. My question is: How does a communicator proceed to estimate what pieces of information will be marshalled, or made salient, in the mind of the audience, in short, which pieces of information are 'calculable'.

Dan Sperber and Deirdre Wilson (1986), from whom the preceding example was borrowed, have an interesting theory of the hearer, which

postulates a variety of pertinent cognitive traits. For example, they postulate that cognizers have a number of rules of deductive inference, but these
are all *elimination* rules (e.g. from 'P and Q' you may infer 'Q') and not
introduction rules (e.g., from 'P' you may infer 'P or Q'). Now assume that
this piece of cognitive psychology is correct. Clearly, it is not known or
believed by the naive speaker. The speaker cannot appeal to any such
theoretical knowledge to make predictions of what is likely to be derived
or calculated by the hearer. Nonetheless, speakers are evidently pretty
good at making such predictions, more precisely, at predicting what kinds
of 'implicatures' will be appreciated by an audience. How do they do
that? Again, I suggest, by simulation. They can simulate in themselves the
states that result from the inference rules, without knowing what those
rules are. Hence, they can project, with fairly substantial reliability, what
hearers will be able to infer and understand.

A related point concerns people's intuitive grasp of what others will
find *funny*.[9] Again it seems far-fetched to suppose that my ability to gauge
what will amuse you is based on a theory of humor (of what amuses
people). I do not possess any general theory of this sort. More plausibly,
I gauge *your* probable reaction to a joke by projecting my own. (There can
be adjustments here for factual information about interpersonal differences,
but this is just a corrective to the basic tactic of simulation.) There are
(arguably) two states of yours that I judge or anticipate through simulation.
I estimate by simulation that you will grasp the intended point of the joke:
a cognitive state. I also judge by simulation that you will be amused by it:
not a purely cognitive state.

Apropos of non-cognitive states, it is worth stressing that a virtue of
the simulation theory is its capacity to provide a uniform account of all
mental state attributions, not only of propositional attitudes but of non-
propositional mental states like pains and tickles. This contrasts with the
rationality approach, which has no resources for explaining the latter. No
principle of *rationality* dictates when a person should feel pain, or what
one should do when in pain. Similarly for tickles. Thus, a rationality (or
charity) approach to propositional attitude interpretation would have to be
supplemented by an entirely different element to account for attributions of
sensations, and perhaps emotions as well. Such bifurcation has less appeal
than the unified account offered by the simulation approach.

In a brief discussion of the simulation idea, Dennett (1987b) finds it very
puzzling. How can it work, he asks, without being a kind of theorizing?
If I make believe I am a suspension bridge and wonder what I will do
when the wind blows, what comes to mind depends on how sophisticated
my *knowledge* is of the physics and engineering of suspension bridges.
Why should making believe that I have your beliefs be any different? Why
should it too not require theoretical knowledge?

To answer this question, we need to say more about the general idea of simulation. For a device to simulate a system is for the former to behave in a way that 'models', or maintains some relevant isomorphism to, the behavior of the latter. This is the sense in which a computer might simulate a weather system or an economy. Now if a person seeks to simulate the weather or the economy, in the sense of mentally constructing or anticipating an actual (or genuinely feasible) sequence of its states, she is very unlikely to be accurate unless she has a good theory of the system. A successful simulation of this kind must be *theory-driven*, let us say. This is Dennett's point. But must all mental simulations be theory-driven in order to succeed? I think not. A simulation of some target systems might be accurate even if the agent lacks such a theory. This can happen if (1) the *process* that drives the simulation is the same as (or relevantly similar to) the process that drives the system, and (2) the initial states of the simulating agent are the same as, or relevantly similar to, those of the target system. Thus, if one person simulates a sequence of mental states of another, they will wind up in the same (or isomorphic) final states as long as (A) they begin in the same (or isomorphic) initial states, and (B) both sequences are driven by the same cognitive process or routine. It is not necessary that the simulating agent have a theory of what the routine is, or how it works. In short, successful simulation can be *process-driven*.

Now in central cases of interpretation, the interpreter is not actually in the very same initial states as the interpretee. While there may be overlap in beliefs and goals, there are typically relevant differences as well. So how can the interpreter succeed via simulation? The critical move, of course, is that the interpreter tries to imagine, or 'feign', the same initial states as the interpretee. She 'pretends' or 'makes believe' she has the relevant initial states, and then performs reasoning operations (or other cognitive operations) to generate successive states in herself. But are these 'pretend' states—the pseudo-beliefs, pseudo-desires, and so forth—relevantly similar to the genuine beliefs and desires that they model? Is it plausible that imagined beliefs and actual beliefs would yield the same, or analogous, outputs when operated upon by the same cognitive operations?[10]

It *is* plausible, I submit. Consider hypothetical, or subjunctive, reasoning. I ask myself, 'Suppose I did action *A*—what would be the result?' How do I proceed to answer this question? It seems that what I do is imagine myself believing the proposition 'I do *A*', and then draw causal inferences from that pseudo-belief together with (certain) antecedent genuine beliefs. Furthermore, it seems that I use the very same inference processes as those I would use on a set of wholly genuine belief inputs. (The output, though, is only a belief in the same hypothetical mood, not a genuine belief.) Similarly, I make contingency plans by executing practical reasoning operations on feigned beliefs in certain contingencies; and these are the same planning operations that I would apply to genuine beliefs in those contingencies. So it seems that 'pretend' belief states *are* relevantly similar to belief states; there are significant isomorphisms. The possibility of isomorphisms between 'genuine' states and imaginatively, or artificially, generated 'copies' is further illustrated in the imagery domain. Roger Shepard, Stephen Kosslyn, and their respective colleagues have produced striking evidence to support the claim that visual images are similar in important respects to genuine visual perceptions (Shepard and Cooper 1982; Kosslyn 1980). To determine the congruence or noncongruence of two shapes, forming a mental image of one being rotated into alignment with the other can be almost as reliable as actually seeing the results of this rotation. This would hardly be possible if imagery were not relevantly similar to genuine perception.[11]

V

Let us explore the psychological defensibility of the simulation approach in more detail. We may first note that several cognitive scientists have recently endorsed the idea of mental simulation as one cognitive heuristic, although these researchers stress its use for knowledge in general, not specifically knowledge of others' mental states. Kahneman and Tversky (1982) propose that people often try to answer questions about the world by an operation that resembles the running of a simulation model. The starting conditions for a 'run', they say, can either be left at realistic default values or modified to assume some special contingency. Similarly, Rumelhart, Smolensky, McClelland, and Hinton (1986) describe the importance of 'mental models' of the world, in particular, models that simulate how the world would respond to one's hypothetical actions. They first apply this idea to actual and imagined conversations, and later describe a PDP (parallel distributed processing) network for playing tic-tac-toe, a network that embodies 'simulations' of the world's (i.e., the opponent's) response to the agent's possible moves.

Since part of my argument rests on the superior plausibility of the simulation approach in accounting for children's interpretational ability, let us next look at recent work by developmental psychologists that bear on this point. The most striking findings are those by Heinz Wimmer and Josef Perner, conjoined with a follow-up study by Simon Baron-Cohen, Alan Leslie, and Uta Frith. Various experimental studies had previously shown that as early as $2\frac{1}{2}$ years, children use a substantial vocabulary about perception, volition, major emotions, and knowledge. But experiments by Wimmer and Perner (1983) strongly indicate that around the ages of four to six, an ability to clearly distinguish between someone else's belief state and reality becomes firmly established. In their study, children between three and nine years of age observed a sketch in which a protagonist put an object into a location X. The children then witnessed that, in the absence of the protagonist, the object was transferred from X to location Y. Since this transfer came as a surprise, they should assume that the protagonist still believed that the object was in X. Subjects were then required to indicate where the protagonist will look for the object on his return. None of the 3–4-year olds, 57 percent of the 4–6-year olds, and 86 percent of the 6–9-year olds pointed correctly to location X. In their related study, Baron-Cohen, Leslie and Frith (1985) studied the ability of autistic children to perform this sort of task. Of critical relevance here are two facts about autistic children. First, the main symptom of autism is impairment in verbal and nonverbal communication. Second, autistic children show a striking poverty of pretend play. Baron-Cohen et al.'s experiment showed that when the tested children were asked where the doll protagonist would look for her marble, 85 percent of the normal children answered correctly, but only 20 percent of the autistic children (with a mean age close to 12 and a relatively high mean IQ of 82) answered correctly. Especially striking was the fact that the test also included a pool of Down's syndrome children, 86 percent of whom answered the crucial question *correctly*. This suggests that the failure of the autistic children is not due to general mental retardation, a trait shared by Down's syndrome children. Rather it is a specific cognitive deficit. Baron-Cohen et al. hypothesize that autistic children as a group fail to acquire a 'theory of mind', i.e., an ability to impute beliefs to others and therefore predict their behavior correctly. This would account for their social and communicational impairment. It might also be related to their lack of pretend play. Perhaps, as Gordon (1986) suggests, all this points to a prepackaged 'module' for simulation directed at other human beings, a module that is impaired in autism.

One of the co-authors of the autism study, Alan Leslie, has sketched a theory that interrelates pretend play and the representation of mental states (Leslie 1987). He points out that pretending is in some ways an odd practice. From an evolutionary point of view, one might expect a high premium on maintaining an accurate and objective view of the world. A child who acts as if dolls have genuine feelings is scarcely acting upon a veridical picture of the world. Yet pretend play emerges at an early age, and becomes more elaborate during development. It is not implausible to conjecture that pretend play is a preliminary exercise of a mechanism the primary function of which is the simulation of real people's mental states. Roughly this theme is articulated both by Leslie and by Paul Harris (1989). Such a mechanism, on the present theory, underlies interpersonal interpretation, prediction, and perhaps communication as well.

Whatever the force of these findings and speculations, there is a straightforward challenge to the psychological plausibility of the simulation approach. It is far from obvious, introspectively, that we regularly place ourselves in another person's shoes and vividly envision what we would do in his circumstances. This is a natural thing to do while watching a tennis match, perhaps, or while listening to someone relating their tragic life story. But the simulation approach ostensibly makes this empathic attitude the standard mode of interpretation. Is that not difficult to accept?

Two replies should be made. First, simulation need not be an introspectively vivid affair. The approach can certainly insist that most simulation is semi-automatic, with relatively little salient phenomenology. It is a psychological commonplace that highly developed skills become automatized, and there is no reason why interpersonal simulation should not share this characteristic. (On the issue of conscious awareness, the simulation theory is no worse off than its competitors. Neither the rationality approach nor the folk-theory theory is at all credible if it claims that appeals to its putative principles are introspectively prominent aspects of interpretation.)

A second point might be that many cases of rapid, effortless interpretation may be devoid of even automatized simulation. When a mature cognizer has constructed, by simulation, many similar instances of certain action-interpretation patterns, she may develop generalizations or other inductively formed representations (schemas, scripts, and so forth) that can trigger analogous interpretations by application of those 'knowledge structures' alone, sans simulation. I have, of course, already acknowledged the role of inductively based predictions of behavior and the need for standard empirical information to make adjustments for individual differences. The present point is a slightly larger concession. It agrees that in many cases the interpreter relies solely (at the time of interpretation) on inductively acquired information. But this information, it suggests, is historically derived from earlier simulations. If this story is right, then simulation remains the fundamental source of interpretation, though not the essence of every act (or even most acts) of interpretation. We might call this the *complex* variant of the simulation approach. It converges somewhat toward the folk-theory theory (though the exact degree of convergence depends on the nature of the inductively based knowledge structures it posits). It still remains distinct, however, (A) because the folk-theory theory makes no allowance for simulation, and (B) because the complex variant postulates simulation as the originating source of (most) interpretation.

Commenting in part on an earlier version of this paper, Paul Churchland (1989) poses two difficulties for the simulation theory. First, he says, simulation is not necessary for understanding others. People who are congenitally deaf, or blind, are quite capable of understanding normal people, and people who have never themselves felt profound grief or rejection can nevertheless provide appropriate interpretations of others who are so afflicted. In general, understanding goes beyond what one has personally experienced. I have already granted, however, that straightforwardly empirical information is required to accommodate individual differences, and these examples are just more extreme illustrations of the point. We must certainly allow for the human capacity to extrapolate from one's own case, to project types of sensory or emotional sensibility that one does not oneself instantiate. This concession does not undermine the point that interpretation primarily starts from the home base of one's own experience.

Churchland further objects that while simulation may account for the prediction of others' behavior, it does not provide for *explanation*. The simulation theory makes the understanding of others depend crucially on having an initial understanding of oneself. But it leaves mysterious, he says, the nature of first person understanding. More specifically, *explanatory* understanding requires appreciation of the *general patterns* that comprehend individual events in both cases. This requires a *theory*, which the simulation approach spurns. In my opinion, however, explanation can consist of telling a story that eliminates various alternative hypotheses about how the event in question came about, or could have come about. This can effectively answer a 'Why'-question, which is the essence of explanation (see van Fraassen 1980, chap. 5). In the case of interpretive explanation this is done by citing a specific set of goals and beliefs, which implicitly rules out the indefinitely many alternative desire-and-belief sets that might have led to the action.

Churchland rejects the deductive nomological theory of explanation on the grounds that it presupposes a sentential, or propositional attitude, account of knowledge representation. He proposes to replace this picture of cognition with a prototype-based picture, especially one that is elaborated within a connectionist framework. He still wishes to count human cognition as significantly *theoretical*, but theory possession is apparently no longer associated with nomologicality. Churchland is welcome to use the term 'theory' in this neological fashion; but it cannot resuscitate the standard version of the folk-theory approach to interpretation. It is only in the usual, nomological construal of theories that I am addressing (and rejecting) that approach. I am pleased to see Churchland also reject that approach, but it seems to have ramifications for his other views that I shall mention below.

VI

Considering the complexity of the human organism, it may well be considered remarkable that we are able to predict human behavior as well as we do. Is this impressive success fully accounted for by the simulation theory? Only, I think, with an added assumption, viz., that the other people, whose behavior we predict, are psychologically very similar to ourselves. Just as the child readily learns a grammar of a natural language because its native grammar-learning structures mirror those of its language-creating mates, so a person can successfully simulate the internal operations of others because they are largely homologous to her own. The fuller picture, then, has strong affinities to Noam Chomsky's emphasis on the role of species-specific traits in mental activity.

Although I view this theme as Chomskyesque, it is also similar to one made by Quine (1969a). Quine asks how the language learner manages to learn the law of English verbal behavior connected with 'yellow'. The answer, he says, is that the learner's quality spacing is enough like his neighbor's that such learning is almost a foregone conclusion: he is making his induction in a 'friendly world'. He is playing a game of chance with favorably loaded dice. Similarly, I am suggesting, people's predictions of other people's behavior, based heavily on attributions of content, are so successful because people operate with the same set of fundamental cognitive constraints. (Notice, I need not say that people are successful at assigning correct contents to people's mental states; that would assume that there is an independent fact of the matter about content, prior to the activity of interpretation. Since some interpretation theorists would reject this thesis, I can confine my claim to successful prediction of *behavior*.)

The constraints I have in mind must be constraints on the specific contents assigned to an agent's propositional attitudes. Without positing such constraints, it is hard to account for the definiteness and interpersonal uniformity in content attributions. There would seem to be too much 'play', too much looseness, in the sorts of abstract constraints that a theorist like Davidson, for example, imposes. Assuming the interpretations of the interpreter to be given, we need to explain why she makes those rather than the innumerable other conceivable interpretations.

In a similar (though not identical) context, Lewis (1983c) worries whether enough constraints on content are imposed by his theory to exclude preposterous and perverse misinterpretations. To exclude perverse interpretations, Lewis says we need a priori presumptions about just what sorts of things are apt to be believed or desired. These presumptions should be thought of as built into our interpretation procedures. Adopting a suggestion of Gary Merrill, Lewis proposes that natural kinds are more eligible for content attributions than non-natural kinds. Taking naturalness to be a graded affair, more natural kinds have greater eligibility for content inclusion than less natural kinds. Principles of content possession should therefore impute a bias toward believing that things are green rather than grue, toward having a basic desire for long life rather than for long-life-unless-one-was-born-on-Monday-and-in-that-case-life-for-an-even-number-of-weeks.

I agree with Lewis that to get things right, i.e., to conform to our actual content attributions, account must be taken of what is 'natural' and 'unnatural'. But only if this means 'natural for us': congenial to human psychology. This is not what Lewis means. By 'natural' Lewis means properties Nature herself deems natural, those categories that are objectively, independently, nonanthropocentrically natural. This is not very plausible. Granted that the kind 'a mass of molecules' is more of a natural kind than, say, 'table', it is still less plausible to attribute beliefs about masses of molecules to scientifically untutored people than beliefs about tables. Or take the hue yellow. From an objective, nonanthropocentric viewpoint, yellow is less natural than other possible spectral or reflectancy categorizations. Nonetheless, it is more plausible to attribute contents involving yellow than more objective categorizations of light frequency. Clearly, it is concepts that are humanly more natural, i.e., psychologically congenial, that are more eligible for content.[12]

What I am suggesting, then, is that uniformity in cross-personal interpretations should be partly explained by psychological preferences for certain modes of categorization and 'entification', or more basically, by operations that generate categorial and entificational preferences. The precise nature of these operations and/or preferences remains to be spelled out by cognitive science. But let me give some examples of what I mean.

Our entification practices include propensities to group together, or unify, certain sets of elements rather than others in a perceptual display. The Gestalt principles of similarity, proximity, closedness, and good continuation are attempts to systematize the mental operations that underpin these unificational practices. The Gestalt principles apply not only in the visual domain, but in the temporal domain as well. Thus, presented with the opening passage of Mozart's fortieth symphony, principles of temporal proximity (and so forth) make it natural to segment the passage into three distinct phrases (I oversimplify here). Other conceivable segmentations are highly unnatural. It is plausible to conjecture that the same Gestalt principles are at work in fixing our conceptual (as opposed to perceptual) intuitions of identity, or unity, of objects through time (see Goldman 1987a).

Another set of categorial preferences feature what Eleanor Rosch calls the 'basic level' of categories (Rosch 1975, 1978). Language (and presumably thought) is full of category hierarchies such as *poodle, dog, mammal, animal, physical object*. Experiments show that the categories in the middle of such hierarchies, in the present case *dog* rather than *poodle* or *physical object*, have a definite psychological primacy.

How do entitative and categorial preferences of the interpreter get deployed in the interpretation process? Two slightly different hypotheses are possible. First, the preferences may be registered directly; that is, the interpreter uses her own categorial preferences to assign content to the interpretee. Second, they might be used in conjunction with the simulation heuristic. In assigning reference and meaning, the interpreter imagines what the agent's concept-forming or proposition-forming devices might generate in the present context, and this imaginative act is structured by the interpreter's own concept-forming and judgment-forming operations.

In either case, the hypotheses I am advancing would account for a substantial degree of uniformity in specific content attributions. It would also mesh with Davidson's theme of belief similarity among interpreters and interpretees, but only subject to important qualifications. The simulation hypothesis assumes that the interpreter tends to impute to the interpretee the same fundamental categories as her own, or at least the same basic category-forming (and proposition-forming) operations. She also tends to project the same basic belief-forming processes. But these practices still leave room for wide divergence in belief content. The simulation procedure can take account of differences in the agent's evidential exposures, and in the special inferential habits, algorithms, and heuristics that he has learned or acquired.[13] Differences along these dimensions can ramify into substantial differences in belief sets.

My emphasis on conspecific psychological traits may suggest the possibility that only other *people* are interpretable by us. That is not a claim I endorse. On the contrary, we certainly think of ourselves as interpreting other animals; and although we may partly deceive ourselves with misplaced anthropomorphism, we do have moderate predictive success. Of course, the use of straightforward inductively gathered information is prominent here. But, as indicated earlier, we also use our own psychology as a home base, and make conservative revisions from that starting point. Perhaps this is why it is more difficult to construct right-seeming interpretations of heterospecifics than conspecifics. Dolphins seem to be highly intelligent and to communicate among themselves, yet no human has constructed a plausible interpretation of their language.

Although my discussion centers on the psychological dimensions involved in content attributions, it by no means precludes an important role for the external world, especially causal relations with the external world, in the choice of semantic assignments to thoughts. In deciding what is the *referent* of an imputed thought, in particular, it seems clear that the interpreter takes into account the thought's causal history. Similarly, it is plausible to suppose that imputation of other semantic dimensions of thought involves mind-world connections. These are plausibly part of the conceptual background with which the interpreter operates. Although I am not addressing these issues, which lie at the heart of much current debate, they are complementary to the themes I am pursuing.

VII

In this final section I briefly address several possible philosophical ramifications of the simulation approach, including the interpretation strategy with which I began.

Does the simulation approach imply a sharp divide between explanations of the mental and the physical? If so, it would vindicate the claim of the hermeneutic tradition, which contrasts understanding of human action with understanding of physical phenomena. No sharp contrast necessarily follows from the simulation theory. For one thing, we have already noted that simulation or mental modeling is sometimes postulated as a cognitive heuristic for representing physical phenomena as well as mental states. Admittedly, this realization of the simulation heuristic would presumably be theory-driven rather than process-driven. Still, this already admits an important parallel. Furthermore, proponents of interpretational simulation need not maintain that nomological explanation of human phenomena is impossible. They just maintain that *commonsense* explanations and predictions of the mental do not (in the main) invoke laws.

A second philosophical issue raised by the simulation theory is the epistemology of other minds. Ostensibly, the theory is a version of the 'analogical' theory of mental state ascription. It seems to impute to interpreters inferences of roughly the following form: 'If he is psychologically like me, he must be in mental state M; he is psychologically like me; therefore, he is in mental state M.' But there is a long-standing suspicion of such arguments from analogy, centering on the second premise. How can the interpreter know (or believe justifiably) that the agent is psychologically like her? Can physical and behavioral similarity support this premise? Is not an analogy based on a single case a thin reed on which to rest?

The best line of reply, I think, is to deny that interpreters must believe the second premise. Many beliefs are formed by mechanisms, or routines, that are built into the cognitive architecture. Although these mechanisms might be described in terms of 'rules' or 'principles', it would be misleading to say that the cognizers believe those rules or principles. For example, it is plausible to say that people form perceptual beliefs (or representations) in accord with Gestalt rules, but implausible to say that they literally believe those rules. They represent certain partly occluded figures as being single, unitary objects when there is sufficient 'continuity' between their perceived parts; but they do not believe the continuity principle itself. In our case, cognizers make interpretations in accordance with a routine that could be formulated by the principle, 'Other people are psychologically like me'. But this is not really a believed 'premise' on which they inferentially base their interpretations.

Could a belief that is produced by such a routine qualify as justified, or as a piece of knowledge, if the rule is not believed? Reliabilism is one species of epistemology that would be congenial to this result. If the routine, or process, is a generally reliable one, then reliabilism (in certain forms) may be prepared to count its output beliefs as justified (see chapter 6). So there is at least one type of epistemology that promises to resolve the epistemic challenge to the simulation theory.[14]

A third noteworthy philosophical point concerns the ramification of abandoning the folk-theory theory. This theory has been a salient premise in the argument for eliminativism about propositional attitudes. Eliminativists standardly begin by emphasizing that the attitudes—and all our commonsense mentalistic notions—are part of a folk psychological theory. They then point to the bleak history of past folk scientific theories, suggesting that the same scenario is in store for folk psychology (see Churchland 1981). Since folk psychology will ultimately prove to have poorer predictive value than scientific psychology, its constructs will need to be replaced or eliminated, just like the constructs of, say, alchemy. However, if it turns out that there is no folk theory, in the sense of a set of commonsense generalizations that define the mental terms, then an important premise for eliminativism is no longer available. (This point has been made by Gordon.)

Let me turn now to what is probably the most pressing philosophical issue posed by the simulation theory. What is the relation, it may be asked, between the simulation approach and what it is for mental ascriptions to be *correct*? The simulation theory purports to give an account of the procedure used in ascribing mental states to others. What light does this shed, however, on the conditions that are *constitutive* of mental state possession (especially possession of the attitudes)? The interpretation strategist hopes to extract from the interpretation procedure some criteria of correctness for mentalistic ascriptions. Certainly the rationality and functionalist theories would generate answers to this question. (Whether or not the answers they generate are correct is another matter. Functionalist definitions, for example, have many familiar problems.) But the simulation theory looks distinctly unpromising on this score. Since simulation is such a fallible procedure, there is little hope of treating 'M is ascribed (or ascribable) to S on the basis of simulation' as constitutive of 'S is in M'. Furthermore, simulation assumes a prior understanding of what state it is that the interpreter ascribes to S. This just re-raises the same question: what state is it that the interpreter is imputing to the agent when she ascribes state M? What does her understanding of the M-concept consist in?

As far as the interpretation strategy is concerned, it indeed appears that if the simulation theory is correct, the interpretation strategy is fruitless. One cannot extract criteria of mentalistic ascription from the practice of interpersonal interpretation if that practice rests on a prior and independent understanding of mentalistic notions. As far as the interpretation strategy goes, then, the moral of the simulation theory is essentially a negative one. It should be recalled, however, that I warned from the outset that the hope of the interpretation strategy may not be well founded.

Since the simulation theory is only a theory of interpretation, a theory of how people apply mental terms to others, it is officially neutral about the *meaning* of these terms. It is even compatible with, say, a functionalist account of their meaning! It is conceivable that what people mean by mental terms is given by functionalism, yet they use simulation as a heuristic procedure for ascertaining or inferring the mental states of others. Although this is compatible with the simulation theory, we have already given independent reasons for concluding that the central presupposition of (commonsense) functionalism, viz., the existence of a folk theory, is not satisfied. Furthermore, other well-known difficulties with functionalism, such as absent qualia problems and (other) threats of liberalism and chauvinism, render its prospects quite bleak (see Block 1980). The time is ripe to reconsider the prospects of the first-person approach to the understanding of mental concepts. It has always seemed plausible, prior to philosophical theorizing, that our naive understanding of mental concepts should prominently involve introspective and not merely causal/relational elements. Some such approach to the concept of the mental would nicely complement the simulation theory of interpretation. However, this topic cannot be pursued here.[15]

Whether or not I have mounted a successful defense of the simulation theory, I hope I have at least persuaded the reader of the importance of getting the descriptive story of interpretive activity right. Although I think that the evidence in favor of the simulation account is substantial, I am even more convinced of the thesis that philosophers (as well as cognitive scientists) must pay closer attention to the psychology of the interpreter. Making that point has been the principal aim of this paper.

Notes

Earlier versions of this paper were presented to the philosophy of mind seminar of the Centre National de la Recherche Scientifique in Paris, a conference on the Chomskyan turn in Jerusalem, the Oxford Philosophical Society, the Society for Philosophy and Psychology, and the philosophy departments at King's College, London and Rutgers University. Commentator and audience comments on all of these occasions were most helpful. I am particularly indebted to Michael Ayers, Michael Bratman, Pascal Engel, Jerry Fodor, Elizabeth Fricker, Samuel Guttenplan, J. Christopher Maloney, Christopher Peacocke, Stephen Schiffer, and Robert van Gulick. Special thanks are due to Holly Smith, who read and commented on several previous drafts.

1. Functionalism, or the folk-theory theory, has not usually been presented under the 'interpretation' label. Nonetheless, I believe it causes no distortion, and indeed provides illumination, to view it in this guise.

2. Not all theories of content are discussed here. Many of these theories are not conveniently formulated as theories of interpretation, i.e., as accounts of the interpreter. For example, the causal, covariational, or information-theoretic approach (Fodor 1987; Dretske 1981a) is normally stated directly as a theory of content, not in terms of the methods or constraints employed by an interpreter. The same holds for the evolutionary, 'selectionist', or learning historical, approaches to content (Millikan 1984; Dennett 1987c; Dretske 1988). Furthermore, some of these approaches (especially in their pure forms) do not seem promising as full theories of content ascription unless they are supplemented by one of the three approaches I discuss. The covariational approach seems best suited to handle only beliefs, and indeed only that fraction of beliefs under 'direct' causal control of their referents. To handle all types of beliefs, and the other attitudes, the approach probably needs to be incorporated into a larger, functional framework (or another such framework). Even Fodor, for example, who defends a covariational theory of content, also endorses a functional account of the attitude types (Fodor 1987, pp. 69–70); and he acknowledges that the content of certain mental representations, viz., the logical vocabulary, should be handled in terms of their functional roles (Fodor 1990, pp. 110–111). Furthermore, many of the foregoing theories would be extremely dubious accounts of how we *ordinarily* understand and ascribe contentful states, which is our present topic. A person can grasp and apply the concept of belief, for example, without any knowledge of, or any commitment to, either evolutionary theory or operant conditioning.

3. Hartry Field (1977) appeals to probabilistic coherence in the context of a theory of content.

4. It may be argued that Jeremy's judgments are not expressions of 'probability' judgments, but merely degrees of inductive support, which need not obey the probability calculus (see Levi 1985). However, even if the Linda-style case does not make the point at hand, other cases involving genuine probabilities could do so.

5. A convenient set of readings on the sure-thing principle appears in Gärdenfors and Sahlin 1988, part III. For a survey of deductive failings, see Anderson 1985, chapter 10. For empirically based misgivings about the charity approach, similar to those expressed here, see Thagard and Nisbett 1983.

6. Putnam 1988 contains some new difficulties for functionalism. But this critique does not challenge the use of functional-style generalizations by interpreters.

7. A classical statement of the Verstehen approach is Collingwood (1946). Other recent writers who find the simulation approach congenial include Heal (1986), Ripstein (1987), Putnam (1978, lecture VI), Nozick (1981, pp. 637–638), Montgomery (1987), and Johnson (1988). Heal and Ripstein, in particular, anticipate a number of points made here. Unfortunately, those papers came to my attention only after this one was complete.

8. The threat of a regress was pointed out by Stephen Schiffer.

9. Here I am indebted to Michael Ayers.

10. This question is raised by Dennett (1987b), and its importance was impressed upon me by J. Christopher Maloney. For helpful discussion, see Ripstein 1987.

11. I am indebted here to Christopher Peacocke. Notice that I am not assuming any sort of 'pictorial' theory of imagery, only the 'perception-similitude' thesis about imagery (see Goldman 1986, chap. 12).

12. This answer would admittedly not serve Lewis's purposes, since he wants (roughly) purely 'physicalistic' constraints. This is implied by his own formulation of the problem of radical interpretation (in his paper of that title), as well as by the fact that he is trying to meet Hilary Putnam's challenge to resolve problems of content indeterminacy from an 'externalist' perspective. Although my answer would not serve Lewis's purposes, the crucial point of my argument is that his own answer just is not satisfactory.

13. Here I place significant weight on my distinction between basic 'processes' and acquired 'methods' in Goldman 1986. It is assumed that the interpreter spontaneously uses the same *processes* as the interpretee, but may differ in the *methods* she deploys.

14. Another variant of the problem of other minds is presented by Wittgenstein and reconstructed by Kripke (1982). According to this problem, if the primary concept of a mental state is derived from my own case, I cannot coherently form even a conception of another person's being in that state. For a good reply to this problem, see Loar 1990.

15. For a first-person, or subjective, rendering of mental content, see Loar 1987. Interestingly, Loar couples his internalist account of content with a 'projective', or simulational, account of understanding others.

Chapter 2
Metaphysics, Mind, and Mental Science

There are two ways that metaphysics and the theory of mind can intersect. First, the theory of mind can be considered one branch of metaphysics. Questions about the fundamental nature of mind are ontological questions. Second, an understanding of certain aspects of the mind can make contributions to various other parts of metaphysics, not just to the ontology of the mind. More precisely, an empirical understanding of the mental operations that help shape our ontological framework can contribute to metaphysics. This second kind of intersection will be the focus of the present discussion.

Let us follow P. F. Strawson in distinguishing descriptive and revisionary metaphysics. "Descriptive metaphysics," he writes, "is content to describe the actual structure of our thought about the world; revisionary metaphysics is concerned to produce a better structure" (Strawson 1959, p. 9). What Strawson calls "the structure of our thought about the world" might usefully be called our *folk ontology*. Folk ontology is the set of fundamental entities, properties, and relations that are posited in our naive, common-sense, prereflective mode of thought.[1] Descriptive metaphysics is the discipline that seeks to describe and understand that folk ontology. This style of metaphysics does not try to decide whether, or to what extent, our folk ontology is viable or correct. It simply seeks to lay bare its content and to understand its roots or sources. Revisionary metaphysics, by contrast, attempts to delineate an ontology that is more in tune with the findings of science and with general theoretical considerations. Thus, descriptive metaphysics tries to give us roughly (but only roughly) what Wilfrid Sellars (1963) calls the "manifest image" of the world, while revisionary metaphysics tries to provide what Sellars calls the "scientific image."

A slightly better contrast than 'descriptive' versus 'revisionary' might be descriptive versus *prescriptive* metaphysics. Prescriptive metaphysics would try to tell us what ontological commitments we *ought* to adopt, given the best available science and philosophy. With this nomenclature, we can leave it open whether, and to what degree, prescriptive metaphysics would have us depart from folk ontology. There is a continuum of possible prescriptive positions, with little or no revision standing at the conservative end of the continuum and radical revision at the other end.

Since descriptive metaphysics is concerned with our naive "conceptual scheme," and since that conceptual scheme is (plausibly) part of, or a product of, our psychology, it should come as no surprise that the discipline of psychology, and the allied cognitive sciences, have important contributions to make to descriptive metaphysics. So at least I shall argue. I shall further argue that the cognitive sciences can make contributions to prescriptive metaphysics. As we learn more about the ways in which our constitution shapes our initial view, we may be forced to revise our prior conception of the (rest of the) world. This has something in common with Thomas Nagel's (1986) notion of "objectification," or "objective ascent," in which we gain a better understanding of the world by seeing how our initial view is the product both of the world and of our own constitution. Now although Nagel is silent on this matter, the cognitive sciences seem to deliver the best available scientific insight into our constitution, or mental architecture. So it seems plausible that the cognitive sciences can make contributions to prescriptive metaphysics. My principal theme, then, is to articulate more fully just how the mental sciences can contribute to both descriptive and prescriptive metaphysics.

I

Let me begin with descriptive metaphysics. The notion of folk ontology, which is at the heart of descriptive metaphysics, suffers from vagueness. Just which types of entities and properties are sufficiently "fundamental" to count as elements of our folk ontology? Exactly where are cuts to be made in fixing what is "naive," "commonsensical," or "prereflective"? These are admittedly difficult questions, which I shall not try to resolve here. The vaguenesses involved are real but not crippling. There are enough clear cases to make it reasonable to proceed, even if at some later juncture more precision is desired.

I should say a few more words about my conception of descriptive metaphysics. On my proposal, descriptive metaphysics would not simply provide a list of the objects to which the "folk" are ontically committed. It would also seek to understand or explain why the folk have that ontology rather than another, i.e., to identify the underlying principles, mechanisms, or constraints that shape their ontological "choices." For example, descriptive metaphysics is interested in whether people's ontic commitments are the result of the lexical ingredients of the language they imbibe from their cultural community or whether it flows directly from their biologically specified cognitive architecture. Different portions of folk ontology may require different treatments on this sort of question. The folk ontology of color, for example, may receive one sort of account, while the folk ontology of mental states, e.g., beliefs, may receive another. Indeed, even a single ontological category may require explanatory elements from multiple sources.

W. V. Quine (1974) engages in what I am calling descriptive metaphysics when he says that people are instinctively "body-minded." By "bodies" Quine means things like rocks, trees, and dogs, which people seem to find natural physical units. They contrast with a more inclusive set of things that consist of "any arbitrary congeries of particle-stages, however spatiotemporally gerrymandered or disperse[d]." (Quine 1974, p. 54) Eli Hirsch also lays stress on people's propensities to prefer certain kinds of units rather than others (Hirsch 1982, 1988). He discusses the following "strange" principle of individuation. If two people A and B are in physical contact exclusively with each other during an interval of time, then there is a "cperson" whose history includes A before the contact, person B during the contact interval, and person A again after the interval. Hirsch calls this a "strange" principle of individuation because it strikes people intuitively as bizarre or unnatural. The same holds for Sydney Shoemaker's "klable" entities, viz., entities having a history consisting in stages of a kitchen table from midnight to noon followed by stages of a living room table from noon to midnight, and so forth (Shoemaker 1979).

I assume that the entities countenanced by our folk ontology include persons, rocks, and tables but not cpersons or klables. This is one thing that descriptive metaphysics would tell us. The deeper question, however, is to understand why the former are included but not the latter. Understanding can be sought in two directions. First, what are the principles or criteria that underlie the "preferred" sorts of unity or identity of objects over time? In other words, what are the general characteristics of table and person unity-schemes that make them preferred to klable and cperson unity-schemes? And what are the analogous characteristics that dictate preferred spatial unity-schemes? Second, what is the source of these "preferred" characteristics or unity-schemes? Are the preferences fixed by linguistic convention, perhaps with an eye to the utility of one type of unity-scheme over others? Or is it some sort of innate feature (or set of constraints) of the human cognitive architecture?

All these questions are ones to which both philosophers and psychologists have devoted considerable attention. No attempt to review this large literature will be undertaken here. However, let me try to sketch how psychological investigations can be helpful. As both Quine and Hirsch point out, insightful and influential proposals were made by the Gestalt psychologists. Focusing primarily on perception, the Gestalt theorists proposed "rules" by which the mind organizes elements into larger perceptual units. Ray Jackendoff (1983) endorses these rules and embeds them into what he calls a "preference rule system." One rule is the rule of *proximity*: in a visual display, elements that are closer together tend (ceteris paribus) to be grouped into a single unit. Another grouping rule is *similarity:* elements more similar to one another tend to be grouped together. Jackendoff, following Wertheimer (1938), stresses that these rules involve graded conditions. The effect of the proximity rule can be enhanced by increasing disparities of distance, or weakened by reducing relative distances.[2] Proximity and similarity can interact as well. When both rules apply they can either reinforce each other, producing strong grouping intuitions, or they can conflict, yielding weak or ambiguous judgments. But the reactions across individuals are strikingly uniform, whether the cases elicit firm or hesitant intuitions.

As formulated, the Gestalt rules are certainly very vague. Not only is there no precise statement of how they interact; even the individual rules are vague. There are many different respects of similarity, for example. Which respects or dimensions are more important or weighty? Until determinate metrics of similarity are developed, vagueness abounds. Nonetheless, I shall assume that human psychology *has* relevant metrics, which justify postulation of the similarity rule, even if many crucial details remain to be specified.

A third Gestalt rule is a preference for *good continuation.* Where grouping choices are made, one is more likely to see a series of dots as a single line if this preserves directionality than if it abruptly changes directionality. The application of this rule, like that of the others, is not restricted to vision. They apply to auditory perception and the other modalities as well. For example, a series of beats on a drum will be grouped in accordance with the rules, and the same grouping will be imposed if the pattern of beats is merely felt, e.g., as taps on the back of the neck.

Gestalt rules have been used by Lerdahl and Jackendoff (1982) to develop a theory of musical representation. The mind imposes a segmentation of musical pitches--rather, a hierarchy of related segmentations—and very different groupings are intuitively quite implausible. Gestalt rules have also been proposed by a number of psychologists as components of a theory of "good parts," i.e., the kinds of decompositions of wholes into smaller units that are psychologically natural or "preferred."[3]

Given the widespread applicability of the Gestalt rules, it seems promising that they should be usable to help explain the cross-temporal unity schemes that people find natural. Indeed, many philosophical discussions of identity over time appeal heavily to some sort of continuity principle. Anthony Quinton (1973, chap. 3) discusses the need for spatial continuity between the object stages, and Robert Nozick (1981, chap. 1) introduces what he calls the "closest continuer" principle. Hirsch (1982) shows convincingly that simple continuity principles do not really work—for example, a watch can persist or "survive" despite complete disassembly and dispersal of its parts at the factory. Nonetheless, Hirsch also proposes a principle of persistence that involves qualitative and spatiotemporal continuity that "minimizes change."

There are many complications about persistence that are not addressed by the Gestalt rules. Chief among these is the role of sortals. It is arguably part of our conception of object identity that what persists through various changes should at least remain an object of the same sort.[4] The Gestalt rules, though, are sortal-neutral; so they may be unable to tell us the full story about persistence. However, perhaps sortal-neutral principles are at work, including the Gestalt rules. Indeed, the infant may need a prior conception of object persistence in order to be capable of learning the sortals that the linguistic community introduces. And the very choice of the community's sortals may be constrained by Gestalt or Gestalt-like rules. I shall not pursue these complex issues here.

I do not mean to leave the impression that the Gestalt rules are the final word by psychologists on the question of temporal or spatial unity. On the contrary, important work is being done on the infant's conception of unity, persistence, and identity. Whereas various recent experiments have suggested that adherence to static Gestalt principles begins to emerge near six months of age, Elizabeth Spelke (1985) found that a "common movement" principle applies at four months. When a partly occluded object moves in certain ways, four-month-old infants perceive the object as a single unit behind its occluder. They perceive the unity of a rod that moves back and forth in a linear translation behind a stationary block, its center never coming into view. They also perceive the unity of a rod that moves in depth. Unity is not perceived if the object is stationary against a stationary background and only the occluder moves, or if the object and the occluder move together. Experiments such as these can shed more light on the innate constraints in our conception of objects.[5]

II

Returning to the Gestalt rules, I want to suggest that these can be applied in an explanatory fashion to some familiar metaphysical puzzles.

Consider the Ship of Theseus. At time t, there is a ship (-stage) $S1$. During the interval from t to t', parts of $S1$ are successively removed and replaced by functionally equivalent parts. At t' there is a ship $S2$ that results from these replacements but has none of $S1$'s original parts. Meanwhile, during most of the interval, the old parts from $S1$ are left in a junkyard. Finally, at t', they are reassembled into another ship, $S3$. With which ship is $S1$ identical (or unified), $S2$ or $S3$?

There is certainly a measure of ambiguity here. Most of us feel a tug in both directions: some temptation to identify (or unify) $S1$ with $S2$ and some temptation to identify it with $S3$. But most people favor $S2$. I propose that these reactions can be explained in terms of the Gestalt rules (in Jackendoff's preference rule construal). The good continuation rule is certainly much better exemplified if $S1$ is unified with $S2$ than if it is unified with $S3$. On the other hand, similarity seems to favor the unification of $S1$ with $S3$. These competing factors account for the measure of irresolution that makes us call the case a puzzle. At the same time, good continuation is weightier, on balance, though not decisively so.

The second metaphysical puzzle concerns what is variously called "teletransportation" or "telecloning." Suppose there is a machine that analyzes a person's body and brain and creates a blueprint from which an exact replica can be constructed. If you are planning a trip from Earth to Mars, or to a planet in a distant galaxy, you might consider the possibility of greatly shortening your trip. The machine could create a blueprint of you, destroy your Earthly body, but simultaneously beam a message to the target planet, where a precise replica would be built from different molecules. The question is: Would the person (-stage) on Mars be *you*? Would it be person-united (identified) with the Earthly person that entered the machine?

Again, intuitions are somewhat conflicted; there are tugs in both directions. On the whole, however, most of us come out in favor of unification. If we felt assured of the procedure's reliability, we would opt for being teletransported to Mars rather than undergo an arduous journey. We feel sufficiently confident that teletransportation preserves identity.

Again, our intuitive reactions to the case can be understood in terms of Gestalt rules. The replica has very adequate qualitative similarity to the person who enters the machine, both physical and psychological similarity. The hitch comes in the abrupt discontinuity. No person-stages occupy the spatiotemporal region between the Earthly and Martian stages. This discontinuity upsets, or at least unsettles, our unification intuitions. *Some* continuation is realized, however, in the path of the radio beams. Conjoined with similarity, this seems to suffice for unification. (Another important factor here, stressed by Shoemaker (1979) is that there is a *causal* connection between the two person-stages.)

In a variant of the central teletransportation case, intuitions turn out rather differently. Consider a case where two replicas are accidentally constructed on Mars (or other such "fission" cases). Here one is inclined to deny unification of *either* replica with the Earthly stage. I suggest that this is due to the fact that when two paths of continuation are equally good, the rule of good continuation generates no acceptable resolution; hence no unification intuition is forthcoming.[6]

Cases in which intuitions are fuzzy, ambiguous, or conflicted can be very agonizing. In a well-known case described by Bernard Williams (1973) where intuitions can be made to conflict over whether a person "survives" a sequence of operations, Williams points out how unsatisfactory it would be for the prospective subject of these operations to be told that it is "conceptually undecidable" whether or not it will be he who suffers certain pains. This may be a reason to try to devise some prescriptive metaphysics that resolves the issue. It may be true, nonetheless, that our folk ontology provides no (firm) basis for such a resolution. Our folk ontology may simply be indeterminate.

Folk ontology may suffer from inconsistency as well as indeterminacy. This can be illustrated in connection with the principles that drive our identification practices. Consider a cross-world variant of the original Ship of Theseus story devised by Hugh Chandler (1975). Suppose possible world $W1$ is as described in the original story, and let A be the initial ship-stage, B the ship-stage continuous with it with all the new parts, and C the ship-stage latterly constructed from the original parts. Next suppose that in possible world $W2$ the story is similar except that when the parts are removed they are not replaced; the ship is simply dismantled and then later reconstructed. Call the earlier ship-stage D and the reconstructed one E. Now our intuitions suggest the following (formulated in terms of identity). Within world $W1$, $A = B$, but $B \neq C$. Within world $W2$, $D = E$. Concerning cross-world identities, it seems plausible to say that $D = A$ and $E = C$. But this set of identity and distinctness claims is inconsistent!

Now some metaphysicians, such as David Lewis (1983e, 1986), want to draw the conclusion that the objects in the different possible worlds should not be identified; there are only counterpart relations across worlds. This is one possible moral to draw if one wants to do prescriptive metaphysics, to construct a "correct" ontology, which presumably must feature no internal contradictions. But if we are only doing descriptive metaphysics, there is no need to draw this sort of moral. Our folk ontology, or the (psychological) constraints that direct it, may simply be liable to such internal contradiction. It is no flaw in a piece of descriptive metaphysics that it portrays our folk ontology in a way that reveals it to have such a liability.

A familiar case in point is Sorites puzzles. These puzzles can plausibly be said to arise because of two cognitive traits: (1) a disposition to create binary, ungraded categories, and (2) a principle of good continuation, which inclines a cognizer to co-classify objects that differ only minutely (on relevant dimensions). Many writers seem to diagnose the Sorites puzzles as arising from defects in our linguistic conventions. But I suspect that the root explanation lies in more deep-seated cognitive traits.

III

Let me turn now to prescriptive metaphysics, especially in its revisionary form. Prescriptive metaphysics is revisionary, on my understanding, if it urges any of the following: (A) the postulation of some entities, properties, or relations (or types of entities, properties, or relations) that are not posited by our folk ontology; (B) the rejection of some (types of) entities (and so forth) that are posited by our folk ontology; or (C) the ascription of an ontological status to certain entities that differs from their assigned status in our folk ontology.

What might rationalize or ground a piece of revisionary metaphysics? From what intellectual sources can such proposals plausibly arise? Historically, some specimens of revisionary metaphysics have stemmed from purely philosophical considerations (or philosophical considerations operating on prior common sense beliefs). McTaggart's (1908) argument for the unreality of time, for example, was purely philosophical, as were Plato's arguments for the existence of the Forms. Similarly, Kant's arguments for the mind-dependence of space and time were purely epistemological: how else could we account for our (presumed) a priori knowledge of geometry and arithmetic? Other historical arguments for revisionary metaphysics have come primarily from physical science. Modern physics tells us that ordinary bodies are not solid, as common sense assumes, but are thoroughly "gappy." Relativity theory dictates the replacement of our commonsense assumptions about space and time with relativistic construals. And quantum mechanics may wreak havoc with many of our folk ontological presumptions.

In other historical cases, the argumentation has been based on a mix of scientific and philosophical considerations. Seventeenth-century claims about the difference in ontological status between primary and secondary qualities stemmed partly from corpuscularian physics and partly from philosophical reflection. Russell appealed to physics in challenging the naive conception of causality; whereas Hume's argument for revising the status of causation was either philosophical or proto-psychological.

Many metaphysicians have been quite unclear as to whether they were proposing descriptive or prescriptive ontological theories; often they have tried some sort of hybrid. Others have claimed to do descriptive metaphysics where this is highly suspect. Berkeley's claim that his idealism was an articulation of common sense deserves little credence; idealism has even less credibility as descriptive metaphysics than as prescriptive metaphysics. Many specific metaphysical claims have been put forward as descriptive by some writers but revisionary (and hence prescriptive) by others. Locke's doctrine that color is merely a disposition in objects to produce sensations in us was presented as a revisionary doctrine, one at variance with naive thought about the matter. Recent philosophers like Colin McGinn, by contrast, present this dispositional theory as an *analysis* of our ordinary conception of color, i.e., as a piece of descriptive metaphysics (see McGinn 1983). My special interest in the rest of the paper is explicitly revisionary metaphysics, especially the ways in which revisionary metaphysics might be based (in part!) on psychology or cognitive science.

It will be useful at this point to survey some alternative ways in which prescriptive metaphysics might be revisionary. For any entity or property that folk ontology posits, what might prescriptive metaphysics say about that entity or property? To put flesh on these alternatives, the example of color is particularly handy.

First, prescriptive metaphysics might deny the existence of this entity or property entirely. In the case of properties, for example, it might deny that there is any scientifically acceptable property that is coextensive with the putative property posited by folk ontology (e.g., the property of being red). This denial, of course, should be backed up by some indication of what counts as a "scientifically acceptable" property. In any case, this would be a nihilistic, or eliminative, brand of revisionism (for the property or entity in question).[7]

Second, without denying the existence of the entity or property in question, prescriptive metaphysics might ascribe to it a different ontological status from the one assigned to it by folk ontology. (There remains the delicate question of what kinds of status ascribed to an entity or property count as *ontological*. I shall not try to settle that here, but shall merely appeal to educated philosophical judgment.) The most familiar move here is to start with a property to which folk ontology ascribes purely objective status, and then to replace it with some subjective, or non-purely-objective, status. For example, folk ontology (arguably) ascribes to red the status of being a property of physical objects, intrinsic to objects, nonrelational, and nonanthropocentric. What might prescriptive metaphysics say on that score?

In principle, it might agree with folk ontology. Indeed, it might assert that red is a natural kind: that people's division of objects into hues (either in perceptual judgment or in language) cuts nature at her joints. This would be a conservative, nonrevisionary assessment. However, this is extremely dubious, given the phenomenon of metamerism. Metamerism shows that the color divisions that humans make are arbitrary or bizarre by the standards of physics. These divisions are a product of our humanly idiosyncratic visual system. Acknowledging this point, a comparatively modest revision would say that colors are objective, but not natural kinds. Since color divisions can be analyzed in terms of purely physical properties, they are not subjective or relational. They are properties of physical objects themselves. But the particular groupings of objects into color categories, and the system of hue categories—the color "space"—can only be specified by adverting to human reactions, to human judgments of similarity and difference. This position has been sketched by J. J. C. Smart (1975) and defended in detail by David Hilbert (1987), who calls it "anthropocentric realism." I shall call it "anthropocentric objectivism." On Hilbert's view, color is surface spectral reflectance: the disposition objects have to reflect varying percentages of the incident light. The spectral reflectance of a surface is a property that any surface has in complete independence of how it appears to any observer, or even the existence of any observers.

Although this view is objectivist and hence conservative, it still departs, in my opinion, from folk ontology, and is therefore revisionary. Folk ontology does not assign to color the status of being anthropocentric. So this kind of theory does propose a change in the ontological status of color.

It should be clear that while part of the scientific research that fuels the theory of color is essentially research in physics, another part is cognitive science. (Psychophysics bridges these two disciplines.) The psychological side of the research is especially prominent in the study of color constancy. Constancy is important in challenging the attempt to identify an object's color (at time t) with the wavelength of the light it reflects (at t); for it shows that in many circumstances perceived color is constant through changes in illumination.[8]

More extreme revisionary proposals than anthropocentric objectivism would be various brands of subjectivism. First there is intrinsic, or non-dispositional, subjectivism, which says that color is a property of mental states, or perhaps of mental objects such as sense-data. Next there are various brands of dispositional subjectivism. These are various versions of the secondary-quality approach, which claims that colors are dispositions of physical objects to produce certain sensations in people. While the reference to subjective sensations is common to these dispositional approaches, they differ in the particular dispositions they specify.

One version of the dispositionalist approach might be existentially mind-dependent. It might say, roughly, that an object O is red if and only if there exist perceivers such that O is disposed to produce R-experiences in them. Another version of the dispositionalist approach would have no such existential commitment; it would say that an object O is red if and only if it would produce R-experiences in certain perceivers if there were any such perceivers. The first variant would imply that nothing is red in a world without the right sort of perceivers; the second variant would have no such implication.

Setting aside this aspect of the dispositionalist approach, still other differences are important. One proposal might seek to make the truth conditions of color-identity statements depend on the appearances that would be produced in *normal* lighting conditions (e.g., sunlight), while another proposal might make the truth conditions of color-identity statements depend on appearances that would be produced in *all* lighting conditions. Scientific facts about color make this a significant distinction.[9] Similarly, one proposal might identify a particular shade, e.g., "unique green," via the responses of an *average* observer. But since there are non-trivial individual differences among observers, a different approach might relativize unique green to an individual.[10]

Of even greater importance for present purposes is the question of whether color categories can be simply relativized to human physiology, or whether they should be relativized to cultural convention embedded in language. Before the publication of Brent Berlin and Paul Kay's book, *Basic Color Terms* (1969), there was a general assumption that the visible spectrum is a paradigm of continuity, and its division into red, yellow, green, and blue (etc.) is an accident of culture. But Berlin and Kay, through cross-cultural studies, provided evidence that these hue labels cluster around certain perceptual foci, which apparently arise from the visual apparatus itself. Thus, color categories seem to be more (humanly) universal and less culturally relative than previously suspected. In trying to pinpoint the ontological status of color, this is an importance difference. Moreover, to resolve the issue, one needs the empirical results of the cognitive sciences.

To amplify this point, let us return to the domain of "objects" and their spatiotemporal identity (or unity) conditions. It is plausible to say that folk ontology represents persons and tables, in contrast with Hirsch's cpersons and Shoemaker's klables, as "natural" objects; that the former are viewed within folk ontology as "genuine" continuants, whereas the latter would be greeted as artificial and contrived in roughly the way that grue and bleen are spontaneously viewed as artificial and contrived. We might formulate this difference by saying that persons and tables, according to folk ontology, have "objecthood" which cpersons and klables lack. But what should prescriptive metaphysics say? Is there a property of objecthood that persons and tables (or the person and table unity-schemes) instantiate but cpersons and klables (or their respective unity-schemes) lack? If so, what is the ontological status of this property?

Some philosophers, e.g., Quine (1969c, 1974, 1981), would prefer a prescriptive metaphysics that grants parity to persons and cpersons, or to tables and klables. They would therefore reject the invidious property of objecthood entirely (quite apart from general nominalist qualms about properties). A different sort of prescriptive metaphysician might try to find room for the (invidious) property of objecthood, but only in a relational, subjective, form. There is little hope of identifying objecthood with any "objective" anthropocentric property, in the way that Hilbert identifies color with surface spectral reflectance. But one could certainly try a "secondary quality" move, and identify objecthood with the disposition of persons, tables, and so forth (or their respective unity-schemes) to elicit from people certain subjective responses, viz., "unity intuitions."[11]

If this or other such moves are made, the question arises whether unity intuitions are mere by-products of accidental (though perhaps rationalizable) features of language, or whether they are the results of more deep-seated properties of human cognitive architecture, such as the Gestalt rules. An answer to this question clearly awaits further research in cognitive science. But this means that the precise story about objecthood may well hinge on the results of cognitive science, just as the precise ontological story about color must be informed by the best available research on cognition.

Apart from these relatively refined metaphysical conclusions, cognitive science can contribute to prescriptive metaphysics in a more coarse-grained fashion. Naive thought, it may be suggested, tacitly embraces a "detectionist" or "apprehensionist" assumption. If we find some objects X and Y phenomenologically discriminable, or if we find ourselves (and others) making certain systematic individuating or classifying judgments, we tend to assume that there must be objective properties that we are detecting, apprehending, or registering. Thus, our folk ontology is highly objectivist. Prescriptive metaphysics must begin with what our folk ontology provides. But if it acquires evidence that supports a constructivist, antidetectionist explanation for our discriminations and judgments, then it has grounds for revisionary conclusions. Now cognitive science is in the business of trying to find explanations of mental phenomena. Although it is not "occupationally" in a position to exclude detectionist explanations (unless one includes all of psychophysics, for example, within cognitive science), it may be in a position to provide explanations of various discriminations and judgments in terms of various psychological processes, faculties, and so forth. This can lend support to constructivist explanations, and thereby undermine the credibility of detectionist assumptions.

The case is analogous to arguments about religious experience and religious belief. The theist claims that the best explanation of such experience and belief is the existence of an external God. The atheist replies that there is an alternate explanation of these phenomena, one that appeals only to psychological and cultural mechanisms. If the latter explanation is more parsimonious, or otherwise provides a "better explanation," then that undermines the God hypothesis. Similarly, if cognitive theory can explain the phenomenological or judgmental events without positing objectively detected properties, then the existence of such properties may be undermined from the standpoint of prescriptive metaphysics.

This is precisely the strategy employed by Hume vis-à-vis causation. Hume offered a proto-psychological theory of "habit" that purported to explain why we believe in causation construed as "necessary connection." He saw this as undermining the naive belief in an objective causal relation. It remains to be seen whether Hume's psychological project can be sustained by theories that are empirically superior to his, or whether analogous psychological theories can be developed for other ontological domains, such as mathematics. In recent work, Noam Chomsky has speculated that mathematical cognition may be a by-product of the language faculty.[12] If this sort of conjecture were confirmed, it could add empirical support to a subjectivist, or quasi-subjectivist, ontology of mathematics. It hardly needs emphasis that no such conclusion can be sustained by the cognitive sciences alone; philosophical considerations will always be pertinent. But the mental sciences can certainly provide a range of relevant evidence.

Here is a further question about prescriptive metaphysics that the cognitive sciences should address. When a theory is both prescriptive and revisionary, it ostensibly implies that we should abjure or abandon some features of our folk ontology. But is such abandonment psychologically feasible? *Can* we abandon our color framework, our basic framework for object individuation, our belief in causation, or in, say, the propositional attitudes? This is a problem that needs to be addressed by psychology. Perhaps the answer is that we can revise our "theoretical" beliefs about such matters while retaining some more primitive stratum of mental representation. This suggestion is promising, but requires more careful investigation by the mental sciences.

There are also questions of a more philosophical sort about the limits of revisability. It would seem, for example, that prescriptive metaphysics could not coherently advocate elimination of the propositional attitudes, because the very business of prescriptive metaphysics is to advocate the adoption of certain propositional attitudes, viz., belief or disbelief in the existence of various entities and properties. However, this worry may not be conclusive. Perhaps prescriptive metaphysics could propose some sort of "replacement" properties for belief and disbelief that would allow itself to stay in business while still being revisionary.

Another possible constraint on revisability, at least of the eliminativist variety, concerns the commitments invoked in the epistemic process of getting evidence to support revision. If we are to use science, for example, in marshalling support for revisionary proposals, we cannot coherently abandon any of the relations to which science appeals. If science invokes the causal relation, or any sort of nomological relation, then it would seem to be ("pragmatically") incoherent to use science to champion the elimination of such relations. These issues concerning the limits of revisability are ones to which prescriptive metaphysics must stay alert; but this is not the occasion to pursue them in further detail.

Notes

I am indebted to Victor Caston, Marian David, Markus Lammenranta, David Lewis, Holly Smith, and Scott Sturgeon for valuable comments and suggestions.
1. It may well be suggested that folk ontology should include not only the entities, properties, and relations to which prereflective thought is ontically committed, but also a certain amount of our naive beliefs about these things. The trouble is that it is hard

to say just which of our beliefs should be included. At a minimum, however, folk ontology should include our (naive) beliefs or presumptions about the ontological status of the objects in question.

2. For examples, see Jackendoff 1983, chap. 8 or Goldman 1987a. My paper is an earlier pass at some of the same themes presented here.

3. For a summary, see Goldman 1986, chap. 11.

4. See Wiggins 1980, chap. 3 and Hirsch 1982, chap. 3.

5. In unpublished lectures, Saul Kripke has pointed to a problem of circularity in using motion as a criterion of cross-temporal identity: the usual understanding of motion seems to presuppose the notion of an object's persistence through time. This issue will not be addressed here.

6. The situation is a bit different in Derek Parfit's "branchline" case, where the machine creates one replica on Mars but neglects to destroy the Earthly person (Parfit 1984, pp. 199–201). There the later Earthly person (-stage) is presumably the only one that is unified with the earlier Earthly person (-stage). This is because it has superior continuity with the earlier stage than does the replica on Mars.

7. Although science has often fueled eliminative proposals, or other types of revisionary proposals, it cannot sustain these proposals without philosophical support. If philosophy tells us, for example, that all scientific theory should be given an instrumentalist construal, then the metaphysical ramifications of science will be considerably muted. However, since I am inclined to be a realist about scientific theory, I am not myself tempted to blunt the power of science as a weapon of metaphysical revision, at least not on instrumentalist grounds.

8. See Hilbert 1987.

9. On the significance of this distinction, see Averill 1985.

10. See Hardin 1988.

11. The secondary-quality move in question here, of course, is a revisionary, not an "analytical," move. The latter I find quite implausible, both for color and for objecthood. I think that our folk ontology is robustly objectivist about both color and objecthood. As a revisionary theory, however, the dispositionalist approach has somewhat greater plausibility.

12. Lecture delivered at a conference in Jerusalem, April 1988.

Chapter 3
Cognition and Modal Metaphysics

Contemporary metaphysics is often driven by two impulses: to articulate our naive, commonsensical ontology and to construct an ontology enlightened by scientific theory and philosophical reflection. As I urged in chapter 2, these impulses should be expressed in two different branches of the subject: *descriptive* and *prescriptive* metaphysics. Careful separation of these branches can forestall confusion and irrelevant argumentation. Descriptive metaphysics would try to describe and explain our ordinary ontological commitments: our "folk ontology." Prescriptive metaphysics would subject these commitments to critical appraisal. It would be prepared to undertake a reformulation of ontology, possibly an extensive redesign of the ontological landscape. In this paper I shall delineate this bipartite approach in more detail, with special attention to the kinds of evidence and argumentation that should be relevant in each branch of the subject.

Chapter 2 also argued that cognitive science can make contributions to metaphysics, not only descriptive metaphysics but prescriptive metaphysics as well. A second purpose of this chapter—indeed, the one that occupies a greater portion of my attention—is to illustrate just how such contributions can be made, specifically, how cognitive science can (help) support *revisions* in ontological stance. The principal example in both of these ventures is modal metaphysics, especially essentialism.

I

Before turning to modal metaphysics, let me briefly consider two other ontological domains: color and time. In each of the latter domains we have sensations or feelings that evoke certain ontological views. However, psychological explanations of the feelings can be offered which, together perhaps with physical information, tend to undermine those views. Prescriptive metaphysics should make use of these explanations and offer a revised set of ontological conclusions.

Let us begin with the case of color. Naive experience suggests that colors are intrinsic, nonrelational properties of physical objects; that each color is a natural kind, whose physical instances are substantially similar along some physical dimension. Although problems with this naive view have been raised for centuries, recent work in color science makes it particularly difficult to maintain. The physical objects to which we ascribe a particular color are not, in general, as similar (in a color relevant way) as we naively suppose. And although color properties appear to be intrinsic and nonrelational, this appearance is substantially an artifact of our specific color receptor and interpretive systems. On reflection, colors are best thought of as highly anthropocentric, or relational, properties.

The human color receptor system is trichromatic, consisting of three types of cones.[1] Each cone type is a broad-band receptor; that is, each responds to a very broad range of light wavelengths. The main difference between the three cone elements is in their sensitivity curves. This difference enables the receptor system to discriminate wavelengths, but it is not always able to discriminate between wavelength mixtures. The receptor output produced by a single wavelength can typically be duplicated by a mixture of three suitably balanced other wavelengths. This is a consequence of the receptor system functioning like an integrator, i.e., like an adding machine that records total sums without keeping track of the component figures. Since the receptor outputs from some wavelength combinations are exactly equal, the system has no way of knowing how the color was generated. This is responsible for metamerism, in which widely disparate wavelength stimuli produce equivalent hue experiences. In addition to metamerism, there is the fact that wavelengths within a given hue category, e.g., blue, can be reflected or emitted by surfaces of radically different chemical compositions. Larry Hardin (1988, pp. 2–7) lists fifteen different physical properties of objects that influence their perceived color. Thus, the blue of the sky, the blueness of water, the blue-looking portion of the rainbow, the blue of sapphire, and the iridescent blue of some beetles all have different causes.

Many other properties of color experience are the products of the opponent-processing system, according to the generally accepted theory of Leo Hurvich and Dorothea Jameson. Six different neural processes are organized into three opponent-process pairs: red-green, blue-yellow, and black-white. The two members of each pair are antagonists, so that excitation of one member automatically inhibits the other. The experience of hue depends on two of the opponent-process pairs: red-green and blue-yellow. Each pair can be likened to a balance scale: if one arm goes down, the other comes up . The hue we see depends upon the position of the two balances.

This system gives rise, for one thing, to *unique* hues. These are hues that are seen as "pure", e.g., a blue that is judged to have no trace of red or green . This characteristic of color experience is an artifact of the opponent-processing system. For example, unique red is not produced by a single wavelength, but only by a mixture of wavelengths. Another set of relationships that is generated (partly) by the opponent-processing system is a set of phenomenal similarities among hues that allow them to be represented in a circular arrangement: the "color circle". There is no systematic relationship in the spectral stimuli, however, that mirrors this circle. Although much of it does parallel the spectral continuum, in "closing" the circle there is a "jump" from the low to the high end of the visible spectrum. Finally, the entire phenomenon of color complementarity is also a manifestation of the opponent-processing system.

The peculiar complex of color experiences and relationships that result from our internal color coding system makes it difficult to reconcile our naive conception of color with external physical reality. Thus, prescriptive metaphysics seems driven toward a different construal of color than our naive ontology. I won't review all of the arguments here, since some of the relevant literature and arguments are summarized and cited in chapter 2.[2] Suffice it to say, first, that it is difficult to make out a case for colors as natural kinds. Metamerism, for example, shows that the set of physical stimuli that can produce any given hue experience are too heterogeneous and gerrymandered to qualify as a natural kind. Again, although one would suppose that an intrinsic physical characteristic of light is responsible for the "uniqueness", or "purity" of certain hues, there seems to be no such characteristic. All this pushes the reflective theorist toward a secondary-quality or anthropocentric construal of color. Colors can only be understood as capacities of physical objects to produce certain sensations in human beings, or other creatures with similar color-receptive apparatus. But this is a move to semisubjectivism. Even this kind of position is difficult to work out in detail, so a further demotion of color to a purely subjective status—as qualifying states of mind—might be necessary.

What do I mean by "demotion"? Ontological demotion occurs when a philosopher assigns an ontological status to a predicate (or singular term) that is "lower" than the one assigned to it by common sense, or by other philosophical views. By "lower" I mean a position closer to the antirealist, irrealist, or nonobjectivist end of the ontological continuum. Without trying to provide a general scale of ontological status, we can cite the following status revisions as examples of ontological demotion: (1) claiming that a predicate does not denote a property at all, but merely expresses a feeling, sentiment, emotion, or attitude (expressivism, or projectivism); (2) claiming that a predicate purports to denote a property but fails to denote one (an "error theory"); (3) claiming that although a predicate succeeds in denoting a property, the extension of that property is empty (contrary to the prevailing view); (4) claiming that the property denoted by a predicate is more "subjective", or less "objective", than is otherwise supposed. There might be analogous kinds of demotion for (putative) "entities" and "facts", in addition to properties. In the case of color, it is usually the fourth, least radical variety of demotion, that is contemplated.

It would be very nice to have a general criterion of when ontological demotion is in order. Formulation of a satisfactory metaphysical principle of this kind would be a valuable achievement. Unfortunately, I have no such principle to offer. I am therefore compelled to proceed in a piecemeal, case-by-case, fashion. Much of the rest of the paper will concern cases in which, by my lights, psychological or cognitivist explanation can (help) support ontological demotion. However, I have no theory of when, precisely, such explanations support demotion. Obviously, it is silly to suppose that *whenever* psychological explanation is possible, demotion is warranted. But in *some* cases ontological demotion seems justified, all things considered.

II

My second example concerns time. One conception of time, often said to articulate the (or a) commonsense understanding of time, represents it as something constantly in flux, as something that gradually "moves", "flows", or "advances" from the past into the future. One familiar expression of this picture is the metaphor of the "river of time". The core of this conception focuses on a privileged moment "now", relative to which events can be classified as either "past", "present", or "future". This classification system is what McTaggart (1908) called the "A-series". According to this conception, there is a "now" that is constantly moving, thereby inducing changes in the status of events from future to present and from present to past.

Here I wish to consider a certain critique of this conception of time, a critique given by Paul Horwich (1987), who derives his account from Izchak Miller's (1984) elucidation of Husserl (1928). This critique grants that we have a *feeling* of the passage of time, but offers a psychological explanation of this feeling to undermine its presumed veridicality. The psychological explanation is not based on *experimental* psychology, so perhaps it doesn't qualify as "cognitive science" in the standard acceptation of that term. But this point is not crucial. The idea is to illustrate how psychological explanations, whatever their methodological pedigree, can provide evidence for the untenability of certain intuitively appealing ontological views.

The Husserl-Miller-Horwich account (see Horwich 1987, pp. 33–36) runs approximately as follows. We are aware of a succession of complex experiences. Each complex experience has the same structure, consisting of memories of the distant past, more recent recollections, sensations, and anticipations projected for various times in the future. Moreover, some of the memories and anticipations are of experiences that themselves contain just those sorts of constituents. For example, I remember that many of the things I now recall were once recalled as not having happened so far in the past, and things I now anticipate were then expected to happen even further in the future than they now are. Thus, an experience represents both a set of events strung out in time and a set of experiences, each of which represents, from different perspectives, the same string of events. In this fashion we are conscious of the same experiential framework being filled with the same contents from different temporal perspectives. It therefore seems as if a single entity—the structure of experience—is in motion relative to the world. If we add the further idea that our experiential framework has a *location*, viz., *now* (the present), we get the conclusion that this location is constantly changing: the "now" moves.

If this psychological explanation is correct, it shows that the feeling of temporal flow could arise from the content of experience alone, without any relevant thing actually flowing. Since the notion of such flow is problematic, the invited inference is to reject the existence of such a "moving *now*". In other words, the psychological story offers a putatively better explanation of the feeling than the hypothesis of its veridicality. Thus, although folk ontology may be committed to a "moving now" conception of time, there is no need for prescriptive metaphysics to endorse such an entity or such a construal of the nature of time. What is suggested, then, is a radical kind of ontological demotion, one of the eliminative, or "error theory", type.

I am comfortable with this conclusion. I hesitate, however, over how it should be generalized. Should we say that whenever a feeling or intuition can be explained internally, there is a presumption against its veridicality? This certainly needs qualification. Internal explanations can commonly be expanded into fuller explanations that cite external factors, perhaps explanations invoking the metaphysical posit in question. Thus, the proposed principle should be qualified to say that the indicated presumption arises only when a feeling or intuition can be given an *autonomous* internal explanation, where an internal explanation is autonomous if it either *excludes* expansion into a fuller explanation citing the metaphysical posit or is *unreceptive* to such expansion. (Receptivity and unreceptivity would need to be spelled out.)

Even this is probably too strong. We need to consider not only the *possibility* of such an explanation but its *plausibility*. The degree of plausibility will depend on our relevant background information. Similarly, in deciding for or against demotion we need to consider any background information, scientific or otherwise, that bears on the initial acceptability of the ontological posit. If the posit is problematic or "queer" relative to this information—like the "moving now" conception of time—then a demotion decision is more easily justified. Thus, psychological explainability is not itself sufficient for demotion. Much depends on how the specific demotion fits with the rest of our ontological and doctrinal commitments. However, with scientific advances and philosophical systematization, posits that are commonsensically congenial may become reflectively unsustainable.

III

I turn now to the topic of modal metaphysics. This takes us from two fairly specialized domains into the heartland of metaphysics, at least recent metaphysics. Here too I shall consider the possibility of psychological explanation and its prospective impact on the prescriptive metaphysics of the domain. First, however, I shall try to show how neglect of the descriptive-prescriptive distinction muddies the waters in modal metaphysics. I shall contrast the methodological implications of my bipartite conception of metaphysics with the methodologies of two leading modal metaphysicians, David Lewis and Saul Kripke. Their respective methodologies have many attractive features, but sometimes suffer from failure to distinguish the two branches of metaphysics. One should not try to assess a candidate methodology without first clarifying the "office" for which it is a candidate. Since there are, in my opinion, two offices to be filled, the qualifications for office are naturally rather different.

Lewis's metaphysical methodology might be called *systematic common-sensism*. The core elements are expressed in the following passage:

> In trying to improve the unity and economy of our total theory ...,
> I am trying to accomplish two things that somewhat conflict. I am
> trying to *improve* that theory, that is to change it. But I am trying to
> improve *that* theory, that is to leave it recognizably the same theory
> we had before. For it is pointless to build a theory, however nicely
> systematized it might be, that it would be unreasonable to believe.
> And a theory cannot earn credence just by its unity and economy.
> What credence it cannot earn, it must inherit.... A worthwhile theory
> must be credible, and a credible theory must be conservative. It
> cannot gain, and it cannot deserve, credence if it disagrees with too
> much of what we thought before. And much of what we thought
> before was just common sense. Common sense is a settled body of
> theory—unsystematic folk theory—which at any rate we *do* believe;
> and I presume that we are reasonable to believe it. (Most of it.) ...
> [T]heoretical conservatism is the only sensible policy.... Part of this
> conservatism is reluctance to accept theories that fly in the face of
> common sense. (Lewis 1986, p. 134)

As suggested above, my methodological disagreements with Lewis stem largely from his failure to distinguish the different missions of descriptive

and prescriptive metaphysics. Although his attachment to common sense—
our initial theory—is eminently reasonable for descriptive metaphysics, it
is quite dubitable for prescriptive metaphysics. Focusing for the moment
on the former, one should neither try to *improve* the folk theory nor make
it more systematic or economical. The proper aim of descriptive metaphysics is simply to describe (and explain) our naive ontology *as it is*, warts and
all, without making it more unified or elegant than it is in the hands of the
folk.

While the yen for theoretical improvement is misplaced within descriptive metaphysics, it finds a proper niche in prescriptive metaphysics. Here,
however, Lewis seems too unprepared for change. He is methodologically
committed to having a theory that is recognizably the old theory we had
before. He is unwilling to divest himself of folk belief, as I would be
prepared to do. This stems, in part, from our epistemological differences.
As a reliabilist, I am prepared for a scenario in which many commonsense
beliefs are convicted of being unreliably caused, thereby rendering the
accepted views unworthy of continued credal commitment. Lewis's epistemic
conservatism makes him leery of major doctrinal revisions. But such revisions sometimes seem to be in order, as in the cases of color and time.

Of course, Lewis's modal metaphysics is usually criticized for going
against common sense. Lewis acknowledges that his extreme modal realism
conflicts with part of common sense, and that this counts against it. He
defends his overall view as *more* consonant with common sense—at least
when the values of economy and unity are factored in—than rival theories.
I would argue against his extreme modal realism in two ways, again
emphasizing the descriptive-prescriptive distinction. As far as descriptive
metaphysics goes, extreme realism is readily refuted by the incredulous
stare, by the acknowledged disagreement with common sense. It cannot be
redeemed by being part of a larger systematic theory, even if that theory
is more consonant with common sense on the whole than rival theories of
equal systematicity. Systematicity is no virtue at all in descriptive metaphysics, since our commonsense doctrines may be highly unsystematic. So
being a component of a systematic theory cannot outweigh violation of
common sense.

When we turn to prescriptive metaphysics, Lewis's extreme modal realism is doubtful on epistemic grounds. We simply have no good reason to
believe it, to believe that there *are* other universes very much like ours. The
mere fact that we *say* things like "there are other ways things could have
been" does not provide good evidence for this (and it wouldn't even if the
language of "concrete universes" provided a good paraphrase for the
language of "ways things could have been", which is doubtful). To suppose
that what we naively say provides good evidence for what exists places

excessive faith in the deliverances of common sense (or common expression).

As further illustration of how the conflation of descriptive and prescriptive missions can obfuscate modal metaphysics, consider the issue of transworld identity versus counterpart theory. Proponents of identity theory are surely right in saying that this approach conforms to our intuitive, commonsensical ways of thinking—certainly to our ordinary ways of *speaking*. As Kripke (1971) argues, when one says that Nixon might have gotten Carswell through, one surely means to be talking about *Nixon*, not a counterpart of Nixon. So crossworld identity theory has the upper hand if we are discussing *descriptive* metaphysics, and that is the branch that parties to the dispute often seem to be addressing. Certainly that is what Kripke is addressing when he rejects Lewis's suggestion that what "we really mean" by the Nixon counterfactual is given by the counterpart translation (Kripke 1971, p. 148).

Now Lewis and others have pointed out certain problems with transworld identity. Since an individual in another possible world may be endowed with properties that he lacks in this world, there is a violation of the principle of the indiscernibility of identicals. This is one standard reason for preferring the counterpart relation to strict identity. But why should this be a reason for preferring counterpart theory *as a reconstruction of naive ontology*? Why assume that the common folk *notice* that strict crossworld identity runs afoul of the indiscernibility of identicals? It is vastly more plausible to suppose that they don't reflect on the implications of their way of conceptualizing the matter. So even assuming the systematic indefensibility of the identity approach, this does not show that people don't ordinarily think in those terms. When we turn to *prescriptive* metaphysics, of course, the problems and paradoxes of transworld identity must be taken seriously—e.g., the paradox posed by Roderick Chisholm (1967). But prescriptive metaphysics is a different branch of the subject. Theories suitable for one branch need not be suitable for the other.

IV

I shall return to Lewis's methodology later, but now I turn to Kripke's. Kripke's methodology comes out most clearly in his discussion of essentialism (Kripke 1971, 1980). He famously contends that Queen Elizabeth II could not have been born of different parents than her actual parents; she could not, for example, have been the child of Mr. and Mrs. Truman. He similarly holds that the composition of an object is essential to it. Given that a particular lectern is made of wood, and not ice, it could not have been made of ice instead. Although we can imagine a qualitatively similar lectern made of ice, it would not be the very same lectern as the original.

What is the evidence that is supposed to support essentialism? Kripke takes intuitions to be the crucial data, intuitions about how one would describe test cases like the foregoing. In discussing the Queen Elizabeth case, he writes, "One can only become convinced of this *by reflection on how you would describe this situation*" (1980, p. 113; italics added); and about the lectern example he says, "*One has a considerable feeling* that it could *not* [have been made of ice] " (1971, p. 152; first italics added). Similarly, in discussing whether there are any possible worlds in which heat would not be molecular motion, the tests he poses are tests about "what we would say" (1971, p. 159). A general statement of the centrality of intuitions occurs in a slightly different context: "Of course, some philosophers think that something's having intuitive content is very inconclusive evidence in favor of it. I think it is very heavy evidence in favor of anything, myself. I really don't know, in a way, what more conclusive evidence one can have about anything, ultimately speaking" (1980, p. 42).[3] So the evidence on which Kripke rests his essentialist claims apparently consists of intuitions about ways to describe relevant situations.[4]

From the perspective of my descriptive-prescriptive distinction, we should ask which branch of metaphysics Kripke means to discuss. Since he doesn't draw any such distinction, this is not clear. If he were confining his discussion to descriptive metaphysics, then the appeal to intuitions—to what we would intuitively say about certain situations—is unquestionably relevant, and pretty convincing. If all (or most) speakers agree with his description about how we are inclined to describe the situations in question, that would strongly support his contention that origin and composition are indeed viewed as essential properties *within our commonsense ontology*. (Actually, this should be qualified. The support will be strong only if *all* the relevant test cases turn out as Kripke claims. That is by no means entirely clear.) However, if Kripke means to be speaking about prescriptive metaphysics, as I think he is (in part), much more needs to be said.

Why should we regard intuitions or feelings as reliable indicators of genuine metaphysical facts? Do the intuitions simply reflect linguistic rules or conventions about the proper way to describe these cases? This would seem to turn the necessities in question into linguistic necessities, which defenders of metaphysical necessity are anxious to avoid. If that is not the intention, what licenses the inference from these intuitions to the putative metaphysical facts? Why should the intuitions be relied upon? Perhaps they are no sounder than the feeling, or intuition, that time flows.

The issue can be crystallized by focusing on exactly what sorts of "facts" essentialism is intended to formulate. Now Kripke, of course, is a stipulationist. Possible worlds, he says, are stipulated, not discovered by powerful telescopes. However, there evidently are limits on what can be stipulated, according to Kripke. If we could stipulate *any* possible world we wished, why couldn't we stipulate one in which Queen Elizabeth is the daughter of Mr. and Mrs. Truman? Why couldn't we stipulate a world in which the original lectern is made of ice? Since Kripke obviously thinks we cannot stipulate *these* worlds, he evidently thinks there are *objective constraints* on what can be stipulated. Apparently, these objective constraints are what the doctrine of essentialism means to capture.

Are there genuinely objective constraints, constraints that "reality itself" dictates, rather than just our language or thought? Or are the only constraints subjective, constraints that are somehow imposed by our thought or language? To suggest that the constraints are purely subjective would be to suggest an ontological "demotion" of essentialism.[5] At least two writers have explicitly made roughly this proposal: J. L. Mackie (1974) and Alan Sidelle (1989). Mackie says that although the necessities formulated by essentialism apply to individual things and natural kinds, "that they so apply is primarily a feature of the way we think and speak" (Mackie 1974, p. 560). Sidelle explicitly opposes a "realist" conception of modality and essence, and proposes a "conventionalist" conception instead.[6] The prospects for some such demotion of essentialism is what I now wish to explore. Notice that we can grant the *truth* of essentialism while still questioning its ontological *status*, just as we can acknowledge the existence of color or the truths of mathematics while still jibbing at their ontological status. Thus, I am not going to deny that, *in some sense*, objects have some of their properties necessarily, but I am going to speculate on the acceptable reading, or interpretation, of this doctrine.

V

What might be a psychological, or cognitivist, story that would account for people's essentialist intuitions? Cognitive science certainly has no specific analysis to offer at this point. Indeed, it has barely addressed the question, to my knowledge. Nonetheless, clues to a fruitful direction of inquiry may be culled from the work of Hans Kamp (1985). Although Kamp's work is not aimed at questions about *de re* modality, and cannot be applied in detail to our topic, it does represent a *kind* of theory that holds prospects for relevant development.

Kamp is interested in discourse representation theory (DR theory). Central to DR theory is the concept of a discourse representation structure (DRS), which has two components: a set of *reference markers*, called the 'universe' of the DRS, and a set of 'conditions', which act as predications on the markers. When a person hears a text, this gives rise to a DRS, which is obtained by applying to the text an algorithmic procedure, a *DRS-construction algorithm*. Thus, suppose someone hears the three-sentence text *T*: "The Defense Secretary is addressing the Union. A professor of mathematics disapproves of him. She is flinging a tomato at him." A construction algorithm is applied to such a sequence of sentences by dealing with them in order of appearance. Application to the first sentence gives rise to some DRS K_1, which includes reference markers x and y, triggered by 'the Defense Secretary' and 'the Union' respectively. When the algorithm then turns to the second sentence, it incorporates its content into K_1. Some of the construction rules that are applied during this stage rely on K_1 for their application. For instance, the rule that deals with the anaphoric pronoun 'him' must choose an antecedent for the pronoun from among the reference markers that are contained in the universe of K_1. In this manner, K_1 acts as context of interpretation for the second sentence in T. The result of applying the algorithm to that sentence is a new DRS K_2. K_2 now captures the joint content of the first two sentences and serves as context of interpretation for the third sentence.

Kamp mostly discusses DRS's as formal structures, but he also thinks that something like these formal structures capture an important facet of cognition, that is, thought. This is the assumption on which I shall proceed. Apparently, then, Kamp hypothesizes that we have mental DRS-construction algorithms, which operate on a presented text to generate a set of mental representations including markers for entities introduced by that text. Information obtained from nontextual sources, e.g., perception, also generate such markers, though Kamp does not attempt to explore these sources. Cognitive states such as beliefs will be characterizable by DRS's. Where two DRS's K_1 and K_2 share the marker x, the two beliefs that these DRS's identify act as "being about the same thing". Note that this is a strictly internal sense in which the two beliefs are about the same thing. It does not require that there be an object in the outside world which makes both beliefs true. But it is intuitively clear that believers often think of their two beliefs as being about the same thing, though such a thought can certainly be mistaken. Thus, you may have, concerning a person known under the name of 'John Williams', both the belief that he is an accomplished guitarist and the belief that he is conductor of the Boston Pops. In fact, these are different individuals, but from an internal perspective they may be about one and the same person.

Of interest to the theory of *de re* modality are the principles that govern our mental representations of individuals as being about the same or different individuals. I propose that we think of this topic as dealing with principles of "mental bookkeeping". If I already have a reference marker, or representation, x, and I now get a new characterization or text, under what circumstances will I introduce a distinct, nonoverlapping marker y, and under what circumstances will I think of this new characterization or text as referring to the previously introduced referent of x? This problem is what needs to be answered by appropriate DRS-construction algorithms.

Before speculating on the possible applicability of these ideas to essentialism, let us examine their applicability to another topic in metaphysics, viz., the doctrine of *haecceitism*. For present purposes I shall understand haecceitism as the doctrine that things have primitive, nonqualitative thisnesses. Robert Adams (1979) gives arguments for this thesis, all involving considerations against the identity of indiscernibles. Much of his discussion concerns objects with spatial properties, like Max Black's (1952) two globes. But let us try to avoid complications involving spatiality; so let us consider an argument offered by Adams that deals primarily with minds (construed, apparently, as disembodied) rather than bodies.

Suppose I have an *almost indiscernible* twin. The only qualitative difference between him and me is that on one night of our lives the firebreathing dragon that pursues me in my nightmare has ten horns, whereas the monster in his dream has only seven. No doubt there is a possible world in which there are almost indiscernible twins of this sort. But if such a world is possible, it seems to follow that a world with *perfectly indiscernible* twins is also possible. For surely I could have existed, and so could my twin, if my monster had had only seven horns, like his. In that case we still would have been distinct though qualitatively indiscernible.

Suppose we find Adams's judgments about his case fully intuitive. What should we conclude? Clearly Adams means us to conclude something about extramental metaphysical facts. But that will strike many of us as problematic. What we certainly are entitled to conclude, however, is that we have cognitive dispositions to "track" individuals through "possible space" in a fashion that is unconstrained by purely qualitative characteristics. That is, we manage to maintain distinctions among mentally represented individuals (myself and my twin) even though they are represented—at least in the final possible world—as qualitatively indiscernible. To use Kamp's framework, we have DRS-construction algorithms that allow us to track distinct individuals even into situations where they are qualitatively indiscernible. An equally striking example of a related sort is Chisholm's Noah-Adam example. In hearing or reading Chisholm's case, one tracks Noah and Adam through a series of possible worlds which culminate in a total reversal of their initial qualitative characteristics. Although this is puzzling, we do seem to have mental capacities to do this. This is something that Kamp's construction algorithms would want to capture, and may be well designed to capture, in a precise way. What we have, then, is an interesting fact about our cognitive life: a fact that might be called *cognitive haecceitism*. This is, of course, a metaphysically more modest doctrine than the one Adams commends to us. It is a doctrine about our cognitive bookkeeping habits, our mental inventory-making propensities.

Should we feel compelled to assent to anything stronger? I demur. I am inclined to accept only a subjectivist, or cognitivist, version of haecceitism;

or at most a semisubjectivist (or "secondary quality") version. The latter version would formulate the thesis in terms of a disposition of *objects* to elicit judgments from us. It might say, roughly, that objects are disposed to be identified or re-identified by us in ways that are not wholly constrained by their qualitative characteristics. Although this is not purely subjectivist, it is clear that the main disposition lies in *us* rather than objects themselves. In any case, both of these versions of haecceitism are obviously less objective than Adams intends; either would be an ontological demotion of haecceitism. Are we compelled to accept something stronger? Not, I think, unless we are entitled to believe that our intuitions about Adams's examples are reliable indicators of intrinsic metaphysical facts (nonqualitative thisnesses). But it seems more plausible to hold that the occurrence of these intuitions are only good evidence of our cognitive bookkeeping traits, not of extramental metaphysical facts.

Let us now return to essentialism. Here too we have intuitions whose content and occurrence ought to be subsumable under appropriately formulated DRS-construction algorithms. These algorithms should imply that when you have a reference marker x for an individual, and you receive a description of an individual whose origin or composition is different from the actual origin or composition of the individual marked by x, then you will introduce a distinct reference marker y. If you already represent Queen Elizabeth with marker x, then the construction algorithm will lead you to construct a distinct marker for an imagined daughter of the Trumans. And similarly in the lectern case. Distinctness of origin or of composition leads to mental representations of distinctness, rather than co-reference (or anaphora).

All this, of course, is something Kripke and other essentialists can cheerfully accept. The crucial question is whether we should now join Kripke and other essentialists in inferring from our anti-coreference intuitions the objectivist essentialism that they want. Certainly we are entitled to conclude that we have cognitive dispositions—which a program like Kamp's would hope to delineate in detail—that lead to the intuitions in question. But are these cognitive traits, or the intuitions they generate, good evidence for the existence of objective, extramental, essentialist facts? Do the intuitions constitute "detectings" of such facts? The availability of purely psychological explanations of the intuitions ostensibly provide a systematic alternative to such "detectivist" explanations.

As in the haecceitism case, we can restrict our acceptance of essentialism to a purely subjectivist reading, or perhaps a semi-subjectivist, or secondary quality, interpretation. According to this doctrine, no further, more objective rendition of essentialism should be endorsed. In the case of color, the traits we commonsensically assign to objects themselves turn out to be sustainable only as relations to (or relational "products" of) our cognitive traits. Similarly, in the present case, what defenders of essentialism typically attribute to modal reality itself may best be seen as cognitive dispositions, or at most as relations between (nonmodal) properties (or descriptions) of objects and our cognitive traits.

The attractiveness of the subjectivist, or semisubjectivist, interpretation of essentialism may be enhanced by comparing it to a similar approach to transtemporal unity. What makes certain objects, or object-stages, transtemporally united with other objects, or object-stages? That is, what makes pairs of objects (or object-stages) parts of a single object-history? Consider cases like the ship of Theseus. Is the original ship transtemporally united with the ship gradually rebuilt from it plank by plank? Or is it united with the ship that was latterly reconstructed from all the original planks? Let's assume that the former answer is correct. What makes this so? Is the correctness of this answer a matter of objective fact that obtains independently of people's dispositions to have intuitive responses of certain sorts to questions of transtemporal unity (or identity)? Or does correctness only arise from patterns of unity judgment that people are disposed to make, or that objects are disposed to elicit from people? I am inclined to endorse the subjectivist answer, or its semisubjectivist cousin (cf. Goldman 1987a, and chapter 2). I am tempted to view essentialism in the same light.

VI

Provision of a psychological explanation of essentialist intuitions is obviously not a proof that there are no (*de re*) modal facts of an extramental sort. Essentialist objectivism is consistent with the availability of such explanations. Extramental modal facts might even stand in some sort of explanatory relation to the events cited in the psychological explanation. For example, assuming that the construction-algorithm story is correct, these construction algorithms might not be innate. They might be acquired by some sort of learning process, and the learning process might include events that are somehow produced by the extra-mental modal facts.[7]

But what sort of learning events and causal relationships are contemplated here? What actual, observed events that might produce the relevant construction algorithms could have been produced by the modal facts in question? More important, even if such a story is not excluded, what *evidence* do we have that any such story is correct? What evidence is there that our possession of these algorithms is somehow related to mind-independent modal facts? The only evidence that has been adduced is our intuitions about cases. And the mere occurrence of these intuitions does not have much probative force once we recognize that there are competing explanations that make no commitment to extramental modal facts. First, there are candidate explanations that are purely psychological and do not invoke any external events. For example, they might claim that the construction algorithms are innate dispositions. Second, there are candidate explanations that invoke certain external events (e.g., events involved in the cognizer's language-learning history) but not extramental *modal* facts. Isn't it more likely (or at a minimum, equally likely) that one of these competing explanatory stories—one that makes no commitment to extramental modal facts—is a better explanation, a more reasonable explanation (all things considered), than some explanatory story that makes such a commitment?

It may be instructive to compare the case of essentialism to that of color and time. In the case of color we not only have information about relevant psychological facts, but also relevant information about the physics of color, i.e., about the physics of light, light sources, and light-reflecting surfaces. Moreover, the latter information supports the subjectivist demotion. In the modal case, by contrast, we have no comparable scientific information about relevant external facts.

Granting this disanalogy, how much does it undercut the argument for demotion in the case of essentialism? Not very much, I think. After all, what sort of information could we expect to obtain in the nature of the case? Even if essentialist objectivism were right, what sort of relevant information would be *scientifically* discoverable? None, it appears. Equally, if subjectivism were true, we would not expect to have any scientific information about (extramental) modal reality. Thus, the absence of scientific information about external facts does not cut one way or the other.

Our evidential situation vis-à-vis *de re* modality is more analogous to that of the "moving now" conception of time. In neither case is there independent, extrapsychological information that supports the demotion. However, in both cases the hypothesized entities or facts are regarded by many as puzzling, suspect, or problematic from the outset. In such cases our ability to explain the putative evidence without countenancing the problematic items (as fully objective) may suffice to support the proposed demotion.

A comparison with other inviting candidates for ontological demotion is also worthwhile. We ordinarily speak of people and jokes as being funny; perhaps we even "perceive" them as funny. Nonetheless, it is easy to be persuaded that a secondary quality account of funniness is in order. Notice, however, that we have no specific physical information that supports this demotion; so this kind of information is not in general required for demotion. Admittedly, this particular demotion also makes no appeal to a detailed psychological story. This is probably because the obvious interpersonal (and intermood) variability in humor responses makes it evident, even in the absence of a detailed psychological theory, that humor is a peculiar product of mental factors. In cases where subjective responses are more uniform, as in the cases of time and essentialism, a detailed psychological story is evidentially more critical. Such a story can make it clear, or at least plausible, that the phenomenon in question is largely an artifact of our specific cognitive constitution.

A demotional treatment of *de re* modality is discomfiting because it seemingly threatens a similar treatment of all modality, including nomic modality. Wouldn't we be reluctant to submit nomic modality or its cousins to such treatment? Let me emphasize, first, that I am only urging demotion for *de re* modality, not for nomic modality, counterfactuals, or the like. Notice, moreover, that our epistemic situation vis-à-vis nomic modality does not closely parallel that of *de re* modality. In the case of nomic necessities we have evidence in the form of observed regularities; we are not restricted to mere intuitions about what we would say. Admittedly, the nature of the relationship between observed, this-world regularities and nomic modalities is problematic. But certainly there is ample opportunity for differential treatment of the two cases.

The moral of the recent discussion is that the chief problem for essentialist objectivism is epistemic. We might restate it this way. The argument for the standard objectivist version of essentialism proceeds from psychological inconceivability to metaphysical impossibility. Since we cannot *conceive* of Queen Elizabeth having a different origin from her actual origin, we conclude that it is metaphysically impossible for Queen Elizabeth to have a different origin. The question is: are our conceptual dispositions— our mental bookkeeping dispositions—reliable evidence for objective metaphysical fact? Is inconceivability a reliable indicator of impossibility? Unless there is some story that underwrites this indicator relationship, the epistemic status of the intuitions is problematic.

On the other hand, if essentialism is given a subjectivist or semisubjectivist reading, the evidential status of intuitions is rendered quite unproblematic.[8] Anti-coreference intuitions are evidence for the dispositional traits in question because they are *positive instances* of those dispositions. Of course, this improvement in epistemic status is earned at the price of demotion in ontological status. But that price may be entirely reasonable. If the epistemic acceptability of essentialism requires the detection of transworld regularities in an extramental realm, this epistemic status may just be unattainable. Only ontological demotion can brighten the epistemic prospects for essentialism.

The problem of epistemic access to modal facts appears most pressing for an extreme realist like Lewis. Lewis claims that this difficulty is exaggerated by wrongly insisting on a *causal* account of modal knowledge (see Lewis 1986, pp. 108ff.). Knowledge of modality, says Lewis, no more requires causal interaction with (nonactual) possible worlds than knowledge of mathematics requires causal interaction with mathematical objects.

But I do not mean to defend a purely causal theory of knowledge. I endorse a *reliabilist* account, which presumably can accommodate mathematical knowledge along with the rest (see chapters 5, 6, and 9, and Goldman 1986). Specifically, I do not mean to require for modal knowledge that our modal intuitions causally interact with modal reality. I do insist, however, that our modal beliefs be reliably formed. If these beliefs are based primarily (or exclusively) on modal intuitions, these intuitions have to be reliable indicators of modal facts. That, however, is problematic.

Now Lewis sometimes intimates that modal knowledge, like mathematical knowledge, can be acquired by abstract reasoning. How would this work in the case of essentialism? In fact, when Lewis comes to specify just how one forms modal opinions, his story is the same intuitional story as Kripke's:

> We try to think how duplicates of things already accepted as possible—for instance, because they are actual—might be arranged to fit the description of an alleged possibility. Having imagined various arrangements—not in complete detail, of course—we consider how they might aptly be described. If things of these kinds were arranged like this, would *that* be a world where Saul Kripke is the son of Rudolf Carnap? (Lewis 1986, p. 114)

Lewis's description of modal reasoning, then, is hardly distinguishable from Kripke's. This brings us back to our recurrent question: why give credence to intuitive reactions? On Lewis's modal ontology, such credence is well placed only if intuitive reactions are correlated with the existence or non-existence of possible worlds of certain sorts (or perhaps accessibility relations among such worlds). We seem to have no reason to believe in this correlation.

Other objectivist interpretations of possible worlds have no better epistemic prospects than Lewis's, as far as I can see. Consider the identification of possible worlds with (maximal) "states of affairs". There is no more reason to suppose that our intuitions are reliable indicators of exactly which "states of affairs" there are than of which "concrete universes". Here I side with Lewis's reservations about these "ersatz" worlds.

Of course, Lewis's methodology also emphasizes the role of systematicity, and I have not criticized this consideration as a proper one for prescriptive metaphysics. To the contrary, I suggested earlier that a demotional decision must partly depend on background theory. We must ask, then, how well we can get along, all things considered, with or without "realist" modality. What the availability of a cognitivist explanation of modal intuitions shows is that we may not *need* objective modal facts to accommodate the existence, or occurrence, of these intuitions. The burden is therefore on the objectivist about modality to show that theoretical considerations make it reasonable nonetheless to countenance such facts.

Whether this burden can be successfully discharged is not something we can pursue on this occasion. At the present time, however, I am inclined to think that the best interpretation of essentialism would give it merely a subjectivist or semisubjectivist reading, linking it fundamentally to our cognitive dispositions. Although this is a demotion from the standard interpretation, it is the most plausible stance for prescriptive metaphysics.

Notes

I am most grateful to Jean Kazez, Holly Smith, and Joseph Tolliver for valuable critical comments and suggestions.

1. For a brief description of the human color system, see Gleitman (1981), pp. 200–213. For a longer treatment, with attention to philosophical issues, see Hardin (1988).

2. For a more recent treatment of difficulties for color physicalism, see Boghossian and Velleman (1991).

3. Admittedly, this passage occurs in a context where the prime topic is the meaningfulness of a certain *notion*. But Kripke's comments seem intended to have a wider application.

4. It is not clear how completely Kripke means to rest his arguments on appeals to intuition. He gives a rather different argument, relying only on considerations of the theory of reference, in footnote 56 of *Naming and Necessity* (p. 114). However, in the preface to the 1980 edition he says that he "had no ambition in this short footnote rigorously to prove 'essentialism from the theory of reference alone'" (p. 1). In any case, my discussion is confined to arguments for essentialism based on appeals to intuition. For critical discussion of arguments based on the theory of reference, see Salmon (1982) and Steward (1990).

5. Actually, a subjectivist rendering of essentialism may not constitute an ontological demotion relative to *ordinary* people's views because ordinary folk may not be objectivists about modality. But subjectivism about essentialism is an ontological demotion relative to most of its *philosophical* defenders.

6. I discovered the Mackie paper when the present paper was well underway and the Sidelle book only after this paper was virtually complete. A number of things Sidelle says, especially about epistemological problems of modality, are similar to things said here. Our positive views, however, differ at least in emphasis: mine being more psychological, his more linguistic. (His are linguistic in the sense of 'pertaining to language', rather than 'pertaining to linguistics'.) However, if my application of Kamp's approach to discourse representation theory that appears in the text were developed in certain ways, perhaps it would approximate Sidelle's "conventionalist" proposal.

7. An analogous point is often made by moral realists in reply to arguments from explanation by moral antirealists. For example, Sturgeon (1985) responds in this fashion to Harman (1977).

8. This point is also stressed by Sidelle (1989, pp. 97, 100).

Part II
Individual Epistemology

Chapter 4
A Causal Theory of Knowing

Since Edmund Gettier (1963) pointed out a certain important inadequacy of the traditional analysis of "S knows that p," several attempts have been made to correct that analysis (see Clark 1963, Sosa 1964, and Lehrer 1965). In this paper I shall offer still another analysis (or a sketch of an analysis) of "S knows that p," one which will avert Gettier's problem. My concern will be with knowledge of empirical propositions only, since I think that the traditional analysis is adequate for knowledge of nonempirical truths.

Consider an abbreviated version of Gettier's second counterexample to the traditional analysis. Smith believes

(q) Jones owns a Ford

and has very strong evidence for it. Smith's evidence might be that Jones has owned a Ford for many years and that Jones has just offered Smith a ride while driving a Ford. Smith has another friend, Brown, of whose whereabouts he is totally ignorant. Choosing a town quite at random, however, Smith constructs the proposition

(p) Either Jones owns a Ford or Brown is in Barcelona.

Seeing that q entails p, Smith infers that p is true. Since he has adequate evidence for q, he also has adequate evidence for p. But now suppose that Jones does *not* own a Ford (he was driving a rented car when he offered Smith a ride), but, quite by coincidence, Brown happens to be in Barcelona. This means that p is true, that Smith believes p, and that Smith has adequate evidence for p. But Smith does not know p.

A variety of hypotheses might be made to account for Smith's not knowing p. Michael Clark, for example, points to the fact that q is false, and suggests this as the reason why Smith cannot be said to know p (Clark 1963). Generalizing from this case, Clark argues that, for S to know a proposition, each of S's grounds for it must be *true*, as well as his grounds for his grounds, etc.[1] I shall make another hypothesis to account for the fact that Smith cannot be said to know p, and I shall generalize this into a new analysis of "S knows that p."

Notice that what *makes p* true is the fact that Brown is in Barcelona, but that this fact has nothing to do with Smith's believing *p*. That is, there is no *causal* connection between the fact that Brown is in Barcelona and Smith's believing *p*. If Smith had come to believe *p* by reading a letter from Brown postmarked in Barcelona, then we might say that Smith knew *p*. Alternatively, if Jones did own a Ford, and his owning the Ford was manifested by his offer of a ride to Smith, and this in turn resulted in Smith's believing *p*, then we would say that Smith knew *p*. Thus, one thing that seems to be missing in this example is a causal connection between the fact that makes *p* true [or simply: the fact that *p*] and Smith's belief of *p*. The requirement of such a causal connection is what I wish to add to the traditional analysis.

To see that this requirement is satisfied in all cases of (empirical) knowledge, we must examine a variety of such causal connections. Clearly, only a sketch of the important kinds of cases is possible here.

Perhaps the simplest case of a causal chain connecting some fact *p* with someone's belief of *p* is that of *perception*. I wish to espouse a version of the causal theory of perception, in essence that defended by H. P. Grice (1961). Suppose that *S* sees that there is a vase in front of him. How is this to be analyzed? I shall not attempt a complete analysis of this, but a necessary condition of *S*'s seeing that there is a vase in front of him is that there be a certain kind of causal connection between the presence of the vase and *S*'s believing that a vase is present. I shall not attempt to describe this causal process in detail. Indeed, to a large extent, a description of this process must be regarded as a problem for the special sciences, not for philosophy. But a certain causal process—viz., that which standardly takes place when we say that so-and-so sees such-and-such—must occur. That our ordinary concept of sight (i.e., knowledge acquired by sight) includes a causal requirement is shown by the fact that if the relevant causal process is absent, we would withhold the assertion that so-and-so *saw* such-and-such. Suppose that, although a vase is directly in front of *S*, a laser photograph[1] is interposed between it and *S*, thereby blocking it from *S*'s view. The photograph, however, is one of a vase (a different vase), and when it is illuminated by light waves from a laser, it looks to *S* exactly like a real vase. When the photograph is illuminated, *S* forms the belief that there is a vase in front of him. Here we would deny that *S sees* that there is a vase in front of him, for his view of the real vase is completely blocked, so that it has no causal role in the formation of his belief. Of course, *S* might *know* that there is a vase in front of him even if the photograph is blocking his view. Someone else, in a position to see the vase, might tell *S* that there is a vase in front of him. Here the presence of the vase might be a causal ancestor of *S*'s belief, but the causal process would not be a (purely) *perceptual* one. *S* could not be said to *see* that there is a vase in front of him.

For this to be true, there must be a causal process, but one of a very special sort, connecting the presence of the vase with S's belief.

I shall here assume that perceptual knowledge of facts is noninferential. This is merely a simplifying procedure, and not essential to my account. Certainly a percipient does not *infer* facts about physical objects from the state of his brain or from the stimulation of his sense organs. He need not know about these goings-on at all. But some epistemologists maintain that we directly perceive only sense data and that we infer physical-object facts from them. This view could be accommodated within my analysis. I could say that physical-object facts cause sense data, that people directly perceive sense data, and that they infer the physical object facts from the sense data. This kind of process would be fully accredited by my analysis, which will allow for knowledge based on inference. But for purposes of exposition it will be convenient to regard perceptual knowledge of external facts as independent of any inference.

Here the question arises about the scope of perceptual knowledge. By perception I can know noninferentially that there is a vase in front of me. But can I know noninferentially that the painting I am viewing is a Picasso? It is unnecessary to settle such issues here. Whether the knowledge of such facts is to be classed as inferential or noninferential, my analysis can account for it. So the scope of noninferential knowledge may be left indeterminate.

I turn next to memory, i.e., knowledge that is based, in part, on memory. Remembering, like perceiving, must be regarded as a causal process. S remembers p at time t only if S's believing p at an earlier time is a cause of his believing p at t. Of course, not every causal connection between an earlier belief and a later one is a case of remembering. As in the case of perception, however, I shall not try to describe this process in detail. This is a job mainly for the scientist. Instead, the kind of causal process in question is to be identified simply by example, by "pointing" to paradigm cases of remembering. Whenever causal processes are of that kind— whatever that kind is, precisely—they are cases of remembering.[2]

A causal connection between earlier belief (or knowledge) of p and later belief (knowledge) of p is certainly a necessary ingredient in memory.[3] To remember a fact is not simply to believe it at t_0 and also to believe it at t_1. Nor does someone's knowing a fact at t_0 and his knowing it at t_1 entail that he remembers it at t_1. He may have perceived the fact at t_0, forgotten it, and then relearned it at t_1 by someone's telling it to him. Nor does the inclusion of a memory "impression"—a feeling of remembering—ensure that one really remembers. Suppose S perceives p at t_0, but forgets it at t_1. At t_2 he begins to believe p again because someone tells him p, but at t_2 he has no memory impression of p. At t_3 we artificially stimulate in S a memory impression of p. It does not follow that S remembers p at t_3. The description of the case suggests that his believing p at t_0 has no causal effect whatever on his believing p at t_3; and if we accepted this fact, we would deny that he remembers p at t_3.

Knowledge can be acquired by a combination of perception and memory. At t_1 the fact p causes S to believe p, by perception. S's believing p at t_0 results, via memory, in S's believing p at t_1. Thus, the fact p is a cause of S's believing p at t_1, and S can be said to know p at t_1. But not all knowledge results from perception and memory alone. In particular, much knowledge is based on *inference*.

As I shall use the term 'inference', to say that S knows p by "inference" does not entail that S went through an explicit, conscious process of reasoning. It is not necessary that he have "talked to himself," saying something like "Since such-and-such is true, p must also be true." My belief that there is a fire in the neighborhood is based on, or inferred from, my belief that I hear a fire engine. But I have not gone through a process of explicit reasoning, saying "There's a fire engine; therefore there must be a fire." Perhaps the word 'inference' is ordinarily used only where explicit reasoning occurs; if so, my use of the term will be somewhat broader than its ordinary use.

Suppose S perceives that there is solidified lava in various parts of the countryside. On the basis of this belief, plus various "background" beliefs about the production of lava, S concludes that a nearby mountain erupted many centuries ago. Let us assume that this is a highly warranted inductive inference, one which gives S adequate evidence for believing that the mountain did erupt many centuries ago. Assuming this proposition is true, does S know it? This depends on the nature of the causal process that induces his belief. If there is a continuous causal chain of the sort he envisages connecting the fact that the mountain erupted with his belief of this fact, then S knows it. If there is no such causal chain, however, S does not know that proposition.

Suppose that the mountain erupts, leaving lava around the countryside. The lava remains there until S perceives it and infers that the mountain erupted. Then S does know that the mountain erupted. But now suppose that, after the mountain has erupted, a man somehow removes all the lava. A century later, a different man (not knowing of the real volcano) decides to make it look as if there had been a volcano, and therefore puts lava in appropriate places. Still later, S comes across this lava and concludes that the mountain erupted centuries ago. In this case, S cannot be said to know the proposition. This is because the fact that the mountain did erupt is not a cause of S's believing that it erupted. A necessary condition of S's knowing p is that his believing p be connected with p by a causal chain.

In the first case, where S knows p, the causal connection may be diagrammed as in figure 4.1. (p) is the fact that the mountain erupted at

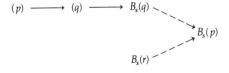

Figure 4.1

such-and-such a time. (q) is the fact that lava is (now) present around the countryside. 'B' stands for a belief, the expression in parentheses indicating the proposition believed, and the subscript designating the believer. (r) is a "background" proposition, describing the ways in which lava is produced and how it solidifies. Solid arrows in the diagram represent causal connections; dotted arrows represent inferences. Notice that, in figure 4.1, there is not only an arrow connecting (q) with S's belief of (q), but also an arrow connecting (p) with (q). In the suggested variant of the lava case, the latter arrow would be missing, showing that there is no continuous causal chain connecting (p) with S's belief of (p). Therefore, in that variant case, S could not be said to know (p).

I have said that p is causally connected to S's belief of p, in the case diagrammed in figure 4.1. This raises the question, however, of whether the inferential part of the chain is itself a causal chain. In other words, is S's belief of q a cause of his believing p? This is a question to which I shall not try to give a definitive answer here. I am inclined to say that inference *is* a causal process, that is, that when someone *bases* his belief of one proposition on his belief of a set of other propositions, then his belief of the latter propositions can be considered a cause of his belief of the former proposition. But I do not wish to rest my thesis on this claim. All I do claim is that, if a chain of inferences is "added" to a causal chain, then the entire chain is causal. In terms of our diagram, a chain consisting of solid arrows plus dotted arrows is to be considered a causal chain, though I shall not take a position on the question of whether the dotted arrows represent causal connections. Thus, in figure 4.1, p is a cause of S's belief of p, whether or not we regard S's belief of q a cause of his belief of p.[4]

Consider next a case of knowledge based on "testimony." This too can be analyzed causally. p causes a person T to believe p, by perception. T's belief of p gives rise to (causes) his asserting p. T's asserting p causes S, by auditory perception, to believe that T is asserting p. S infers that T believes p, and from this, in turn, he infers that p is a fact. There is a continuous causal chain from p to S's believing p, and thus, assuming that each of S's inferences is warranted, S can be said to know p.

This causal chain is represented in figure 4.2. 'A' refers to an act of asserting a proposition, the expression in parentheses indicating the propo-

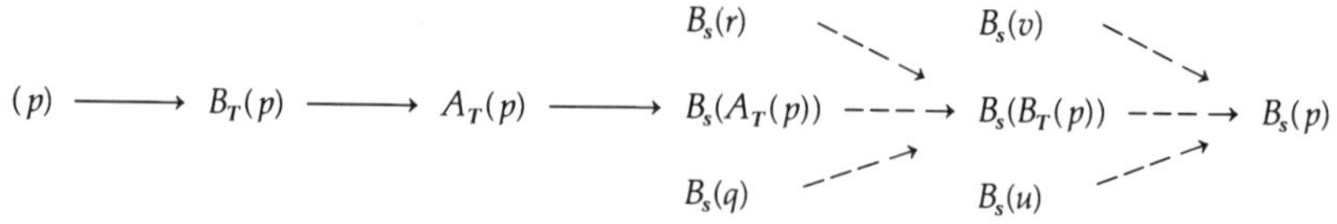

$$B_s(r) \quad \searrow \qquad B_s(v) \quad \searrow$$

$$(p) \longrightarrow B_T(p) \longrightarrow A_T(p) \longrightarrow B_s(A_T(p)) \dashrightarrow B_s(B_T(p)) \dashrightarrow B_s(p)$$

$$B_s(q) \quad \nearrow \qquad B_s(u) \quad \nearrow$$

Figure 4.2

sition asserted and the subscript designating the agent. (q), (r), (u), and (v) are background propositions. (q) and (r), for example, pertain to T's sincerity; they help S conclude, from the fact that T asserted p, that T really believes p.

In this case, as in the lava case, S knows p because he has correctly reconstructed the causal chain leading from p to the evidence for p that S perceives, in this case, T's asserting (p). This correct reconstruction is shown in the diagram by S's inference "mirroring" the rest of the causal chain. Such a correct reconstruction is a necessary condition of knowledge based on inference. To see this, consider the following example. A newspaper reporter observes p and reports it to his newspaper. When printed, however, the story contains a typographical error so that it asserts not-p. When reading the paper, however, S fails to see the word 'not', and takes the paper to have asserted p. Trusting the newspaper, he infers that p is true. Here we have a continuous causal chain leading from p to S's believing p; yet S does not know p. S thinks that p resulted in a report to the newspaper about p and that this report resulted in its printing the statement p. Thus, his reconstruction of the causal chain is mistaken. But, if he is to know p, his reconstruction must contain no mistakes. Though he need not reconstruct *every* detail of the causal chain, he must reconstruct all the important links.[5] An additional requirement for knowledge based on inference is that the knower's inferences be warranted. That is, the propositions on which he bases his belief of p must genuinely confirm p very highly, whether deductively or inductively. Reconstructing a causal chain merely by lucky guesses does not yield knowledge.

With the help of our diagrams, we can contrast the traditional analysis of knowing with Clark's (1963) analysis and contrast each of these with my own analysis. The traditional analysis makes reference to just three features of the diagrams. First, it requires that p be true; i.e., that (p) appear in the diagram. Second, it requires that S believe p; i.e., that S's belief of p appear in the diagram. Third, it requires that S's inferences, if any, be warranted; i.e., that the sets of beliefs that are at the tails of dotted arrows must jointly highly confirm the belief at the head of these arrows. Clark proposes a further requirement for knowledge. He requires that *each* of the beliefs in S's chain of inference be *true*. In other words, whereas the traditional analysis requires a fact to correspond to S's belief of p, Clark requires that a fact correspond to *each* of S's beliefs on which he bases his belief of p. Thus, corresponding to each belief on the right side of the diagram there must be a fact on the left side. (My diagrams omit facts corresponding to the "background" beliefs.)

As Clark's analysis stands, it seems to omit an element of the diagrams that my analysis requires, viz., the arrows indicating causal connections. Now Clark might reformulate his analysis so as to make implicit reference to these causal connections. If he required that the knower's beliefs include *causal beliefs* (of the relevant sort), then his requirement that these beliefs be true would amount to the requirement that there *be* causal chains of the sort I require. This interpretation of Clark's analysis would make it almost equivalent to mine, and would enable him to avoid some objections that have been raised against him. But he has not explicitly formulated his analysis this way, and it therefore remains deficient in this respect.

Before turning to the problems facing Clark's analysis, more must be said about my own analysis. So far, my examples may have suggested that, if S knows p, the fact that p is a cause of his belief of p. This would clearly be wrong, however. Let us grant that I can know facts about the future. Then, if we required that the known fact cause the knower's belief, we would have to countenance "backward" causation. My analysis, however, does not face this dilemma. The analysis requires that there be a causal *connection* between p and S's belief, not necessarily that p be a *cause* of S's belief. p and S's belief of p can also be causally connected in a way that yields knowledge if both p and S's belief of p have a *common* cause. This can be illustrated as follows.

T intends to go downtown on Monday. On Sunday, T tells S of his intention. Hearing T say he will go downtown, S infers that T really does intend to go downtown. And from this S concludes that T will go downtown on Monday. Now suppose that T fulfills his intention by going downtown on Monday. Can S be said to know that he would go downtown? If we ever can be said to have knowledge of the future, this is a reasonable candidate for it. So let us say S did know that proposition. How can my analysis account for S's knowledge? T's going downtown on Monday clearly cannot be a cause of S's believing, on Sunday, that he would go downtown. But there is a fact that is the common cause of T's going downtown and of S's belief that he would go downtown, viz., T's intending (on Sunday) to go downtown. This intention resulted in his going downtown and also resulted in S's believing that he would go downtown. This causal connection between S's belief and the fact believed allows us to say that S *knew* that T would go downtown.

The example is diagrammed in figure 4.3. (p) = T's going downtown on Monday. (q) = T's intending (on Sunday) to go downtown on Monday.

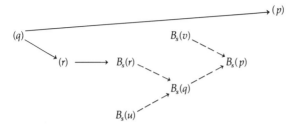

Figure 4.3

$(r) = T$'s telling S (on Sunday) that he will go downtown on Monday. (u) and (v) are relevant background propositions pertaining to T's honesty, resoluteness, etc. The diagram reveals that q is a cause both of p and of S's belief of p. Cases of this kind I shall call *Pattern 2* cases of knowledge. Figures 4.1 and 4.2 exemplify *Pattern 1* cases of knowledge.

Notice that the causal connection between q and p is an essential part of S's knowing p. Suppose, for example, that T's intending (on Sunday) to go downtown does not result in, or cause, T's going downtown on Monday. Suppose that T, after telling S that he would go downtown, changes his mind. Nevertheless, on Monday he is kidnapped and forced, at the point of a gun, to go downtown. Here both q and p actually occur, but they are not causally related. The diagram in figure 4.3 would have to be amended by deleting the arrow connecting (q) with (p). But if the rest of the facts of the original case remain the same, S could not be said to know p. It would be false to say that S knew, on Sunday, that T would go downtown on Monday.

Pattern 2 cases of knowledge are not restricted to knowledge of the future. I know that smoke was coming out of my chimney last night. I know this because I remember perceiving a fire in my fireplace last night, and I infer that the fire caused smoke to rise out of the chimney. This case exemplifies Pattern 2. The smoke's rising out of the chimney is not a causal factor of my belief. But the fact that there was a fire in the fireplace was a cause both of my belief that smoke was coming out of the chimney and of the fact that smoke was coming out of the chimney. If we supplement this case slightly, we can make my knowledge exemplify *both* Pattern 1 and Pattern 2. Suppose that a friend tells me today that he perceived smoke coming out of my chimney last night and I base my continued belief of this fact on his testimony. Then the fact was a cause of my current belief of it, as well as an *effect* of another fact that caused my belief. In general, numerous and diverse kinds of causal connections can obtain between a given fact and a given person's belief of that fact.

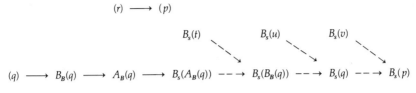

Figure 4.4

Let us now examine some objections to Clark's analysis and see how the analysis presented here fares against them. John Turk Saunders and Narayan Champawat (1964) have raised the following counterexample to Clark's analysis:

> Suppose that Smith believes
>
> (p)   Jones owns a Ford
>
> because his friend Brown whom he knows to be generally reliable and honest yesterday told Smith that Jones had always owned a Ford. Brown's information was correct, but today Jones sells his Ford and replaces it with a Volkswagen. An hour later Jones is pleased to find that he is the proud owner of two cars: he has been lucky enough to win a Ford in a raffle. Smith's belief in p is not only justified and true, but is fully grounded, e.g., we suppose that each link in the ... chain of Smith's grounds is true.

Clearly Smith does not know p; yet he seems to satisfy Clark's analysis of knowing.

Smith's lack of knowledge can be accounted for in terms of my analysis. Smith does not know p because his believing p is not causally related to p, Jones's owning a Ford *now*. This can be seen by examining figure 4.4. In the diagram, (p) = Jones's owning a Ford now; (q) = Jones's having always owned a Ford (until yesterday); (r) = Jones's winning a Ford in a raffle today. (t), (u), and (v) are background propositions. (v), for example, deals with the likelihood of someone's continuing to own the same car today that he owned yesterday. The subscript 'B' designates Brown, and the subscript 'S' designates Smith. Notice the absence of an arrow connecting (p) with (q). The absence of this arrow represents the absence of a causal relation between (q) and (p). Jones's owning a Ford in the past (until yesterday) is not a cause of his owning one now. Had he continued owning the same Ford today that he owned yesterday, there would be a causal connection between q and p and, therefore, a causal connection between p and Smith's believing p. This causal connection would exemplify Pattern 2. But, as it happened, it is purely a coincidence that Jones owns a Ford today as well as yesterday. Thus, Smith's belief of p is not connected with *p* by Pattern 2, nor is there any Pattern 1 connection between them. Hence, Smith does not know *p*.

If we supplement Clark's analysis as suggested above, it can be saved from this counterexample. Though Saunders and Champawat fail to mention this explicitly, presumably it is one of Smith's beliefs that Jones's owning a Ford yesterday would *result* in Jones's owning a Ford now. This was undoubtedly one of his grounds for believing that Jones owns a Ford now. (A complete diagram of *S*'s beliefs relevant to *p* would include this belief.) Since this belief is false, however, Clark's analysis would yield the correct consequence that Smith does not know *p*. Unfortunately, Clark himself seems not to have noticed this point, since Saunders and Champawat's putative counterexample has been allowed to stand.

Another sort of counterexample to Clark's analysis has been given by Saunders and Champawat and also by Keith Lehrer. This is a counterexample from which his analysis cannot escape. I shall give Lehrer's (1965) example of this sort of difficulty. Suppose Smith bases his belief of

(*p*)   Someone in his office owns a Ford

on his belief of four propositions

(*q*)   Jones owns a Ford

(*r*)   Jones works in his office

(*s*)   Brown owns a Ford

(*t*)   Brown works in his office

In fact, Smith knows *q*, *r*, and *t*, but he does not know *s* because *s* is false. Since *s* is false, not *all* of Smith's grounds for *p* are true, and, therefore, on Clark's analysis, Smith does not know *p*. Yet clearly Smith does know *p*. Thus, Clark's analysis is *too strong*.

Having seen the importance of a causal chain for knowing, it is fairly obvious how to amend Clark's requirements without making them too weak. We need not require, as Clark does, that *all* of *S*'s grounds be true. What is required is that enough of them be true to ensure the existence of at least *one* causal connection between *p* and *S*'s belief of *p*. In Lehrer's example, Smith thinks that there are two ways in which he knows *p*: via his knowledge of the conjunction of *q* and *r*, and via his knowledge of the conjunction of *s* and *t*. He does not know *p* via the conjunction of *s* and *t*, since *s* is false. But there is a causal connection, via *q* and *r*, between *p* and Smith's belief of *p*. And this connection is enough.

Another sort of case in which one of *S*'s grounds for *p* may be false without preventing him from knowing *p* is where the false proposition is a dispensable background assumption. Suppose *S* bases his belief of *p* on

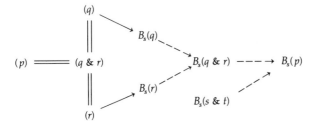

Figure 4.5

seventeen background assumptions, but only sixteen of these are true. If these sixteen are strong enough to confirm p, then the seventeenth is dispensable. S can be said to know p though one of his grounds is false.

Our discussion of Lehrer's example calls attention to the necessity of a further clarification of the notion of a "causal chain." I said earlier that causal chains with admixtures of inferences are causal chains. Now I wish to add that causal chains with admixtures of logical connections are causal chains. Unless we allow this interpretation, it is hard to see how facts like "Someone in the office owns a Ford" or "All men are mortal" could be *causally* connected with beliefs thereof.

The following principle will be useful: If x *is logically related to y and if y is a cause of z, then x is a cause of z.* Thus, suppose that q causes S's belief of q and that r causes S's belief of r. Next suppose that S infers $q \& r$ from his belief of q and of r. Then the facts q and r are causes of S's believing $q \& r$. But the fact $q \& r$ is logically related to the fact q and to the fact r. Therefore, using the principle enunciated above, the fact $q \& r$ is a cause of S's believing $q \& r$.

In Lehrer's case another logical connection is involved: a connection between an existential fact and an instance thereof. Lehrer's case is diagrammed in figure 4.5. In addition to the usual conventions, logical relationships are represented by double solid lines. As the diagram shows, the fact p—someone in Smith's office owning a Ford—is logically related to the fact $q \& r$—Jones's owning a Ford and Jones's working in Smith's office. The fact $q \& r$ is, in turn, logically related to the fact q and to the fact r. q causes S's belief of q and, by inference, his belief of $q \& r$ and of p. Similarly, r is a cause of S's belief of p. Hence, by the above principle, p is a cause of S's belief of p. Since Smith's inferences are warranted, even setting aside his belief of $s \& t$, he knows p.

In a similar way, universal facts may be causes of beliefs thereof. The fact that all men are mortal is logically related to its instances: John's being mortal, George's being mortal, Oscar's being mortal, etc. Now suppose that S perceives George, John, Oscar, etc., to be mortal (by seeing them die). He infers from these facts that all men are mortal, an inference which,

I assume, is warranted. Since each of the facts, John is mortal, George is mortal, Oscar is mortal, etc., is a cause of S's believing that fact, each is also a cause of S's believing that all men are mortal. Moreover, since the universal fact that all men are mortal is logically related to each of these particular facts, this universal fact is a cause of S's belief of it. Hence, S can be said to know that all men are mortal. In analogous fashions, S can know various other logically compound propositions.

We can now formulate the analysis of knowing as follows:

> S knows that p if and only if *the fact p is causally connected in an "appropriate" way with S's believing p.*

"Appropriate," knowledge-producing causal processes include the following:

1. perception
2. memory
3. a causal chain, exemplifying either Pattern 1 or 2, which is correctly reconstructed by inferences, each of which is warranted (background propositions help warrant an inference only if they are true)[6]
4. combinations of 1, 2, and 3

We have seen that this analysis is *stronger* than the traditional analysis in certain respects: the causal requirement and the correct-reconstruction requirement are absent from the older analysis. These additional requirements enable my analysis to circumvent Gettier's counterexamples to the traditional one. But my analysis is *weaker* than the traditional analysis in another respect. In at least one popular interpretation of the traditional analysis, a knower must be able to justify or give evidence for any proposition he knows. For S to know p at t, S must be able, at t, to *state* his justification for believing p, or his grounds for p. My analysis makes no such requirement, and the absence of this requirement enables me to account for cases of knowledge that would wrongly be excluded by the traditional analysis.

I know now, for example, that Abraham Lincoln was born in 1809.[7] I originally came to know this fact, let us suppose, by reading an encyclopedia article. I believed that this encyclopedia was trustworthy and that its saying Lincoln was born in 1809 must have resulted from the fact that Lincoln was indeed born in 1809. Thus, my original knowledge of this fact was founded on a warranted inference. But now I no longer remember this inference. I remember that Lincoln was born in 1809, but not that this is stated in a certain encyclopedia. I no longer have any pertinent beliefs that highly confirm the proposition that Lincoln was born in 1809. Nevertheless, I know this proposition now. My original knowledge of it was preserved until now by the causal process of memory.

Defenders of the traditional analysis would doubtlessly deny that I really do know Lincoln's birth year. This denial, however, stems from a desire to protect their analysis. It seems clear that many things we know were originally learned in a way that we no longer remember. The range of our knowledge would be drastically reduced if these items were denied the status of knowledge.

Other species of knowledge without explicit evidence could also be admitted by my analysis. Notice that I have not closed the list of "appropriate" causal processes. Leaving the list open is desirable, because there may be some presently controversial causal processes that we may later deem "appropriate" and, therefore, knowledge-producing. Many people now doubt the legitimacy of claims to extrasensory perception. But if conclusive evidence were to establish the existence of causal processes connecting physical facts with certain persons' beliefs without the help of standard perceptual processes, we might decide to call such beliefs items of knowledge. This would be another species of knowledge in which the knower might be unable to justify or defend his belief. My analysis allows for the possibility of such knowledge, though it doesn't commit one to it.

Special comments are in order about knowledge of our own mental states. This is a very difficult and controversial topic, so I hesitate to discuss it, but something must be said about it. Probably there are some mental states that are clearly distinct from the subject's belief that he is in such a state. If so, then there is presumably a causal process connecting the existence of such states with the subject's belief thereof. We may add this kind of process to the list of "appropriate" causal processes. The more difficult cases are those in which the state is hardly distinguishable from the subject's believing that he is in that state. My being in pain and my believing that I am in pain are hardly distinct states of affairs. If there is no distinction here between the believing and the believed, how can there be a causal connection between them? For the purposes of the present analysis, we may regard identity as a "limiting" or "degenerate" case of a causal connection, just as zero may be regarded as a "limiting" or "degenerate" case of a number. It is not surprising that knowledge of one's own mental state should turn out to be a limiting or degenerate case of knowledge. Philosophers have long recognized its peculiar status. While some philosophers have regarded it as a paradigm case of knowledge, others have claimed that we have no "knowledge" of our mental states at all. A theory of knowledge that makes knowledge of one's own mental states rather different from garden-variety species of knowledge is, in so far forth, acceptable and even welcome.

In conclusion, let me answer some possible objections to my analysis. It might be doubted whether a causal analysis adequately provides the meaning of the word 'knows' or of the sentence (-schema) "S knows p." But

I am not interested in giving the *meaning* of "S knows p"; only its *truth conditions*. I claim to have given one correct set of truth conditions for "S knows p." Truth conditions of a sentence do not always provide its meaning. Consider, for example, the following truth-conditions statement: "The sentence 'Team T wins the baseball game' is true if and only if team T has more runs at the end of the game than the opposing team." This statement fails to provide the meaning of the sentence 'Team T wins the baseball game'; for it fails to indicate an essential part of the meaning of that sentence, viz., that to win a game is to achieve the presumed goal of playing it. Someone might fully understand the truth conditions given above and yet fail to understand the meaning of the sentence because he has no understanding of the notion of "winning" in general.

Truth conditions should not be confused with verification conditions. My analysis of "S knows p" does not purport to give procedures for *finding out* whether a person (including oneself) knows a given proposition. No doubt, we sometimes do know that people know certain propositions, for we sometimes know that their beliefs are causally connected (in appropriate ways) with the facts believed. On the other hand, it may often be difficult or even impossible to find out whether this condition holds for a given proposition and a given person. For example, it may be difficult for me to find out whether I really do remember a certain fact that I seem to remember. The difficulties that exist for finding out whether someone knows a given proposition do not constitute difficulties for my analysis, however.

In the same vein it should be noted that I have made no attempt to answer skeptical problems. My analysis gives no answer to the skeptic who asks that I start from the content of my own experience and then prove that I know there is a material world, a past, etc. I do not take this to be one of the jobs of giving truth conditions for "S knows that p."

The analysis presented here flies in the face of a well-established tradition in epistemology, the view that epistemological questions are questions of logic or justification, not causal or genetic questions. This traditional view, however, must not go unquestioned. Indeed, I think my analysis shows that the question of whether someone knows a certain proposition is, in part, a causal question, although, of course, the question of what the correct analysis is of "S knows that p" is not a causal question.

Notes

I wish to thank members of the University of Michigan Philosophy Department, several of whom made helpful comments on earlier versions of this paper.

1. If a laser photograph (hologram) is illuminated by light waves, especially waves from a laser, the effect of the hologram on the viewer is exactly as if the object were being seen. It preserves three-dimensionality completely, and even gives appropriate parallax effects as the viewer moves relative to it. Cf. Leith and Upatnieks (1965).

2. For further defense of this kind of procedure, with attention to perception, cf. Grice. (1961).

3. Causal connections can hold between states of affairs, such as believings, as well as between events. If a given event or state, in conjunction with other events or states,"leads to" or "results in" another event or state (or the same state obtaining at a later time), it will be called a "cause" of the latter. I shall also speak of "facts" being causes.

4. A fact can be a cause of a belief even if it does not *initiate* the belief. Suppose I believe that there is a lake in a certain locale, this belief having started in a manner quite unconnected with the existence of the lake. Continuing to have the belief, I go to the locale and perceive the lake. At this juncture, the existence of the lake becomes a cause of my believing that there is a lake there. This is analogous to a table top that is supported by four legs. When a fifth leg is inserted flush beneath the table top, it too becomes a cause of the table top's not falling. It has a causal role in the support of the table top even though, before it was inserted, the table top was adequately supported.

5. Clearly we cannot require someone to reconstruct every detail, since this would involve knowledge of minute physical phenomena, for example, of which ordinary people are unaware. On the other hand, it is difficult to give criteria to identify which details, in general, are "important." This will vary substantially from case to case.

6. Perhaps background propositions that help warrant S's inference must be *known* by S, as well as true. This requirement could be added without making our analysis of "S knows that p" circular. For these propositions would not include p. In other words, the analysis of knowledge could be regarded as recursive.

7. This kind of case is drawn from an unpublished manuscript of Gilbert Harman.

Chapter 5
Discrimination and Perceptual Knowledge

This paper presents a partial analysis of perceptual knowledge, an analysis that will, I hope, lay a foundation for a general theory of knowing. The envisaged theory, like that of Chapter 4, would seek to explicate the concept of knowledge by reference to the causal processes that produce (or sustain) belief. Unlike the earlier theory, however, it would abandon the requirement that a knower's belief that p be causally connected with the fact, or state of affairs, that p.

What kinds of causal processes or mechanisms must be responsible for a belief if that belief is to count as knowledge? They must be mechanisms that are, in an appropriate sense, "reliable." Roughly, a cognitive mechanism or process is reliable if it not only produces true beliefs in actual situations, but would produce true beliefs, or at least inhibit false beliefs, in relevant counterfactual situations. The theory of knowledge I envisage, then, would contain an important counterfactual component.

To be reliable, a cognitive mechanism must enable a person to *discriminate* or *differentiate* between incompatible states of affairs. It must operate in such a way that incompatible states of the world would generate different cognitive responses. Perceptual mechanisms illustrate this clearly. A perceptual mechanism is reliable to the extent that contrary features of the environment (e.g., an object's being red, versus its being yellow) would produce contrary perceptual states of the organism, which would, in turn, produce suitably different beliefs about the environment. Another belief-governing mechanism is a reasoning mechanism, which, given a set of antecedent beliefs, generates or inhibits various new beliefs. A reasoning mechanism is reliable to the extent that its functional procedures would generate new true beliefs from antecedent true beliefs.

My emphasis on discrimination accords with a sense of the verb 'know' that has been neglected by philosophers. The O.E.D. lists one (early) sense of 'know' as "*to distinguish* (one thing) *from* (another)," as in "I know a hawk from a handsaw" (*Hamlet*) and "We'll teach him to know Turtles from Jayes" (*Merry Wives of Windsor*). Although it no longer has great currency, this sense still survives in such expressions as "I don't know him from Adam," "He doesn't know right from left," and other phrases that readily come to mind. I suspect that this construction is historically important and can be used to shed light on constructions in which 'know' takes propositional objects. I suggest that a person is said to know that p just in case he *distinguishes* or *discriminates* the truth of p from relevant alternatives.

A knowledge attribution imputes to someone the discrimination of a given state of affairs from possible alternatives, but not necessarily all logically possible alternatives. In forming beliefs about the world, we do not normally consider all logical possibilities. And in deciding whether someone knows that p (its truth being assumed), we do not ordinarily require him to discriminate p from all logically possible alternatives. Which alternatives are, or ought to be considered, is a question I shall not fully resolve in this paper, but some new perspectives will be examined. I take up this topic in section I.

I

Consider the following example. Henry is driving in the countryside with his son. For the boy's edification Henry identifies various objects on the landscape as they come into view. "That's a cow," says Henry, "That's a tractor," "That's a silo," "That's a barn," etc. Henry has no doubt about the identity of these objects; in particular, he has no doubt that the last-mentioned object is a barn, which indeed it is. Each of the identified objects has features characteristic of its type. Moreover, each object is fully in view, Henry has excellent eyesight, and he has enough time to look at them reasonably carefully, since there is little traffic to distract him.

Given this information, would we say that Henry *knows* that the object is a barn? Most of us would have little hesitation in saying this, so long as we were not in a certain philosophical frame of mind. Contrast our inclination here with the inclination we would have if we were given some additional information. Suppose we are told that, unknown to Henry, the district he has just entered is full of papier-mâché facsimiles of barns. These facsimiles look from the road exactly like barns, but are really just façades, without back walls or interiors, quite incapable of being used as barns. They are so cleverly constructed that travelers invariably mistake them for barns. Having just entered the district, Henry has not encountered any facsimiles; the object he sees is a genuine barn. But if the object on that site were a facsimile, Henry would mistake it for a barn. Given this new information, we would be strongly inclined to withdraw the claim that Henry *knows* the object is a barn. How is this change in our assessment to be explained?[1]

Note first that the traditional justified-true-belief account of knowledge is of no help in explaining this change. In both cases Henry truly believes (indeed, is certain) that the object is a barn. Moreover, Henry's "justification" or "evidence" for the proposition that the object is a barn is the same in both cases. Thus, Henry should either know in both cases or not know in both cases. The presence of facsimiles in the district should make no difference to whether or not he knows.

My old causal analysis cannot handle the problem either. Henry's belief that the object is a barn is caused by the presence of the barn; indeed, the causal process is a perceptual one. Nonetheless, we are not prepared to say, in the second version, that Henry knows.

One analysis of propositional knowledge that might handle the problem is Peter Unger's (1968) non-accidentality analysis. According to this theory, S knows that p if and only if it is not at all accidental that S is right about its being the case that p. In the initial description of the example, this requirement appears to be satisfied; so we say that Henry knows. When informed about the facsimiles, however, we see that it is accidental that Henry is right about its being a barn. So we withdraw our knowledge attribution. The "non-accidentality" analysis is not very satisfying, however, for the notion of "non-accidentality" itself needs explication. Pending explication, it isn't clear whether it correctly handles all cases.

Another approach to knowledge that might handle our problem is the "indefeasibility" approach (Lehrer and Paxson 1969, and Klein 1971). On this view, S knows that p only if S's true belief is justified *and* this justification is not defeated. In an unrestricted form, an indefeasibility theory would say that S's justification j for believing that p is defeated if and only if there is some true proposition q such that the conjunction of q and j does not justify S in believing that p. In slightly different terms, S's justification j is defeated just in case p would no longer be evident for S if q were evident for S. This would handle the barn example, presumably, because the true proposition that there are barn facsimiles in the district is such that, if it were evident for Henry, then it would no longer be evident for him that the object he sees is a barn.

The trouble with the indefeasibility approach is that it is too strong, at least in its unrestricted form. On the foregoing account of "defeat," as Gilbert Harman shows (1973, p. 152), it will (almost) always be possible to find a true proposition that defeats S's justification. Hence, S will never (or seldom) know. What is needed is an appropriate restriction on the notion of "defeat," but I am not aware of an appropriate restriction that has been formulated thus far.

The approach to the problem I shall recommend is slightly different. Admittedly, this approach will raise problems analogous to those of the indefeasibility theory, problems which will not be fully resolved here. Nevertheless, I believe this approach is fundamentally on the right track.

What, then, is my proposed treatment of the barn example? A person knows that p, I suggest, only if the actual state of affairs in which *p* is true is *distinguishable* or *discriminable* by him from a relevant possible state of affairs in which p is false. If there is a relevant possible state of affairs in which p is false and which is indistinguishable by him from the actual state of affairs, then he fails to know that p. In the original description of the barn case there is no hint of any relevant possible state of affairs in which the object in question is not a barn but is indistinguishable (by Henry) from the actual state of affairs. Hence, we are initially inclined to say that Henry knows. The information about the facsimiles, however, introduces such a relevant state of affairs. Given that the district Henry has entered is full of barn facsimiles, there is a relevant alternative hypothesis about the object, viz., that it is a facsimile. Since, by assumption, a state of affairs in which such a hypothesis holds is indistinguishable by Henry from the actual state of affairs (from his vantage point on the road), this hypothesis is not "ruled out" or "precluded" by the factors that prompt Henry's belief. So, once apprised of the facsimiles in the district, we are inclined to deny that Henry knows.

Let us be clear about the bearing of the facsimiles on the case. The presence of the facsimiles does not "create" the possibility that the object Henry sees is a facsimile. Even if there were no facsimiles in the district, it would be possible that the object on that site is a facsimile. What the presence of the facsimiles does is make this possibility *relevant*; or it makes us *consider* it relevant.

The qualifier 'relevant' plays an important role in my view. If knowledge required the elimination of all logically possible alternatives, there would be no knowledge (at least of contingent truths). If only *relevant* alternatives need to be precluded, however, the scope of knowledge could be substantial. This depends, of course, on which alternatives are relevant.

The issue at hand is directly pertinent to the dispute—at least one dispute—between skeptics and their opponents. In challenging a claim to knowledge (or certainty), a typical move of the skeptic is to adduce an unusual alternative hypothesis that the putative knower is unable to preclude: an alternative compatible with his "data." In the skeptical stage of his argument, Descartes says that he is unable to preclude the hypothesis that, instead of being seated by the fire, he is asleep in his bed and dreaming, or the hypothesis that an evil and powerful demon is making it appear to him as if he is seated by the fire. Similarly, Bertrand Russell points out that, given any claim about the past, we can adduce the "skeptical hypothesis" that the world sprang into being five minutes ago, exactly as it then was, with a population that "remembered" a wholly unreal past (Russell 1921, pp. 159–160).

One reply open to the skeptic's opponent is that these skeptical hypotheses are just "idle" hypotheses, and that a person can know a proposition even if there are "idle" alternatives he cannot preclude. The problem, of course, is to specify when an alternative is "idle" and when it is "serious" ("relevant"). Consider Henry once again. Should we say that the possibility of a facsimile before him is a serious or relevant possibility if there are no facsimiles in Henry's district, but only in Sweden? Or if a single such facsimile once existed in Sweden, but none exist now?

There are two views one might take on this general problem. The first view is that there is a "correct" answer, in any given situation, as to which alternatives are relevant. Given a complete specification of Henry's situation, a unique set of relevant alternatives is determined: either a set to which the facsimile alternative belongs or one to which it doesn't belong. According to this view, the semantic content of 'know' contains (implicit) rules that map any putative knower's circumstances into a set of relevant alternatives. An analysis of 'know' is incomplete unless it specifies these rules. The correct specification will favor either the skeptic or the skeptic's opponent.

The second view denies that a putative knower's circumstances uniquely determine a set of relevant alternatives. At any rate, it denies that the semantic content of 'know' contains rules that map a set of circumstances into a single set of relevant alternatives. According to this second view, the verb 'know' is simply not so semantically determinate.

The second view need not deny that there are *regularities* governing the alternative hypotheses a speaker (i.e., an attributor or denier of knowledge) thinks of, and deems relevant. But these regularities are not part of the semantic content of 'know'. The putative knower's circumstances do not *mandate* a unique selection of alternatives; but psychological regularities govern which set of alternatives are in fact selected. In terms of these regularities (together with the semantic content of 'know'), we can explain the observed use of the term.

It is clear that some of these regularities pertain to the (description of the) putative knower's circumstances. One regularity might be that the more *likely* it is, given the circumstances, that a particular alternative would obtain (rather than the actual state of affairs), the more probable it is that a speaker will regard this alternative as relevant. Or, the more *similar* the situation in which the alternative obtains to the actual situation, the more probable it is that a speaker will regard this alternative as relevant. It is not only the circumstances of the putative knower's situation, however, that influence the choice of alternatives. The speaker's own linguistic and psychological context are also important. If the speaker is in a class where Descartes's evil demon has just been discussed, or Russell's five-minute-old-world hypothesis, he may think of alternatives he would not otherwise think of and will perhaps treat them seriously. This sort of regularity is entirely ignored by the first view.

What I am calling the "second" view might have two variants. The first variant can be imbedded in Robert Stalnaker's (1972) framework for pragmatics. In this framework, a proposition is a function from possible worlds into truth values; the determinants of a proposition are a sentence and a (linguistic) context. An important contextual element is what the utterer of a sentence presupposes, or takes for granted. According to the first variant of the second view, a sentence of the form 'S knows that p' does not determine a unique proposition. Rather, a proposition is determined by such a sentence together with the speaker's presuppositions concerning the relevant alternatives.[2] Skeptics and nonskeptics might make different presuppositions (both presuppositions being "legitimate"), and, if so, they are simply asserting or denying different propositions.

One trouble with this variant is its apparent implication that, if a speaker utters a knowledge sentence without presupposing a fully determinate set of alternatives, he does not assert or deny any proposition. That seems too strong. A second variant of the second view, then, is that sentences of the form 'S knows that p' express vague or indeterminate propositions (if they express "propositions" at all), which can, but need not, be made more determinate by full specification of the alternatives. A person who *assents* to a knowledge sentence says that S discriminates the truth of p from relevant alternatives; but he may not have a distinct set of alternatives in mind. (Similarly, according to Paul Ziff (1960), a person who says something is "good" says that it answers to *certain* interests; but he may not have a distinct set of interests in mind.) Someone who *denies* a knowledge sentence more commonly has one or more alternatives in mind as relevant, because his denial may stem from a particular alternative S cannot rule out. But even the denier of a knowledge sentence need not have a full set of relevant alternatives in mind.

I am attracted by the second view under discussion, especially its second variant. In the remainder of the paper, however, I shall be officially neutral. In other words, I shall not try to settle the question of whether the semantic content of 'know' contains rules that map the putative knower's situation into a unique set of relevant alternatives. I leave open the question of whether there is a "correct" set of relevant alternatives, and if so, what it is. To this extent, I also leave open the question of whether skeptics or their opponents are "right." In defending my analysis of 'perceptually knows', however, I shall have to discuss particular examples. In treating these examples I shall assume some (psychological) regularities concerning the selection of alternatives. Among these regularities is the fact that speakers do not *ordinarily* think of "radical" alternatives, but are caused to think of such alternatives, and take them seriously, if the putative knower's circumstances call attention to them. Since I assume that radical or unusual alternatives are not ordinarily entertained or taken seriously, I may appear to side with the opponents of skepticism. My official analysis, however, is neutral on the issue of skepticism.

II

I turn now to the analysis of 'perceptually knows'. Suppose that Sam spots Judy on the street and correctly identifies her as Judy, i.e., believes she is Judy. Suppose further that Judy has an identical twin, Trudy, and the possibility of the person's being Trudy (rather than Judy) is a relevant alternative. Under what circumstances would we say that Sam knows it is Judy?

If Sam regularly identifies Judy as Judy and Trudy as Trudy, he apparently has some (visual) way of discriminating between them (though he may not know how he does it, i.e., what cues he uses). If he does have a way of discriminating between them, which he uses on the occasion in question, we would say that he *knows* it is Judy. But if Sam frequently mistakes Judy for Trudy, and Trudy for Judy, he presumably does not have a way of discriminating between them. For example, he may not have sufficiently distinct (visual) memory "schemata" of Judy and Trudy. So that, on a particular occasion, sensory stimulation from either Judy *or* Trudy would elicit a Judy-identification from him. If he happens to be right that it is Judy, this is just accidental. He doesn't *know* it is Judy.

The crucial question in assessing a knowledge attribution, then, appears to be the truth value of a counterfactual (or set of counterfactuals). Where Sam correctly identifies Judy as Judy, the crucial counterfactual is: "If the person before Sam were Trudy (rather than Judy), Sam would believe her to be Judy." If this counterfactual is true, Sam doesn't know it is Judy. If this counterfactual is false (and all other counterfactuals involving relevant alternatives are also false), then Sam may know it is Judy.

This suggests the following analysis of (noninferential) perceptual knowledge.

> S (noninferentially) *perceptually knows that p* if and only if
> 1. S (noninferentially) perceptually believes that p,
> 2. p is true, and
> 3. there is no relevant contrary q of p such that, if q were true (rather than p), then S would (still) believe that p.

Restricting attention to relevant possibilities, these conditions assert in effect that the only situation in which S would believe that p is a situation in which p is true. In other words, S's believing that p is sufficient for the truth of p. This is essentially the analysis of noninferential knowledge proposed by D. M. Armstrong (1968, 1973), though without any restriction to "relevant" alternatives.

This analysis is too restrictive. Suppose Oscar is standing in an open field containing Dack the dachshund. Oscar sees Dack and (noninferentially) forms a belief in (P):

(P)   The object over there is a dog.

Now suppose that (Q):

(Q)   The object over there is a wolf.

is a relevant alternative to (P) (because wolves are frequenters of this field). Further suppose that Oscar has a tendency to mistake wolves for dogs (he confuses them with malamutes, or German shepherds). Then if the object Oscar saw were Wiley the wolf, rather than Dack the dachshund, Oscar would (still) believe (P). This means that Oscar fails to satisfy the proposed analysis with respect to (P), since (3) is violated. But surely it is wrong to deny—for the indicated reasons—that Oscar *knows* (P) to be true. The mere fact that he would erroneously take a wolf to be a dog hardly shows that he doesn't know a *dachshund* to be a dog! Similarly, if someone looks at a huge redwood and correctly believes it to be a tree, he is not disqualified from knowing it to be a tree merely because there is a very small plant he would wrongly believe to be a tree, i.e., a bonsai tree.

The moral can be formulated as follows. If Oscar believes that a dog is present because of a certain way he is "appeared to," then this true belief fails to be knowledge if there is an alternative situation in which a non-dog produces the same belief by means of the same, or a very similar, appearance. But the wolf situation is not such an alternative: although it would produce in him the same belief, it would not be by means of the same (or a similar) appearance. An alternative that disqualifies a true perceptual belief from being perceptual knowledge must be a "perceptual equivalent" of the actual state of affairs (see Hintikka 1969 on "perceptual alternatives"). A *perceptual equivalent* of an actual state of affairs is a possible state of affairs that would produce the same, or a sufficiently similar, perceptual experience.

The relation of perceptual equivalence must obviously be relativized to *persons* (or organisms). The presence of Judy and the presence of Trudy might be perceptual equivalents for Sam, but not for the twins' own mother (to whom the twins look quite different). Similarly, perceptual equivalence must be relativized to *times*, since perceptual discriminative capacities can be refined or enhanced with training or experience, and can deteriorate with age or disease.

How shall we specify alternative states of affairs that are candidates for being perceptual equivalents? First, we should specify the *object* involved. (I assume for simplicity that only one object is in question.) As the Judy-

Trudy case shows, the object in the alternative state of affairs need not be identical with the actual object. Sometimes, indeed, we may wish to allow non-actual possible objects. Otherwise our framework will be unable in principle to accommodate some of the skeptic's favorite alternatives, e.g., those involving demons. If the reader's ontological sensibility is offended by talk of possible objects, I invite him to replace such talk with any preferred substitute.

Some alternative states of affairs involve the same object but different properties. Where the actual state of affairs involves a certain ball painted blue, an alternative might be chosen involving the same ball painted green. Thus, specification of an alternative requires not only an object, but properties of the object (at the time in question). These should include not only the property in the belief under scrutiny, or one of its contraries, but other properties as well, since the property in the belief (or one of its contraries) might not be sufficiently determinate to indicate what the resultant percept would be like. For full generality, let us choose a *maximal set of* (nonrelational) *properties*. This is a set that would exhaustively characterize an object (at a single time) in some possible world.[3]

An object plus a maximal set of (nonrelational) properties still does not fully specify a perceptual alternative. Also needed are relations between the object and the perceiver, plus conditions of the environment. One relation that can affect the resultant percept is *distance*. Another relational factor is *relative orientation*, both of object vis-à-vis perceiver and perceiver vis-à-vis object. The nature of the percept depends, for example, on which side of the object faces the perceiver, and on how the perceiver's bodily organs are oriented, or situated, vis-à-vis the object. Thirdly, the percept is affected by the current state of the *environment*, e.g., the illumination, the presence or absence of intervening objects, and the direction and velocity of the wind.

To cover all such elements, I introduce the notion of a *distance-orientation-environment* relation, for short, a *DOE relation*. Each such relation is a conjunction of relations or properties concerning distance, orientation, and environmental conditions. One DOE relation is expressed by the predicate 'x is 20 feet from y, the front side of y is facing x, the eyes of x are open and focused in y's direction, no opaque object is interposed between x and y, and y is in moonlight'.

Since the health of sensory organs can affect percepts, it might be argued that this should be included in these relations, thereby opening the condition of these organs to counterfactualization. For simplicity I neglect this complication. This does not mean that I don't regard the condition of sensory organs as open to counterfactualization. I merely omit explicit incorporation of this factor into our exposition.

We can now give more precision to our treatment of perceptual equivalents. Perceptual states of affairs will be specified by ordered triples, each consisting of (1) an object, (2) a maximal set of nonrelational properties, and (3) a DOE relation. If S perceives object b at t and if b has all the properties in a maximal set J and bears DOE relation R to S at t, then the actual state of affairs pertaining to this perceptual episode is represented by the ordered triple $\langle b, J, R \rangle$. An alternative state of affairs is represented by an ordered triple $\langle c, K, R^* \rangle$, which may (but need not) differ from $\langle b, J, R \rangle$ with respect to one or more of its elements.

Under what conditions is an alternative $\langle c, K, R^* \rangle$ a perceptual equivalent of $\langle b, J, R)$ for person S at time t? I said that a perceptual equivalent is a state of affairs that would produce "the same, or a very similar" perceptual experience. That is not very committal. Must a perceptual equivalent produce exactly the same percept? Given our intended use of perceptual equivalence in the analysis of perceptual knowledge, the answer is clearly No. Suppose that a Trudy-produced percept would be qualitatively distinct from Sam's Judy-produced percept, but similar enough for Sam to mistake Trudy for Judy. This is sufficient grounds for saying that Sam fails to have knowledge. Qualitative identity of percepts, then, is too strong a requirement for perceptual equivalence.

How should the requirement be weakened? We must not weaken it too much, for the wolf alternative might then be a perceptual equivalent of the dachshund state of affairs. This would have the unwanted consequence that Oscar doesn't know Dack to be a dog.

The solution I propose is this. If the percept produced by the alternative state of affairs would not differ from the actual percept in any respect that is causally relevant to S's belief, this alternative situation is a perceptual equivalent for S of the actual situation. Suppose that a Trudy-produced percept would differ from Sam's Judy-produced percept to the extent of having a different eyebrow configuration. (A difference in shape between Judy's and Trudy's eyebrows does not ensure that Sam's percepts would "register" this difference. I assume, however, that the eyebrow difference would be registered in Sam's percepts.) But suppose that Sam's visual "concept" of Judy does not include a feature that reflects this contrast. His Judy-concept includes an "eyebrow feature" only in the sense that the absence of eyebrows would inhibit a Judy-classification. It does not include a more determinate eyebrow feature, though: Sam hasn't learned to associate Judy with distinctively shaped eyebrows. Hence, the distinctive "eyebrow shape" of his actual (Judy-produced) percept is not one of the percept-features that is causally responsible for his believing Judy to be present. Assuming that a Trudy-produced percept would not differ from his actual percept in any *other* causally relevant way, the hypothetical Trudy-situation is a perceptual equivalent of the actual Judy-situation.

Consider now the dachshund-wolf case. The hypothetical percept produced by a wolf would differ from Oscar's actual percept of the dachshund in respects that are causally relevant to Oscar's judgment that a dog is present. Let me elaborate. There are various kinds of objects, rather different in shape, size, color, and texture, that would be classified by Oscar as a dog. He has a number of visual "schemata," we might say, each with a distinctive set of features, such that any percept that "matches" or "fits" one of these schemata would elicit a "dog" classification. (I think of a schema not as a "template," but as a set of more-or-less abstract—though iconic—features.[4]) Now, although a dachshund and a wolf would each produce a dog-belief in Oscar, the percepts produced by these respective stimuli would differ in respects that are causally relevant to Oscar's forming a dog-belief. Since Oscar's dachshund-schema includes such features as having an elongated, sausagelike shape, a smallish size, and droopy ears, these features of the percept are all causally relevant, when a dachshund is present, to Oscar's believing that a dog is present. Since a hypothetical wolf-produced percept would differ in these respects from Oscar's dachshund-produced percept, the hypothetical wolf state of affairs is not a perceptual equivalent of the dachshund state of affairs for Oscar.

The foregoing approach requires us to relativize perceptual equivalence once again, this time to the belief in question, or the property believed to be exemplified. The Trudy-situation is a perceptual equivalent for Sam of the Judy-situation *relative to the property of being* (identical with) *Judy.* The wolf-situation is not a perceptual equivalent for Oscar of the dachshund-situation *relative to the property of being a dog.*

I now propose the following definition of perceptual equivalence:

> If object b has the maximal set of properties J and is in DOE relation R to S at t, if S has some percept P at t that is perceptually caused by b's having J and being in R to S at t, and if P noninferentially causes S to believe (or sustains S in believing) of object b that it has property F, then
>
> $\langle c, K, R^* \rangle$ *is a perceptual equivalent of* $\langle b, J, R \rangle$ *for S at t relative to property F if and only if*
>
> 1. if at t object c had K and were in R^* to S, then this would perceptually cause S to have some percept P^* at t,
> 2. P^* would cause S noninferentially to believe (or sustain S in believing) of object c that it has F, and
> 3. P^* would not differ from P in any respect that is causally relevant to S's F-belief.

Since I shall analyze the *de re, relational,* or *transparent* sense of 'perceptually knows', I shall want to employ, in my analysis, the *de re* sense of 'believe'. This is why such phrases as 'believe ... *of object b*' occur in the definition of perceptual equivalence. For present purposes, I take for granted the notion of (perceptual) *de re* belief. I assume, however, that the object *of which* a person perceptually believes a property to hold is the object he perceives, i.e., the object that "perceptually causes" the percept that elicits the belief. The notion of *perceptual causation* is another notion I take for granted. A person's percept is obviously caused by many objects (or events), not all of which the person is said to perceive. One problem for the theory of perception is to explicate the notion of perceptual causation, that is, to explain which of the causes of a percept a person is said to perceive. I set this problem aside here (but see Goldman 1977). A third notion I take for granted is the notion of a (noninferential) *perceptual belief*, or perceptual "taking." Not all beliefs that are noninferentially caused by a percept can be considered perceptual "takings"; "indirectly" caused beliefs would not be so considered. But I make no attempt to delineate the requisite causal relation.

Several other comments on the definition of perceptual equivalence are in order. Notice that the definition is silent on whether J or K contains property F, i.e., whether F is exemplified in either the actual or the alternative states of affairs. The relativization to F (in the definiendum) implies that an F-belief is produced in both situations, not that F is exemplified (in either or both situations). In applying the definition to cases of putative knowledge, we shall focus on cases where F belongs to J (so S's belief is true in the actual situation) but does not belong to K (so S's belief is false in the counterfactual situation). But the definition of perceptual equivalence is silent on these matters.

Though the definition does not say so, I assume it is possible for object c to have all properties in K, and possible for c to be in R^* to S while having all properties in K. I do not want condition 1 to be vacuously true, simply by having an impossible antecedent.

It might seem as if the antecedent of (1) should include a further conjunct, expressing the supposition that object b is absent. This might seem necessary to handle cases in which, if c were in R^* to S, but b remained in its actual relation R to S, then b would "block" S's access to c. (For example, b might be an orange balloon floating over the horizon, and c might be the moon.) This can be handled by the definition as it stands, by construing R^*, where necessary, as including the absence of object b from the perceptual scene. (One cannot *in general* hypothesize that b is absent, for we want to allow object c to be identical with b.)

The definition implies that there is no temporal gap between each object's having its indicated properties and DOE relation and the occurrence of the corresponding percept. This simplification is introduced because no general requirement can be laid down about how long it takes for the stimulus energy to reach the perceiver. The intervals in the actual and alternative states may differ because the stimuli might be at different distances from the perceiver.

III

It is time to turn to the analysis of perceptual knowledge, for which the definition of perceptual equivalence paves the way. I restrict my attention to perceptual knowledge of the possession, by physical objects, of nonrelational properties. I also restrict the analysis to *noninferential* perceptual knowledge. This frees me from the complex issues introduced by inference, which require separate treatment.

It may be contended that all perceptual judgment is based on inference and, hence, that the proposed restriction reduces the scope of the analysis to nil. Two replies are in order. First, although cognitive psychology establishes that percepts are affected by cognitive factors, such as "expectancies," it is by no means evident that these causal processes should be construed as inferences. Second, even if we were to grant that there is in fact no noninferential perceptual belief, it would still be of epistemological importance to determine whether noninferential perceptual knowledge of the physical world is conceptually possible. This could be explored by considering merely possible cases of noninferential perceptual belief, and seeing whether, under suitable conditions, such belief would count as knowledge.

With these points in mind, we may propose the following (tentative) analysis:

> At t S noninferentially perceptually knows of object b that it has property F if and only if
>
> 1. for some maximal set of nonrelational properties J and some DOE relation R, object b has (all the members of) J at t and is in R to S at t,
> 2. F belongs to J,
> 3. A. b's having J and being in R to S at t perceptually causes S at t to have some percept P,[5]
>   B. P noninferentially causes S at t to believe (or sustains S in believing) of object b that it has property F, and
>   C. there is no alternative state of affairs $\langle c, K, R^* \rangle$ such that
>   i. $\langle c, K, R^* \rangle$ is a relevant perceptual equivalent of $\langle b, J, R \rangle$ for S at t relative to property F, and
>   ii. F does not belong to K.

Conditions 1 and 2 jointly entail the truth condition for knowledge: S knows b to have F (at t) only if b does have F (at t). Condition 3B contains the belief condition for knowledge, restricted, of course, to (noninferential) perceptual belief. The main work of the conditions is done by 3C. It requires that there be no relevant alternative that is (i) a perceptual equivalent to the actual state of affairs relative to property F, and (ii) a state of affairs in which the appropriate object lacks F (and hence S's F-belief is false).

How does this analysis relate to my theme of a "reliable discriminative mechanism"? A perceptual cognizer may be thought of as a two-part mechanism. The first part constructs percepts (a special class of internal states) from receptor stimulation. The second part operates on percepts to produce beliefs. Now, in order for the conditions of the analysans to be satisfied, each part of the mechanism must be sufficiently discriminating, or "finely tuned." If the first part is not sufficiently discriminating, patterns of receptor stimulation from quite different sources would result in the same (or very similar) percepts, percepts that would generate the same beliefs. If the second part is not sufficiently discriminating, then even if different percepts are constructed by the first part, the same beliefs will be generated by the second part. To be sure, even an undiscriminating bipartite mechanism may produce a belief that, luckily, is true; but there will be other, counterfactual, situations in which such a belief would be false. In this sense, such a mechanism is unreliable. What our analysis says is that S has perceptual knowledge if and only if not only does his perceptual mechanism produce true belief, but there are no relevant counterfactual situations in which the same belief would be produced via an equivalent percept and in which the belief would be false.

Let me now illustrate how the analysis is to be applied to the barn example, where there are facsimiles in Henry's district. Let $S =$ Henry, $b =$ the barn Henry actually sees, and $F =$ the property of being a barn. Conditions 1 through 3B are met by letting J take as its value the set of all nonrelational properties actually possessed by the barn at t, R take as its value the actual DOE relation the barn bears to Henry at t, and P take as its value the actual (visual) percept caused by the barn. Condition 3C is violated, however. There is a relevant triple that meets subclauses (i) and (ii), i.e., the triple where $c =$ a suitable barn facsimile, $K =$ a suitable set of properties (excluding, of course, the property of being a barn), and $R^* =$ approximately the same DOE relation as the actual one. Thus, Henry does not (noninferentially) perceptually *know* of the barn that it has the property of being a barn.

In the dachshund-wolf case, $S =$ Oscar, $b =$ Dack the dachshund, and $F =$ being a dog. The first several conditions are again met. Is 3C met as well? There is a relevant alternative state of affairs in which Wiley the wolf is believed by Oscar to be a dog, but lacks that property. This state of affairs doesn't violate 3C, however, since it isn't a *perceptual equivalent* of the actual situation relative to being a dog. So this alternative doesn't disqualify Oscar from knowing Dack to be a dog.

Is there another alternative that *is* a perceptual equivalent of the actual situation (relative to being a dog)? We can imagine a DOE relation in which fancy devices between Wiley and Oscar distort the light coming from Wiley and produce in Oscar a Dack-like visual percept. The question here, however, is whether this perceptual equivalent is *relevant*. Relevance is determined not only by the hypothetical object and its properties, but also by the DOE relation. Since the indicated DOE relation is highly unusual, this will count (at least for a nonskeptic) against the alternative's being relevant and against its disqualifying Oscar from knowing.[6]

The following "Gettierized" example, suggested by Marshall Swain, might appear to present difficulties. In a dark room there is a candle several yards ahead of S which S sees and believes to be ahead of him. But he sees the candle only indirectly, via a system of mirrors (of which he is unaware) that make it appear as if he were seeing it directly.[7] We would surely deny that S knows the candle to be ahead of him. (This case does not really fit our intended analysandum, since the believed property F is relational. This detail can be ignored, however.) Why? If we say, with Harman, that all perceptual belief is based on inference, we can maintain that S infers that the candle is ahead of him from the premise that he sees whatever he sees *directly*. This premise being false, S's knowing is disqualified on familiar grounds.

My theory suggests another explanation, which makes no unnecessary appeal to inference. We deny that S knows, I suggest, because the system of mirrors draws our attention to a perceptual equivalent in which the candle is *not* ahead of S, i.e., a state of affairs where the candle is behind S but reflected in a system of mirrors so that it appears to be ahead of him. Since the actual state of affairs involves a system of reflecting mirrors, we are impelled to count this alternative as relevant, and hence to deny that S knows.

Even in ordinary cases, of course, where S sees a candle directly, the possibility of reflecting mirrors constitutes a perceptual equivalent. In the ordinary case, however, we would not count this as relevant; we would not regard it as a "serious" possibility. The Gettierized case impels us to take it seriously because there the actual state of affairs involves a devious system of reflecting mirrors. So we have an explanation of why people are credited with knowing in ordinary perceptual cases but not in the Gettierized case.

The following is a more serious difficulty for our analysis. S truly believes something to be a tree, but there is a relevant alternative in which an electrode stimulating S's optic nerve would produce an equivalent percept, which would elicit the same belief. Since this is assumed to be a relevant alternative, it ought to disqualify S from knowing. But it doesn't satisfy our definition of a perceptual equivalent, first because the electrode would not be a perceptual cause of the percept (we would not say that S *perceives* the electrode), and second because S would not believe *of the electrode* (nor of anything else) that it is a tree. A similar problem arises where the alternative state of affairs would involve S's having a hallucination.

To deal with these cases, we could revise our analysis of perceptual knowledge as follows. (A similar revision in the definition of perceptual equivalence would do the job equally well.) We could reformulate 3C to say that there must neither be a relevant perceptual equivalent of the indicated sort (using our present definition of perceptual equivalence) *nor* a relevant alternative situation in which an equivalent percept occurs and prompts a *de dicto* belief that something has F, but where there is nothing that *perceptually* causes this percept and nothing *of which* F is believed to hold. In other words, knowledge can be disqualified by relevant alternative situations where S doesn't perceive anything and doesn't have any *de re* (F-) belief at all. I am inclined to adopt this solution, but will not actually make this addition to the analysis.

Another difficulty for the analysis is this. Suppose Sam's "schemata" of Judy and Trudy have hitherto been indistinct, so Judy-caused percepts sometimes elicit Judy-beliefs and sometimes Trudy-beliefs, and similarly for Trudy-caused percepts. Today Sam falls down and hits his head. As a consequence a new feature is "added" to his Judy-schema, a mole-associated feature. From now on he will believe someone to be Judy only if he has the sort of percept that would be caused by a Judy-like person with a mole over the left eye. Sam is unaware that this change has taken place and will remain unaware of it, since he isn't conscious of the cues he uses. Until today, neither Judy nor Trudy has had a left-eyebrow mole; but today Judy happens to develop such a mole. Thus, from now on Sam can discriminate Judy from Trudy. Does this mean that he will *know* Judy to be Judy when he correctly identifies her? I am doubtful.

A possible explanation of Sam's not knowing (on future occasions) is that Trudy-with-a-mole is a relevant perceptual equivalent of Judy. This is not Trudy's actual condition, of course, but it might be deemed a relevant possibility. I believe, however, that the mole case calls for a further restriction, one concerning the *genesis* of a person's propensity to form a certain belief as a result of a certain percept. A merely fortuitous or accidental genesis is not enough to support knowledge. I do not know exactly what requirement to impose on the genesis of such a propensity. The mole case intimates that the genesis should involve certain "experience" with objects, but this may be too narrow. I content myself with a very vague addition to our previous conditions, which completes the analysis:

4. S's propensity to form an F-belief as a result of percept P has an appropriate genesis.

Of course this leaves the problem unresolved. But the best I can do here is identify the problem.

IV

A few words are in order about the intended significance of my analysis. One of its purposes is to provide an alternative to the traditional "Cartesian" perspective in epistemology. The Cartesian view combines a theory of knowledge with a theory of justification. Its theory of knowledge asserts that S knows that p at t only if S is (fully, adequately, etc.) justified at t in believing that p. Its theory of justification says that S is justified at t in believing that p only if either (A) p is self-warranting for S at t, or (B) p is (strongly, adequately, etc.) supported or confirmed by propositions each of which is self-warranting for S at t. Now propositions about the state of the external world at t are not self-warranting. Hence, if S knows any such proposition p at t, there must be some other propositions which strongly support p and which are self-warranting for S at t. These must be propositions about S's mental state at t and perhaps some obvious necessary truths. A major task of Cartesian epistemology is to show that there is some such set of self-warranting propositions, propositions that support external-world propositions with sufficient strength.

It is impossible to canvass all attempts to fulfill this project; but none have succeeded, and I do not think that any will. One can conclude either that we have no knowledge of the external world or that Cartesian requirements are too demanding. I presuppose the latter conclusion in offering my theory of perceptual knowledge. My theory requires no justification for external-world propositions that derives entirely from self-warranting propositions. It requires only, in effect, that beliefs in the external world be suitably caused, where "suitably" comprehends a process or mechanism that not only produces true belief in the actual situation, but would not produce false belief in relevant counterfactual situations. If one wishes, one can so employ the term 'justification' that belief causation of *this* kind counts as justification. In this sense, of course, my theory does require justification. But this is entirely different from the sort of justification demanded by Cartesianism.

My theory protects the possibility of knowledge by making Cartesian-style justification unnecessary. But it leaves a door open to skepticism by its stance on relevant alternatives. This is not a failure of the theory, in my opinion. An adequate account of the term 'know' should make the temptations of skepticism comprehensible, which my theory does. But it should also put skepticism in a proper perspective, which Cartesianism fails to do.

In any event, I put forward my account of perceptual knowledge not primarily as an antidote to skepticism, but as a more accurate rendering of what the term 'know' actually means. In this respect it is instructive to test my theory and its rivals against certain metaphorical or analogical uses of 'know'. A correct definition should be able to explain extended and figurative uses as well as literal uses, for it should explain how speakers arrive at the extended uses from the central ones. With this in mind, consider how tempting it is to say of an electric-eye door that it "knows" you are coming (at least that *something* is coming), or "sees" you coming. The attractiveness of the metaphor is easily explained on my theory: the door has a reliable mechanism for discriminating between something being before it and nothing being there. It has a "way of telling" whether or not something is there: this "way of telling" consists in a mechanism by which objects in certain DOE relations to it have differential effects on its internal state. By contrast, note how artificial it would be to apply more traditional analyses of 'know' to the electric-eye door, or to other mechanical detecting devices. How odd it would be to say that the door has "good reasons," "adequate evidence," or "complete justification" for thinking something is there; or that it has "the right to be sure" something is there. The oddity of these locutions indicates how far from the mark are the analyses of 'know' from which they derive.

The trouble with many philosophical treatments of knowledge is that they are inspired by Cartesian-like conceptions of justification or vindication. There is a consequent tendency to overintellectualize or overrationalize the notion of knowledge. In the spirit of naturalistic epistemology (cf. Quine 1969b), I am trying to fashion an account of knowing that focuses on more primitive and pervasive aspects of cognitive life, in connection with which, I believe, the term 'know' gets its application. A fundamental facet of animate life, both human and infra-human, is telling things apart, distinguishing predator from prey, for example, or a protective habitat from a threatening one. The concept of knowledge has its roots in this kind of cognitive activity.

Notes

An early version of this paper was read at the 1972 Chapel Hill Colloquium. Later versions were read at the 1973 University of Cincinnati Colloquium and at a number of other philosophy departments. For comments and criticism, I am especially indebted to Holly Smith, Bruce Aune, Jaegwon Kim, Louis Loeb, and Kendall Walton.

1. [Note added in this edition.] The barn facsimile example was originally suggested to me as a puzzle by Carl Ginet. Gail Stine (1976) also uses the example, which she would have heard when I read a version of this paper at Wayne State University in about 1974.

2. Something like this is suggested by Fred Dretske (1970). [Addendum for this edition:] I should emphasize that Dretske himself uses the phrase 'relevant alternatives', probably its first occurrence in the literature.

3. I have in mind here purely qualitative properties. Properties like *being identical with Judy* would be given by the selected object. If the set of qualitative properties (at a given time) implied which object it was that had these properties, then specification of the object would be redundant, and we could represent states of affairs by ordered pairs of maximal sets of (qualitative) properties and DOE relations. Since this is problematic, however, I include specification of the object as well as the set of (qualitative) properties.

4. For a discussion of iconic schemata, see Posner 1973, chap. 3.

5. Should (3A) be construed as implying that *every* property in *J* is a (perceptual) cause of *P*? No. Many of *b*'s properties are exemplified in its interior or at its backside. These are not causally relevant, at least in visual perception. (3A) must therefore be construed as saying that *P* is (perceptually) caused by *b*'s having (jointly) *all* the members of *J*, and leaving open which, among these members, are individually causally relevant. It follows, however, that (3A) does not require that *b's-having-F*, in particular, is a (perceptual) cause of *P*, and this omission might be regarded as objectionable. "Surely," it will be argued, "*S* perceptually knows *b* to have *F* only if *b's-having-F* (perceptually) causes the percept." The reason I omit this requirement is the following. Suppose *F* is the property of being a dog. Can we say that *b's-being-a-dog* is a cause of certain light waves' being reflected? This is very dubious. It is the molecular properties of the surface of the animal that are causally responsible for this transmission of light, and hence for the percept.

   One might say that, even if the percept needn't be (perceptually) caused by *b's-having-F*, it must at least be caused by microstructural properties of *b* that ensure *b's*-having-F. As the dog example again illustrates, however, this is too strong. The surface properties of the dog that reflect the light waves do not *ensure* that the object is a dog, either logically or nomologically. Something could have that surface (on one side) and still have a non-dog interior and backside. The problem should be solved, I think, by reliance on whether there are relevant perceptual equivalents. If there are no relevant perceptual equivalents in which *K* excludes being a dog, then the properties of the actual object that are causally responsible for the percept suffice to yield knowledge. We need not require either that the percept be (perceptually) caused by *b's-having-F*, nor by any subset of *J* that "ensures" *b's-having-F*.

6. It is the "unusualness" of the DOE relation that inclines us not to count the alternative as relevant; it is not the mere fact that the DOE relation differs from the actual one. In general, our analysis allows knowledge to be defeated or disqualified by alternative situations in which the DOE relation differs from the DOE relation in the actual state of affairs. Our analysis differs in this respect from Fred Dretske (1971). Dretske's analysis, which ours resembles on a number of points, considers only those counterfactual situations in which everything that is "logically and causally independent of the state of affairs expressed by *P*" is the same as in the actual situation. (*P* is the content of *S*'s belief.) This implies that the actual DOE relation cannot be counterfactualized, but must be held fixed. (It may also imply—depending what *P* is—that one cannot counterfactualize the perceived object nor the full set of properties *J*.) This unduly narrows the class of admissible alternatives. Many *relevant* alternatives, that do disqualify knowledge, involve DOE relations that differ from the actual DOE relation.

7. Harman (1973, pp. 22–23) has a similar case. In that case, however, *S* does not see the candle; it is not a cause of his percept. Given our causal requirement for perceptual knowledge, that case is easily handled.

Chapter 6
What Is Justified Belief?

The aim of this paper is to sketch a theory of justified belief. What I have in mind is an explanatory theory, one that explains in a general way why certain beliefs are counted as justified and others as unjustified. Unlike some traditional approaches, I do not try to prescribe standards for justification that differ from, or improve upon, our ordinary standards. I merely try to explicate the ordinary standards, which are, I believe, quite different from those of many classical, e.g., 'Cartesian', accounts.

Many epistemologists have been interested in justification because of its presumed close relationship to knowledge. This relationship is intended to be preserved in the conception of justified belief presented here. In previous papers on knowledge (chapters 4 and 5, and Goldman 1975), I have denied that justification is necessary for knowing, but there I had in mind 'Cartesian' accounts of justification. On the account of justified belief suggested here, it *is* necessary for knowing, and closely related to it.

The term 'justified', I presume, is an evaluative term, a term of appraisal. Any correct definition or synonym of it would also feature evaluative terms. I assume that such definitions or synonyms might be given, but I am not interested in them. I want a set of substantive conditions that specify when a belief is justified. Compare the moral term 'right'. This might be defined in other ethical terms or phrases, a task appropriate to meta-ethics. The task of normative ethics, by contrast, is to state substantive conditions for the rightness of actions. Normative ethics tries to specify non-ethical conditions that determine when an action is right. A familiar example is act-utilitarianism, which says an action is right if and only if it produces, or would produce, at least as much net happiness as any alternative open to the agent. These necessary and sufficient conditions clearly involve no ethical notions. Analogously, I want a theory of justified belief to specify in non-epistemic terms when a belief is justified. This is not the only kind of theory of justifiedness one might seek, but it is one important kind of theory and the kind sought here.

In order to avoid epistemic terms in our theory, we must know which terms are epistemic. Obviously, an exhaustive list cannot be given, but here are some examples: 'justified', 'warranted', 'has (good) grounds', 'has reason (to believe)', 'knows that', 'sees that', 'apprehends that', 'is probable' (in an epistemic or inductive sense), 'shows that', 'establishes that', and 'ascertains that'. By contrast, here are some sample non-epistemic expressions: 'believes that', 'is true', 'causes', 'it is necessary that', 'implies', 'is deducible from', and 'is probable' (either in the frequency sense or the propensity sense). In general, (purely) doxastic, metaphysical, modal, semantic, or syntactic expressions are not epistemic.

There is another constraint I wish to place on a theory of justified belief, in addition to the constraint that it be couched in non-epistemic language. Since I seek an explanatory theory, i.e., one that clarifies the underlying source of justificational status, it is not enough for a theory to state 'correct' necessary and sufficient conditions. Its conditions must also be appropriately deep or revelatory. Suppose, for example, that the following sufficient condition of justified belief is offered: 'If S senses redly at t and S believes at t that he is sensing redly, then S's belief at t that he is sensing redly is justified.' This is not the kind of principle I seek; for, even if it is correct, it leaves unexplained *why* a person who senses redly and believes that he does, believes this justifiably. Not every state is such that if one is in it and believes one is in it, this belief is justified. What is distinctive about the state of sensing redly, or 'phenomenal' states in general? A theory of justified belief of the kind I seek must answer this question, and hence it must be couched at a suitably deep, general, or abstract level.

A few introductory words about my *explicandum* are appropriate at this juncture. It is often assumed that whenever a person has a justified belief, he knows that it is justified and knows what the justification is. It is further assumed that the person can state or explain what his justification is. On this view, a justification is an argument, defense, or set of reasons that can be given in support of a belief. Thus, one studies the nature of justified belief by considering what a person might *say* if asked to defend, or justify, his belief. I make none of these sorts of assumptions here. I leave it an open question whether, when a belief *is* justified, the believer *knows* it is justified. I also leave it an open question whether, when a belief is justified, the believer can *state* or *give* a justification for it. I do not even assume that when a belief is justified there is something 'possessed' by the believer which can be called a 'justification' . I do assume that a justified belief gets its status of being justified from some processes or properties that make it justified. In short, there must be some justification-conferring processes or properties. But this does not imply that there must be an argument, or reason, or anything else, 'possessed' at the time of belief by the believer.

I

A theory of justified belief will be a set of principles that specify truth-conditions for the schema ⌐S's belief in *p* at time *t* is justified⌐, i.e., conditions for the satisfaction of this schema in all possible cases. It will be convenient to formulate candidate theories in a recursive or inductive format, which would include (A) one or more base clauses, (B) a set of recursive clauses (possibly null), and (C) a closure clause. In such a format, it is permissible for the predicate 'is a justified belief' to appear in recursive clauses. But neither this predicate, nor any other epistemic predicate, may appear in (the antecedent of) any base clause.[1]

Before turning to my own theory, I want to survey some other possible approaches to justified belief. Identification of problems associated with other attempts will provide some motivation for the theory I shall offer. Obviously, I cannot examine all, or even very many, alternative attempts. But a few sample attempts will be instructive.

Let us concentrate on the attempt to formulate one or more adequate base-clause principles.[2] Here is a classical candidate:

(1) If *S* believes *p* at *t*, and *p* is indubitable for *S* (at *t*), then *S*'s belief in *p* at *t* is justified.

To evaluate this principle, we need to know what 'indubitable' means. It can be understood in at least two ways. First, '*p* is indubitable for *S*' might mean: '*S* has no *grounds* for doubting *p*'. Since 'ground' is an epistemic term, however, principle (1) would be inadmissible on this reading, for epistemic terms may not legitimately appear in the antecedent of a base clause. A second interpretation would avoid this difficulty. One might interpret '*p* is indubitable for *S*' psychologically, i.e., as meaning '*S* is psychologically incapable of doubting *p*'. This would make principle (1) admissible, but would it be correct? Surely not. A religious fanatic may be psychologically incapable of doubting the tenets of his faith, but that doesn't make his belief in them justified. Similarly, during the Watergate affair, someone may have been so blinded by the aura of the presidency that even after the most damaging evidence against Nixon had emerged he was still incapable of doubting Nixon's veracity. It doesn't follow that his belief in Nixon's veracity was justified.

A second candidate base-clause principle is this:

(2) If *S* believes *p* at *t*, and *p* is self-evident, then *S*'s belief in *p* at *t* is justified.

To evaluate this principle, we again need an interpretation of its crucial term, in this case 'self-evident'. On one standard reading, 'evident' is a synonym for 'justified'. '*Self*-evident' would therefore mean something like 'directly justified', 'intuitively justified', or 'nonderivatively justified'. On this reading 'self-evident' is an epistemic phrase, and principle (2) would be disqualified as a base-clause principle.

However, there are other possible readings of 'p is self-evident' on which it isn't an epistemic phrase. One such reading is: 'It is impossible to understand p without believing it'.[3] According to this interpretation, trivial analytic and logical truths might turn out to be self-evident. Hence, any belief in such a truth would be a justified belief, according to (2).

What does 'it is *impossible* to understand p without believing it' mean? Does it mean '*humanly* impossible'? That reading would probably make (2) an unacceptable principle. There may well be propositions which humans have an innate and irrepressible disposition to believe, e.g., 'Some events have causes'. But it seems unlikely that people's inability to refrain from believing such a proposition makes every belief in it justified.

Should we then understand 'impossible' to mean 'impossible in principle', or 'logically impossible'? If that is the reading given, I suspect that (2) is a vacuous principle. I doubt that even trivial logical or analytic truths will satisfy this definition of 'self-evident'. Any proposition, we may assume, has two or more components that are somehow organized or juxtaposed. To understand the proposition one must 'grasp' the components and their juxtaposition. Now in the case of *complex* logical truths, there are (human) psychological operations that suffice to grasp the components and their juxtaposition but do not suffice to produce a belief that the proposition is true. But can't we at least *conceive* of an analogous set of psychological operations even for simple logical truths, operations which perhaps are not in the repertoire of human cognizers but which might be in the repertoire of some conceivable beings? That is, can't we conceive of psychological operations that would suffice to grasp the components and componential-juxtaposition of these simple propositions but do not suffice to produce *belief* in the propositions? I think we can conceive of such operations. Hence, for any proposition you choose, it will possible for it to be understood without being believed.

Finally, even if we set these two objections aside, we must note that self-evidence can at best confer justificational status on relatively few beliefs, and the only plausible group are beliefs in necessary truths. Thus, other base-clause principles will be needed to explain the justificational status of beliefs in contingent propositions.

The notion of a base-clause principle is naturally associated with the idea of 'direct' justifiedness, and in the realm of contingent propositions first-person-current-mental-state propositions have often been assigned this role. In Roderick Chisholm's terminology, this conception is expressed by the notion of a '*self-presenting*' state or proposition. The sentence 'I am thinking', for example, expresses a self-presenting proposition. (At least I shall *call* this sort of content a 'proposition', though it only has a truth value given some assignment of a subject who utters or entertains the content and a time of entertaining.) When such a proposition is true for person S at time *t*, S is justified in believing it at *t*: in Chisholm's terminology, the proposition is 'evident' for S at *t*. This suggests the following base-clause principle.

(3)   If *p* is a self-presenting proposition, and *p* is true for S at *t*, and S believes *p* at *t*, then S's belief in *p* at *t* is justified.

What, exactly, does 'self-presenting' mean? Chisholm (1977, p. 22) offers this definition: "*h* is self-presenting for S at *t* = ₔf. *h* is true at *t*; and necessarily, if *h* is true at *t*, then *h* is evident for S at *t*." Unfortunately, since 'evident' is an epistemic term, 'self-presenting' also becomes an epistemic term on this definition, thereby disqualifying (3) as a legitimate base clause. Some other definition of self-presentingness must be offered if (3) is to be a suitable base-clause principle.

Another definition of self-presentation readily comes to mind. 'Self-presentation' is an approximate synonym of 'self-intimation', and a proposition may be said to be self-intimating if and only if whenever it is true of a person that person believes it. More precisely, we may give the following definition.

(SP)   Proposition *p* is self-presenting if and only if: necessarily, for any S and any *t*, if *p* is true for S at *t*, then S believes *p* at *t*.

On this definition, 'self-presenting' is clearly not an epistemic predicate, so (3) would be an admissible principle. Moreover, there is initial plausibility in the suggestion that it is *this* feature of first-person-current-mental-state proposition—viz., their truth guarantees their being believed—that makes beliefs in them justified.

Employing this definition of self-presentation, is principle (3) correct? This cannot be decided until we define self-presentation more precisely. Since the operator 'necessarily' can be read in different ways, there are different forms of self-presentation and correspondingly different versions of principle (3). Let us focus on two of these readings: a *'nomological'* reading and a *'logical'* reading. Consider first the nomological reading. On this definition a proposition is self-presenting just in case it is nomologically necessary that if *p* is true for S at *t*, then S believes *p* at *t*.[4]

Is the nomological version of principle (3)—call it '(3ₙ)'—correct? Not at all. We can imagine cases in which the antecedent of (3ₙ) is satisfied but we would not say that the belief is justified. Suppose, for example, that p is the proposition expressed by the sentence 'I am in brain-state B', where 'B' is shorthand for a certain highly specific neural state description. Further suppose it is a nomological truth that anyone in brain-state B will ipso facto *believe* he is in brain-state *B*. In other words, imagine that an occurrent belief with the content 'I am in brain-state *B*' is realized whenever one is in brain-state *B*.[5] According to (3_N), any such belief is justified. But that is clearly false. We can readily imagine circumstances in which a person goes into brain-state *B* and therefore has the belief in question, though this belief is by no means justified. For example, we can imagine that a brain surgeon operating on *S* artifically induces brain-state *B*. This results, phenomenologically, in *S*'s suddenly believing—out of the blue—that he is in brain-state *B*, without any relevant antecedent beliefs. We would hardly say, in such a case, that *S*'s belief that he is in brain-state *B* is justified.

Let us turn next to the logical version of (3)—call it '(3_L)'—in which a proposition is defined as self-presenting just in case it is logically necessary that if *p* is true for *S* at *t*, then *S* believes *p* at *t*. This stronger version of principle (3) might seem more promising. In fact, however, it is no more successful than (3_N). Let *p* be the proposition 'I am awake' and assume that it is logically necessary that if this proposition is true for some person *S* and time *t*, then *S* believes *p* at *t*. This assumption is consistent with the further assumption that *S* frequently believes *p* when it is false, e.g., when he is dreaming. Under these circumstances, we would hardly accept the contention that *S*'s belief in this proposition is always justified. But nor should we accept the contention that the belief is justified when it is *true*. The truth of the proposition logically guarantees that the belief is *held*, but why should it guarantee that the belief is *justified*?

The foregoing criticism suggests that we have things backwards. The idea of self-presentation is that truth guarantees belief. This fails to confer justification because it is compatible with there being belief without truth. So what seems necessary—or at least sufficient—for justification is that belief should guarantee truth. Such a notion has usually gone under the label of '*infallibility*', or '*incorrigibility*'. It may be defined as follows.

(INC)   Proposition *p* is incorrigible if and only if: necessarily, for any *S* and any *t*, if *S* believes *p* at *t*, then *p* is true for *S* at *t*.

Using the notion of incorrigibility, we may propose principle (4).

(4)   If *p* is an incorrigible proposition, and *S* believes *p* at *t*, then *S*'s belief in *p* at *t* is justified.

As was true of self-presentation, there are different varieties of incorrigibility, corresponding to different interpretations of 'necessarily'. Accordingly, we have different versions of principle (4). Once again, let us concentrate on a nomological and a logical version, (4_N) and (4_L) respectively.

We can easily construct a counterexample to (4_N) along the lines of the belief-state/brain-state counterexample that refuted (3_N). Suppose it is nomologically necessary that if anyone believes he is in brain-state *B* then it is true that he is in brain-state B, for the only way this belief-state is realized is through brain-state B itself. It follows that 'I am in brain-state B' is a nomologically incorrigible proposition. Therefore, according to (4_N), whenever anyone believes this proposition at any time, that belief is justified. But we may again construct a brain surgeon example in which someone comes to have such a belief but the belief isn't justified.

Apart from this counterexample, the general point is this. Why should the fact that S's believing p guarantees the truth of p imply that S's belief is justified? The nature of the guarantee might be wholly fortuitous, as the belief-state/brain-state example is intended to illustrate. To appreciate the point, consider the following related possibility. A person's mental structure might be such that whenever he believes that p will be true (of him) a split second later, then p is true (of him) a split second later. This is because, we may suppose, his believing it brings it about. But surely we would not be compelled in such a circumstance to say that a belief of this sort is justified. So why should the fact that S's believing p guarantees the truth of p *precisely at the time of belief* imply that the belief is justified? There is no intuitive plausibility in this suppositon.

The notion of logical incorrigibility has a more honored place in the history of conceptions of justification. But even principle (4_L), I believe, suffers from defects similar to those of (4_N). The mere fact that belief in p logically guarantees its truth does not confer justificational status on such a belief.

The first difficulty with (4_L) arises from logical or mathematical truths. Any true proposition of logic or mathematics is logically necessary. Hence, any such proposition p is logically incorrigible, since it is logically necessary that, for any S and any t, if S believes p at t then p is true (for S at t). Now assume that Nelson believes a certain very complex mathematical truth at time t. Since such a proposition is logically incorrigible, (4_L) implies that Nelson's belief in this truth at t is justified. But we may easily suppose that this belief of Nelson is not at all the result of proper mathematical reasoning, or even the result of appeal to trustworthy authority. Perhaps Nelson believes this complex truth because of utterly confused reasoning, or because of hasty and ill-founded conjecture. Then his belief is not justified, contrary to what (4_L) implies.

The case of logical or mathematical truths is admittedly peculiar, since the truth of these propositions is assured independently of any beliefs. It might seem, therefore, that we can better capture the idea of 'belief logically guaranteeing truth' in cases where the propositions in question are *contingent*. With this in mind, we might restrict (4_L) to *contingent* incorrigible propositions. Even this amendment cannot save (4_L), however, since there are counterexamples to it involving purely contingent propositions.

Suppose that Humperdink has been studying logic—or, rather, pseudo-logic—from Elmer Fraud, whom Humperdink has no reason to trust as a logician. Fraud has enunciated the principle that any disjunctive proposition consisting of at least forty distinct disjuncts is very probably true. Humperdink now encounters the proposition p, a contingent proposition with forty disjuncts, the seventh disjunct being 'I exist'. Although Humperdink grasps the proposition fully, he doesn't notice that it is entailed by 'I exist'. Rather, he is struck by the fact that it falls under the disjunction rule Fraud has enunciated (a rule I assume Humperdink is not *justified* in believing). Bearing this rule in mind, Humperdink forms a belief in p. Now notice that p is logically incorrigible. It is logically necessary that if anyone believes p, then p is true (of him at that time). This simply follows from the fact that, first, a person's believing anything entails that he exists, and second, 'I exist' entails p. Since p is logically incorrigible, principle (4_L) implies that Humperdink's belief in p is justified. But surely, given our example, that conclusion is false. Humperdink's belief in p is not at all justified.

One thing that goes wrong in this example is that while Humperdink's belief in p logically implies its truth, Humperdink doesn't *recognize* that his believing it implies its truth. This might move a theorist to revise (4_L) by adding the requirement that S 'recognize' that p is logically incorrigible. But this, of course, won't do. The term 'recognize' is obviously an epistemic term, so the suggested revision of (4_L) would result in an inadmissible base clause.

II

Let us try to diagnose what has gone wrong with these attempts to produce an acceptable base-clause principle. Notice that each of the foregoing attempts confers the status of 'justified' on a belief without restriction on *why* the belief is held, i.e., on what *causally initiates* the belief or *causally sustains* it. The logical versions of principles (3) and (4), for example, clearly place no restriction on causes of belief. The same is true of the nomological versions of (3) and (4), since nomological requirements can be satisfied by simultaneity or cross-sectional laws, as illustrated by our brain-state/belief-state examples. I suggest that the absence of causal requirements accounts for the failure of the foregoing principles. Many of our counterexamples are ones in which the belief is caused in some strange or unacceptable way, e.g., by the accidental movement of a brain surgeon's hand, by reliance on an illicit, pseudo-logical principle, or by the blinding aura of the presidency. In general, a strategy for defeating a noncausal principle of justifiedness is to find a case in which the principle's antecedent is satisfied but the belief is caused by some faulty belief-forming process. The faultiness of the belief-forming process will incline us, intuitively, to regard the belief as unjustified. Thus, correct principles of justified belief must be principles that make causal requirements, where 'cause' is construed broadly to include sustainers as well as initiators of belief (i.e., processes that determine, or help to overdetermine, a belief's continuing to be held.)[6]

The need for causal requirements is not restricted to base-clause principles. Recursive principles will also need a causal component. One might initially suppose that the following is a good recursive principle: 'If S justifiably believes q at t, and q entails p, and S believes p at t, then S's belief in p at t is justified'. But this principle is unacceptable. S's belief in p doesn't receive justificational status simply from the fact that p is entailed by q and S justifiably believes q. If what causes S to believe p at t is entirely different, S's belief in p may well not be justified. Nor can the situation be remedied by adding to the antecedent the condition that S justifiably believes that q entails p. Even if he believes this, and believes q as well, he might not put these beliefs together. He might believe p as a result of some other, wholly extraneous, considerations. So once again, conditions that fail to require appropriate causes of a belief don't guarantee justifiedness.

Granted that principles of justified belief must make reference to causes of belief, what kinds of causes confer justifiedness? We can gain insight into this problem by reviewing some faulty processes of belief-formation, i.e., processes whose belief-outputs would be classed as unjustified. Here are some examples: confused reasoning, wishful thinking, reliance on emotional attachment, mere hunch or guesswork, and hasty generalization. What do these faulty processes have in common? They share the feature of *unreliability*: they tend to produce *error* a large proportion of the time. By contrast, which species of belief-forming (or belief-sustaining) processes are intuitively justification-conferring? They include standard perceptual processes, remembering, good reasoning, and introspection. What these processes seem to have in common is *reliability*: the beliefs they produce are generally true. My positive proposal, then, is this. The justificational status of a belief is a function of the reliability of the process or processes that cause it, where (as a first approximation) reliability consists in the tendency of a process to produce beliefs that are true rather than false.

To test this thesis further, notice that justifiedness is not a purely categorical concept, although I treat it here as categorical in the interest of simplicity. We can and do regard certain beliefs as more justified than others. Furthermore, our intuitions of comparative justifiedness go along with our beliefs about the comparative reliability of the belief-causing processes.

Consider perceptual beliefs. Suppose Jones believes he has just seen a mountain goat. Our assessment of the belief's justifiedness is determined by whether he caught a brief glimpse of the creature at a great distance, or whether he had a good look at the thing only thirty yards away. His belief in the latter sort of case is (ceteris paribus) more justified than in the former sort of case. And, if his belief is true, we are more prepared to say he *knows* in the latter case than in the former. The difference between the two cases seems to be this. Visual beliefs formed from brief and hasty scanning, or where the perceptual object is a long distance off, tend to be wrong more often than visual beliefs formed from detailed and leisurely scanning, or where the object is in reasonable proximity. In short, the visual processes in the former category are less reliable than those in the latter category. A similar point holds for memory beliefs. A belief that results from a hazy and indistinct memory impression is counted as less justified than a belief that arises from a distinct memory impression, and our inclination to classify those beliefs as *'knowledge'* varies in the same way. Again, the reason is associated with the comparative reliability of the processes. Hazy and indistinct memory impressions are generally less reliable indicators of what actually happened; so beliefs formed from such impressions are less likely to be true than beliefs formed from distinct impressions. Further, consider beliefs based on inference from observed samples. A belief about a population that is based on random sampling, or on instances that exhibit great variety, is intuitively more justified than a belief based on biased sampling, or on instances from a narrow sector of the population. Again, the degree of justifiedness seems to be a function of reliability. Inferences based on random or varied samples will tend to produce less error or inaccuracy than inferences based on nonrandom or nonvaried samples.

Returning to a categorical concept of justifiedness, we might ask just *how* reliable a belief-forming process must be in order that its resultant beliefs be justified. A precise answer to this question should not be expected. Our conception of justification is *vague* in this respect. It does seem clear, however, that *perfect* reliability isn't required. Belief-forming processes that *sometimes* produce error still confer justification. It follows that there can be justified beliefs that are false.

I have characterized justification-conferring processes as ones that have a 'tendency' to produce beliefs that are true rather than false. The term 'tendency' could refer either to *actual* long-run frequency, or to a 'propensity', i.e., outcomes that would occur in merely *possible* realizations of the process. Which of these is intended? Unfortunately, I think our ordinary conception of justifiedness is vague on this dimension too. For the most part, we simply assume that the 'observed' frequency of truth versus error would be approximately replicated in the actual long run, and also in relevant counterfactual situations, i.e., ones that are highly 'realistic', or conform closely to the circumstances of the actual world. Since we ordinarily assume these frequencies to be roughly the same, we make no concerted effort to distinguish them. Since the purpose of my present theorizing is to capture our ordinary conception of justifiedness, and since our ordinary conception is vague on this matter, it is appropriate to leave the theory vague in the same respect.

We need to say more about the notion of a belief-forming 'process'. Let us mean by a 'process' a *functional operation* or procedure, i.e., something that generates a *mapping* from certain states—'inputs'—into other states—'outputs'. The outputs in the present case are states of believing this or that proposition at a given moment. On this interpretation, a process is a *type* as opposed to a *token*. This is fully appropriate, since it is only types that have statistical properties such as producing truth 80 percent of the time; and it is precisely such statistical properties that determine the reliability of a process. Of course, we also want to speak of a process as *causing* a belief, and it looks as if types are incapable of being causes. But when we say that a belief is caused by a given process, understood as a functional procedure, we may interpret this to mean that it is caused by the particular *inputs* to the process (and by the intervening events 'through which' the functional procedure carries the inputs into the output) on the occasion in question.

What are some examples of belief-forming 'processes' construed as functional operations? One example is reasoning processes, where the inputs include antecedent beliefs and entertained hypotheses. Another example is functional procedures whose inputs include desires, hopes, or emotional states of various sorts (together with antecedent beliefs). A third example is a memory process, which takes as input beliefs or experiences at an earlier time and generates as output beliefs at a later time. For example, a memory process might take as input a belief at t_1 that Lincoln was born in 1809 and generate as output a belief at t_n that Lincoln was born in 1809. A fourth example is perceptual processes. Here it isn't clear whether inputs should include states of the environment, such as the distance of the stimulus from the cognizer, or only events within or on the surface of the organism, e.g., receptor stimulations. I shall return to this point in a moment.

A critical problem concerning our analysis is the degree of generality of the process-types in question. Input-output relations can be specified very broadly or very narrowly, and the degree of generality will partly determine the degree of reliability. A process-type might be selected so narrowly that only one instance of it ever occurs, and hence the type is either completely reliable or completely unreliable. (This assumes that reliability is a function of *actual* frequency only.) If such narrow process-types were selected, beliefs that are intuitively unjustified might be said to result from perfectly reliable processes; and beliefs that are intuitively justified might be said to result from perfectly unreliable processes.

It is clear that our ordinary thought about process-types slices them broadly, but I cannot at present give a precise explication of our intuitive principles. One plausible suggestion, though, is that the relevant processes are *content-neutral*. It might be argued, for example, that the process of *inferring p whenever the Pope asserts p* could pose problems for our theory. If the Pope is infallible, this process will be perfectly reliable; yet we would not regard the belief-outputs of this process as justified. The content-neutral restriction would avert this difficulty. If relevant processes are required to admit as input beliefs (or other states) with *any* content, the aforementioned process will not count, for its input beliefs have a restricted propositioned content, viz., *'the Pope asserts p'*.

In addition to the problem of 'generality' or 'abstractness' there is the previously mentioned problem of the *'extent'* of belief-forming processes. Clearly, the causal ancestry of beliefs often includes events outside the organism. Are such events to be included among the 'inputs' of belief-forming processes? Or should we restrict the extent of belief-forming processes to *'cognitive'* events, i.e., events within the organism's nervous system? I shall choose the latter course, though with some hesitation. My general grounds for this decision are roughly as follows. Justifiedness seems to be a function of how a cognizer deals with his environmental input, i.e., with the goodness or badness of the operations that register and transform the stimulation that reaches him. ('Deal with', of course, does not mean *purposeful* action; nor is it restricted to *conscious* activity.) A justified belief is, roughly speaking, one that results from cognitive operations that are, generally speaking, good or successful. But *'cognitive'* operations are most plausibly construed as operations of the cognitive faculties, i.e., 'information-processing' equipment *internal* to the organism.

With these points in mind, we may now advance the following base-clause principle for justified belief.

> (5)   If S's believing p at t results from a reliable cognitive belief-forming process (or set of processes), then S's belief in p at t is justified.

Since 'reliable belief-forming process' has been defined in terms of such notions as belief, truth, statistical frequency, and the like, it is not an epistemic term. Hence, (5) is an admissible base clause.

It might seem as if (5) promises to be not only a successful base clause, but the only principle needed whatever, apart from a closure clause. In other words, it might seem as if it is a necessary as well as a sufficient condition of justifiedness that a belief be produced by reliable cognitive belief-forming processes. But this is not quite correct, given our provisional definition of 'reliability'.

Our provisional definition implies that a reasoning process is reliable only if it generally produces beliefs that are true, and similarly, that a memory process is reliable only if it generally yields beliefs that are true.

But these requirements are too strong. A reasoning procedure cannot be expected to produce true belief if it is applied to false premises. And memory cannot be expected to yield a true belief if the original belief it attempts to retain is false. What we need for reasoning and memory, then, is a notion of *'conditional reliability'*. A process is conditionally reliable when a sufficient proportion of its output-beliefs are true *given that its input-beliefs are true*.

With this point in mind, let us distinguish *belief-dependent* and *belief-independent* cognitive processes. The former are processes some of whose inputs are belief-states.[7] The latter are processes *none* of whose inputs are belief-states. We may then replace principle (5) with the following two principles, the first a base-clause principle and the second a recursive-clause principle.

(6_A)   If S's belief in p at t results ('immediately') from a belief-independent process that is (unconditionally) reliable, then S's belief in p at t is justified.

(6_B)   If S's belief in p at t results ("immediately") from a belief-dependent process that is (at least) conditionally reliable, and if the beliefs (if any) on which this process operates in producing S's belief in p at t are themselves justified, then S's belief in p at t is justified.[8]

If we add to (6_A) and (6_B) the standard closure clause, we have a complete theory of justified belief. The theory says, in effect, that a belief is justified if and only it is *'well formed'*, i.e., it has an ancestry of reliable and/or conditionally reliable cognitive operations. (Since a dated belief may be over-determined, it may have a number of distinct ancestral trees. These need not all be full of reliable or conditionally reliable processes. But at least one ancestral tree must have reliable or conditionally reliable processes throughout.)

The theory of justified belief proposed here, then, is an *historical or genetic* theory. It contrasts with the dominant approach to justified belief, an approach that generates what we may call (borrowing a phrase from Robert Nozick) *'current time-slice'* theories. A current time-slice theory makes the justificational status of a belief wholly a function of what is true of the cognizer *at the time* of belief. An historical theory makes the justificational status of a belief depend on its prior history. Since my historical theory emphasizes the reliability of the belief-generating processes, it may be called *'historical reliabilism'*.

The most obvious examples of current time-slice theories are 'Cartesian' foundationalist theories, which trace all justificational status (at least of contingent propositions) to current mental states. The usual varieties of coherence theories, however, are equally current time-slice views, since they too make the justificational status of a belief wholly a function of *current* states of affairs. For coherence theories, however, these current states include all other beliefs of the cognizer, which would not be considered relevant by Cartesian foundationalism. Have there been other historical theories of justified belief? Among contemporary writers, Quine and Popper have historical epistemologies, though the notion of 'justification' is not their avowed *explicandum*. Among historical writers, it might seem that Locke and Hume had genetic theories of sorts. But I think that their genetic theories were only theories of ideas, not of knowledge or justification. Plato's theory of recollection, however, is a good example of a genetic theory of knowing.[9] And it might be argued that Hegel and Dewey had genetic epistemologies (if Hegel can be said to have had a clear epistemology at all).

The theory articulated by (6_A) and (6_B) might be viewed as a kind of 'foundationalism,' because of its recursive structure. I have no objection to this label, as long as one keeps in mind how different this 'diachronic' form of foundationalism is from Cartesian, or other 'synchronic' varieties of, foundationalism.

Current time-slice theories characteristically assume that the justificational status of a belief is something which the cognizer is able to know or determine at the time of belief. This is made explicit, for example, by Chisholm (1977, pp. 17, 114–116). The historical theory I endorse makes no such assumption. There are many facts about a cognizer to which he lacks 'privileged access', and I regard the justificational status of his beliefs as one of those things. This is not to say that a cognizer is necessarily ignorant, at any given moment, of the justificational status of his current beliefs. It is only to deny that he necessarily has, or can get, knowledge or true belief about this status. Just as a person can know without knowing that he knows, so he can have justified belief without knowing that it is justified (or believing justifiably that it is justified).

A characteristic case in which a belief is justified though the cognizer doesn't know that it's justified is where the original evidence for the belief has long since been forgotten. If the original evidence was compelling, the cognizer's original belief may have been justified; and this justificational status may have been preserved through memory. But since the cognizer no longer remembers how or why he came to believe, he may not know that the belief is justified. If asked now to justify his belief, he may be at a loss. Still, the belief *is* justified, though the cognizer can't demonstrate or establish this.

The historical theory of justified belief I advocate is connected in spirit with the causal theory of knowing presented in chapter 4.[10] I had this in mind when I remarked near the outset of the paper that my theory of justified belief makes justifiedness come out closely related to knowledge.

Justified beliefs, like pieces of knowledge, have appropriate histories; but they may fail to be knowledge either because they are false or because they founder on some other requirement for knowing of the kind discussed in the post-Gettier knowledge-trade.

There is a variant of the historical conception of justified belief that is worth mentioning in this context. It may be introduced as follows. Suppose S has a set B of beliefs at time t_0, and some of these beliefs are *un*justified. Between t_0 and t_1 he reasons from the entire set B to the conclusion p, which he then accepts at t_1. The reasoning procedure he uses is a very sound one, i.e., one that is conditionally reliable. There is a sense or respect in which we are tempted to say that S's belief in p at t_1 is 'justified'. At any rate, it is tempting to say that the *person* is justified in believing p at t. Relative to his antecedent cognitive state, he did as well as could be expected: the *transition* from his cognitive state at t_0 to his cognitive state at t_1 was entirely sound. Although we may acknowledge this brand of justifiedness—it might be called '*terminal-phase reliabilism*'—it is not a kind of justifiedness so closely related to knowing. For a person to know proposition p, it is not enough that the *final phase* of the process that leads to his belief in p be sound. It is also necessary that some entire history of the process be sound (i.e., reliable or conditionally reliable).

Let us return now to the historical theory. In the next section of the paper, I shall adduce reasons for strengthening it a bit. Before looking at these reasons, however, I wish to review two quite different objections to the theory.

First, a critic might argue that *some* justified beliefs do not derive their justificational status from their causal ancestry. In particular, it might be argued that beliefs about one's current phenomenal states and intuitive beliefs about elementary logical or conceptual relationships do not derive their justificational status in this way. I am not persuaded by either of these examples. Introspection, I believe, should be regarded as a form of retrospection. Thus, a justified belief that I am 'now' in pain gets its justificational status from a relevant, though brief, causal history.[11] The apprehension of logical or conceptual relationships is also a cognitive process that occupies time. The psychological process of 'seeing' or 'intuiting' a simple logical truth is very fast, and we cannot introspectively dissect it into constituent parts. Nonetheless, there are mental operations going on, just as there are mental operations that occur in idiots savants, who are unable to report the computational processes they in fact employ.

A second objection to historical reliabilism focuses on the reliability element rather than the causal or historical element. Since the theory is intended to cover all possible cases, it seems to imply that for any cognitive process C, if C is reliable in possible world W, then any belief in W that results from C is justified. But doesn't this permit easy counter-

examples? Surely we can imagine a possible world in which wishful thinking is reliable. We can imagine a possible world where a benevolent demon
so arranges things that beliefs formed by wishful thinking usually come
true. This would make wishful thinking a reliable process in that possible
world, but surely we don't want to regard beliefs that result from wishful
thinking as justified.

There are several possible ways to respond to this case and I am unsure
which response is best, partly because my own intuitions (and those of
other people I have consulted) are not entirely clear. One possibility is to
say that in the possible world imagined, beliefs that result from wishful
thinking *are* justified. In other words we reject the claim that wishful
thinking could never, intuitively, confer justifiedness.[12]

However, for those who feel that wishful thinking couldn't confer justifiedness, even in the world imagined, there are two ways out. First, it may
be suggested that the proper criterion of justifiedness is the propensity of a
process to generate beliefs that are true in a *nonmanipulated environment*, i.e.,
an environment in which there is no purposeful arrangement of the world
either to accord or conflict with the beliefs that are formed. In other words,
the suitability of a belief forming process is only a function of its success in
'natural' situations, not situations of the sort involving benevolent or ma-
levolent demons, or any other such manipulative creatures. If we reformulate
the theory to include this qualification, the counterexample in question will
be averted.

Alternatively, we may reformulate our theory, or reinterpret it, as follows.
Instead of construing the theory as saying that a belief in possible world *W*
is justified if and only if it results from a cognitive process that is reliable in
W, we may construe it as saying that a belief in possible world *W* is
justified if and only if it results from a cognitive process that is reliable *in
our world*. In short, our conception of justifiedness is derived as follows. We
note certain cognitive processes in the actual world, and form beliefs about
which of these are reliable. The ones we believe to be reliable are then
regarded as justification-conferring processes. In reflecting on hypothetical
beliefs, we deem them justified if and only if they result from processes
already picked out as justification-conferring, or processes very similar to
those. Since wishful thinking is not among these processes, a belief formed
in a possible world *W* by wishful thinking would not be deemed justified,
even if wishful thinking is reliable *in W*. I am not sure that this is a correct
reconstruction of our intuitive conceptual scheme, but it would accommodate the benevolent demon case, at least if the proper thing to say in that
case is that the wishful-thinking-caused beliefs are unjustified.

Even if we adopt this strategy, however, a problem still remains. Suppose that wishful thinking turns out to be reliable *in the actual world!*[13] This
might be because, unbeknownst to us at present, there is a benevolent

demon who, lazy until now, will shortly start arranging things so that our wishes come true. The long-run performance of wishful thinking will be very good, and hence even the new construal of the theory will imply that beliefs resulting from wishful thinking (in *our* world) are justified. Yet this surely contravenes our intuitive judgment on the matter.

Perhaps the moral of the case is that the standard format of a 'conceptual analysis' has its shortcomings. Let me depart from that format and try to give a better rendering of our aims and the theory that tries to achieve that aim. What we really want is an explanation of why we count, or would count, certain beliefs as justified and others as unjustified. Such an explanation must refer to our beliefs about reliability, not to the actual facts. The reason we count beliefs as justified is that they are formed by what we believe to be reliable belief-forming processes. Our beliefs about which belief-forming processes are reliable may be erroneous, but that does not affect the adequacy of the explanation. Since we believe that wishful thinking is an unreliable belief-forming process, we regard beliefs formed by wishful thinking as unjustified. What matters, then, is what we believe about wishful thinking, not what is true (in the long run) about wishful thinking. I am not sure how to express this point in the standard format of conceptual analysis, but it identifies an important point in understanding our theory.

III

Let us return, however, to the standard format of conceptual analysis, and let us consider a new objection that will require some revisions in the theory advanced until now. According to our theory, a belief is justified in case it is caused by a process that is in fact reliable, or by one we generally believe to be reliable. But suppose that although one of S's beliefs satisfies this condition, S has no reason to believe that it does. Worse yet, suppose S has reason to believe that his belief is caused by an *un*reliable process (although *in fact* its causal ancestry is fully reliable). Wouldn't we deny in such circumstances that S's belief is justified? This seems to show that our analysis, as presently formulated, is mistaken.

Suppose that Jones is told on fully reliable authority that a certain class of his memory beliefs are almost all mistaken. His parents fabricate a wholly false story that Jones suffered from amnesia when he was seven but later developed *pseudo*-memories of that period. Though Jones listens to what his parents say and has excellent reason to trust them, he persists in believing the ostensible memories from his seven-year-old past. Are these memory beliefs justified? Intuitively, they are not justified. But since these beliefs result from genuine memory and original perceptions, which are adequately reliable processes, our theory says that these beliefs are justified.

Can the theory be revised to meet this difficulty? One natural suggestion is that the actual reliability of a belief's ancestry is not enough for justified-ness; in addition, the cognizer must be *justified in believing* that the ancestry of his belief is reliable. Thus one might think of replacing (6_A), for example, with (7). (For simplicity, I neglect some of the details of the earlier analysis.)

(7) If S's belief in p at t is caused by a reliable cognitive process, and S justifiably believes at t that his p-belief is so caused, then S's belief in p at t is justified.

It is evident, however, that (7) will not do as a base clause, for it contains the epistemic term 'justifiably' in its antecedent.

A slightly weaker revision, without this problematic feature, might next be suggested, viz.,

(8) If S's belief in p at t is caused by a reliable cognitive process, and S believes at t that his p-belief is so caused, then S's belief in p at t is justified.

But this won't do the job. Suppose that Jones believes that his memory beliefs are reliably caused despite all the (trustworthy) contrary testimony of his parents. Principle (8) would be satisfied, yet we wouldn't say that these beliefs are justified.

Next, we might try (9), which is stronger than (8) and, unlike (7), formally admissible as a base clause.

(9) If S's belief in p at t is caused by a reliable cognitive process, and S believes at t that his p-belief is so caused, and this meta-belief is caused by a reliable cognitive process, then S's belief in p at t is justified.

A first objection to (9) is that it wrongly precludes unreflective crea-tures—creatures like animals or young children, who have no beliefs about the genesis of their beliefs—from having justified beliefs. If one shares my view that justified belief is, at least roughly, *well-formed* belief, surely animals and young children can have justified beliefs.

A second problem with (9) concerns its underlying rationale. Since (9) is proposed as a substitute for (6_A), it is implied that the reliability of a belief's own cognitive ancestry does not make it justified. But, the suggestion seems to be, the reliability of a *meta-belief*'s ancestry confers justifiedness on the first-order belief. Why should that be so? Perhaps one is attracted by the idea of a 'trickle-down' effect: if an $n + 1$-level belief is justified, its justification trickles down to an n-level belief. But even if the trickle-down theory is correct, it doesn't help here. There is no assurance from the satisfaction of (9)'s antecedent that the meta-belief itself is *justified*.

To obtain a better revision of our theory, let us reexamine the Jones case. Jones has strong evidence against certain propositions concerning his past. He doesn't *use* this evidence, but if he were to use it properly, he would stop believing these propositions. Now the proper use of evidence would be an instance of a (conditionally) reliable process. So what we can say about Jones is that he fails to use a certain (conditionally) reliable process that he could and should have used. Admittedly, had he used this process, he would have 'worsened' his doxastic states: he would have replaced some true beliefs with suspension of judgment. Still, he couldn't have known this in the case in question. So, he failed to do something which, epistemically, he should have done. This diagnosis suggests a fundamental change in our theory. The justificational status of a belief is not only a function of the cognitive processes *actually* employed in producing it; it is also a function of processes that could and should be employed.

With these points in mind, we may tentatively propose the following revision of our theory, where we again focus on a base-clause principle but omit certain details in the interest of clarity.

(10)   If S's belief in p at t results from a reliable cognitive process, and there is no reliable or conditionally reliable process available to S which, had it been used by S in addition to the process actually used, would have resulted in S's not believing p at t, then S's belief in p at t is justified.

There are several problems with this proposal. First, there is a technical problem. One cannot use an additional belief-forming (or doxastic-state-forming) process *as well as* the original process if the additional one would result in a different doxastic state. One wouldn't be using the original process at all. So we need a slightly different formulation of the relevant counterfactual. Since the basic idea is reasonably clear, however, I won't try to improve on the formulation here. A second problem concerns the notion of *'available'* belief-forming (or doxastic-state-forming) processes. What is it for a process to be 'available' to a cognizer? Were scientific procedures 'available' to people who lived in prescientific ages? Furthermore, it seems implausible to say that all 'available' processes ought to be used, at least if we include such processes as gathering *new* evidence. Surely a belief can sometimes be justified even if additional evidence gathering would yield a different doxastic attitude. What I think we should have in mind here are such additional processes as calling previously acquired evidence to mind, assessing the implications of that evidence, etc. This is admittedly somewhat vague, but here again our ordinary notion of justifiedness is vague, so it is appropriate for our analysans to display the same sort of vagueness.

This completes the sketch of my account of justified belief. Before concluding, however, it is essential to point out that there is an important use of 'justified' that is not captured by this account but can be captured by a closely related one.

There is a use of 'justified' in which it is not implied or presupposed that there is a *belief* that is justified. For example, if S is trying to decide whether to believe p and asks our advice, we may tell him that he is 'justified' in believing it. We do not thereby imply that he *has* a justified *belief*, since we know he is still suspending judgment. What we mean, roughly, is that he *would* or *could* be justified if he were to believe p. The justificational status we ascribe here cannot be a function of the causes of S's believing p, for there is no belief by S in p. Thus, the account of justifiedness we have given thus far cannot explicate *this* use of 'justified'. (It doesn't follow that this use of 'justified' has no connection with causal ancestries. Its proper use may depend on the causal ancestry of the cognizer's cognitive state, though not on the causal ancestry of his believing p.)

Let us distinguish two uses of 'justified': an *ex post* use and an *ex ante* use. The *ex post* use occurs when there exists a belief, and we say of *that belief* that it is (or isn't) justified . The *ex ante* use occurs when no such belief exists, or when we wish to ignore the question of whether such a belief exists. Here we say of the *person*, independent of his doxastic state vis-à-vis p, that p is (or isn't) suitable for him to believe.[14]

Since we have given an account of *ex post* justifiedness, it will suffice if we can analyze *ex ante* justifiedness in terms of it. Such an analysis, I believe, is ready at hand. S is *ex ante* justified in believing p at t just in case his total cognitive state at t is such that from that state he could come to believe p in such a way that this belief would be *ex post* justified. More precisely, he is *ex ante* justified in believing p at t just in case a reliable belief-forming operation is available to him such that the application of that operation to his total cognitive state at t would result, more or less immediately, in his believing p and this belief would be *ex post* justified. Stated formally, we have the following:

> (11)   Person S is *ex ante* justified in believing p at t if and only if there is a reliable belief-forming operation available to S which is such that if S applied that operation to his total cognitive state at t, S would believe p at t-plus-delta (for a suitably small delta) and that belief would be *ex post* justified.

For the analysans of (11) to be satisfied, the total cognitive state at t must have a suitable causal ancestry. Hence, (11) is implicitly an historical account of *ex ante* justifiedness.

As indicated, the bulk of this paper was addressed to *ex post* justifiedness. This is the appropriate analysandum if one is interested in the connection between justifiedness and knowledge, since what is crucial to whether a person *knows* a proposition is whether he has an actual *belief* in the proposition that is justified. However, since many epistemologists are interested in *ex ante* justifiedness, it is proper for a general theory of justification to try to provide an account of that concept as well. Our theory does this quite naturally, for the account of *ex ante* justifiedness falls out directly from our account of *ex post* justifiedness.

Notes

Research on this paper was begun while the author was a fellow of the John Simon Guggenheim Memorial Foundation and of the Center for Advanced Study in the Behavioral Sciences. I am grateful for their support. I have received helpful comments and criticism from Holly Smith, Mark Kaplan, Fred Schmitt, Stephen Stich, and many others at several universities where earlier drafts of the paper were read.

1. Notice that the choice of a recursive format does not prejudice the case for or against any particular theory. A recursive format is perfectly general. Specifically, an explicit set of necessary and sufficient conditions is just a special case of a recursive format, i.e., one in which there is no recursive clause.

2. Many of the attempts I shall consider are suggested by material in William Alston 1971.

3. Such a definition (though without the modal term) is given, for example, by W. V. Quine and J. S. Ullian (1970, p. 21). Statements are said to be self-evident just in case "to understand them is to believe them".

4. I assume, of course, that 'nomologically necessary' is *de re* with respect to 'S' and 't' in this construction. I shall not focus on problems that may arise in this regard, since my primary concerns are with different issues.

5. This assumption violates the thesis that Davidson calls 'The Anomalism of the Mental'. Cf. Davidson 1970. But it is unclear that this thesis is a necessary truth. Thus, it seems fair to assume its falsity in order to produce a counterexample. The example neither entails nor precludes the mental-physical identity theory.

6. Keith Lehrer's example of the gypsy lawyer is intended to show the inappropriateness of a causal requirement. (See Lehrer 1974, pp. 124–125.) But I find this example unconvincing. To the extent that I clearly imagine that the lawyer fixes his belief solely as a result of the cards, it seems intuitively wrong to say that he *knows*—or has a *justified belief*—that his client is innocent.

7. This definition is not exactly what we need for the purposes at hand. As Ernest Sosa points out, introspection will turn out to be a belief-dependent process since sometimes the input into the process will be a belief (when the introspected content is a belief). Intuitively, however, introspection is not the sort of process which may be merely conditionally reliable. I do not know how to refine the definition so as to avoid this difficulty, but it is a small and isolated point.

8. It may be objected that principles (6_A) and (6_B) are jointly open to analogues of the lottery paradox. A series of processes composed of reliable but less-than-perfectly-reliable processes may be extremely unreliable. Yet applications of (6_A) and (6_B) would confer justifiedness on a belief that is caused by such a series. In reply to this objection, we might simply indicate that the theory is intended to capture our ordinary notion of justifiedness, and this ordinary notion has been formed without recognition of this kind of problem. The theory is not wrong *as* a theory of the ordinary (naive) conception of justifiedness. On the other hand, if we want a theory to do more than capture the ordinary conception of justifiedness, it might be possible to strengthen the principles to avoid lottery-paradox analogues.

9. I am indebted to Mark Pastin for this point.
10. The reliability aspect of the theory also has its precursors in my earlier papers on knowing: Goldman 1975 and chapter 5.
11. The view that introspection is retrospection was taken by Ryle, and before him (as Charles Hartshorne points out to me) by Hobbes, Whitehead, and possibly Husserl.
12. Of course, if people in world W learn *inductively* that wishful thinking is reliable, and regularly base their beliefs on this inductive inference, it is quite unproblematic and straightforward that their beliefs are justified. The only interesting case is where their beliefs are formed *purely* by wishful thinking, without using inductive inference. The suggestion contemplated in this paragraph of the text is that, in the world imagined, even pure wishful thinking would confer justifiedness.
13. I am indebted here to Mark Kaplan.
14. The distinction between *ex post* and *ex ante* justifiedness is similar to Roderick Firth's distinction between *doxastic* and *propositional* warrant. See Firth 1978.

Chapter 7
Strong and Weak Justification

It is common in recent epistemology to distinguish different senses, or conceptions, of epistemic justification. The proposed oppositions include the objective/subjective, internalist/externalist, regulative/nonregulative, resource-relative/resource-independent, personal/verific, and deontological/evaluative conceptions of justification.[1] In some of these cases, writers regard both members of the contrasting pair as legitimate; in other cases only one member. In this paper I want to propose another contrasting pair of conceptions of justification, and hold that *both* are defensible and legitimate. The contrast will then be used to construct a modified version of reliabilism, one which handles certain problem cases more naturally than my previous versions of reliabilism.

I

I should begin by acknowledging the undesirability of multiplying senses of any term beyond necessity. Lacking good evidence for multivocality of a target analysandum, a unified analysis should be sought. But sometimes there is indeed good evidence for multivocality. Here is a case in point for the term 'justified'.

Consider a scientifically benighted culture, of ancient or medieval vintage. This culture employs certain highly unreliable methods for forming beliefs about the future and the unobserved. Their methods appeal to the doctrine of signatures, to astrology, and to oracles. Members of the culture have never thought of probability theory or statistics, never dreamt of anything that could be classed as 'experimental method'.[2] Now suppose that on a particular occasion a member of this culture forms a belief about the outcome of an impending battle by using one of the aforementioned methods, say, by consulting zodiacal signs in a culturally approved fashion. Call this method M. Is this person's belief justified, or warranted?

One feels here a definite tension, a tug in opposite directions. There is a strong temptation to say, no, this belief is not justified or warranted. Yet from a different perspective one feels inclined to say, yes, the belief is justified.

The attraction of the negative answer is easily explained. It is natural to regard a belief as justified only if it is generated by proper, or adequate, methods. But method M certainly looks improper and inadequate. This point can be reinforced in the following way. Epistemologists have widely supposed—and I concur—that a necessary condition for having knowledge is having justified belief. But the belief under consideration has no chance to qualify as knowledge, assuming it is wholly based on zodiacal signs. Even if it happens to be true, even if there is nothing 'Gettierized' about the case, the believer cannot be credited with *knowing* (beforehand) the outcome of the battle. The natural explanation is that his belief fails to be justified.

Why, then, is some attraction felt toward a positive answer? This seems to stem from the cultural plight of our believer. He is situated in a certain spatio-historical environment. Everyone else in this environment uses and trusts method M. Moreover, our believer has good reasons to trust his cultural peers on many matters, and lacks decisive reasons for distrusting their confidence in astrology. While it is true that a scientifically trained person, set down in this same culture, could easily find ways to cast doubt on method M, our believer is not so trained, and has no opportunity to acquire such training. It is beyond his intellectual scope to find flaws in M. Thus, we can hardly *fault* him for using M, nor fault him therefore for believing what he does. The belief in question is epistemically *blameless*, and that seems to explain why we are tempted to call it *justified*.[3]

As this case illustrates, there are two distinct ideas or conceptions of epistemic justification. On one conception, a justified belief is (roughly) a *well-formed* belief, a belief formed (or sustained) by proper, suitable, or adequate methods, procedures, or processes. On another conception, a justified belief is a *faultless, blameless*, or *nonculpable* belief. As our example suggests, the first of these conceptions is stronger, or more stringent, than the second. It requires the belief to be formed by methods that are *actually* proper or adequate, whereas the second conception makes no such requirement. I therefore call the first conception the *strong* conception and the second the *weak*. Each of these seems to me a legitimate conception. Each captures some chunks of intuition involving the term 'justified' (in its epistemic applications).

Granting the distinction between strong and weak justification, my next task is to delineate more precisely the conditions attached to these respective conceptions. Before turning to this, however, let me mention another distinction relevant to the theory of justified belief.

In *Epistemology and Cognition* I propose a distinction between belief-forming *processes* and belief-forming *methods* (Goldman 1986, pp. 92–95). 'Processes' are basic psychological processes, roughly, wired-in features of our native cognitive architecture. 'Methods' are learnable algorithms, heuristics, or procedures for forming beliefs, such as procedures that appeal to instrument readings, or statistical analyses. All beliefs are formed partly by processes. We cannot do anything in the cognitive realm without using basic psychological operations. Learned methods, by contrast, are not universally required, although the vast majority of an adult's beliefs are probably indebted to such methods. Now *fully* justified beliefs, I propose, must be formed by adequate processes and adequate methods, if methods are used at all. (At least this is so for strong justification.) But it is possible to form a belief by a combination of adequate process and inadequate method, or by a combination of inadequate process and adequate method. I therefore distinguish two levels of justifiedness: primary justifiedness, corresponding to the level of processes, and secondary justifiedness, corresponding to the level of methods. A complete account of justifiedness must present conditions for both of these levels.

The strong/weak distinction I have introduced enters at each level: the level of processes and the level of methods. So let me try to sketch conditions of strong and weak justification for each level separately. I begin with the level of methods.

II

Strong justification at the level of methods requires the use of *proper* or *adequate* methods. What makes a method proper or adequate? A natural and appealing answer is a reliabilist answer: a method is proper or adequate just in case it is reliable, i.e., leads to truth a sufficiently high percent of the time. This answer meshes perfectly with our intuitions about the scientifically benighted believer. His belief is not strongly justified precisely because the method of consulting zodiacal signs is not a reliable way of getting truths about the outcomes of battles.

What exactly is meant by calling a method or process 'reliable' needs further discussion. I shall address this issue in due course. Another sort of issue, however, needs comment. High reliability may not suffice for method-level justifiedness because even highly reliable methods may be *less* reliable than other available methods. Some people might argue for a *maximum* reliability condition, not merely a *satisficing* reliability condition. I am going to set this matter aside. There are enough other questions to be dealt with in this paper, and the proposed switch to maximum reliability would not seriously affect the other epistemological topics on which I shall focus.

However, I do not mean to imply that use of a highly reliable method is sufficient for method-level, or secondary, justifiedness. Two other conditions are necessary. First, it is necessary that the method have been *acquired* in a suitable fashion. If a person adopts a method out of the blue, and by chance it happens to be reliable, his use of that method does not confer secondary justifiedness. The method must be acquired by other methods, or ultimately processes, that are either reliable or meta-reliable. A further necessary condition of secondary justifiedness is that the believer's cognitive state, at the time he uses the method, should not *undermine* the correctness, or adequacy, of the method. Very roughly, it should not be the case that the believer *thinks* that the method is unreliable, nor is he justified in regarding the method as unreliable. Of course, the latter condition should be spelled out in nonjustificational terms, something I undertake (sketchily) in Goldman 1986 (pp. 62–63, 111–112) but will not repeat here.

Roderick Chisholm (1982, p. 29) expresses the worry that the reliable-method condition is too *easy* to satisfy. He considers the case of a man who comes to believe that there are nine planets by reading the tea leaves. Now suppose that this reading took place on a Friday afternoon at 2:17, and suppose that nobody on any other occasion consults tea leaves about the number of planets at 2:17 on a Friday afternoon. Then, says Chisholm, this man followed a method that always leads to truth, a method one could describe by saying, 'To find out anything about the number of planets, consult tea leaves at 2:17 on a Friday afternoon.'

Notice, however, that *this* is not plausibly the method the man has *used*. For a method to be used, it must be represented in the cognizer's head (though not necessarily consciously). But presumably neither the day of the week nor the time of day was part of the recipe for belief formation that the man represented in his head. Although we can introduce those features into a description of his action, it doesn't follow that they were parts of the method *he used*.[5] But the method he *did* use—consulting the tea leaves—is not reliable.

Admittedly, a cognizer *might* incorporate these temporal factors into a method, and such a method could be reliable (at least in the sense Chisholm specifies). But use of this reliable method would not suffice for secondary (method-level) justifiedness. As indicated, the believer must acquire the method in a suitable fashion. That condition is (apparently) not met in Chisholm's example. If a new example were constructed in which it *is* met, then I think the cognizer's belief *would*, intuitively, be justified.

The plausibility of the reliability approach can be bolstered by considering degrees of justifiedness. Although my main analysandum is the categorical notion of justified belief, a brief digression on the comparative notion may be instructive. Chisholm (1966, 1977) has rightly stressed the idea of multiple grades of epistemic status. Can such a notion be captured within reliabilism? Quite naturally, I believe. Ceteris paribus, one belief is better justified than another belief just in case the methods (or processes) that generate (or sustain) the former are more reliable than those that generate the latter.

A simple example will illustrate this idea. Suppose one student does a long addition problem by adding columns from top to bottom, in the canonical fashion. This student arrives at a belief in the answer. A second student goes through the same procedure, yielding the same answer, but then 'checks her work' by doing it all over again. Or perhaps she does the problem the second time by proceeding bottom-up, or by using a calculator. In any event, she uses a *compound* method, M_2, which contains the first method, M_1, as its first component. The compound method involves forming a belief only when both procedures yield the same answer. It is plausible to say that both students have justified beliefs, but that the second has a *more* justified, or *better* justified, belief than her classmate. Why? The natural answer is: method M_2 is more reliable than M_1. Indeed, the difference in degree of justifiedness seems to correspond precisely to the difference in reliability of the methods. If the compound method has only marginally greater reliability, then it yields, intuitively, only marginally greater justifiedness. If the compound method has substantially greater reliability, justifiedness is substantially increased. This supports the idea that reliability is the underlying ingredient in justifiedness.

III

Returning from this digression, but staying at the level of methods, I turn now from strong to weak justification. The weak notion of justification, it will be recalled, is that of blameless, or nonculpable, belief. We must be careful here, however. A well-formed belief, whose method is well acquired and non-undermined, is also presumably blameless. So the strong notion of justifiedness entails blamelessness. But I want the notions of strong and weak justification to be *opposing* notions. This means that the weak notion of justification that interests me is not precisely that of blamelessness, but the narrower notion of *mere* blamelessness. That is, the weak notion is that of *ill-formed*-but-blameless belief.

With this point clarified, let me propose some conditions for weakly justified belief (at the level of methods). More precisely, I shall try to provide only some *sufficient* conditions for weak justifiedness, not necessary conditions. S's belief in p is weakly justified (at the secondary level) if (1) the method M by which the belief is produced is unreliable (i.e., not sufficiently reliable), but (2) S does not believe that M is unreliable, and (3) S neither possesses, nor has available to him/her, a reliable way of telling that M is unreliable. (By this I mean that S has neither reliable method nor reliable process which, if applied to his/her present cognitive state, would lead S to believe that M is unreliable.) It is plausible that a further condition should also be added, viz., (4) there is no process or method *S believes* to be reliable which, if used, would lead *S* to believe that *M* is unreliable.

The proposed conditions seem to capture our case of the scientifically benighted cognizer. That cognizer's belief in the outcome of the impending battle is in fact ill-formed, i.e., formed by an unreliable method. But he does not believe that his method is unreliable. Moreover, there is no reliable method (or process) in his possession, or available to him, that would lead him to believe that his astrology-based method is unreliable. Finally, there is no method or process he *believes* to be reliable that would lead him to this judgment.

Our judgment of the benighted cognizer does depend, admittedly, on exactly what he knows, or has been told, about the accuracy of past astrology-based predictions, especially battle predictions. If he is told that in *all* such cases the predictions were falsified, we would surely deny that his use of the astrology-based method is defensible. After all, he does possess a native process of *induction*, which can be applied to such data! But let the case be one in which he receives relatively few well-substantiated reports of battle outcomes. Some of these corroborate the prior predictions, as chance would dictate. Where outcomes reportedly go against the predictions, the community's astrology experts explain that the predictions had been based on misapplications of the method. The experts have techniques for 'protecting' their theory from easy falsification, and only sophisticated methodologies or astronomical theories would demonstrate the indefensibility of such tactics; but these are not available. (Needless to say, if this particular example of a benighted cognizer does not fully suit the reader, other examples to make the same point might readily be constructed.)

Clearly, the truth of the contention that no way of detecting the target method's unreliability is *possessed* or *available* to a cognizer depends on exactly how the terms 'possessed' and 'available' are understood. It might be argued, for instance, that sophisticated scientific methodology is always in fact 'available' to people, even when such a methodology is not in use by members of their culture. The proper response, I suggest, is that the notions of availability and possession are vague and variable. They are open to a number of interpretations, each reasonably plausible and pertinent in at least some contexts.

The vagueness or variability of 'possession' has been stressed in connection with *evidence* possession by Richard Feldman (1988); I also mention it a bit in Goldman 1986 (p. 204). At one extreme, possessing, or having, a piece of evidence at a given time could mean consciously thinking of that evidence. At another extreme, it could mean having that evidence stored somewhere in memory, however difficult it may be to retrieve or access the item. An intermediate view would be that a piece of evidence is 'possessed' only if it is either in consciousness or *easily* accessible from memory.

Similar ambiguities arise for the term 'available'. But here there are not only different possible locations *in the head* but different locations and degrees of accessibility in the *social* world. Is a piece of evidence socially 'available' no matter how difficult or costly it would be to find it? There are no clear-cut answers here, neither in the case of *evidence* nor in the case of *methods*, which is what directly concerns me here. Different speakers (and listeners) use varying standards, depending on context and intention. So it is best to leave the notions of possession and availability in their natural, vague state, rather than try to provide artificial precision. It follows, of course, that the notion of weak justification inherits this vagueness. But there is plenty of evidence that epistemic concepts, including justification and knowledge, *have* this kind of vagueness.[6] However, under very natural and commonly used standards, no process or method is possessed or available to our benighted cognizer for telling that his astrology-based battle-predicting method is unreliable. Hence, his battle predictions based on that method are weakly justified. (This probably follows as well from one very moderate constraint I shall later impose on 'availability'.)

IV

Let me turn now to primary justifiedness: justifiedness at the level of processes. In this treatment I shall adopt the simple format for presenting reliabilism that I used in chapter 6, rather than the preferable but more unwieldy format of process-permitting rule systems found in Goldman 1986. However, I shall later opt for the preferable rule-system format.

The proposed account of *strong* justification at the primary level closely parallels the account at the secondary level. A belief of person S is strongly justified at the primary level if and only if (1) it is produced (or sustained) by a sufficiently reliable cognitive process, and (2) that the producing process is reliable is not undermined by S's cognitive state.

The proposed conditions for *weak* justification at the primary level also parallel those at the secondary level. S's belief is weakly justified at the primary level if (1) the cognitive process that produces the belief is unreliable, but (2) S does not believe that the producing process is un- reliable, and (3) S neither possesses, nor has available to him/her, a reliable way of telling that the process is unreliable. Finally, a further condition may be appropriate: (4) there is no process or method S *believes* to be reliable which, if used, would lead S to believe that the process is unreliable. Once again, interpretation of the terms 'possession' and 'available' is subject to variation. I shall not try to give a unique interpretation to these vague terms. As indicated earlier, though, I shall shortly impose one plausible constraint on availability.

V

I want to turn immediately now to an example of central interest, the case of a cognizer in a Cartesian demon world. Focus on the perceptual beliefs of such a cognizer. These beliefs are regularly or invariably false, but they are caused by the same internal processes that cause our perceptual beliefs. In the Cartesian demon world, however, those processes are unreliable. (I assume that either there is just a lone cognizer using those processes in that world or that the demon fools enough people to render those processes insufficiently reliable.) Then according to the proposed account of *strong* justifiedness, the cognizer's beliefs are not justified.

This sort of case is an ostensible problem for reliabilism, because there is a strong temptation to say that a cognizer in a demon world *does* have justified perceptual beliefs. The course of his experience, after all, may be indistinguishable from the course of your experience or mine, and we are presumably justified in holding our perceptual beliefs. So shouldn't his beliefs be justified as well?[7]

Under the present theory the treatment of the demon case is straightforward. The victim of the demon fails to have *strongly* justified beliefs, but he does have *weakly* justified beliefs. While his beliefs are not *well formed*, they are *blameless* and *nonculpable*. His cognitive processes are not reliable (in his world), but (A) he does not believe that they are unreliable, (B) he has no reliable way of telling this, and (C) there is no method or process he *believes* to be reliable that would lead him to this conclusion. So on the weak conception of justifiedness, the resulting beliefs are justified.

Is it really true that the demon victim has no reliable way of telling that his perceptual processes are unreliable? What seems fairly clear is that none of his cognitive processes we normally deem reliable would lead him to the conclusion that his perceptual processes are unreliable. Surely if he uses his memories of past perceptual beliefs, memories of subsequent 'validations' of these by further perceptual checks, and then makes a standard inductive generalization, he will conclude that his perceptual processes *are* reliable. However, it might be contended that a reliable method is *available* to him that would yield the conclusion that his processes are unreliable. This is the 'single-output' method that would have him start with his antecedent corpus of beliefs and produce the conclusion, 'My perceptual processes are unreliable'. This single-output method is reliable since the one belief it produces is true!

I make two replies to this proposal. First, to call this is a 'method' is surely to trivialize the notion of a method. I admit, though, that I have no convenient way of restricting methods that would rule this out. (*Perhaps* all single-output formulas should be excluded; but I am unsure of this.) However, even if we persist in calling this a 'method', there is little plausibility in saying that it is *available* to the demon victim. Availability should not be construed as mere in-principle constructibility and usability. It must at least be required that the cognizer could naturally be led to that method by some processes and/or methods he already employs, operating on his actual beliefs and experiences. But that is false in the present case. All his antecedent beliefs, processes, and methods run *against* the acceptance of this single-output 'method'. So there is no relevant sense in saying that this method is possessed by, or available to, this cognizer. Hence, his perceptual beliefs are indeed weakly justified.

VI

It is clear that this version of reliabilism accommodates the intuition that the demon victim has justified beliefs—at least on one conception of justification. What relation does this version bear to other versions of reliabilism? In Goldman 1986 a reliabilist theory is proposed that handles the demon-world case rather differently. That theory is formulated in terms of right systems of process-permitting rules. A belief qualifies as justified (at the process level) just in case it is produced by processes that conform with some right rule system. (A non-undermining proviso is also included.) A rule system is right just in case it is reliable, i.e., compliance with that rule system would produce beliefs with a sufficiently high truth ratio.

These formulations do not resolve all questions of interpretation about the theory. Suppose we ask whether a belief B, in some possible world W, is justified. The answer depends on whether the processes that cause B in W are permitted by a right rule system. But is the rightness of a rule system a function of the system's reliability in W? Or is it fixed in some other way?

In Goldman 1986 (p. 107) I suggest that rightness of rule systems is rigid. A given rule system is either right in all possible worlds or wrong in all possible worlds; it does not vary across worlds. Furthermore, rightness is not determined by the system's reliability in the *actual* world, for example, but rather by its reliability in what I call *normal worlds*. A very special sense of 'normal worlds' is delineated. A normal world is understood as a world consistent with our general *beliefs* about the actual world, beliefs about the sorts of objects, events, and changes that occur in the actual world. The upshot of this theory is that the appraisal of a demon victim's beliefs does not depend on whether his perceptual belief-forming processes are reliable in the demon world, but on whether they are reliable in normal worlds. Since they presumably *are* reliable in normal worlds, even this victim's beliefs qualify as justified according to the theory. Moreover, even if it should turn out that the actual world is a demon world, and our own beliefs are systematically illusory, these beliefs would (or could) still be justified. As long as the processes are reliable in normal worlds—which in this scenario does not include the actual world—these beliefs will be justified.

The normal-worlds version of reliabilism has the virtue of saving intuitions about justification in demon-world cases. It also has other attractions. It seems to me natural to expect that reliability should be assessed in normal situations (or worlds) rather than all possible situations. When one says of a car that it is very reliable, one doesn't imply that it will start and run smoothly in *all* weather conditions; not at −50 degrees Fahrenheit, for example. One only implies that it will start in *normal* conditions.[8] However, this sense of 'normalcy' probably refers to *typical* situations. It doesn't imply anything like my *doxastic* sense of 'normalcy'. What might rationalize the doxastic sense? In writing *Epistemology and Cognition*, I had planned a chapter on concepts. One thesis I planned to defend is that our concepts are constructed against certain background assumptions, comprised of what we believe about what typically happens in the actual world. I expected this approach to concepts to underpin the doxastic-normalcy conception of reliability. Unfortunately, I did not manage to work out such an approach in detail.

In any case, there are a number of problems facing the account of justification that focuses on normal worlds (construed doxastically). First, *which* general beliefs about the actual world are relevant in fixing normal worlds? There seem to be too many choices. Second, whichever general beliefs are selected, it looks as if dramatically different worlds might conform to these beliefs. Does a rule system count as right only if it has a high truth ratio in *all* those worlds?[9] Third, when the theory says that normal worlds are fixed by the general beliefs *we* have about the actual world, what is the referent of 'we'?[10] Is it *everyone* in the actual world, i.e., the whole human race? Different members of the human race have dramatically divergent general beliefs. How are the pertinent general beliefs to be extracted?

Finally, even if these problems could be resolved, it isn't clear that the normal-worlds approach gets things right. Consider a possible non-normal world *W*, significantly different from ours. In *W* people commonly form beliefs by a process that has a very high truth ratio in *W*, but would not have a high truth ratio in normal worlds. Couldn't the beliefs formed by the process in *W* qualify as justified?[11]

To be concrete, let the process be that of forming beliefs in accord with feelings of clairvoyance. Such a process presumably does not have a high truth ratio in the actual world; nor would it have a high truth ratio in normal worlds. But suppose *W* contains clairvoyance waves, analogous to sound or light waves. By means of clairvoyance waves people in *W* accurately detect features of their environment just as we detect features of our environment by light and sound. Surely, the clairvoyance belief-forming processes of people in world *W can* yield justified beliefs.

For all the foregoing reasons. it seems wise to abandon the normal-worlds version of reliabilism. Fortunately, this does not leave reliabilism incapable of meeting the demon-world problem. The present version of reliabilism accommodates the intuition that demon-world believers have justified beliefs by granting that they have *weakly* justified beliefs.

If the normal-worlds interpretation of rightness is abandoned, what should be put in its place (in the account of *strong* justification)? As the foregoing example suggests, it is probably unwise to rigidify rightness; better to let it vary from world to world. Perhaps the best interpretation is the most straightforward one: a rule system is right in *W* just in case it has a high truth ratio in *W*.

There are reasons, however, why reliabilism cannot rest content with this interpretation. I shall mention them briefly, although I cannot fully address the issues they raise. First, some rule system might be used rather sparsely in a given world, say the actual world. Its performance in that world might therefore be regarded as a poor indication of its true colors: either too favorable or too unfavorable. For this reason, it seems advisable to assess its rightness in *W* not simply by its performance in *W*, but by its performance in a set of worlds very close to *W*. In other words, we should be interested in the probability of a rule system yielding truths in the propensity, or modal frequency, interpretation of probability.[12]

A similar conclusion is mandated by a related consideration. There are many different possible ways of complying with, or instantiating, a given rule system. Even if we take the outside environment as fixed, some rules might be used frequently in one scenario but infrequently in another. (Remember, the rules are *permission* rules; they do not say what processes *must* be used, or when.) These different scenarios, or compliance profiles, would presumably generate different truth ratios. The multiplicity of compliance profiles is noted in Goldman 1986 (p. 395, note 23), where it is acknowledged that new refinements in the reliability theory are needed. Several plausible developments readily suggest themselves. First, one might require that *all* compliance profiles, even the lowest, should generate a specified, tolerably high, truth ratio. Alternatively, one might propose one or another weaker requirement, e.g., that the mean compliance profile, or the modal profile (in the statistical sense), should have a certain high truth ratio. Although I won't examine these ideas further, all are in the spirit of reliabilism.

Another technical problem is worth mentioning. *Epistemology and Cognition* formulates reliabilism in terms of rule *systems* because many single processes would not have determinate truth ratios. Consider an inference process, or a memory process, for example. Whether it yields true or false beliefs depends on the truth values of the prior beliefs which it takes as inputs. Thus, only an entire system of processes, or a system of process-permitting rules, holds the prospect of having associated truth ratios. However, a problem now arises. If you start with a given system, R, that has a very high truth ratio, adding a single unreliable rule might not reduce the truth ratio very much. So R^*, obtained from R by adding such a rule, might still pass the reliability test. But if R^* contains a poor rule, we don't want to count it as right. Let us call this the epistemic *free-rider* problem.

I propose the following solution. It is not enough that a rule system itself have a sufficiently high truth ratio (in whatever fashion this gets spelled out or refined). It must also be required that none of its *subsets* should have an *in*sufficiently high truth ratio. Since the unit set of a member rule is a subset of the rule system, this requirement disbars rule systems with any individually unreliable rules.

VII

Let me leave these detailed points about the strong conception of justifiedness, and consider a worry about its general contours.[13] In particular, let me focus on the 'world-bound' character of reliabilism, as it emerges in the present formulation of strong justifiedness. Since the rightness of a rule system is now allowed to vary from world to world, even from one experientially indistinguishable world to another, it looks as if there is an element of *luck* in whether a belief is strongly justified or not. If we are in the world we *think* we are in, our perceptual beliefs are (in the main) strongly justified. If we are in a demon world, on the other hand, our perceptual beliefs are not strongly justified. But these two worlds are experientially indistinguishable. So it seems to be a matter of luck whether or not our beliefs are strongly justified. But can invidious epistemic judgments properly rest on luck?

Note first that luck is a generally acknowledged component in other epistemic achievements, specifically *knowledge*. Justification does not logically imply truth, so even if one has a justified belief it is still a matter of luck whether one gets truth, and hence a matter of luck whether one attains knowledge. A similar moral follows from Gettier examples. People in experientially indistinguishable worlds might differ in their knowledge attainments because their true justified beliefs are Gettierized in one of the worlds but not the other. Since luck is a component in knowledge, why should it be shocking to find it in justifiedness?

The critic might retort that while it is conscionable to let luck figure in knowledge. it is unconscionable to let it figure in justification, which is an evaluative notion. But, I reply, should luck be excluded from evaluative contexts? Several writers have pointed out that it seems to enter into moral and legal evaluation (see Williams 1976 and Nagel 1979). Two equally reckless truck drivers, one who unluckily strikes a child and one who does not, may incur different amounts of disapprobation and punishment. A similar point might be made in a slightly different vein about aesthetic evaluation. We can evaluate a painter's artistic feats even while admitting that these feats are partly due to luck: the luck of natural talent and the good fortune of excellent training.

But shouldn't there be *some* style of justificational evaluation that eliminates or minimizes luck? This seems plausible. It is precisely what is captured with the concept of weak justification. So the present theory also makes room for anti-luck cravings.

VIII

Does my duplex theory of justification amount to an acknowledgment that internalism is partly correct? Is it a partial abandonment of externalism? I find this hard to answer because the terms 'internalism' and 'externalism' do not have generally accepted definitions. Internalism might be the view that whether you are justified in believing a proposition is directly accessible to you from the internal perspective, or by immediate reflection. If this is how internalism is defined, though, it is not clear that the weak conception of justification is a brand of internalism. Whether you possess a way of telling, or have available a way of telling that certain belief-forming processes are reliable or unreliable may not be something directly accessible to you by immediate reflection. I also doubt whether the weak conception of justification would fully appeal to internalists. Most internalists, I suspect, would like a more demanding conception of justification.

So I do not know whether the duplex theory of justification amounts to a marriage of externalism and internalism. I have no objection to this union, if that indeed is what it is. The important point is that it captures many intuitions about justified belief and does so in a broadly reliabilist framework.

Notes

This paper was read at the 1986 NEH Summer Institute on the Theory of Knowledge and at a conference in honor of Roderick Chisholm at Brown University. It has benefited from audience comments on both occasions.

1. Objective and subjective senses are distinguished in Pollock (1979) and Goldman (1986), the latter using the terms 'real' and 'apparent' justification. Externalist and internalist conceptions are discussed by Armstrong (1973), Goldman (1980), BonJour (1980, 1985), and Alston (1986). The regulative and non-regulative options are discussed by Kornblith (1983), Goldman (1980, 1986), and Pollock (1986). Resource-

relative and resource-independent conceptions are distinguished in Goldman (1986). Lehrer (1981) presents the personal and verific conceptions. Alston (1985) delineates deontological and evaluative conceptions (among many others).

2. Alston (1985) has a similar example of 'cultural isolation'.

3. Justifiedness as freedom from blameworthiness is one of the conceptions discussed by Alston (1985). A related conception of justifiedness as freedom from (epistemic) irresponsibility is presented by Kornblith (1983) and BonJour (1985).

4. A process or method is meta-reliable if, roughly, the methods (or processes) it tends to produce or preserve are mostly reliable. There are, however, a variety of alternative ways of spelling out the spirit of this idea. See Goldman (1986), pp. 27, 52–53, 115–116, 374–377.

5. Similarly, just because a perceptual belief is formed on a Friday, or in an environment with rose-tinted light, this does not mean that the cognizer has used *processes* of 'perceptual belief-formation on a Friday', or 'perceptual belief-formation in rose-tinted light'. In general, external circumstances such as date, time of day, physical objects in the environment, conditions of observation, etc. are not parts of a person's *cognitive processes*. The reason for this is not quite the same, however, as the reason in the case of methods. It isn't because these factors are not represented in the cognizer's head; processes in my sense are not the sorts of things that are represented explicitly in the head. Rather, they are *general operating characteristics* of the cognitive system. This is what restricts them to purely internal features or mechanisms. Many examples of process types given in the critical literature on reliabilism violate the exclusion of external factors, e.g., most cases discussed by Alvin Plantinga (1986, pp. 10–11). Observance of this exclusion does not by itself, of course, solve the 'generality problem' confronting reliabilism. But exclusion of external conditions is essential to understanding the kind of referent that the term 'cognitive process' is intended to have.

6. For a persuasive discussion of one dimension of contextual vagueness, see S. Cohen (1986); also Sosa (1974) and Dretske (1981b).

7. This point has been emphasized by a number of writers, including Pollock (1984), S. Cohen (1984), Lehrer and Cohen (1983), Ginet (1985), Foley (1985), and Luper-Foy (1985).

8. This example is due to Matthias Steup.

9. This point was raised by Alvin Plantinga, in correspondence.

10. This point was raised by Ernest Sosa in a lecture at the NEH Summer Institute on the Theory of Knowledge, Boulder, Colorado, 1986.

11. This general point, and the core of the example that follows, is due to Stewart Cohen, in correspondence.

12. See van Fraassen (1980), chap. 6.

13. A different kind of objection should be addressed as well. I maintain that strong justification, involving generally reliable methods and processes, is necessary for knowledge. But Richard Foley (1985, p. 195) raises the following objection. It is possible for someone to know that a demon has been deceiving most people and himself as well, but no longer is deceiving him. He can then know by means of his perceptual processes, even though these processes are not generally reliable (nor usually reliable *for him*). I grant that a person in such a situation can have knowledge, but I deny that it would be obtained purely perceptually. Rather, it would be obtained *by inference* from the person's knowledge that the demon is *currently* allowing his visual processes to function properly (i.e., reliably). Foley does not specify how knowledge about the demon's new practice might be obtained, but it is compatible with the imagined example that this knowledge be obtained by reliable processes, as reliabilism requires. From such knowledge about the demon's new practice, plus the fact that it now looks to the person

as if, say, there is a javelina in the bush (a belief acquired by reliable introspection), the cognizer can reliably infer that there *is* a javelina in the bush. Thus, as Foley says, knowledge acquired with the help of perceptual processes is possible, even if these processes are not generally reliable; but this does not contravene reliabilism.

Chapter 8
Psychology and Philosophical Analysis

It is often said that philosophical analysis is an a priori enterprise. Since it prominently features thought experiments designed to elicit the meaning, or semantic properties, of words in one's own language, it seems to be a purely reflective inquiry, requiring no observational or empirical component. I too have sometimes acquiesced in this sort of view. While arguing that certain phases of epistemology require input from psychology and other cognitive sciences, I have granted that the more 'conceptual' stages of epistemology are strictly philosophical and (hence) non-empirical (Goldman 1986). In this paper I want to qualify this position. I shall suggest that psychological theories can have a bearing on philosophical analysis; they can support the plausibility or implausibility of specific analyses. To many philosophers, of course, the thesis that empirical cognitive sciences can help shed light on lexical meanings is hardly newsworthy. However, I hope that some of the details of my considerations will be instructive.

Although my conception of philosophical analysis is expressly lexicalist, there are other conceptions afloat. On some views, the objects of analysis are natural kinds, or properties, and the aim of the enterprise is to reveal their (metaphysical) essences. We are to discover what consciousness or justice *are*, not what the words 'consciousness' or 'justice' mean. I shall not argue here for the lexicalist approach, except to say that it seems appropriate at least for the class of epistemological examples that primarily concern me here. Whatever one thinks about justice or consciousness as possible natural kinds, it is dubious that knowledge or justificational status are natural kinds.

Certain arguments for an empirical construal of analysis are fairly straightforward. Suppose that the semantic properties of a lexical item L are given by an intension, i.e., a function from possible worlds into sets of objects (or ordered n-tuples of objects). It looks as if the statement that a given term L (in a specified language) has a specific intension N is a contingent statement. So it seems likely that empirical means are needed to determine the truth value of any hypothesis about L's intension. Furthermore, the process of verifying any such hypothesis is inductive. At any given time, philosophers or linguists will have examined intuitive reactions to only a finite number of examples. Even if a hypothesis has been verified by all cases thus far examined, there may still be unthought-of counterexamples. Of course, inductive methodology should not be equated with empirical methodology. Mathematical subject matter can be approached inductively (in a broad sense) without being thereby approached empirically (see Lakatos 1976). However, consulting linguistic intuition seems to be an empirical method, or at least a convenient informal substitute for a proper empirical method. The more proper method would (arguably) consist of eliciting verbal responses from informants, not only oneself but other competent speakers of the language. There is no great gap, then, between traditional philosophical methodology and the methods of empirical cognitive sciences.

There are familiar arguments, several due to Hilary Putnam (1975), for denying that mentalistic elements wholly fix meanings, and hence for denying that the cognitive sciences can settle issues of meaning. Putnam's emphasis on the social division of linguistic labor and on the referential, or environmental, aspects of meaning, raises doubts about whether meaning is related to 'what is in the head'. But while these points may show that meaning does not wholly reside in the head, they still leave room for the mental in the determination of meaning. With respect to quasi-technical words like 'beech' or 'elm', only the mental conditions of experts (or reasonably competent speakers) are relevant to their meanings. As far as the environment is concerned, it cannot replace considerations of linguistic intuitions and the mental materials which generate them. To make an initial fix on which stuff in the environment counts as water, linguistic intuitions and their underlying source are pertinent. Putnam should concede this much since his own claims about the role of the environment in determining reference or meaning appeal to intuitions about 'reference' and 'meaning'.

How can we motivate the suggestion that cognitive theories can have a bearing on philosophical analysis? Most of the work in cognitive science that ostensibly bears on philosophical analysis is the body of work on concepts and categories.[1] However, it is a thorny matter to interpret and evaluate the implications of this research. I shall therefore focus the bulk of my attention, not on the core of this literature, but on an adjacent aspect of mental processing that is of special interest for a certain item of philosophical analysis. I shall argue that an appreciation of this psychological phenomenon provides support for a certain account of the epistemic term 'know', i.e., the 'relevant alternatives' account.

According to the relevant alternatives theory, 'knows p' means (roughly) 'believes p truly on the basis of evidence that eliminates all relevant alternatives to p'.[2] A critical component of this analysis is the qualifier 'relevant'. Skeptics have long argued that there is very little, if any, knowledge because people cannot rule out certain logically possible alternatives. But the analysis in question does not require all alternatives to be eliminated, only all relevant ones. And perhaps the skeptical alternatives are not relevant. However, the term 'relevant' is quite vague, and nobody has yet spelled out the precise contours of relevance. Is the analysis defensible despite this vagueness? Or does the theory suffer from unacceptable obscurity, ad-hoc-ness, or even occultness, as it is sometimes charged?[3]

A valuable framework for assessing the account is provided by David Lewis (1983d), who reminds us how widespread is the phenomenon of vagueness, and how vagueness is often resolved by conversational context. Austin's sentence 'France is hexagonal' is true enough (i.e., true over a large enough part of its delineations of vagueness) to be acceptable in some conversational contexts, but not others. It is acceptable under low, but not high, standards of precision. Lewis argues that conversational principles include a 'rule of accommodation' that would have us honor the prerogative of the speaker to raise or lower the standards. He also calls attention to the vagueness of modal terms like 'can' and 'must'. These do not often express absolute (i.e., 'logical' or 'metaphysical') possibility, but rather various relative modalities. Not all the possibilities there enter into consideration. Ignoring possibilities that violate laws of nature, we get the physical modalities; ignoring those that are known not to obtain, we get the epistemic modalities; and so forth.[4] Stewart Cohen (1986, 1987, 1988) applies Lewis's conversational perspective to defend the relevant alternatives account of knowledge, and argues for the vagueness of another epistemic expression, 'having good reasons', on further grounds.

It is not clear, however, that conversational considerations resolve all the issues here. First, it is doubtful that listeners always defer to speakers. Certainly commonsense epistemologists do not defer to skeptics when the latter exhibit relaxation of standards of relevance. Second, there are many cases that need to be covered where there is minimal conversation, certainly not enough to fix standards. In cases where nobody has asserted or denied that a target person knows, but where we query an informant on the matter, he will commonly have an intuition. Since this cannot be traced to conversational constraints on the range of relevant alternatives, there must be further factors at work. Third, while there is some measure of vagueness in the term 'know', there are also strong uniformities of intuition, as witnessed by the high degree of consensus in Gettier cases. How can the relevant alternatives approach handle these uniformities (without appealing, as other theories do, to false 'lemmas', or the like)?

One type of answer is 'objectivist': it claims, for example, that the difference between relevant and irrelevant alternatives resides in the kinds of possibilities that actually exist in the objective situation, or in objective probabilities (see Dretske 1981b and S. Cohen 1988). But there are problems with these proposals. In the barn facsimile case (chapter 5), the objective probability of the sighted object being a facsimile may be zero, given all the facts of the case (plus an assumption of determinism, if you will). Nonetheless, where there are lots of facsimiles in the neighborhood, there is a strong inclination to deny knowledge. As far as objective possibility goes, in a case where there are no facsimiles anywhere, it may still be 'objectively possible' (e.g., technologically possible) for one to be on the site, but we would probably not consider this a relevant alternative. Further difficulties are posed by cases of 'evidence one does not possess'. In Gilbert Harman's case of the unopened misleading letters implying that Donald left Italy for San Francisco, we are strongly tempted to deny that you know that Donald is in Italy (Harman 1973, p. 143). But there is no serious possibility or probability of Donald having gone to San Francisco.

If an objectivist approach to relevance does not succeed, what account can be given of relevance? How should we go about trying to provide one? The question as I see it is one of trying to give a plausible, parsimonious explanation of people's (linguistic) intuitions. Presumably, the intuitions of an informant, or judge, are the product of (at least) three factors: (A) (his grasp of) the meaning of 'know', (B) his beliefs about the state of the putative knower in the target example, and (C) various of his other beliefs, background information, and so forth, which I shall lump together under the term 'context'. Although the analyst is primarily trying to pinpoint the contribution of (A), she needs to assess the contributions of the other factors as well. It is at this juncture that psychology becomes germane. Suppose that psychology tells us that context effects loom large in cognitive life. Then we should be alert to the possibility that factor (C) could play a large role, and might combine with the relevant-alternatives component of (A) to account for informants' intuitions. This is the account I shall defend.

A variety of findings in assorted psychological domains indicate that context has a critical impact on cognizers' judgments and categorizations. Here is a sampling of such findings. E. M. Roth and E. J. Shoben (1983) found that judgments of prototypicality for lexical items are affected by linguistic context. Which members of the category 'beverage' are most typical: coffee, tea, or milk? After reading about two secretaries taking a midmorning break, subjects ranked coffee as the most typical, followed by tea and then milk. But after reading about a truck driver stopping at a truck stop, subjects ranked them in the order of coffee, then milk, and then tea. Amos Tversky (1977) has shown that judgments of similarity are affected by context. Subjects were asked to say which of three countries was most similar to Austria. In one case the choice set consisted of {Sweden, Poland, and Hungary}; in another it was {Sweden, Norway, and Hungary}. In the first case, a plurality of subjects chose Sweden as most similar to Austria, presumably because, in this choice-set context, Poland and Hungary were grouped as 'Eastern bloc' countries, making Sweden more similar to Austria by contrast to that pair. In the second case, a majority of subjects chose Hungary as most similar to Austria presumably because, in this different context, Sweden and Norway were grouped as Scandinavian countries, making Hungary more similar to Austria by being non-Scandinavian. Third, the widely researched 'priming' phenomenon is a species of context effect. In lexical decision tasks, subjects are asked to decide whether briefly presented items are words or not. It is found that less time is required to decide that an item is a word if it is preceded by an associated word. For instance, 'butter' is more rapidly judged to be a word when preceded by (the 'prime') 'bread'. Furthermore, this priming effect is obtained even when the subject is unaware of the associative relations between the prime and the target. This is taken as evidence of an automatic and ubiquitous phenomenon of associative spread of activation in memory.

How might context effects help explain intuitions about knowledge? Contextual factors can enter the picture in two ways. First, elements of the target example can affect the judge's choice of relevant alternatives; and second, elements in the judge's conversational context can affect his choice. (Of course, background information is always operative as well.) In the barn facsimile example, the presence of barn facsimiles in the neighborhood can 'prime' the possibility of the sighted object (in fact a barn) being a facsimile instead. Similarly, in one of the original Gettier (1963) cases where the target proposition is the disjunction, 'Either Jones owns a Ford or Brown is in Barcelona', the stipulated fact that Jones does not own a Ford and that Brown is only coincidentally in Barcelona can 'prime' the possibility that neither Jones owns a Ford nor Brown is in Barcelona. This is an alternative not eliminated by the evidence. Context effects can also provide an explanation for the unpossessed evidence example. Even though Donald has no plans to leave Italy during the summer, the mere presence of the phony letter postmarked in San Francisco can make salient the possibility of his being there instead.[5] With respect to conversational context, if the speaker is in a philosophy class discussing skepticism, various radical counterpossibilities may be prompted and made 'live' by the discussion. But when he goes about his everyday affairs, as Hume observed, these radical possibilities recede in salience and seriousness. This is what psychological context effects would lead one to expect. In general, it looks as if uniformities of intuitions about knowledge could be predicted from the psychology of context effects together with the relevant-alternatives account of the meaning of 'know'. This illustrates how empirical psychology might lend credibility (or incredibility) to specific philosophical analyses.

It must be conceded, however, that the little I have said about context effects would not make really firm predictions about intuitions. The psychological story needs to be spelled out more fully. There are the beginnings of such work, dealing with spontaneous propensities to generate counterfactual possibilities, and the stimulus factors that influence the choice of what to counterfactualize, i.e., what is relatively 'mutable' or 'immutable' (see Kahneman and Miller 1986). Epistemic terms like 'know', and modal terms like 'could' and 'might', have semantic features that trigger possibility searches, but the precise directions and depth of the exploration depend on psychological propensities. Philosophers are trained to imagine and construct 'theoretical' or 'logical' possibilities. For most people, though, the range of counterpossibilities that are considered, and certainly those that are 'live' or salient, is narrowly constrained. Raw recruits to philosophy have to be trained (brainwashed?) to expand their range of alternatives.

Suppose, then, that people have a propensity to conduct mental 'possibility searches', and there are fairly rigid patterns in the directions and depth of their searches.[6] These patterns of direction and depth might induce a metric of seriousness on classes of possibilities. Such a metric might generate the observed interpersonal uniformities in intuitive judgments of 'knowledge' (especially in hypothetical cases, where the facts are clearly stipulated). It would also explain why skeptical alternatives do not normally function (outside special contexts) to inhibit knowledge attributions. These alternatives are simply too remote, given the usual direction-and-depth properties of possibility searches.[7]

If these sorts of psychological details could be filled in, we would then have a theory of 'relevant alternatives' that ought to satisfy those who find this notion occult or ad hoc. Would it be a theory that should be inserted into the definition, or the semantics, of 'know'? I am inclined to think not; better to construe it as part of the 'pragmatics' of 'know'. Of course, this would imply that the skeptic's denial of knowledge is not semantically excluded. But I do not find this objectionable, for it would make intelligible the power of the skeptic's challenge. The skeptic is not semantically confused; he just exercises an aberrant pattern of possibility exploration.

This approach seems to leave unanswered what many regard as the crucial question: 'Does a person in a specified case *really* know?'. However, to assume that there is always a determinate answer to this question assumes that either the linguistic meaning of 'knows', or the meaning together with attendant pragmatic factors (including the speaker's intention), fix a proposition with determinate truth conditions. Although philosophers widely make this sort of assumption, it should not be accepted uncritically. But it raises large issues, for which this is not a suitable occasion.

Some people might contend that the psychological properties governing possibility searches should be (somehow) reflected in the semantic contents of 'know'. I have no knock-down argument against this. (Nor do I have a set of general principles for deciding how to apportion explanations of intuitions to semantic versus nonsemantic factors.) But I could accept this suggestion as grist for my mill, for it would still require psychological investigation to help specify the semantics of 'know'.

The psychological perspective being advocated can guide us toward a broader understanding of a familiar puzzle about knowledge. The closure principle for knowledge asserts that if S knows p, and S knows that p entails q, then S knows q. Or better, consider a slightly weaker principle: if S knows p, and S knows that p entails q, then S can know q (see Gleb 1988). But this principle seems to conflict with intuitions about certain cases. It is intuitively plausible that I know I am in Tucson, Arizona, but not that I know (or that I can know) that I am not an envatted brain in London undergoing desert landscape experiences (see Dretske 1970 and Nozick 1981). The alternatives-elimination approach to knowledge conforms with this violation of closure, for I have no way of eliminating the chief alternative to the latter proposition, viz., that I *am* an envatted brain in London.

It might be surprising that the relevant alternatives approach meshes with closure violation. Let RA(p) be the set of relevant alternatives for p and RA(q) be the set of relevant alternatives for q; and suppose that p entails q. Then if 'know' is to be 'logically well behaved', RA(q) should be a subset of RA(p). Hence, if there is some member of RA(q) which the putative knower cannot eliminate, there is also a member of RA(p) which he cannot eliminate. Yet precisely this seems to be violated: 'I am an envatted brain in London (etc.)' apparently belongs to the relevant alternative set for the entailed proposition (using normal procedures of possibility search), but does not belong to the set for the entailing proposition.

If we adopt the psychological diagnosis of our knowledge intuitions, we can make sense of this puzzle. Since alternative-possibility searches are keyed by the topic in question, why expect 'logically good behavior' from them? Why should we expect the alternatives triggered by 'I am in Tucson' to include all the alternatives triggered by 'I am not an envatted brain in London'? It should not be surprising that the envatted brain alternative exceeds the depth-and-direction limits for 'I am in Tucson' but not the limits for 'I am not an envatted brain in London'.

Psychologists discover analogously 'messy' or anomalous behavior in other judgmental contexts. For example, people seem to evaluate choices or outcomes by making comparisons to a reference point, as the following example from R. Thaler (1980) highlights (also see Tversky and Kahneman 1981). Gasoline stations have the option of calling a credit card price of $1.00 per gallon a 'surcharge' on a 96 cent base price, or calling $1.00 the normal price and labelling 96 cents a cash 'discount'. But consumers are more likely to be willing to pay the $1.00 price in the latter case, where they merely pass up an improvement from the induced anchor point, than they are in the former case, where they would view $1.00 as a ' loss' from the induced reference point. Another demonstration of the anomalous effects of an anchor point comes from Paul Slovic, who found that a strictly inferior bet was rated as more attractive than a superior one, because of different induced reference points (Slovic 1985, cited in Kahneman and Miller 1986).

That our psychological apparatus should generate logically 'messy' behavior should come as no surprise. The familiar Sorites puzzles are predictable from a psychological perspective. We seem to have two mechanisms for forming categories and making categorization judgments. There is a mechanism that favors (at least cheerfully accepts) binary, as opposed to graded, categorizations. There also seems to be a principle of 'good continuation', which dictates a preference for coclassifying objects that differ only minutely (on relevant dimensions). This pair of psychological principles lead to the Sorites puzzles. In a similar vein, I suggest, there are psychological traits that breed anomalous judgments about knowledge. We should not reject an analysis of 'know' because it has this consequence; on the contrary, we should expect it of an accurate analysis.

For my second illustration of the relevance of psychology (or cognitive science more broadly), I want to explore (all too briefly) the implications for epistemic analysis of a certain cognitive approach to concepts. This approach is best represented by Charles Fillmore's 'frame semantics', but the approach is also developed by other linguists and psychologists.[8] A frame is a system of concepts related in such a way that to understand one of them you have to understand the whole structure into which they fit. The specific thrust of Fillmore's frame theory is that many lexical items are introduced and understood against the background of a certain type of situation, a set of institutional practices, or perhaps a simplified or schematized set of regularities. The mental representation of such a type of situation is sometimes called an 'idealized cognitive model' (ICM). Fillmore suggests that a definition of the lexical item can only be given, or understood, against the presupposition of the relevant ICM. In more familiar philosophical terminology, the lexical item is 'theory laden'.

Here is a standard example. The term 'bachelor' is defined in the context of a simplified world view in which all people are marriageable at a certain age, mostly marry at that age, and stay married to the same spouse. In this simplified world, a bachelor is simply any unmarried male past marriageable age. Outside the simplified world, questions of applicability of 'bachelor' become ambiguous. Does the Pope (or any priest) count as a bachelor? A thrice-married divorcé? An unmarried male with a long-term (heterosexual or homosexual) relationship? These certainly do not fit the prototype of a bachelor, and it is doubtful that they genuinely qualify as such, although they do fit the standard definition.

What seems to happen here is that a prototype arises that is logically independent of the standard definition, and this prototype heavily controls our intuitions if and when we query the term's application outside its originally intended frame. (Here I depart from the express content of Fillmore's story.) The prototype of a bachelor is that of a man who leads, and has always led, a relatively solitary and independent lifestyle, without any close bonding relationship, doing his own cooking and other chores traditionally performed by a wife. Neither a thrice-married divorcé, nor an unmarried man with a long-term coupling, nor even a priest, resembles this prototype very closely. On the other hand, a legally married man who lives apart from his wife for years without establishing any other continuous relationship, who does his own cooking, etc., comes quite close to the prototype of a bachelor; and there is some temptation to call him that. Indeed, men often speak of 'batching it' when their wife (and children) go off for a long trip or holiday.

I want to apply the frame-semantics approach to a range of cases specially relevant to evaluative domains. In many areas of discourse, practices of evaluation arise in situations where certain regularities obtain, or are assumed to obtain. In the standard situation, the evaluated forms of conduct have characteristic consequences, which comprise the basis or rationale for their positive or negative assessment. In athletic contexts, for example, fairness, courtesy, and graceful acceptance of results tend to produce relatively smooth games, (comparatively) good relations among players, and satisfaction all around. (At least this is the idealized model.) Since these are valued consequences, a positive evaluation is placed on this form of conduct. It is called 'sporting', or 'sportsmanlike', behavior. What happens, now, if we consider the same kind of conduct in an altogether different context, where most players are highly contentious, and do not respect fairness, courtesy, or graceful acceptance of results? They expect players to cheat as much as possible, and to complain strenuously when they lose; they get satisfaction from trying to exceed their opponents in trickery. In this setting, fairness, courtesy, and gracefulness do not contribute to the general pleasure of the game, do not have the same valued consequences as in the 'source' situation. Does it seem intuitively right (to us) to call such conduct 'sporting' or 'sportsmanlike'? I think it does, at least to a considerable degree. Apparently, the intrinsic features of the conduct have been partly 'detached' from their evaluative basis or rationale. What substantially drives our intuitions is the style of conduct itself. I should emphasize that this is a matter of degree. There is still a vector in the opposite direction, rooted in the original basis or rationale, to withhold the terms 'sporting' or 'sportsmanlike'.

Let me extend this idea to the epistemological sphere, in particular to the evaluative term 'justified' (or 'warranted'). In earlier work, I have argued that our intuitive classification of beliefs as justified and unjustified is based on their mode of generation. In particular, beliefs produced by processes or methods with a high truth ratio are called 'justified', and those produced by processes or methods with relatively low truth ratios are called 'unjustified' (see chapter 6 and Goldman, 1986). This proposal was based on examination of cases. Beliefs formed by perception, memory, and 'good' reasoning are all considered justified, and these modes of production apparently share the characteristic of (relatively) high truth ratio (reliability). Beliefs formed by wishful thinking, by hasty generalization, or by felt experiences of clairvoyance, are classified as unjustified, and these modes of production apparently share the property of low truth ratio (unreliability).

This story can be embedded in Fillmore's frame-semantical approach. What should be made explicit is that the concepts of justified and unjustified belief are introduced against the background of a model (possibly idealized or simplified—indeed, possibly false of the actual world) in which perception, memory, and 'good' reasoning are reliable, whereas wishful thinking, guesswork, and hasty generalization are unreliable, or much less reliable. High truth ratio is the valued attribute, and in the ICM this attribute is instantiated by perception, memory, and good reasoning, but not by wishful thinking and so forth. However, this attribute may not hold of the same processes outside the ICM. We can imagine possible worlds (inhabited by Cartesian demons) in which perception is not reliable. And we can imagine possible worlds (perhaps inhabited by guardian angels) in which wishful thinking is reliable.

What is our intuition about perceptually formed beliefs in Cartesian demon worlds, where perception is an unreliable process? Most people are inclined to say that these beliefs are justified. Similarly, there is moderate, though by no means universal, inclination to say that wishful-thinking-formed beliefs are unjustified even in a guardian-angel world, where a benevolent angel makes most wishes come true. These results are analogous to the sportsmanship cases. The particular forms of conduct substantially direct our intuitions about cases outside the original model. The original basis, or rationale, for selecting those forms of conduct is not clearly ascendant. The matter is not wholly clear, however. What about clairvoyance in worlds where clairvoyance is reliable, due to forms of energy that don't exist in our world? Are clairvoyantly produced beliefs justified in such a world? There is certainly some temptation to say so, which testifies to the role that the reliability basis still plays in our semantic intuitions. And some people feel inclined to say that wishful thinking in a guardian-angel world would be justified.

In any case, what I suggest is that the correctness of a theory about the basis is not undermined simply because the elements in that basis are not the dominant force in driving intuitions outside the source situation. Intuitions outside the source situation—especially in 'remote', hypothetical cases—are not trustworthy indicators of the originating rationale. To this extent, philosophical theorists should retain a measure of caution in interpreting the results of far-flung thought experiments. They should look more closely at the contexts, or frames, in which words get their initial foothold (a moral with a Wittgensteinian flavor). Since philosophers are commonly most interested in the fundamental basis or rationale, they should be prepared to find it playing only a background role in fixing semantic intuitions. Its theoretical importance is not diminished by this 'recessive' role in semantic interplay.[9]

Notes

Thanks to Robert Cummins, Mike Harnish, Christopher Maloney, and especially Holly Smith for valuable and timely comments.

1. See E. E. Smith and Medin (1981) or E. E. Smith (1988) for a useful survey of this literature.
2. See Dretske (1970, 1981a, 1981b), and Goldman (chapter 5, 1986). Similar suggestions were made earlier by Austin (1961).
3. See Sosa (1986).
4. On the meanings of some modal terms, see Kratzer (1977).
5. Salience is emphasized in S. Cohen 1988. That paper appeared just as I was nearing completion of this one, so I have not been able to study it thoroughly. Like Cohen's other papers cited above, however, its themes are quite close to some defended here.
6. One example of preferred direction is given by Miller and Johnson-Laird (1976, p. 264). The cognitive effect of negation—x is not a table, y is not a cook—is to leave most people still thinking in terms of the same genus, but searching for another species. If x is not a table, perhaps it is a chair; if y is not a cook, perhaps he is a waiter. Other properties of 'semantic fields' may also be operative here.
7. Related themes about the ease or difficulty of possibility generation are developed in Goldman 1986, sections 11.5 and 11.6.
8. See Fillmore (1982a, 1982b), Lakoff (1987), and Murphy and Medin (1985).
9. There is an affinity between the approach outlined here and the theory of justification based on 'normal worlds' that I present in Goldman 1986. Indeed, I regard the present account as a more felicitous—though sketchy and exploratory—formulation of the idea that was guiding my thinking in that earlier treatment. Unfortunately, matters are further complicated by the fact that there are, I believe, two related but distinct senses of 'justified' (see chapter 7). There is a 'strong' sense of 'justified belief', having roughly the content: 'belief formed properly, adequately, or soundly'. There is also a second, 'weak' sense of 'justified belief', viz., 'blameless, or nonculpable, belief'. On the account proposed in chapter 7, our positive evaluation of the demon-world beliefs may be guided by the weak sense. A person's perceptual beliefs in a demon world are justified in the sense of being blameless: although they are not reliably formed, one has no way of telling that they are not reliably formed. In the present paper, I ignore the 'weak' sense entirely.

Chapter 9

Epistemic Folkways and Scientific Epistemology

What is the mission of epistemology, and what is its proper methodology? Such meta-epistemological questions have been prominent in recent years, especially with the emergence of various brands of "naturalistic" epistemology. In this paper, I shall reformulate and expand upon my own meta-epistemological conception (most fully articulated in Goldman 1986), retaining many of its former ingredients while reconfiguring others. The discussion is by no means confined, though, to the meta-epistemological level. New substantive proposals will also be advanced and defended.

Let us begin, however, at the meta-epistemological level, by asking what role should be played in epistemology by our ordinary epistemic concepts and principles. By some philosophers' lights, the sole mission of epistemology is to elucidate commonsense epistemic concepts and principles: concepts like knowledge, justification, and rationality, and principles associated with these concepts. By other philosophers' lights, this is not even part of epistemology's aim. Ordinary concepts and principles, the latter would argue, are fundamentally naive, unsystematic, and uninformed by important bodies of logic and/or mathematics. Ordinary principles and practices, for example, ignore or violate the probability calculus, which ought to be the cornerstone of epistemic rationality. Thus, on the second view, proper epistemology must neither *end* with naive principles of justification or rationality, nor even *begin* there.

My own stance on this issue lies somewhere between these extremes. To facilitate discussion, let us give a label to our commonsense epistemic concepts and norms; let us call them our *epistemic folkways*. In partial agreement with the first view sketched above, I would hold that *one* proper task of epistemology is to elucidate our epistemic folkways. Whatever else epistemology might proceed to do, it should at least have its roots in the concepts and practices of the folk. If these roots are utterly rejected and abandoned, by what rights would the new discipline call itself 'epistemology' at all? It may well be desirable to reform or transcend our epistemic folkways, as the second of the views sketched above recommends. But it is essential to preserve continuity; and continuity can only be recognized if we have a satisfactory characterization of our epistemic folkways. Actually, even if one rejects the plea for continuity, a description of our epistemic folkways is in order. How would one know what to criticize, or what needs to be transcended, in the absence of such a description? So a first mission of epistemology is to describe or characterize our folkways.

Now a suitable description of these folk concepts, I believe, is likely to depend on insights from cognitive science. Indeed, identification of the semantic contours of many (if not all) concepts can profit from theoretical and empirical work in psychology and linguistics. For this reason, the task of describing or elucidating folk epistemology is a *scientific* task, at least a task that should be informed by relevant scientific research.

The second mission of epistemology, as suggested by the second view above, is the formulation of a more adequate, sound, or systematic set of epistemic norms, in some way(s) transcending our naive epistemic repertoire. How and why these folkways might be transcended, or improved upon, remains to be specified. This will partly depend on the contours of the commonsense standards that emerge from the first mission. On my view, epistemic concepts like knowledge and justification crucially invoke psychological faculties or processes. Our folk understanding, however, has a limited and tenuous grasp of the processes available to the cognitive agent. Thus, one important respect in which epistemic folkways should be transcended is by incorporating a more detailed and empirically based depiction of psychological mechanisms. Here too epistemology would seek assistance from cognitive science.

Since both missions of epistemology just delineated lean in important respects on the deliverances of science, specifically cognitive science, let us call our conception of epistemology *scientific epistemology*. Scientific epistemology, we have seen, has two branches: *descriptive* and *normative*. While descriptive scientific epistemology aims to describe our ordinary epistemic assessments, normative scientific epistemology continues the practice of making epistemic judgments, or formulating systematic principles for such judgments.[1] It is prepared to depart from our ordinary epistemic judgments, however, if and when that proves advisable. (This overall conception of epistemology closely parallels the conception of metaphysics articulated in chapters 2 and 3. The descriptive and normative branches of scientific epistemology are precise analogues of the descriptive and prescriptive branches of metaphysics, as conceptualized there.) In the remainder of this paper, I shall sketch and defend the particular forms of descriptive and normative scientific epistemology that I favor.

II

Mainstream epistemology has concentrated much of its attention on two concepts (or terms): knowledge and justified belief. The preceding essay primarily illustrates the contributions that cognitive science can make to an understanding of the former; this essay focuses on the latter. We need not mark this concept exclusively by the phrase 'justified belief'. A family of phrases pick out roughly the same concept: 'well-founded belief', 'reasonable belief', 'belief based on good grounds', and so forth. I shall propose an account of this concept that is in the reliabilist tradition, but departs at a crucial juncture from other versions of reliabilism. My account has the same core idea as Ernest Sosa's *intellectual virtues* approach, but incorporates some distinctive features that improve its prospects.[2]

The basic approach is, roughly, to identify the concept of justified belief with the concept of belief obtained through the exercise of intellectual virtues (excellences). Beliefs acquired (or retained) through a chain of "virtuous" psychological processes qualify as justified; those acquired partly by cognitive "vices" are derogated as unjustified. This, as I say, is a *rough* account. To explain it more fully, I need to say things about the psychology of the epistemic evaluator, the possessor and deployer of the concept in question. At this stage in the development of semantical theory (which, in the future, may well be viewed as part of the "dark ages" of the subject), it is difficult to say just what the relationship is between the meaning or "content" of concepts and the form or structure of their mental representation. In the present case, however, I believe that an account of the form of representation can contribute to our understanding of the content, although I am unable to formulate these matters in a theoretically satisfying fashion.

The hypothesis I wish to advance is that the epistemic evaluator has a mentally stored set, or list, of cognitive virtues and vices. When asked to evaluate an actual or hypothetical case of belief, the evaluator considers the processes by which the belief was produced, and matches these against his list of virtues and vices. If the processes match virtues only, the belief is classified as justified. If the processes are matched partly with vices, the belief is categorized as unjustified. If a belief-forming scenario is described that features a process not on the evaluator's list of either virtues or vices, the belief may be categorized as neither justified nor unjustified, but simply *non*justified. Alternatively (and this alternative plays an important role in my story), the evaluator's judgment may depend on the (judged) *similarity* of the novel process to the stored virtues and vices. In other words, the "matches" in question need not be perfect.

This proposal makes two important points of contact with going theories in the psychology of concepts. First, it has some affinity to the *exemplar* approach to concept representation (cf. Medin and Schaffer 1978; Smith and Medin 1981; Hintzman 1986). According to that approach, a concept is mentally represented by means of representations of its positive instances, or perhaps types of instances. For example, the representation of the concept *pants* might include a representation of a particular pair of faded blue jeans and/or a representation of the type *blue jeans*. Our approach to the concept of justification shares the spirit of this approach insofar as it posits a set of examples of virtues and vices, as opposed to a mere abstract characterization—e.g., a definition—of (intellectual) virtue or vice. A second affinity to the exemplar approach is in the appeal to a similarity, or matching, operation in the classification of new target cases. According to the exemplar approach, targets are categorized as a function of their similarity to the positive exemplars (and dissimilarity to the foils). Of course, similarity is invoked in many other approaches to concept deployment as well (see E. E. Smith 1990). This makes our account of justification consonant with the psychological literature generally, whether or not it meshes specifically with the exemplar approach.

Let us now see what this hypothesis predicts for a variety of cases. To apply it, we need to make some assumptions about the lists of virtues and vices that typical evaluators mentally store. I shall assume that the virtues include belief formation based on sight, hearing, memory, reasoning in certain "approved" ways, and so forth. The vices include intellectual processes like forming beliefs by guesswork, wishful thinking, and ignoring contrary evidence. *Why* these items are placed in their respective categories remains to be explained. As indicated, I plan to explain them by reference to reliability. Since the account will therefore be, at bottom, a reliabilist type of account, it is instructive to see how it fares when applied to well-known problem cases for standard versions of reliabilism.

Consider first the demon-world case. In a certain possible world, a Cartesian demon gives people deceptive visual experiences, which systematically lead to false beliefs. Are these vision-based beliefs justified? Intuitively, they are. The demon's victims are presented with the same sorts of visual experiences that we are, and they use the same processes to produce corresponding beliefs. For most epistemic evaluators, this seems sufficient to induce the judgment that the victims' beliefs are justified. Does our account predict this result? Certainly it does. The account predicts that an epistemic evaluator will match the victims' vision-based processes to one (or more) of the items on his list of intellectual virtues, and therefore judge the victims' beliefs to be justified.

Turn next to Laurence BonJour's (1985) cases in which hypothetical agents are assumed to possess a perfectly reliable clairvoyant faculty. Although these agents form their beliefs by this reliable faculty, BonJour contends that the beliefs are not justified; and apparently most (philosophical) evaluators agree with that judgment. This result is not predicted by simple forms of reliabilism.[3] What does our present theory predict? Let us consider the four cases in two groups. In the first three cases (Samantha, Casper, and Maud), the agent has contrary evidence that he or she ignores. Samantha has a massive amount of apparently cogent evidence that the president is in Washington, but she nonetheless believes (through clairvoyance) that the president is in New York City. Casper and Maud each has large amounts of ostensibly cogent evidence that he/she has no reliable clairvoyant power, but they rely on such a power nonetheless. Here our theory predicts that the evaluator will match these agent's belief-forming processes to the vice of ignoring contrary evidence. Since the processes include a vice, the beliefs will be judged to be unjustified.

BonJour's fourth case involves Norman, who has a reliable clairvoyant power but no reasons for or against the thesis that he possesses it. When he believes, through clairvoyance, that the president is in New York City, while possessing no (other) relevant evidence, how should this belief be judged? My own assessment is less clear in this case than the other three cases. I am tempted to say that Norman's belief is *non*justified, not that it is thoroughly *un*justified. (I construe unjustified as "having negative justificational status", and nonjustified as "lacking positive justificational status".) This result is also readily predicted by our theory. On the assumption that I (and other evaluators) do not have clairvoyance on my list of virtues, the theory allows the prediction that the belief would be judged neither justified nor unjustified, merely nonjustified. For those evaluators who would judge Norman's belief to be *un*justified, there is another possible explanation in terms of the theory. There is a class of putative faculties, including mental telepathy, ESP, telekinesis, and so forth that are scientifically disreputable. It is plausible that evaluators view any process of basing beliefs on the supposed deliverances of such faculties as vices. It is also plausible that these evaluators judge the process of basing one's belief on clairvoyance to be *similar* to such vices. Thus, the theory would predict that they would view a belief acquired in this way as unjustified.[4]

Finally, consider Alvin Plantinga's (1988) examples that feature disease-triggered or mind-malfunctioning processes. These include processes engendered by a brain tumor, radiation-caused processes, and the like. In each case Plantinga imagines that the process is reliable, but reports that we would not judge it to be justification conferring. My diagnosis follows the track outlined in the Norman case. At a minimum, the processes imagined by Plantinga fail to match any virtue on a typical evaluator's list. So the beliefs are at least nonjustified. Furthermore, evaluators may have a prior representation of pathological processes as examples of cognitive vices. Plantinga's cases might be judged (relevantly) similar to these vices, so that the beliefs they produce would be declared unjustified.

In some of Plantinga's cases, it is further supposed that the hypothetical agent possesses countervailing evidence against his belief, which he stead-fastly ignores. As noted earlier, this added element would strengthen a judgment of unjustifiedness according to our theory, because ignoring contrary evidence is an intellectual vice. Once again, then, our theory's predictions conform with reported judgments.

Let us now turn to the question of how epistemic evaluators acquire their lists of virtues and vices. What is the basis for their classification? As already indicated, my answer invokes the notion of reliability. Belief-form-ing processes based on vision, hearing, memory, and ("good") reasoning are deemed virtuous because they (are deemed to) produce a high ratio of true beliefs. Processes like guessing, wishful thinking, and ignoring con-trary evidence are deemed vicious because they (are deemed to) produce a low ratio of true beliefs.

We need not assume that each epistemic evaluator chooses his/her catalogue of virtues and vices by direct application of the reliability test. Epistemic evaluators may partly inherit their lists of virtues and vices from other speakers in the linguistic community. Nonetheless, the hypothesis is that the selection of virtues and vices rests, ultimately, on assessments of reliability.

It is not assumed, of course, that all speakers have the same lists of intellectual virtues and vices. They may have different opinions about the reliability of processes, and therefore differ in their respective lists.[5] Or they may belong to different subcultures in the linguistic community, which may differentially influence their lists. Philosophers sometimes seem to assume great uniformity in epistemic judgments. This assumption may stem from the fact that it is mostly the judgments of philosophers them-selves that have been reported, and they are members of a fairly homoge-neous subculture. A wider pool of "subjects" might reveal a much lower degree of uniformity. That would conform to the present theory, however, which permits individual differences in catalogues of virtues and vices, and hence in judgments of justifiedness.

If virtues and vices are selected on the basis of reliability and unrelia-bility, respectively, why doesn't a hypothetical case introducing a novel reliable process induce an evaluator to add that process to his list of virtues, and declare the resulting belief justified? Why, for example, doesn't he add clairvoyance to his list of virtues, and rule Norman's beliefs to be justified?

I venture the following explanation. First, people seem to have a trait of *categorial conservatism*. They display a preference for "entrenched" catego-ries, in Nelson Goodman's (1955) phraseology, and do not lightly supple-ment or revise their categorial schemes. An isolated single case is not enough. More specifically, merely imaginary cases do not exert much influence on categorial structures. People's cognitive systems are responsive to live cases, not purely fictional ones. Philosophers encounter this when their students or nonphilosophers are unimpressed with science fiction-style counterexamples. Philosophers become impatient with this response because they presume that possible cases are on a par (for counterexample purposes) with actual ones. This phenomenon testifies, however, to a psychological propensity to take an invidious attitude toward purely imaginary cases.

To the philosopher, it seems both natural and inevitable to take hypothetical cases seriously, and if necessary to restrict one's conclusions about them to specified "possible worlds". Thus, the philosopher might be inclined to hold, "If reliability is the standard of intellectual virtue, shouldn't we say that clairvoyance is a virtue *in the possible worlds* of BonJour's examples, if not a virtue in general?" This is a natural thing for philosophers to say, given their schooling, but there is no evidence that this is how people naturally think about the matter. There is no evidence that "the folk" are inclined to relativize virtues and vices to this or that possible world.

I suspect that concerted investigation (not undertaken here) would uncover ample evidence of conservatism, specifically in the normative realm. In many traditional cultures, for example, loyalty to family and friends is treated as a cardinal virtue.[6] This view of loyalty tends to persist even through changes in social and organizational climate, which undermine the value of unqualified loyalty. Members of such cultures, I suspect, would continue to view personal loyalty as a virtue even in *hypothetical* cases where the trait has stipulated unfortunate consequences.

In a slightly different vein, it is common for both critics and advocates of reliabilism to call attention to the relativity of reliability to the domain or circumstances in which the process is used. The question is therefore raised, what is the relevant domain for judging the reliability of a process? A critic like John Pollock (1986, pp. 118–119), for example, observes that color vision is reliable on earth but unreliable in the universe at large. In determining the reliability of color vision, he asks, which domain should be invoked? Finding no satisfactory reply to this question, Pollock takes this as a serious difficulty for reliabilism. Similarly, Sosa (1988 and 1991) notes that an intellectual structure or disposition can be reliable with respect one field of propositions but unreliable with respect to another, and reliable in one environment but unreliable in another. He does not view this as a difficulty for reliabilism, but concludes that any talk of intellectual virtue must be relativized to field and environment.

Neither of these conclusions seems apt, however, for purposes of *description* of our epistemic folkways. It would be a mistake to suppose that ordinary epistemic evaluators are sensitive to these issues. It is likely—or at least plausible—that our ordinary apprehension of the intellectual virtues is rough, unsystematic, and insensitive to any theoretical desirability of relativization to domain or environment. Thus, as long as we are engaged in the description of our epistemic folkways, it is no criticism of the account that it fails to explain what domain or environment is to be used. Nor is it appropriate for the account to introduce relativization where there is no evidence of relativization on the part of the folk.

Of course, we do need an explanatory story of how the folk arrive at their selected virtues and vices. And this presumably requires some reference to the domain in which reliability is judged. However, there may not be much more to the story than the fact that people determine reliability scores from the cases they personally "observe". Alternatively, they *may* regard the observed cases as a sample from which they infer a truth ratio in some wider class of cases. It is doubtful, however, that they have any precise conception of the wider class. They probably don't address this theoretical issue, and don't do (or think) anything that commits them to any particular resolution of it. It would therefore be wrong to expect descriptive epistemology to be fully specific on this dimension.

A similar point holds for the question of process individuation. It is quite possible that the folk do not have highly principled methods for individuating cognitive processes, for "slicing up" virtues and vices. If that is right, it is a mistake to insist that descriptive epistemology uncover such methods. It is no flaw in reliabilism, considered as descriptive epistemology, that it fails to unearth them. It may well be desirable to develop sharper individuation principles for purposes of normative epistemology (a matter we shall address in section III). But the missions and requirements of descriptive and normative epistemology must be kept distinct.

This discussion has assumed throughout that the folk have lists of intellectual virtues and vices. What is the evidence for this? In the moral sphere ordinary language is rich in virtues terminology. By contrast, there are few common labels for intellectual virtues, and those that do exist— 'perceptiveness', 'thoroughness', 'insightfulness', and so forth—are of limited value in the present context. I propose to identify the relevant intellectual virtues (at least those relevant to *justification*) with the belief-forming capacities, faculties, or processes that would be accepted as answers to the question "How does X know?". In answer to this form of question, it is common to reply, "He saw it", "He heard it", "He remembers it", "He infers it from such-and-such evidence", and so forth. Thus, basing belief on seeing, hearing, memory, and (good) inference are in the collection of what the folk regard as intellectual virtues. Consider, for contrast, how anomalous it is to answer the question "How does X know?" with "By guesswork", "By wishful thinking", or "By ignoring contrary evidence". This indicates that *these* modes of belief formation—guessing, wishful thinking, ignoring contrary evidence—are standardly regarded as intellectual *vices*.

They are not ways of obtaining knowledge, nor ways of obtaining justified belief.

Why appeal to "knowledge"-talk rather than "justification"-talk to identify the virtues? Because 'know' has a greater frequency of occurrence than 'justified', yet the two are closely related. Roughly, justified belief is belief acquired by means of the same sorts of capacities, faculties, or processes that yield knowledge in favorable circumstances (i.e., when the resulting belief is true and there are no Gettier complications, or no relevant alternatives).

To sum up the present theory, let me emphasize that it depicts justificational evaluation as involving two stages. The first stage features the acquisition by an evaluator of some set of intellectual virtues and vices. This is where reliability enters the picture. In the second stage, the evaluator applies his list of virtues and vices to decide the epistemic status of targeted beliefs. At this stage, there is no direct consideration of reliability.

There is an obvious analogy here to rule utilitarianism in the moral sphere. Another analogy worth mentioning is Saul Kripke's (1980) theory of *reference-fixing*. According to Kripke, we can use one property to fix a reference to a certain entity, or type of entity; but once this reference has been fixed, that property may cease to play a role in identifying the entity across various possible worlds. For example, we can fix a reference to heat as the phenomenon that causes certain sensations in people. Once heat has been so picked out, this property is no longer needed, or relied upon, in identifying heat. A phenomenon can count as heat in another possible world where it doesn't cause those sensations in people. Similarly, I am proposing, we initially use reliability as a test for intellectual quality (virtue or vice status). Once the quality of a faculty or process has been determined, however, it tends to retain that status in our thinking. At any rate, it isn't reassessed each time we consider a fresh case, especially a purely imaginary and bizarre case like the demon world. Nor is quality relativized to each possible world or environment.

The present version of the virtues theory appears to be a successful variant of reliabilism, capable of accounting for most, if not all, of the most prominent counterexamples to earlier variants of reliabilism.[7] The present approach also makes an innovation in naturalistic epistemology. Whereas earlier naturalistic epistemologists have focused exclusively on the psychology of the epistemic agent, the present paper (along with the preceding essay) also highlights the psychology of the epistemic evaluator.

III

Let us turn now to *normative* scientific epistemology. It was argued briefly in section I that normative scientific epistemology should preserve continuity with our epistemic folkways. At a minimum, it should rest on the same types of evaluative criteria as those on which our commonsense epistemic evaluations rest. Recently, however, Stephen Stich (1990) has disputed this sort of claim. Stich contends that our epistemic folkways are quite idiosyncratic and should not be much heeded in a reformed epistemology. An example he uses to underline his claim of idiosyncracy is the notion of justification as rendered by my "normal worlds" analysis in Goldman 1986. With hindsight, I would agree that that particular analysis makes our ordinary notion of justification look pretty idiosyncratic. But that was the fault of the analysis, not the analysandum. On the present rendering, it looks as if the folk notion of justification is keyed to dispositions to produce a high ratio of true beliefs in the actual world, not in "normal worlds"; and there is nothing idiosyncratic about that. Furthermore, there seem to be straightforward reasons for thinking that true belief is worthy of positive valuation, if only from a pragmatic point of view, which Stich also challenges. The pragmatic utility of true belief is best seen by focusing on a certain subclass of beliefs, viz., beliefs about one's own *plans of action*. Clearly, true beliefs about which courses of action would accomplish one's ends will help secure these ends better than false beliefs. Let proposition $P =$ "Plan N will accomplish my ends" and proposition $P' =$ "Plan N' will accomplish my ends". If P is true and P' is false, I am best off believing the former and not believing the latter. My belief will guide my choice of a plan, and belief in the true proposition (but not the false one) will lead me to choose a plan that *will* accomplish my ends. Stich has other intriguing arguments that cannot be considered here, but it certainly appears that true belief is a perfectly sensible and stable value, not an idiosyncratic one.[8] Thus, I shall assume that normative scientific epistemology should follow in the footsteps of folk practice and use reliability (and other truth-linked standards) as a basis for epistemic evaluation.

If scientific epistemology retains the fundamental standard(s) of folk epistemic assessment, how might it diverge from our epistemic folkways? One possible divergence emerges from William Alston's (1988) account of justification. Although generally sympathetic with reliabilism, Alston urges a kind of constraint not standardly imposed by reliabilism (at least not process reliabilism.) This is the requirement that the processes from which justified beliefs issue must have as their input, or basis, a state *of which the cognizer is aware* (or can easily become aware). Suppose that Alston is right about this as an account of our folk conception of justification. It may well be urged that this ingredient needn't be retained in a scientifically sensitive epistemology. In particular, it may well be claimed that one thing to be learned from cognitive science is that only a small proportion of our cognitive processes operate on consciously accessible inputs. It could therefore be argued that a reformed conception of intellectually virtuous processes should dispense with the "accessibility" requirement.

Alston aside, the point of divergence I wish to examine concerns the psychological units that are chosen as virtues or vices. The lay epistemic evaluator uses casual, unsystematic, and largely introspective methods to carve out the mental faculties and processes responsible for belief formation and revision. Scientific epistemology, by contrast, would utilize the resources of cognitive science to devise a more subtle and sophisticated picture of the mechanisms of belief acquisition. I proceed now to illustrate how this project should be carried out.

An initial phase of the undertaking is to sharpen our conceptualization of the types of cognitive units that should be targets of epistemic evaluation. Lay people are pretty vague about the sorts of entities that qualify as intellectual virtues or vices . In my description of epistemic folkways, I have been deliberately indefinite about these entities, calling them variously "faculties", "processes", "mechanisms", and the like. How should systematic epistemology improve on this score?

A first possibility, enshrined in the practice of historical philosophers, is to take the relevant units to be cognitive *faculties*. This might be translated into modern parlance as *modules*, except that this term has assumed a rather narrow, specialized meaning under Jerry Fodor's (1983) influential treatment of modularity. A better translation might be (cognitive) *systems*, e.g., the visual system, long-term memory, and so forth. Such systems, however, are also suboptimal candidates for units of epistemic analysis. Many beliefs are the outputs of two or more systems working in tandem. For example, a belief consisting in the visual classification of an object ("That is a chair") may involve matching some information in the visual system with a category stored in long-term memory. A preferable unit of analysis, then, might be a *process*, construed as the sort of entity depicted by familiar flow charts of cognitive activity. This sort of diagram depicts a sequence of operations (or sets of parallel operations), ultimately culminating in a belief-like output. Such a sequence may span several cognitive systems. This is the sort of entity I had in mind in previous publications (especially Goldman 1986) when I spoke of "cognitive processes".

Even this sort of entity, however, is not a fully satisfactory unit of analysis. Visual classification, for example, may occur under a variety of degraded conditions. The stimulus may be viewed from an unusual orientation; it may be partly occluded, so that only certain of its parts are visible; and so forth. Obviously, these factors can make a big difference to the reliability of the classification process. Yet it is one and the same process that analyzes the stimulus data and comes to a perceptual "conclusion". So the same process can have different degrees of reliability depending on a variety of parameter values. For purposes of epistemic assessment, it would be instructive to identify the parameters and parameter values that are critically relevant to degrees of reliability. The virtues and vices might then be associated not with processes per se, but with processes operating *with specified parameter values*. Let me illustrate this idea in connection with visual perception.

Consider Irving Biederman's (1987, 1990) theory of object recognition, recognition-by-components (RBC). The core idea of Biederman's theory is that a common concrete object like a chair, a giraffe, or a mushroom is mentally represented as an arrangement of simple primitive volumes called *geons* (*geometrical ions*). These geons, or primitive "components" of objects, are typically symmetrical volumes lacking sharp concavities, such as blocks, cylinders, spheres, and wedges. A set of twenty-four types of geons can be differentiated on the basis of dichotomous or trichotomous contrasts of such attributes as curvature (straight versus curved), size variation (constant versus expanding), and symmetry (symmetrical versus asymmetrical). These twenty-four types of geons can then be combined by means of six relations (e.g., top-of, side-connected, larger-than, etc.) into various possible multiple-geon objects. For example, a cup can be represented as a cylindrical geon that is side-connected to a curved, handle-like geon, whereas a pail can be represented as the same two geons bearing a different relation: the curved, handle-like geon is at the top of the cylindrical geon.

Simplifying a bit, the RBC theory of object recognition posits five stages of processing. (1) In the first stage, low-level vision extracts edge characteristics, such as L's, Y-vertices, and arrows. (2) On the basis of these edge characteristics, viewpoint-independent attributes are detected, such as curved, straight, size-constant, size-expanding, etc. (3) In the next stage, selected geons and their relations are activated. (4) Geon activation leads to the activation of object models, that is, familiar models of simple types of objects, stored in long-term memory. (5) The perceived entity is then "matched" to one of these models, and thereby identified as an instance of that category or classification. (In this description of the five stages, all processing is assumed to proceed bottom-up, but in fact Biederman also allows for elements of top-down processing.)

Under what circumstances, or what parameter values, will such a sequence of processing stages lead to *correct*, or *accurate*, object identification? Biederman estimates that there are approximately 3,000 common basic-level, or entry-level, names in English for familiar concrete objects. However, people are probably familiar with approximately ten times that number of object models because, among other things, some entry-level terms (such as *lamp* and *chair*) have several readily distinguishable object models. Thus, an estimate of the number of familiar object models would be on the order of 30,000.

Some of these object models are simple, requiring fewer than six components to appear complete; others are complex, requiring six to nine components to appear complete. Nonetheless, Biederman gives theoretical considerations and empirical results suggesting that an arrangement of only *two* or *three* geons almost always suffices to specify a simple object and even most complex ones. Consider the number of possible two-geon and three-geon objects. With twenty-four possible geons, Biederman says, the variations in relations can produce 186,624 possible two-geon objects. A third geon with its possible relations to another geon yields over 1.4 billion possible three-geon objects. Thus, if the 30,000 familiar object models were distributed homogeneously throughout the space of possible object models, Biederman reasons, an arrangements of two or three geons would almost always be sufficient to specify any object. Indeed, Biederman puts forward a *principle of geon recovery*: If an arrangement of two or three geons can be recovered from the image, objects can be quickly recognized even when they are occluded, rotated in depth, novel, extensively degraded, or lacking in customary detail, color, and texture.

The principle of three-geon sufficiency is supported by the following empirical results. An object such as an elephant or an airplane is complex, requiring six or more geons to appear complete. Nonetheless, when only three components were displayed (the others being occluded), subjects still made correct identifications in almost 80 percent of the nine-component objects and more than 90 percent of the six-component objects. Thus, the reliability conferred by just three geons and their relations is quite high. Although Biederman doesn't give data for recovery of just one or two geons of complex objects, presumably the reliability is much lower. Here we presumably have examples of parameter values—(1) number of components in the complete object, and (2) number of recovered components—that make a significant difference to reliability. The same process, understood as an instantiation of one and the same flow diagram, can have different levels of reliability depending on the values of the critical parameters in question. Biederman's work illustrates how research in cognitive science can identify both the relevant flow of activity and the crucial parameters. The quality (or "virtue") of a particular (token) process of belief-acquisition depends not only on the flow diagram that is instantiated, but on the parameter values instantiated in the specific tokening of the diagram.

Until now reliability has been my sole example of epistemic quality. But two other dimensions of epistemic quality—which also invoke truth or accuracy—should be added to our evaluative repertoire. These are *question-answering power* and *question-answering speed*. (These are certainly reflected in our epistemic folkways, though not well reflected in the concepts of knowledge or justification.) If a person asks himself a question, such as "What kind of object is that?" or "What is the solution to this algebra problem?", there are three possible outcomes: (A) he comes up with *no answer* (at least none that he believes), (B) he forms a belief in an answer which is *correct*, and (C) he forms a belief in an answer which is *incorrect*. Now reliability is the ratio of cases in category (B) to cases in categories (B) and (C), that is, the proportion of true beliefs to beliefs. Question-answering *power*, on the other hand, is the ratio of (B) cases to cases in categories (A), (B), and (C). Notice that it is possible for a system to be highly reliable but not very powerful. An object-recognition system that never yields outputs in category (C) is perfectly reliable, but it may not be very powerful, since most of its outputs could fall in (A) and only a few in (B). The human (visual) object-recognition system, by-contrast, is very powerful as well as quite reliable. In general, it is power and not just reliability that is an important epistemic desideratum in a cognitive system or process.

Speed introduces another epistemic desideratum beyond reliability and power. This is another dimension on which cognitive science can shed light. It might have been thought, for example, that correct identification of complex objects like an airplane or an elephant requires more time than simple objects such as a flashlight or a cup. In fact, there is no advantage for simple objects, as Biederman's empirical studies indicate. This lack of advantage for simple objects could be explained by the geon theory in terms of parallel activation: geons are activated in parallel rather than through a serial trace of the contours of the object. Whereas more geons would require more processing time under a serial trace, this is not required under parallel activation.

Let us turn now from perception to learning, especially language learning. Learnability theory (Gold 1967; Osherson, Stob, and Weinstein 1985) uses a criterion of learning something like our notion of power, viz., the ability or inability of the learning process to arrive at a correct hypothesis after some fixed period of time. This is called *identification in the limit*. In language learning, it is assumed that the child is exposed to some information in the world, e.g., a set of sentences parents utter, and the learning task is to construct a hypothesis that correctly singles out the language being spoken. The child is presumed to have a learning strategy: an algorithm that generates a succession of hypotheses in response to accumulating evidence. What learning strategy might lead to success? *That* children learn their native language is evident to common sense. But *how* they learn it—what algorithm they possess that constitutes the requisite intellectual virtue—is only being revealed through research in cognitive science.

We may distinguish two types of evidence that a child might receive about its language (restricting attention to the language's grammar): positive evidence and negative evidence. Positive evidence refers to information about which strings of words *are* grammatical sentences in the language, and negative evidence refers to information about which strings of words are *not* grammatical sentences. Interestingly, it appears that children do not receive (much) negative evidence. The absence of negative evidence makes the learning task much harder. What algorithm might be in use that produces success in this situation?

An intriguing proposal is advanced by Robert Berwick (1986; cf. Pinker 1990). In the absence of negative evidence, the danger for a learning strategy is that it might hypothesize a language that is a superset of the correct language, i.e., one that includes all grammatical sentences of the target language plus some additional sentences as well. Without negative evidence, the child will be unable to learn that the "extra" sentences are incorrect, i.e., don't belong to the target language. A solution is to avoid ever hypothesizing an overly general hypothesis. Hypotheses should be *ordered* in such a way that the child always guesses the narrowest possible hypothesis or language at each step. This is called the *subset principle*. Berwick finds evidence of this principle at work in a number of domains, including concepts, sound systems, and syntax. Here, surely, is a kind of intellectual disposition that is not dreamed of by the "folk".

IV

We have been treating scientific epistemology from a purely reliabilist, or veritistic (truth-linked), vantage point. It should be stressed, however, that scientific epistemology can equally be pursued from other evaluative perspectives. You need not be a reliabilist to accept the proposed role of cognitive science in scientific epistemology. Let me illustrate this idea with the so-called *responsibilist* approach, which characterizes a justified or rational belief as one that is the product of epistemically responsible action (Kornblith 1983; Code 1987), or perhaps epistemically responsible processes (Talbott 1990). Actually, this conception of justification is approximated by my own *weak* conception of justification, as presented in chapter 7. Both depict a belief as justified as long as its acquisition is *blameless* or *nonculpable*. Given limited resources and limited information, a belief might be acquired nonculpably even though its generating processes are not virtuous according to the reliabilist criterion.

Let us start with a case of Hilary Kornblith. Kornblith argues that the justificational status of a belief does not depend exclusively on the *reasoning* process that produces that belief. Someone might reason perfectly well from the evidence he possesses, but fail to be epistemically responsible because he neglects to acquire certain further evidence. Kornblith gives the case of Jones, a headstrong young physicist eager to hear the praise of his colleagues. After Jones presents a paper, a senior colleague makes an objection. Unable to tolerate criticism, Jones pays no attention to the objection. The criticism is devastating, but it makes no impact on Jones's beliefs because he does not even hear it. Jones's conduct is epistemically irresponsible. But his reasoning process from the evidence he actually possesses—which does not include the colleague's evidence—may be quite impeccable.

The general principle suggested by Kornblith's example seems to be something like this. Suppose that an agent (1) believes P, (2) does not believe Q, and (3) would be unjustified in believing P if he did believe Q. If, finally, he is *culpable* for failing to believe Q (for being ignorant of Q), then he is unjustified in believing P. In Kornblith's case, P is the physics thesis that Jones believes. Q consists in the criticisms of this thesis presented by Jones's senior colleague. Jones does not believe Q, but if he did believe Q, he would be unjustified in believing P. However, although Jones does not believe Q, he is culpable for failing to believe it (for being ignorant of these criticisms), because he *ought* to have paid attention to his colleague and acquired belief in Q. Therefore, Jones's belief in P is unjustified.

The provision that the agent be *culpable* for failing to believe Q is obviously critical to the principle in question. If the criticisms of Jones's thesis had never been presented within his hearing, nor published in any scientific journal, then Jones's ignorance of Q would not be culpable. And he might well be justified in believing P. But in Kornblith's version of the case, it seems clear that Jones *is* culpable for failing to believe Q, and that is why he is unjustified in believing P.

Under what circumstances is an agent culpable for failing to believe something? That is a difficult question. In a general discussion of culpable ignorance, Holly Smith (1983) gives an example of a doctor who exposes an infant to unnecessarily high concentrations of oxygen and thereby causes severe eye damage. Suppose that the latest issue of the doctor's medical journal describes a study establishing this relationship, but the doctor hasn't read this journal. Presumably his ignorance of the relationship would be culpable; he *should* have read his journal. But suppose that the study had appeared in an obscure journal to which he does not subscribe, or had only appeared one day prior to this particular treatment. Is he still culpable for failing to have read the study by the time of the treatment?

Smith categorizes her example of the doctor as a case of *deficient investigation*. The question is (both for morals and for epistemology), What amounts and kinds of investigation are, in general, sufficient or deficient? We may distinguish two types of investigation: (1) investigation into the physical world (including statements that have been made by other agents), and (2) investigation into the agent's own storehouse of information, lodged in long-term memory. Investigation of the second sort is particularly relevant to questions about the role of cognitive science, so I shall concentrate here on this topic. Actually, the term 'investigation' is not wholly apt when it comes to long-term memory. But it is adequate as a provisional delineation of the territory.

To illustrate the primary problem that concerns me here, I shall consider two examples drawn from the work of Amos Tversky and Daniel Kahneman. The first example pertains to their study of the "conjunction fallacy" (Tversky and Kahneman 1983). Suppose that a subject assigns a higher probability to a conjunction like "Linda is a bank teller and is active in the feminist movement" than to one of its own conjuncts, "Linda is a bank teller". According to the standard probability calculus, no conjunction can have a higher probability than one of its conjuncts. Let us assume that the standard probability calculus is, in some sense, "right". Does it follow that a person is irrational, or unjustified, to make probability assignments that violate this calculus? This is subject to dispute. One might argue that it does not follow, in general, from the fact that M is an arbitrary mathematical truth, that anyone who believes something contrary to M is ipso facto irrational or unjustified. After all, mathematical facts are not all so transparent that it would be a mark of irrationality (or the like) to fail to believe any of them. However, let us set this issue aside. Let us imagine the case of a subject who has studied probability theory and learned the conjunction rule in particular. Let us further suppose that this subject would retract at least one of his two probability assignments if he recognized that they violate the conjunction rule. (This is by no means true of all subjects that Tversky and Kahneman studied.) Nonetheless, our imagined subject fails to think of the conjunction rule in connection with the Linda example. Shall we say that the failure to recover the conjunction rule from long-term memory is a *culpable omission*, one that makes his maintenance of his probability judgments unjustified? Is this like the example of Jones who culpably fails to learn of his senior colleague's criticism? Or is it a case of nonculpable nonrecovery of a relevant fact, a fact that is, in some sense, "within reach", but legitimately goes unnoticed?

This raises questions about when a failure to recover or activate something from long-term memory is culpable, and that is precisely a problem that invites detailed reflection on mechanisms of memory retrieval. This is not a matter to which epistemologists have devoted much attention, partly because little has been known about memory retrieval until fairly recently. But now that cognitive science has at least the beginnings of an understanding of this phenomenon, normative epistemology should give careful attention to that research. Of course, we cannot expect the issue of culpability to be resolved directly by empirical facts about cognitive mechanisms. Such facts are certainly relevant, however.

The main way that retrieval from memory works is by *content addressing* (cf. Potter 1990). Content addressing means starting retrieval with part of the content of the to-be-remembered material, which provides an "address" to the place in memory where identical or similar material is located. Once a match has been made, related information laid down by previously encoded associations will be retrieved, such as the name or appearance of the object. For example, if you are asked to think of a kind of bird that is yellow, a location in memory is addressed where "yellow bird" is located. "Yellow bird" has previously been associated with "canary", so the latter information is retrieved. Note, however, that there are some kinds of information that cannot be used as a retrieval address, although the information is in memory. For example, what word for a family relationship (e.g., *grandmother*) ends in *w*? Because you have probably never encoded that piece of information explicitly, you may have trouble thinking of the word (hint: not *niece*). Although it is easy to move from the word in question (*nephew*) to "word for a family relationship ending in *w*", it is not easy to move in the opposite direction.

Many subjects who are given the Linda example presumably have not established any prior association between such pairs of propositions ("Linda is a bank teller and is active in the feminist movement" and "Linda is a bank teller") and the conjunction rule. Furthermore, in some versions of the experiment, subjects are not given these propositions adjacent to one another. So it may not occur to the subject even to *compare* the two probability judgments, although an explicit comparison would be more likely to address a location in memory that contains an association with the conjunction rule. In short, it is not surprising, given the nature of memory retrieval, that the material provided in the specified task does not automatically yield retrieval of the conjunction rule for the typical subject.

Should the subject deliberately search memory for facts that might retrieve the conjunction rule? Is omission of such deliberate search a culpable omission? Perhaps, but how much deliberate attention or effort ought to be devoted to this task? (Bear in mind that agents typically have numerous intellectual tasks on their agendas, which vie for attentional resources.) Furthermore, what form of search is obligatory? Should memory be probed with the question, "Is there any rule of probability theory that my (tentative) probability judgments violate?" This is a plausible search probe for someone who has already been struck by a thought of the conjunction rule and its possible violation, or whose prior experiences with probability experiments make him suspicious. But for someone who has not already retrieved the conjunction rule, or who has not had experiences with probability experiments that alert him to such "traps", what reason is there to be on the lookout for violations of the probability calculus? It is highly questionable, then, that the subject engaged in "deficient investigation" in failing to probe memory with the indicated question.

Obviously, principles of culpable retrieval failure are not easy to come by. Any principles meriting our endorsement would have to be sensitive to facts about memory mechanisms.

A similar point can be illustrated in connection with the so-called *availability heuristic*, which was formulated by Tversky and Kahneman (1973) and explored by Richard Nisbett and Lee Ross (1980). A cognizer uses the availability heuristic when he estimates the frequency of items in a category by the instances he can *bring to mind* through memory retrieval, imagination, or perception. The trouble with this heuristic, as the abovementioned researchers indicate, is that the instances one brings to mind are not necessarily well correlated with objective frequency. Various *biases* may produce discrepancies: biases in initial sampling, biases in attention, or biases in manner of encoding or storing the category instances.

Consider some examples provided by Nisbett and Ross: one hypothetical example and one actual experimental result. (1) (Hypothetical example) An Indiana businessman believes that a disproportionate number of Hoosiers are famous. This is partly because of a bias in initial exposure, but also because he is more likely to notice and remember when the national media identify a famous person as a Hoosier. (2) (Actual experiment) A group of subjects consistently errs in judging the relative frequency of words with R in first position versus words with R in third position. This is an artifact of how words are encoded in memory (as already illustrated in connection with *nephew*). We don't normally code words by their third letters, and hence words having R in the third position are less "available" (from memory) than words beginning with R. But comparative availability is not a reliable indicator of actual frequency.

Nisbett and Ross (p. 23) view these uses of the availability heuristic as normative errors. "An indiscriminate use of the availability heuristic," they write, "clearly can lead people into serious judgmental errors." They grant, though, that in many contexts perceptual salience, memorability, and imaginability may be relatively unbiased and well correlated with true frequency or causal significance. They conclude: "The normative status of using the availability heuristic ... thus depend[s] on the judgmental domain and context. People are not, of course, totally unaware that simple availability criteria must sometimes be discounted. For example, few people who were asked to estimate the relative number of moles versus cats in their neighborhood would conclude 'there must be more cats because I've seen several of them but I've never seen a mole.' Nevertheless, as this book documents, people often fail to distinguish between legitimate and superficially similar, but illegitimate, uses of the availability heuristic."

We can certainly agree with Nisbett and Ross that the availability heuristic can often lead to incorrect estimates of frequency. But does it follow that uses of the heuristic are often *illegitimate* in a sense that implies the epistemic *culpability* of the users? One might retort, "These cognizers are using all the evidence that they possess, at least *consciously* possess. Why are they irresponsible if they extrapolate from this evidence?" The objection apparently lurking in Nisbett and Ross's minds is that these cognizers *should* be aware that they are using a systematically biased heuristic. This is a piece of evidence that they *ought* to recognize. And their failure to recognize it, and/or their failure to take it into account, makes their judgmental performance culpable. Nisbett and Ross's invocation of the cat/mole example makes the point particularly clear. If someone can appreciate that the relative number of cats and moles *he has seen* is not a reliable indicator of the relative number of cats and moles in the neighborhood, surely he can be expected to appreciate that the relative number of famous Hoosiers *he can think of* is not a reliable indicator of the proportion of famous people who are Hoosiers!

Is it so clear that people *ought* to be able to appreciate the biased nature of their inference pattern in the cases in question? Perhaps it seems transparent in the mole and Hoosier cases; but consider the letter *R* example. What is (implicitly) being demanded here of the cognizer? First, he must perform a feat of meta-cognitive analysis: he must recognize that he is inferring the relative proportion of the two types of English words from his own constructed samples of these types. Second, he must notice that his construction of these samples depends on the way words are encoded in memory. Finally, he must realize that this implies a bias in ease of retrieval. All these points may seem obvious in hindsight, once pointed out by researchers in the field. But how straightforward or obvious are these matters if they haven't already been pointed out to the subject? Of course, we currently have no "metric" of straightforwardness or obviousness. That is precisely the sort of thing we need, however, to render judgments of culpability in this domain. We need a systematic account of how difficult it is, starting from certain information and preoccupations, to generate and apprehend the truth of certain relevant hypotheses. Such an account clearly hinges on an account of the inferential and hypothesis-generating strategies that are natural to human beings. This is just the kind of thing that cognitive science is, in principle, capable of delivering. So epistemology must work hand in hand with the science of the mind. The issues here are not purely scientific, however. Judgments of justifiedness and unjustifiedness, on the responsibilist conception, require assessments of culpability and nonculpability. Weighing principles for judgments of culpability is a matter for philosophical attention. (One question, for example, is how much epistemic culpability depends on voluntariness.) Thus, a mix of philosophy and psychology is needed to produce acceptable principles of justifiedness.

Notes

I wish to thank Tom Senor, Holly Smith, and participants in a conference at Rice University for helpful comments on earlier versions of this paper.

1. Normative scientific epistemology corresponds to what I elsewhere call *epistemics* (see Goldman 1986). Although epistemics is not restricted to the assessment of *psychological* processes, that is the topic of the present paper. So we are here dealing with what I call *primary epistemics*.

2. Sosa's approach is spelled out most fully in Sosa 1985, 1988, and 1991.

3. My own previous formulations of reliabilism have not been so simple. Both "What Is Justified Belief?" (chapter 6 of this volume) and *Epistemology and Cognition* (Goldman 1986) had provisions—e.g., the non-undermining provision of *Epistemology and Cognition*—that could help accommodate BonJour's examples. It is not entirely clear, however, how well these qualifications succeeded with the Norman case, described below.

4. Tom Senor presented the following example to his philosophy class at the University of Arkansas. Norman is working at his desk when out of the blue he is hit (via clairvoyance) with a very distinct and vivid impression of the president at the Empire State Building. The image is phenomenally distinct from a regular visual impression but is in some respects similar and of roughly equal force. The experience is so overwhelming that Norman just can't help but form the belief that the president is in New York. About half of Senor's class judged that in this case Norman justifiably believes that the president is in New York. Senor points out, in commenting on this paper, that their judgments are readily explained by the present account, because the description of the clairvoyance process makes it sufficiently similar to vision to be easily "matched" to that virtue.

5. Since some of these opinions may be true and others false, people's lists of virtues and vices may have varying degrees of accuracy. The "real" status of a trait as a virtue or vice is independent of people's opinions about that trait. However, since the enterprise of descriptive epistemology is to describe and explain evaluators' judgments, we need to advert to the traits they *believe* to be virtues or vices, i.e., the ones on their mental lists.

6. Thanks to Holly Smith for this example. She cites Riding 1989 (chap. 6) for relevant discussion.

7. It should be noted that this theory of justification is intended to capture what I call in chapter 7 the *strong* conception of justification. The complementary conception of *weak* justification will receive attention in section IV of this essay.

8. For further discussion of Stich, see Goldman 1991.

Part III
Social Epistemology

Chapter 10
Foundations of Social Epistemics

1. Introduction

Epistemology has historically been preoccupied with individual knowers and their minds. This preoccupation has a plausible rationale. Knowers are individuals, and knowledge is generated by mental processes and lodged in the mind-brain. Thus, despite isolated attempts to dispense with the knowing subject (e.g., Popper 1972), it is entirely fitting for epistemology to be concerned with individual knowers and their minds.

But concentration on the individual to the exclusion of the social is inappropriate. The bulk of an adult's worldview is deeply indebted to her social world. It can largely be traced to social interactions, to influences exerted by other knowers, primarily through the vehicle of language. It is imperative, then, for epistemology to have a social dimension. How this social dimension should be conceived and structured, however, is far from apparent. No well-entrenched epistemological tradition provides such a structure. This paper lays the foundation for one such structure, for one conception of social epistemology.

In a recent book, *Epistemology and Cognition* (Goldman 1986), I develop a conception of epistemology as a multidisciplinary subject, orchestrated and directed by philosophy but requiring contributions from other fields as well. I call this multidisciplinary conception *epistemics*. *Epistemology and Cognition* focuses on one branch of epistemics: primary individual epistemics. That branch centers on basic processes of the mind-brain, and is therefore allied with the cognitive sciences. In this paper I elaborate the conception of the social branch of epistemics and say a few words about its disciplinary alliances.

2. The Evaluative Task of Social Epistemics

To begin thinking about social epistemology, consider the profile of belief-states of a community, group, or culture. Under 'belief-states' I mean to include varying degrees of confidence as well as full-fledged 'acceptance'. For simplicity, though, I concentrate on states of binary, all-or-none belief.

One possible conception of social epistemology is purely descriptive and explanatory. It might describe belief-profiles of different groups and seek explanations of them in terms of social interchange. A diachronic perspective is especially inviting: a group's belief-profile at time $t + 1$ might be explained by its profile at time t together with communication transactions during the interval. Many disciplines and subdisciplines are currently engaged in studying belief-profiles from approximately this perspective. History, sociology, anthropology, political science, social psychology, and so on explore science, scholarship, political opinion, and popular culture with a view to understanding ideational change.

My conception of social epistemology has some affinities with these disciplines, but the epistemological aim is not coterminous with theirs. These disciplines have strictly descriptive and explanatory goals, while the central aim of epistemology is normative, evaluative, or critical. It does not merely aim to say how and why belief-profiles change or evolve, but to appraise such changes along some epistemologically relevant dimensions. Mechanisms of intellectual influence interest the social epistemologist, but not for their own sake. The epistemologist wishes to investigate epistemologically relevant properties of the mechanisms. What those epistemic properties are remains to be specified.

Despite this difference of emphasis, I do favor a wide scope for social epistemology. On my view all social influences on belief are of potential interest to social epistemology, whatever the contents of the beliefs. Such breadth of scope might be viewed with suspicion in some quarters. Isn't this approach all too congenial to the so-called 'strong program' in the sociology of science (Bloor 1976; Barnes 1977)? According to the strong program, social factors are explanatorily relevant to *all* scientific activity. Critics of this program reply that a sociological explanation of scientific belief is in order only when the target scientist contravenes the norms of scientific rationality. This is made explicit by Larry Laudan (1977, p. 202) in what he calls the *arationality assumption*: "the sociology of knowledge may step in to explain beliefs if and only if those beliefs cannot be explained in terms of their rational merits". The arationality assumption establishes a division of labor between the historian of ideas and the sociologist of knowledge: the latter may step in only when there is some deviation from the norm of rationality. In William Newton-Smith's (1981) formulation, sociology is only for deviants.

I take exception to this arationality assumption. There is no reason why one and the same belief, scientific or otherwise, cannot be explained both in rational and in social terms. This leaves very wide scope, in principle, for social explanations of belief. I agree with Laudan that it is very unlikely that there are laws governing belief that feature *exclusively* sociological variables in their antecedents. Social or sociological factors could not provide a 'complete' explanation of belief. But there is no reason why social factors cannot influence belief-formation in conjunction with other, indisputably rational, factors. Perhaps their influence may be exerted via the mediation of psychological events that figure in a rational explanation (for example, in what Newton-Smith (1981), calls a 'minirat' explanation). Something like this is granted by Laudan too in a more recent paper (Laudan 1984). He acknowledges the possibility of a 'sociology of the rational', that would explain, for example, why different conceptions of rationality evolve in different cultures. I would go further, however, and point out that rationality might partly consist in certain forms of social interchange. Some styles of debate and mutual criticism, some modes of doxastic response to the arguments of others, may be partly constitutive of rationality. So there is no tension between social and rational belief-causation.

Let me cite some commonplace types of social explanations that are compatible with rational explanations of belief. First, suppose a belief is formed rationally as a function of several competing hypotheses and the available evidence. The hypotheses surveyed, however, were generated by a number of different scientists, each working in his own research tradition, partly spurred and influenced by the competition of rival research traditions. In this case, disciplinary fragmentation—a certain social fact—is part of the origin of the competing hypotheses that the working scientist considers. Second, a partial cause of the scientist's entry into the discipline may be the financial or reputational incentives of organized science. This reward structure, of course, does not by itself explain the scientific content of an explanandum belief. But it is one of many operative causes that ultimately lead to the belief. Third, the rational formation of a belief involves the application of a suitable methodology, which the target scientist employs. Whence this methodology? The scientist may have learned it from his mentors, who in turn acquired it from other members of the scientific community, who (perhaps rationally) enforce that methodology as a condition for respect and acceptance within that intellectual matrix (cf. Whitley 1984). In all these cases, the many causes of the belief include some social factors; but these in no way undermine a rational explanation of the belief.

My concurrence with the Edinburgh school on the wide scope for social factors is potentially misleading, for its adherents often seem to have a more specific agenda with which I disagree. They seem to think that scientific beliefs can generally be explained by certain kinds of social factors, ones that would normally be counted as external to the proper conduct of science, such as ideological or political interests, or influences of the general intellectual milieu. Here I part company with them. In the case studies to which strong programmers often appeal, a central issue is whether the predominant influences on scientific belief have been 'external' or 'internal' to the discipline. (See Forman 1971 and Shapin 1975, for examples.) I generally side here with the 'internalist' historical accounts rather than the 'externalist' ones. (See Hendry 1980 and Cantor 1975 for rebuttals of Forman and Shapin, respectively.) This does not mean that I oppose social explanations in these cases. Internal explanations can be social explanations; intradisciplinary influences can be interpersonal influences. It is a mistake to assimilate the external/internal distinction to the social/asocial distinction. (It should be acknowledged that this point is sometimes expressly stated by strong programmers. See Bloor 1973, pp. 190–91, Bloor 1976, p. 4, and Shapin 1982, p. 197. However, they seem to have a marked preference for external explanations.)

Notice that nothing in my epistemological position forces me to take one or another side of the internal/external dispute. My view of the historical facts is, therefore, incidental. In fact, it would not conflict with my epistemological stance even if there were no interesting social explanations of many beliefs. All I wish to defend is the *potential* scope of social factors. Details of particular historical events have no implications for this position.

Other matters of disagreement, however, are more critical to the theoretical issues of this paper. For example, I think it is important to deny the strong program's contention that explanations of a belief cannot refer to its truth, or the state of affairs that makes it true (on this point, see Newton-Smith 1981, pp. 252–253). Even more significantly, I strongly disagree with the Edinburgh school's endorsement of epistemic relativism. This topic will be treated at length in later sections.

I have defended the role of social factors in belief *explanation*. But is this critical for the epistemologist, who is concerned primarily with *normative* assessment? Shouldn't the epistemologist restrict attention to questions of scientific methodology, to canons of logic and evidence? While the epistemologist may acknowledge the social roots of belief, even scientific belief, why is this acknowledgment epistemologically significant? How can it affect matters of epistemic evaluation or appraisal?

Although this question is addressed at length later, some preliminary answers may be given here. Our previous examples provide hints of evaluative subject-matter. Consider the existence of rival research traditions, of ongoing competition, in a discipline. The epistemologist may be interested in evaluating the merits of such competition. The aim here is not to evaluate any specific belief, as rational or irrational, for example. (Rationality is not the only possible dimension of epistemic appraisal.) The epistemologist may be interested in the epistemic consequences of intellectual rivalry. Is such rivalry epistemically beneficial, and if so, how and why? A similar point holds for the social and economic reward structures that characterize modern science and other fact-finding institutions. The existence and nature of such structures are stressed and explored by sociologists (e.g., Merton 1973). What interests the epistemologist are the epistemic consequences of such structures.

It should also be stressed that social epistemology is not restricted to the epistemology of science or scientists. It includes the epistemology of the common person. Far from confining attention to belief-profiles of specialists, it can be concerned with belief-profiles of entire cultures. Lay people often form beliefs about scientific subjects and on policy issues closely linked to scientific matters. But lay people have neither the time, the interest, nor the training to utilize technical methodologies that specialists employ in forming beliefs on these matters. Rather, their belief-formation relies heavily on judgments of authority. The epistemological question here is: what are the proper procedures for appeal to authorities? How should community decisions reflect expert opinion? Here too we have normative questions about social or inter-personal structures that fall in the bailiwick of epistemology.

3. Relativism, Consensualism, and Expertism

In section 2 I argued for an evaluative approach to social epistemology. But what, exactly, are the objects to be evaluated? And what is the basis, criterion, or standard by which evaluations should be made? In this section I consider a variety of possible targets and bases for evaluation and briefly indicate my preference. My own choice is explored more fully in sections 4 and 5.

There are at least three possible targets of evaluation for social epistemology: (A) beliefs of individuals, (B) social belief-profiles, and (C) social practices, procedures, and institutions. The candidacy of (B) and of (C) needs no explanation, but what about (A)? How could an *individual's* belief be an object of evaluation for *social* epistemology? Quite simply, a belief might be evaluated by reference to some properties of the community to which the individual belongs. Has the belief been generated by methods of which the community approves? Does it agree in content with other people's beliefs? Samples of these approaches will be examined, as well as approaches invoking (B) and (C) as evaluative targets.

Let me turn next to alternative bases of evaluation for social epistemology. One possible basis, as just indicated, is the set of methods endorsed by the community or group. A second possible basis is *consensus*, either the existence or promotion of consensus, or agreement with consensual opinions. This second, *consensualist*, basis bears a similarity to the first basis, except that consensualism concerns agreement in belief *content* whereas the first basis concerns agreement in *method*. The third type of basis is *expertism*. It would evaluate objects either in terms of promotion of

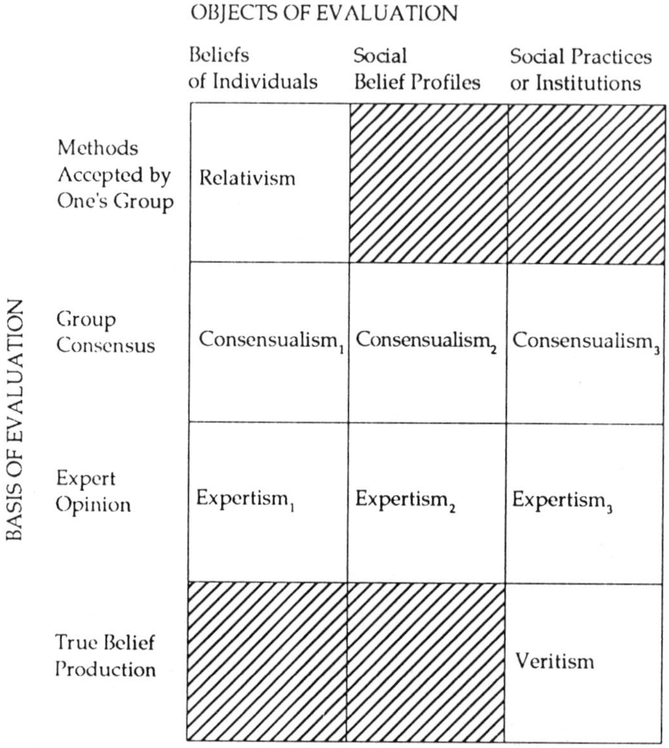

OBJECTS OF EVALUATION

Figure 10.1

expertise or in terms of agreement with expert opinion. The fourth basis I call *veritism*. It would make evaluations by reference to the production of true belief.

Combining the three possible objects of evaluation with the four possible bases for evaluation, a 3 × 4 matrix of possible positions can be generated, as shown in figure 10.1. However, I construct no intelligible portraits of social epistemology that correspond to the middle and right squares of row 1 nor to the left and middle squares of row 4. This leaves us with eight possible positions.

In addition to objects and bases (or standards) of evaluation, an important question for any evaluative subject is its *terms* of evaluation. In epistemology, several terms are widely in use, including 'rational' and 'warranted' (or 'justified'). Of the eight possible positions that have been generated, some are more naturally articulated with one evaluative term and others with another. I shall comment on the most plausible evaluative term for each of the eight positions.

Let me now explore these eight positions in some detail. The upper left square represents a position I call *relativism*. (Another possible label is *parochialism*.) Relativism consists of three theses: (A) There are no universal, context-free, super-cultural, or transhistorical standards by which to judge different belief-forming methods. (This thesis might be called *nihilism*, or *anti-universalism*.) (B) Whatever methods a group accepts are *right for them*. (C) An individual's belief is *socially warranted* (or rational) if and only if this belief is formed (or sustained) by methods that are accepted by the individual's group.

I am not sure this position is fully endorsed by any identifiable theorist. Some theorists, such as Barry Barnes and David Bloor (1982) and Richard Rorty (1979), clearly endorse thesis (A), the nihilist or anti-universalist strand of this position. They also appear to endorse (B). But it is debatable whether they endorse (C). Rorty, however, favors an account of rationality and epistemic authority in terms of "what society lets us say"; he identifies "the community as source of epistemic authority" (Rorty 1979, pp. 174, 188). So perhaps he accepts the entire version of relativism I am describing. There are also affinities with Thomas Kuhn (1970), who sees the scientific community's current paradigm as the only available instrument by which to appraise a member scientist's beliefs.

One difficulty with relativism is that a believer may belong to several communities, which have conflicting sets of approved methods. A scientist, for example, may belong to (a) a general culture, (b) a certain scientific discipline, and (c) a faction within that discipline which champions a distinctive methodology. A given belief of his may conform with his own faction's tenets, but violate methodological strictures accepted by most members of the discipline. How is the belief to be evaluated?

The relativist may retreat to the view that the belief is warranted *relative* to one community and unwarranted *relative* to another. But this adds a further dimension of relativization not in the initial formulation. Suppose we consider this kind of relativism, however, as a candidate framework for social epistemology. How interesting and significant a framework would it be?

It strikes me as quite uninteresting and impoverished. What would the tasks of social epistemology consist in, on this approach? They would consist in (i) identifying a given community's methods, and (ii) determining whether any specified individual has complied with or violated those methods. This combination of tasks is suited, perhaps, to the historian, the sociologist, or the anthropologist. But it has little resemblance to any traditional philosophical mission of epistemology.

The relativist may argue that, nonetheless, this is the only defensible evaluative mission. What grounds are there for such a claim? One proffered ground might be *descriptive* epistemic relativism, the doctrine that different groups and communities, especially at different historical periods, have in fact endorsed different intellectual methodologies. This descriptive thesis is, of course, uncontroversial. But the present thesis of evaluative relativism hardly follows from it. Mere historical diversity does not entail that the only proper standard of evaluation for a believer's performance is the methods of his or her group.

A second possible rationale for theses (B) and (C) of evaluative relativism is its thesis (A), nihilism or anti-universalism. According to nihilism there are no *other*, super-cultural, standards for evaluating a believer's performance (or any other potential object of social-epistemological evaluation). So the only remaining sensible benchmark are the methods of the believer's own group. (Surely it makes no sense to evaluate a believer's performance by the methods of some other group, especially a culturally or temporally inaccessible group.) The plausibility of evaluative relativism thus hinges, in large measure, on the defensibility of epistemic nihilism. But I shall argue that nihilism is mistaken. There are universal, context-free, standards of evaluation.

Let me turn now to the consensualist approach to social epistemology, represented by row 2 of our matrix. Clear-cut endorsements of consensualism are hard to find, though many discussions hint at it. In the logical positivist literature, and elsewhere, science is often touted as exemplary because of its *intersubjectivity*, where this is often understood as the ability to settle disputes among subjects. Settling a dispute, in turn, is the generation of agreement or consensus among disputants. One unambiguous statement of this position is by John Ziman: "The goal of science ... is to achieve the maximum degree of *consensuality*" (Ziman 1978, p. 6).

Three different versions of consensualism correspond to the three entries in row 2, which differ in their evaluative objects. The column 1 version focuses on individual beliefs. It says that an individual belief is warranted if and only if it accords with the consensus in the believer's community. The column 2 version focuses on social belief-profiles as objects of evaluation. A social belief-profile is deemed rational if and only if it has a high degree of consensus. The column 3 variant takes social practices and institutions as evaluative targets. Consensualism in this form maintains that practices and institutions are rational to the extent that they produce consensus.

I have mentioned one possible attraction of consensualism: its connection with dispute settling. One other possible attraction is its resemblance to coherentism, which might make it appealing to those who find coherentism congenial. To develop this theme, a theorist might begin by distinguishing two species of warrant (both applicable to individual beliefs): *individual warrant* and *social warrant*. Each kind of warrant could then receive a coherentist treatment. Intrapersonal coherence could be advanced as a theory of individual warrant while interpersonal coherence—agreement with one's peers—would provide a theory of social warrant. (However, these types of coherence are not really the same. Interpersonal coherence is shared belief in the same propositions, whereas intrapersonal coherence is belief in a set of different but appropriately related propositions, e.g., consistent propositions, mutually supporting propositions, or the like.) On an alternative line of development, coherence could be advanced as a theory of rationality for individual beliefs, while consensus is endorsed as a theory of rationality for social belief-profiles.

Whatever the initial force of these attractions, consensualism in any form is plagued with problems. Let us start with consensualism$_1$ which takes individual beliefs as the target of evaluation. Let us assume that the *term* of evaluation, for which consensualism is the candidate standard, is 'socially warranted'. (The idea here is that a belief might be socially warranted but not individually warranted, or conversely. Whether these two types of warrant are supposed to be commensurable, and if so how, is moot.) The first problem here is the previously encountered one of how to identify the relevant community. A cognizer typically belongs to many communities. Belief P may match the consensus in one community but conflict with the preponderance of opinion in another. Which community fixes the belief's social warrant?

Second, assuming the first problem can be resolved, suppose that the cognizer does not *believe* that P matches the community's viewpoint, although in fact it does. Is his belief in P still socially warranted? Or, third, suppose he *thinks* his belief matches the consensus but it does not. Fourth, suppose that the cognizer, S, (correctly) believes that members of his community generally accept P, but he has excellent reasons for thinking they have been duped. Is S still socially warranted in believing P?

As the second and third problems indicate, it is questionable whether actual *facts* of social consensus determine something called 'social warrant'. It seems, instead, as if a person's warrant is a function of his *beliefs*. Actual social consensus or dissensus cannot confer warrant status if the cognizer is unaware of that consensus. Moreover, even if the cognizer is aware of consensus, as the fourth problem indicates, he may have reasons that override it.

These problems raise doubts whether there is even a clear preanalytic notion of social warrant. Notice that there is relatively little use of such a phrase in common currency. It may be misguided to suppose that there is such a prior notion for social epistemology to explicate. I shall not invoke such a notion in erecting my own conception of social epistemics.

A final problem for consensualism$_1$ is that an individual cognizer might be aware of a general consensus on proposition P but also believe there is a small but authoritative minority who all accept not-P. It is doubtful that such a cognizer is socially warranted in believing P.

This last problem recurs for consensualism$_2$, which takes social belief-profiles as the objects of evaluation. This version is most naturally formulated as a purported explication of the term 'rationality' rather than 'warrant'. But is a high degree of consensus really sufficient for the rationality of a belief-profile? Suppose again that a tiny minority with great expertise all deny P's truth. The great majority, while aware of this dissent, persist in believing P. Is the resulting belief-profile nonetheless rational? According to consensualism, it is; but that is counterintuitive.

Another difficulty for consensualism$_2$ is that consensus per se is not a reliable sign of rationality. It depends on how consensus is reached. All sorts of methods can yield consensus: brainwashing, the threat of the rack or burning at the stake, totalitarian control of the sources of information. Consensus reached by these means does not guarantee rationality.

This objection weighs equally against consensualism$_3$, which applies the approach to social procedures or institutions. The power of procedures or institutions to produce consensus is hardly a sure indication of rationality. Brainwashing, the tools of the Inquisition, and official censorship may have the power to yield consensus, but they are not paradigms of rational procedure. Taking all these objections together, they are weighty grounds against consensualism as an approach to evaluative social epistemology.

Since some of the most serious objections to consensualism rest on its neglect of expert authority, it is natural to turn next to expertism. Like consensualism, expertism can appear in three guises, depending on its target of evaluation. Expertism$_1$ calls an individual's belief socially warranted if and only if it accords with expert opinion in that individual's community. Expertism$_2$ calls a group's belief-profile socially rational just in case the whole profile reflects the opinions of its constituent experts. Expertism$_3$ rates a social procedure or institution rational to the degree that it promotes the general acceptance of expert opinion.

Two features of expertism should be mentioned as possible sources of appeal. First, in relying on the opinions of others to form one's own beliefs, it is obvious that some people should be relied upon more than others. They may have observed the event in question, or have relevant technical knowledge. A rational cognizer should take these factors into account. Second, there is an appealing analogy between expertism and traditional foundationalism. Foundationalism is a theory of individual warrant or rationality that stresses the authoritativeness of certain beliefs, so-called basic beliefs. Expertism could be viewed as an analogue of foundationalism at the social level, in which the opinions of experts play the role of socially basic beliefs. From a social point of view, the beliefs of experts are 'immediately' warranted. Novices' beliefs can inherit social warrant by relying on experts' opinions. (The significance of intellectual authority has recently been stressed by Hardwig 1985, and Welbourne 1981.)

While expertism is more promising than consensualism, it has several problems and deficiencies. First, there are questions that parallel those facing consensualism. Is a cognizer's social warrant a function of experts' actual opinions, or what the cognizer *thinks* about their opinions? If the experts actually believe P but the cognizer is unaware that they do, is he still socially warranted in believing P? If the cognizer thinks they believe P but actually they do not, is he socially warranted in believing P? The only natural answer, I think, is to make the cognizer's social warrant a function of what he believes. But then one wonders whether this is a genuinely distinctive kind of warrant, different from ordinary 'individual' warrant. This point can be pressed by noticing that an expert can be viewed as simply a special case of a natural sign, or indicator, of the truth value of P. If a cognizer believes the putative expert's opinion to be a reliable indicator of P's truth value, he should take that into account in framing his own belief. But this is just a special case of reasoning from indicators. It is not clear that any special kind of warrant—social warrant—emerges from such cases. This bolsters my previously expressed doubts about whether there is any separate notion of social warrant in need of analysis.

The foregoing comments apply to expertism$_1$. What about expertism$_2$? The plausibility of expertism$_2$ partly depends on the interpretation of 'expert'. Does 'expert' mean a person whose opinion (on a given topic) *really is* the best available guide to the truth? Or does it only mean a person who has a *reputation* for being a reliable truth guide? If we take the reputational interpretation, it is not clear that the rationality of a belief-profile is guaranteed by its reflecting expert opinion. What if the so-called experts do not deserve their reputations? Then it is not obvious that the community is being fully rational in agreeing with them. The theory has more plausibility if an expert is understood in the first sense, as someone who is genuinely a reliable guide to truth. (Here again, though, one might wonder whether de facto expertise is relevant. What if the rest of the community is ignorant of who the real experts are? The community as a whole just happens to share their opinions by coincidence. Is the group's belief-profile still guaranteed to be rational? I think not.)

Let us call the first kind of expertism, which appeals to genuine experts, *objective expertism*, and the second kind, which appeals to (deserved or undeserved) reputations for expertise, *subjective*, or *reputational, expertism*. As indicated, I believe that objective expertism has some plausibility. Not so much plausibility, perhaps, as a theory of 'social warrant', but nonetheless as a (partial) standard for social epistemology. A little reflection should show, however, that objective expertism derives its plausibility from a more fundamental value. It is epistemically desirable for a group to reflect expert opinion because this increases the likelihood of the group's having *true beliefs*. If attainment of true beliefs is taken as the *fundamental* epistemic desideratum, then expertism has plausibility as a *derivative* theory.

I use the term *veritism* for the approach that rates true belief as the ultimate epistemic aim. This is the fourth approach I consider. Objective expertism can be seen as a corollary of veritism, since conforming to the opinions of genuine experts is a good means to true belief. Even subjective, or reputational, expertism can be viewed as derivative from veritism. After all, people need some principle to guide them in trying to realize veritistic ends. In the absence of anything better, they might be told to conform their opinions to those of the people they *deem* experts. Finally, even consensualism can best be defended on veritistic grounds. To the extent that societal consensus is a reliable guide to truth, it makes sense to abide by that consensus. Of course, societal consensus is not always a good guide to truth, and that is precisely one of consensualism's weaknesses. But it might make sense as a derivative rule of thumb, in the absence of anything better. It is indefensible, however, as a fundamental criterion of epistemic worth (or of social warrant or rationality).

While objective expertism has merit for the indicated reason, it is at best a *partial* approach to social epistemology. First, there are possible situations in which there are no experts. Here social epistemology would have nothing to say if it were confined to expertism. It might be replied that there must always be experts: if not experts in some absolute sense— people whose reliability on the topic exceeds a specified threshold—at least people who are *comparatively* expert—i.e., more expert than their peers. However, even comparative experts may not exist. The community may have nobody with any opinion at all on the topic. We would still want principles of social epistemology to apply in such cases. Second, whatever expertise already exists in a community, social epistemology need not be restricted to the adjustment of lay belief to expert opinion. A plausible province for social epistemology is the creation and improvement of institutions for *increasing* the level of expertise. Third, expertism only gives advice to non-experts. What should the experts themselves do? Are there no social procedures for becoming expert, or enhancing one's expertise? Surely such procedures are not precluded; and if they exist, they belong to the realm of social epistemology. For many reasons, then, objective expertism does not exhaust social epistemology. (There are also problems inherent in a more precise formulation of expertism. What should be done, for example, when experts disagree? Although I do not try to address this systematically, the following paragraphs are relevant.)

Before leaving the topic of expertism, it is worth illustrating the idea with two examples, one of objective and one of subjective expertism. The example of objective expertism is drawn from a formal treatment of optimizing group judgmental accuracy, by Lloyd Shapley and Bernard Grofman (1984). Shapley and Grofman are interested in the general problem of group decision making, in particular, how best to assign voting weights to group members to optimize a group decision. A special case is where a group chooses whether to believe a given proposition or its negation. (This concerns the notion of aggregate, or collective, belief, which I have not expressly treated. I shall accept this notion without further comment.) Shapley and Grofman show that if individual choices— opinions, in our special case—are mutually independent, and if the a priori likelihood that either of the two choices (beliefs) is correct is one half, then a decision rule which maximizes the probability of the group's getting the truth is a weighted voting rule. In particular, an optimal voting rule must assign weights w_i so that the following constraint is met:

$$w_i \propto \log\left(\frac{p_i}{1 - p_i}\right),$$

where p_i represents the probability that member i has a true opinion. For example, if there is a five member group whose respective probabilities of being correct are 0.9, 0.9, 0.6, 0.6, 0.6, then one optimum weighting scheme assigns these members the weights 0.392, 0.392, 0.072, 0.072, 0.072.

Now if one individual has a higher probability of being correct (having a true opinion) than another, the former has greater objective expertise on the subject. So the foregoing formula for selecting a decision rule (a certain type of social procedure) is designed to fix a group belief by weighting greater expertise more heavily. Shapley and Grofman prove that such a decision rule is conductive to group accuracy, i.e., maximizes the probability of getting a true group belief. In other words, assigning appropriate weights to expertise conduces to veritistic ends. Although Shapley and Grofman do not give much explicit attention to truth and veritism—their scheme is more abstract and general—their model certainly exemplifies the choice of a social procedure under the aegis of veritism.

The second example I shall give, an example of subjective expertism, is the approach of Keith Lehrer and Carl Wagner (1981). (Another example of subjective expertism is found in Stich and Nisbett 1980.) The Lehrer-Wagner theory looks like a consensualist approach, since it lays great emphasis on the rational transformation of initially disparate opinions (subjective probabilities) into consensus. But the source of rationality is each person's (repeated) revision of his subjective probability in accord with weights he assigns to others and their subjective probabilities. Now the weights a person assigns represent his assessments of the competence, reliability, or expertise, of the members in question. Lehrer and Wagner deliberately place few constraints on how these assessments are made.

There is no guarantee, then, that the weights (or degrees of 'respect') have any correspondence to genuine competence or expertise. This is why I call their approach one of subjective, or reputational, expertism.

This is not an appropriate occasion for detailed appraisal of this approach. I merely repeat my earlier suggestion that the plausibility of the approach is best seen as a corollary of veritism. Its limitations are also best appreciated from a veritistic perspective. I conclude that veritism represents the most adequate general approach to social epistemology, and is the one I favor for social epistemics. However, I do not favor it as an account of social 'rationality' or 'warrant'. A more positive account of its contours is presented in the next two sections.

4. Veritism

There is much more to be said in defense of veritism as the principal approach to social epistemology. The chief rationale, quite simply, is that the goal of truth is the common denominator of intellectual pursuits, whatever methods or practices are championed as the best means to this end. True belief is the shared aim of the Inquisitor and the scientist, of the creationist and the evolutionist, and of all the competing research programs that populate the agonistic arena of science. The Inquisitor thinks he knows the truth already, that his victims are well served by being brought to this truth, despite the severity of the measures. The scientist thinks there is no better road to true belief than that of free, uncoerced inquiry. However vast the gulf between these philosophies, they share the goal of truth.

It would be foolish to suppose, of course, that every defender of a favored orthodoxy preaches it with *sincere* belief in its truth or truth-fostering powers. Many an ideology, discourse structure, and conceptual scheme has been embraced in the interest of power rather than an interest in truth, as sundry theorists such as Marxists, Nietzsche, and Michel Foucault have stressed. Still, proponents of such positions must fly their public claims under the banner of truth, or eventual truth attainment. They know this is the *presumptive* aim of intellectual claims. To admit that one's favored methods or policies are mere self- or class-serving fictions, that they have no genuine propensity to conduct people on a path toward truth, is an admission of intellectual bankruptcy. The goal of truth must be honored even in the breach, just as the goal of winning must be simulated even by an athlete who seeks to 'throw' the contest.

Veritism does not deny that people engaged in intellectual pursuits often have extraverific motives for what they do and say. Fame, esteem, and fortune are not even necessarily illegitimate motives; they are epistemically illegitimate only where they *conflict* with the pursuit of truth. But to the degree that social or professional frameworks encourage the *sacrifice* of truth to the satisfaction of these extraneous ends, to that degree such frameworks are deficient from an intellectual standpoint. Veritism does not claim that every existing practice that nominally aspires to intellectual ends in fact optimizes their attainment. It only claims that this is a proper benchmark for grading these practices, precisely because it is their presumptive, or default, goal.

Workers in the social studies of knowledge commonly bracket the issue of truth. (One exception here is Donald Campbell, whose approach has points of contact with veritism. See Campbell 1986.) In analyzing particular cultures and scientific movements, historians, sociologists, and anthropologists typically shy away from questions of truth. This is understandable. Light can be shed on the relation between certain social variables and theory acceptance without addressing a theory's truth value. However, while truth can be set aside in the social *explanation* of belief, truth is not irrelevant in the *epistemic appraisal* of ideational practices. Furthermore, while scholars of the intellect commonly ignore the truth values of the theoretical commitments of their protagonists, these same scholars themselves aspire to truth in their own scientific or historical assertions. They aim at truth in their purely descriptive account of the groups and controversies in question, and they aim at correct explanations of doctrinal changes. For example, when Martin Rudwick (1985) traces the Devonian controversy (in part) through a "gradient of ascribed competences", he is claiming that competence ascriptions in fact played a causal role in changing bodies of opinion. This is a claim he presumably believes to be true, and he would resist attempts to show the non-existence or causal irrelevance of the pertinent competence ascriptions. Thus, while students of science and culture may properly abstract from the truth of the ideational contents they study, they do not and should not extrude the question of truth from their own propositions about the growth, prevalence, and extinction of people's ideational contents.

In the philosophy of science, some writers question the role of truth in scientific theorizing. But even these 'empiricists' or 'antirealists' acknowledge that a crucial test of competing theories is their ability to predict and retrodict observational data correctly, i.e., truly. So the value of truth is again acknowledged, though with some diminution of the domain.

Other philosophers downgrade the role of truth in science and culture for slightly different reasons. Richard Rorty argues for replacing objective truth as a goal of inquiry with merely "keeping the conversation going" (Rorty 1979, p. 377). No doubt it would be wrong to deny that conversation is sometimes conducted for its own sake; and conversationalists often seek the satisfaction of affiliative needs, or emotional release, more than the imparting of truths. The sheer pleasure of language is also a primary motivator of everyday talk, as well as literary expression. So not all human communication or cultural activity aims at truth and truth alone. However, epistemology is not concerned with all facets of interpersonal or cultural activity. It focuses wholly on the intellectual sphere, and on intellectual ends; here the emphasis on truth is entirely in order.

This is not to deny that many an institution or practice can be evaluated along multiple dimensions, both intellectual and nonintellectual. Judicial practices, such as rules of admissible evidence, may be judged in part by their effect on accuracy of verdicts. But they can also be judged by their impact on civil liberties. Practices which are good or bad from an intellectual standpoint may have different qualities from a political, legal, or moral standpoint. Epistemology concentrates on the intellectual perspective without necessarily taking a stand on how the interest of the intellect should finally be balanced against possibly competing interests. Some practices, such as guarantees of freedom of speech, may be justified by reference to *both* intellectual and moral considerations; but these considerations should be kept distinct.

Some philosophers would acknowledge the centrality of truth in a theory of inquiry but dispute the role of true *belief*. Karl Popper (1972) has endorsed the aim of truth, but minimizes the place of subjective states in epistemology. He propounds a conception of epistemology that is concerned with a purely objective realm of entitites—problems, theories, and arguments as such, i.e., objective entities quite apart from any mental or physical realization. The theory of science and culture, however, cannot confine itself to 'third-world' objects. The problems, theories, and arguments that exist 'objectively' are not all that matter to the state of science at a given juncture. It also matters who appreciates the problems, accepts the theories, and is persuaded by the arguments. Considered objectively, both good and bad theories 'exist', as do powerful and completely specious arguments. The critical question is what impact or reception these theories and arguments have on scientists and other cognizers. Social epistemology is therefore concerned with the promotion of true *belief*, not the mere existence of true contents, which may be rejected or ignored by scientists and laymen alike.

Thus far I have spoken rather vaguely about veritism and the aim of truth acquisition. It is time to be more precise. One question concerns the objects of evaluation under the veritistic approach. As I have indicated, the chosen targets of evaluation are social practices and institutions. But these are to be evaluated by their consequences for social belief-profiles. Social practices are epistemically desirable to the extent that they promote epistemically preferred belief-profiles. A second question concerns the precise term of epistemic appraisal under the veritistic approach. Here I am not entirely decided. I reject the terms 'warranted', 'justified', or 'rational' as the vocabulary of choice. They are either inappropriate, excessively vague, or excessively narrow. But I have no single term or expression that captures the relevant dimension or dimensions of appraisal. *Intellectual strength* is the best phrase I can think of; but it is not perfect. 'Intellectual virtue', or 'epistemic virtue', are other possibilities, though the latter is lacking in antecedent associations.

Unwillingness to be committed to a unique *term* of appraisal does not undermine the veritistic conception of social epistemics, as long as veritistic *standards* are formulated by which social practices can be assessed. There are, indeed, a number of distinct truth-linked standards, any or all of which can be used to appraise social institutions and practices. Five different standards can usefully be distinguished: (1) reliability, (2) power, (3) fecundity, (4) speed, and (5) efficiency.

The *reliability* of a practice is measured by the ratio of truths to total number of beliefs a practice would foster. In this reckoning, it is belief tokens that matter. Ten people believing one proposition determine ten beliefs. (Perhaps the duration of beliefs should also be incorporated into the calculus; but I set that aside.)

By *power* I mean the problem-solving, or question-answering, power of a practice (see chapter 9 and Goldman 1986, chap. 6). This is measured by the ability of a practice to help cognizers find and believe true answers to the questions that interest them. Reliability and power are not identical. A reliable practice helps prevent error but it does not necessarily combat ignorance. A practice that generates very few answers to questions of interest may still have a high truth ratio. But a high truth ratio is not sufficient for power. A powerful practice is one that is comparatively effective (at least in the long run) in generating true answers, and beliefs in these answers, not merely maintaining a small proportion of false beliefs.

As defined, the term 'power' retains some ambiguity. On one reading, a practice might qualify as powerful if, for a high proportion of questions asked, it secures true answers for at least *one* questioner. On a second reading, a practice would qualify as powerful only if it generates knowledge (or true belief) in these answers on the part of *many* questioners. To capture the second interpretation, I introduce the term *fecundity*.

Fecundity is an important standard for social epistemics. A culture's scientific practices might be relatively powerful in the sense that they precipitate the discovery of many scientific truths by a small body of scientific elite. But public education in the culture may be weak, so the bulk of the populace is mired in superstition and ignorance. Such a culture's practices or institutions are wanting in fecundity, which is surely *one* measure of a culture's intellectual strength.

The last two truth-linked standards are question-answering *speed* and question-answering *efficiency*. The former is the relative speed of getting correct answers. The second standard, efficiency, incorporates the element of *cost*. When people want answers to complex or previously unanswered questions, resources are typically required to get those answers. More efficient practices are ones that promote answer acquisition at lower cost. They might conserve costs by collaboration and division of labor, for example. The economics of information is certainly an important topic in the theory of information and should not be omitted from the agenda of social epistemics.

How should this array of truth-linked standards be incorporated into veritism? Two routes might be taken. One would simply acknowledge this multiplicity of standards and use 'intellectual strength' as an umbrella term for the set, without trying to weld them into a single criterion or measure. No complete ordering of possible social belief-profiles would be contemplated. Alternatively, one might try to effect a complete ordering, which would require assigning weights to each separate standard (as well as making them more precise). Some arbitrariness would be inevitable, but perhaps that isn't a tragedy. In this paper, I do not try to choose between these strategies. I continue to speak loosely of veritism without opting for any resolution of this problem.

Despite the resulting vagueness, veritism retains plenty of content by contrast with alternative approaches. One contrasting approach not thus far mentioned is *adaptiveness*. A social practice might be rated positively because it promotes survival or fitness, either the survival and fitness of individual group members or the survival of the group qua social entity. Functional explanations in sociology and anthropology frequently take this approach, and it might be invoked as an evaluative stratagem as well. A religious practice, for example, might be graded highly because of its favorable effect on social solidarity. However, this sort of grading is not expressive of the *intellectual* dimension, the dimension traditionally associated with epistemology's mission. There is no tight connection, at least no necessary connection, between intellectual strength and adaptiveness. The science of nuclear fission is intellectually powerful, but it may be inimical to adaptiveness. For good or ill, intellectual strength is a virtue (or set of virtues) distinct from adaptiveness.

I should emphasize that there is nothing fundamentally new about social epistemics, conceived veritistically, except the name. The philosophical task is that of giving a rational reconstruction of what people have long said and done in the socio-intellectual arena. Organized science establishes institutional practices to avoid fraud and fabrication. The adversary process is instituted in the Anglo-American legal system to promote more accurate fact-finding. The free marketplace of ideas is defended in the expectation that free competition is the best means of uncovering truth. All these familiar practices and institutions are traditionally and plausibly rationalized on veritistic grounds. So they are practices that arise from the execution of social epistemics, though not under that label. My attempt to formulate this conception is just an attempt to reconstruct and systematize an enterprise that already has a long history.

5. The Scope of Social Epistemics

Although I have said a few words about objects of evaluation for social epistemics, a fuller treatment is needed to fix the relationship between social and individual epistemics. A useful way to proceed is to start with a taxonomy of belief determinants. Not all belief determinants are proper objects of epistemic evaluation, but it is instructive to note which of them are, and of these which are objects for *social* epistemics.

Here is a taxonomy of factors that can influence beliefs. This taxonomy has no privileged status, but it can help carve out the territories of the parts of epistemics. The starred items represent types of factors that are evaluative objects for social epistemics.

1. Environmental objects and events
2. Basic cognitive processes
3. Nonsocial belief-forming methods
4.* Social belief-forming methods
5.* Patterns of communicational behavior
6.* Institutional rules and structures
7. Nomological regularities

Let me clarify each of these taxa, taking them in order.

Environmental objects and events serve as perceptual stimuli, and give rise to beliefs via perceptual processes. They are, therefore, prime causal factors in the determination of belief. However, no epistemology grades environmental stimuli as epistemically good or bad, permissible or impermissible. So they are not objects of evaluation for any part of epistemics.

The second category, basic cognitive processes, includes processes of perception, memory, attention, concept formation, problem solving, learning, and reasoning. By 'basic' processes, I mean (roughly) natural or native processes, not algorithms, techniques, or heuristics that are acquired through experience or explicit tutelage. In Goldman 1986 I have argued that basic processes are suitable objects of epistemic evaluation. In particular, they comprise the domain for *primary* individual epistemics.

The third category, nonsocial belief-forming methods, is meant to delineate the province of *secondary* individual epistemics. A method, as I use the term, is a learnable algorithm, technique, or procedure for arriving at beliefs. It can either be a highly generic, topic-neutral, procedure or a very task-specific one. Methods range from proof-techniques in logic to procedures for performing and interpreting a spectrographic analysis. A special class of methods are ones that appeal, in whole or part, to the assertions, utterances, and beliefs of other people. These are what I call *social* methods, which are *excluded* from the third category. I want to reserve the class of social methods for the sphere of social—or 'tertiary'—epistemics. Only *nonsocial* methods constitute the objects of appraisal for secondary epistemics.

The fourth category consists of social belief-forming methods: modes of doxastic response to the opinions and messages of others. Within this category are patterns of doxastic response to various argumentative and rhetorical styles, methods of assessing people's trustworthiness, and so on. What distinguishes *social* methods is that their *inputs* are opinions or communicational acts of other people, or the cognizer's beliefs about these. The *outputs* of social belief-forming methods need not have any social content. (On the other hand, nonsocial belief-forming methods can have social contents in their outputs.) I acknowledge that the resulting demarcation between social and nonsocial methods may not be very sharp; some methods may mix social and nonsocial inputs. But we should not expect the boundary between social and individual epistemology to be perfectly well defined.

(Since the boundary between social and nonsocial methods is not sharp, perhaps *all* belief-forming methods could be treated under secondary epistemics. It would then turn out that part of social epistemics would be subsumed under secondary epistemics. This is a conceivable approach, though not my preferred one.)

Social *belief-forming* methods do not exhaust the objects of social, or tertiary, epistemics. (The term 'tertiary' is not intended invidiously, of course, it is just a natural complement to the other numeric labels.) Social epistemics also seeks to evaluate patterns and strategies of communicational behavior. What verbal techniques does the speaker use to try to persuade his audience? What patterns of questioning, challenging, rebutting, and criticizing does he employ against an interlocutor? What communicational media and formats are available for his use, and which does he select? These various patterns and strategies comprise the fifth category of belief determinants.

The sixth category features institutional rules and structures that affect the flow of communication and fix the processes of collective belief-formation. These can play a critical role in determining which messages are sent by which sources, over what communication channels, and to what class of potential receivers. Except for informal, face-to-face situations, where speech opportunities are largely unconstrained, potential message senders need to pay or vie for the use of communication channels. Advertisers must pay for commercial space; speakers in parliamentary bodies must be recognized by the chair; public figures must produce messages that are deemed newsworthy; authors and researchers must have their work accepted by publishers and professional journals. All the institutional rules and structures that govern the choice of message conveyance play a critical role in information flow, and ultimately in belief production.

In certain specialized settings elaborate formal rules control information flow. Take a judicial system, for example. It aims, among other things, to produce verdicts of guilt or innocence. The American judicial system typically involves several parties: a judge, a pair of opposing legal teams, and a jury. Communications are made under a set of formal procedures, presided over by the judge. Juries then debate the case and produce a verdict. Among the rules incorporated in this institutional set-up are rules governing: (i) the size of the jury; (ii) the process of juror selection and exclusion; (iii) jury decisions (e.g., unanimity versus majority rule); (iv) admissible evidence; (v) the privileged attorney-client relation and advocacy responsibilities; and (vi) the burden of proof and the instructions given to jurors (e.g., to convict only when guilt is established "beyond reasonable doubt"). All such institutional rules and structures are candidates for evaluation within social epistemics (see chapter 11).

The seventh category is not really a class of causal factors, but laws governing the causal network by which the preceding factors are linked with beliefs. In addition to psychological laws, there might be laws of economics that subsume the buying and selling of information, or principles of cultural transmission analogous to principles of biological inheritance (see Cavalli-Sforza and Feldman 1981, and Boyd and Richerson 1985). None of these laws or regularities would be *evaluated* by social epistemics. But they would be of interest to the social epistemologist in trying to determine the effects of this or that set of belief-influencing factors (see chapter 12).

As explained in Section 4, the standards for evaluating the relevant social practices are veritistic ones. Social epistemics would assess alternative practices in categories 4, 5, and 6. It would enlist the help of sundry social and behavioral sciences in ascertaining the impact of alternative practices on social belief-profiles. It would then rate these practices on veritistic grounds.

In traditional epistemology and philosophy of science, emphasis has been placed on specification of *optimal* or *ideal* methods and practices. But my proposal for social epistemics (as well as for other portions of epistemics) would advocate an assessment of all possible methods and practices. It is important to identify suboptimal practices because the optimal ones may not be feasible for every group; or they may be costly in terms of some competing, nonveritistic values. To assess whether verific interests should be sacrificed to another value, one would like to know how serious the veritistic loss is likely to be. (Indeed, one of my so-called veritistic standards—efficiency—already requires a calculation of verific gain per some sort of unit of cost.)

How is my delineation of social epistemics related to traditional definitions of the scope of epistemology, philosophy of science, and other studies of science? Epistemology and philosophy of science have tended to focus on categories 2 and 3, though without a systematic distinction between native and learned procedures. Philosophy of science has standardly focused on what I would call methods, especially methods of collecting and assessing evidence. In my categorization, then, traditional philosophy of science is (largely) secondary epistemics. Other disciplines that study science—especially the history and sociology of science—come closer to social epistemics insofar as they explore the kinds of practices and institutions in categories 4, 5, and 6. However, these disciplines characteristically ignore evaluative questions, and especially abstain from veritistic forms of evaluation.

6. Against Nihilism

Veritism stands in clear contrast to evaluative relativism, in particular, to the doctrine of nihilism or anti-universalism that is embedded within relativism. It is to be expected, then, that relativists would find veritism unacceptable. Other theorists can also be expected to question veritism on various counts. Let us therefore anticipate some points of concern and controversy.

Barnes and Bloor (1982) enunciate their relativistic position as follows: "For the relativist there is no sense attached to the idea that some standards or beliefs are really rational as distinct from merely locally accepted as such. Because he thinks that there are no context-free or super-cultural norms of rationality he does not see rationally and irrationally held beliefs as making up two distinct and qualitatively different classes of things" (Barnes and Bloor 1982, pp. 27–28).

Actually, the Barnes and Bloor formulation does not precisely clash with the theses of social epistemics, because they dispute the possibility of evaluating *beliefs* in terms of *rationality*, while social epistemics seeks neither to evaluate beliefs per se nor to evaluate them in terms of rationality. However, the denial of context-free or super-cultural norms can be carried over to social practices and institutions. Relativism may deny that there are any context-free or super-cultural criteria or standards for judging social practices and institutions.

One point that seems critical to the present form of relativism is the claim of an irreducible plurality, or multiplicity, of evaluative standards. Of course, veritism also posits multiple standards: reliability, power, fecundity, speed, and efficiency. However, each of these is supposed to be super-cultural, or culture-neutral. So veritism clearly conflicts with the anti-universalistic component of relativism.

There is another important respect, though, in which veritism can be pluralistic. Veritism can admit that many alternative social practices or institutions may be equally reliable, equally powerful, equally fecund, and so on. Veritism is not committed to a uniquely optimal set of social practices. (See Goldman 1986, section 4.3, for an analogous point about pluralism in individual epistemology.) Since traditions and conditions may vary from culture to culture, it may also turn out that what is veritistically optimal for one culture is not optimal for another.

Veritism is compatible with pluralism in another way too: it does not require every individual to use the same methods. Let a *group method* M^* be a set of methods (or method bundles) $\{M_1, \ldots, M_i, \ldots, M_n\}$, where M_i is the method (or method bundle) used by member i. A group method is *homogeneous* just in case all members of the group use the same method (or method bundle). A group method is *heterogeneous* if two or more members use different methods (method bundles). Now there is nothing in veritism that precludes heterogeneous group methods. Indeed, it could turn out that heterogeneous group methods are preferable on veritistic grounds. Alternatively, we can think of a group method as a policy of encouraging or promoting individuals to use various methods. Then Paul Feyerabend's anarchism (Feyerabend 1975), which ostensibly opposes all methods, can be reconstrued as an endorsement of a single group policy, viz., "Encourage the proliferation of diverse methods among different members." On either construal, veritism can in principle agree with Feyerabend's anarchism, or with Husain Sarkar's approach of method multiplicity (Sarkar 1983).

However, the nihilist might not be assuaged by veritism's compatibility with pluralism. The very idea of any super-cultural standard might be regarded as indefensible. What, then, is my defense of veritistic standards? Very simply, truth-linked standards are the standards implicit in the process of inquiry, and in the very notion of 'intellectual' aims and assessments. Individual intelligence is (at least partly) a matter of facility at problem solving, of finding and believing true answers to the questions one wants to answer (see Goldman 1986, chap. 6). Similarly, social intelligence is a matter of social practices and institutions that foster social problem solving. Getting true answers is, roughly speaking, what *defines* the aims of the intellect. So *all* cultures, communities, or groups that possess the notion of intellectual appraisal *eo ipso* accept truth-linked standards, however much they differ about the methods for *applying* those standards. Needless to say, few cultures, communities, or groups have exclusively intellectual aims. Science and academe are the distinctive subcultures in which intellectual aims are paramount. In most other communities and groups, intellectual aims are subservient to other aims. But insofar as intellectual aims are distinctly identified, truth-linked standards come into play. This is not a point on which cultures differ from one another.

There are, however, three quite different sources of discontent with veritism I have not yet identified. These are associated with charges of (A) circularity, (B) emptiness, and (C) uselessness.

The circularity critique runs as follows. Since 'truth' must be *defined* in terms of intellectual methods, it cannot, on pain of circularity, appear in a criterion for such methods. This sort of objection has been lodged by Hilary Putnam (1983) in discussing the reliability approach to rationality (or justification). But this claim presupposes that truth is definable epistemically, or nonrealistically. If realism about truth is correct, as I argue it is (cf. Goldman 1986, chap. 7), the point collapses. On a proper understanding of 'truth', it is not defined by reference to methods of truth determination, or verification. Hence, there is no circularity in having truth-linked criteria of method appraisal.

The objection from emptiness runs a bit differently. All veritistic standards, it is claimed, assume there are truths or facts, independent of what groups of people believe. But there are no such facts. So-called facts are mere constructions by groups of inquirers. On one variant of this theme, the alleged constructive process can actually be observed in the scientific laboratory. Science is not a matter of discovering pre-existing facts; it is just a process of *negotiation*. Facts are things to be negotiated, or fabricated, not discovered. So goes the argument of scientific 'constructivists', such as Bruno Latour and Steve Woolgar (1979) and Karin Knorr-Cetina (1981).

A full discussion of this claim cannot be undertaken here. In the present context I rest content with two points. First, the sociologist who studies life in a scientific laboratory does not observe the negotiation of scientific *facts*. What is observed is only the negotiation of scientific assertions or beliefs, i.e., what the scientists agree to *say* or *believe* about the facts. That there are 'negotiation' processes in social belief-fixation hardly demonstrates that there are no facts of the matter independent of this negotiation.

Second, the prevalence of negotiation is readily explained in a fashion congenial to veritism. Scientists negotiate with each other because they accord one another a certain degree of respect as experts, as people who stand a chance of being right comparable to their own. They have every reason to heed one another's opinion, and try to arrive at a cognitive judgment that meets, as far as possible, with general approval. The negotiation process is best understood, then, on the assumption that there are facts in the world, and that the several members stand a better chance of 'getting' the facts if they heed the opinions of others.

The third objection against veritism is that of *uselessness*. The whole point of a criterion in the realm of social epistemology, it is argued, is to use or apply the criterion. This means determining the (degree of) intellectual goodness or badness of different social practices. If there is no mutually agreed upon way of applying a criterion, it is useless. Yet this is precisely what obtains for veritism if, and to the extent that, descriptive relativism is true. Where communities differ in their intellectual practices, they will differ about how to apply a veritistic criterion. Any attempt to reach a consensus, or settle a dispute, about the veritistic properties of a specified social practice will be in vain. Hence any veritistic criterion is useless. This objection merits treatment in a separate section.

7. The Problem of Applicability

Let me first clarify what I mean by a 'criterion', or 'standard', of appraisal. I mean simply a condition that specifies a characteristic or magnitude that *makes* the objects in question (comparatively) good or bad. The term 'criterion' is sometimes used in a different sense, in the sense of a verification procedure, or way of telling, whether an object possesses a given characteristic or realizes a given magnitude to a specified degree. But the term is not so intended here. Specification of a good-making characteristic is a conceptually prior task, to be distinguished from the task of finding verification or determination procedures. (For further clarification of these points, in the context of a theory of justification, see Goldman 1986, section 4.2.)

Given this understanding of a standard, or criterion, it is no criticism of veritistic standards that they are not themselves determination, or application, procedures. However, granting that a criterion is not intended to be a verification procedure, wouldn't it be a salient defect of veritistic criteria if they were not applicable, if there were no associated procedures for determining whether any selected social practices satisfy them (to this or that degree)? Doesn't the nonapplicability critique still carry weight?

In considering this critique, we need to look more closely at what is meant by 'applicability', or 'determination procedure'. One thing that might be meant by a 'determination procedure' is a *decision procedure*. This, in turn, has two possible interpretations. In one common and very strong interpretation, a decision procedure is a method which guarantees both (A) that the user will arrive (after finitely many steps) at an answer (belief) about whether any targeted object satisfies the standard, and (B) the resulting answer (belief) will be *correct*.

Is it a reasonable constraint on a standard that it have an associated decision procedure? No, this is an excessively stringent requirement, certainly on the strong reading of 'decision procedure'. Even first-order logic does not have a decision procedure in this sense. Furthermore, it is doubtful whether *any* proffered standard for social epistemology would have a decision procedure. Consider even the standard of consensualism, where applicability seems quite promising. Is there a procedure associated with consensualism that guarantees that it will yield correct answers to the question of whether a given group agrees (unanimously or to any specific degree) on a given topic? In light of the possibility that some people may suppress their true opinion—or just in light of the general problem of ascertaining people's beliefs—there is no such guarantee. So veritistic standards do not seem inferior to other possible standards in respect of (strong) applicability.

Suppose we weaken the sense of 'decision procedure' by deleting clause (B), the requirement of correctness. What we are then left with, however, is much too easy to satisfy. If there is no requirement of correctness of application, an acceptable determination procedure might simply be, "Answer 'yes' to all even-numbered queries of application and 'no' to the remainder."

Presumably, then, some sort of correctness desideratum should be part of a determination procedure. But how much correctness, and how universal must the scope of application be? These questions indicate that the very notion of a determination procedure is rather vague. Until this vagueness is reasonably resolved, there is no plausible demonstration that veritistic criteria cannot have associated determination procedures.

In formulating the envisaged nonapplicability objection, there was another strand in the argument that I have not yet confronted. There was the suggestion that an acceptable standard ought to be *mutually* applicable, i.e., applicable by different communities to their mutual satisfaction. But can veritistic standards be used to settle disputes, or reach a consensus, about specified social practices? The picture presupposed here is something like this. An assemblage of representatives from different intellectual traditions confront the epistemologist with the entreaty: "Give us a criterion for choosing (or ranking) social practices that will lead us to (complete) agreement in this choice." The contention is that veritistic standards do not comply with this entreaty.

But why should the epistemologist accept this version of the challenge? Why suppose there is any criterion satisfying the condition that even people from highly disparate intellectual traditions will come to (complete) agreement when applying it? Different intellectual traditions may have all sorts of idiosyncracies and foibles. They may do (what they call) 'science' in different fashions; they may even use different logics (e.g., classical versus intuitionistic). So why suppose that any single criterion could be used to settle disputes? Furthermore, why is it necessarily a deficiency in a criterion that it could not settle all disputes? As long as it could be used *correctly*, by people who antecedently employ suitable processes and methods, what more can reasonably be required? Obviously, the *use* of any criterion requires employment of previously available processes and methods (at least nonsocial methods). If the processes and methods certain people bring to the criterion are bad enough, they won't apply the method correctly, and the results of their applications will conflict with the applications of others. But why is that a fault of the criterion?

The objector may still not be assuaged. All right, he may reply, perhaps *total* agreement on application is too much to expect for any criterion. But what about the possibility of producing a moderate amount of agreement? Isn't this a good-making trait of a criterion?

Two comments are in order here. First, it has not been shown that veritism fails to satisfy this more relaxed requirement. It will all depend on the range of intellectual traditions envisaged as participants and on how much agreement is a 'moderate' amount. Depending on how these parameters are fixed, the requirement may or may not continue to seem reasonable. If other candidate criteria continue to run afoul of the requirement, which they may, its reasonability would be moot.

I have a more serious objection to this maneuver, however. It seems to me fundamentally misguided to impose usability or applicability of a criterion as a test of (comparative) adequacy. Why should we consider replacing veritism—which has many arguments in its favor—with some other criterion, simply because the latter is more usable?

The point can be illustrated by the familiar story about a man who is poking around on the ground under a lamppost. A friend approaches and asks him what he is doing. He answers that he is looking for his watch, which he lost in the bushes across the street. When the friend asks why is looking here, when he lost the watch over there, the man replies, "because the light is better here". The moral of the story is obvious. The ease of applying a criterion, or its propensity to yield greater agreement, is no reason to suppose it is a *better*, or *correct*, criterion. Ease of application has no clear relevance to correctness, just as better light under the lamppost is not a relevant reason for looking there.

Although I refrain from building any particular determination procedure into the content of veritism, it should not be inferred that I have no preferred group of determination procedures of my own, which I expect to be shared by many of my readers. On the contrary, I presume that the best available set of procedures for determining the veritistic properties of social practices are various procedures of the sundry empirical and mathematical sciences. It is precisely because such sciences are needed to *apply* the veritistic standards that I regard social epistemics as an alliance between philosophy and various scientific disciplines.

This acknowledgment, however, may be seized upon to register a new criticism against veritism, a regress charge. Suppose a group wishes to decide which social practices to adopt, and consults veritistic critieria.

Won't it have to use some social practices in order to apply the criteria, such as the social practices embedded in current social science? But which practices is it allowed to use? Here, again, it looks like it should consult the criterion. But 'consulting' the criterion means applying it; and this requires the use of social practices. So a vicious regress seems to loom.

Two points are germane to this problem. First, the problem as stated holds as much for nonveritistic as veritistic criteria. It does not cut invidiously against the latter. Second, the regress can really be averted. For one thing, judgments about the best social methods or practices do not necessarily depend on the use of *social* methods or practices. Individuals might arrive at these judgments privately, through the use of basic processes and nonsocial methods only. Of course, if they seek to implement these practices within a group, there will have to be some form of communication, hence some social practice. But judgments about the epistemic properties of social practices do not *require* social practices. Finally, it is a mistake to suppose that social practices must be *chosen* at every stage in order to apply a criterion. Social practices may simply *evolve*, without deliberate consultation with a criterion. So there is no cogent argument for a vicious regress. (See similar remarks of mine in Goldman 1980, section IX.)

A final criticism of veritism is one from necessary self-endorsement. Veritistic criteria, the argument runs, ensure that whatever methods or practices are already in place will be approved. If we use practice P to assess the truth values of the beliefs that result from P, won't we necessarily conclude that P performs beautifully? But what value does such a verdict have? None. Since there is no possibility of a practice impugning itself under veritism, veritism is worthless as a standard of appraisal. To use Rorty's epithet, it is purely "Whiggish" (cf. Rorty 1979, chap. 7; also Firth 1981).

The first point to make, in reply, is that self-endorsement is not obviously a flaw. Self-endorsement is a special case of what Robert Nozick (1981) calls 'self-subsumption'. He argues persuasively, in various contexts, that self-subsumption is not a defect. Admittedly, if a practice or method were *necessarily* self-endorsing, we might question the significance of any application of it that yields a self-endorsement. However, veritistic criteria are by no means necessarily self-endorsing

How might a social practice or method, applied to a veritistic criterion, yield a self-impugning judgment? Consider a decision rule à la Shapley and Grofman (1984), which incorporates certain voting weights for making collective judgments. Suppose this decision rule *violates* the log formula Shapley and Grofman present. It is still possible that a group using this decision rule should collectively decide that only decision rules satisfying the Shapley-Grofman formula optimize accuracy, and should be adopted instead. In this situation, the decision rule would generate a self-refuting, or self-impugning, judgment.

There are, then, no sound objections to the veritistic approach to social epistemology. Given the intuitively powerful reasons in its favor, it provides an attractive foundation for social epistemics.

Note

Research leading to this paper was undertaken, in part, under a grant from the National Science Foundation (SES-8204737) and during release time provided by the Social and Behavioral Sciences Research Institute of the University of Arizona. For helpful comments on earlier drafts, I wish to thank Fred Schmitt, Holly Smith, and participants in the NEH Institute on the Theory of Knowledge (summer, 1986).

Chapter 11

Epistemic Paternalism: Communication Control in Law and Society

A popular principle in epistemology and the philosophy of science is the requirement of total evidence (RTE). A weak version of this principle may be stated as follows:

> (W-RTE)   A cognitive agent X should always fix his beliefs or subjective probabilities in accordance with the total evidence in his possession at the time.[1]

This version says nothing about acquiring or collecting evidence, only about the use of evidence already in one's possession. A stronger version of RTE, however, addresses evidence gathering as well:

> (S-RTE)   A cognitive agent X should collect and use all available evidence that can be collected and used (at negligible cost).[2]

This principle had best be understood in purely epistemic terms, rather than moral or legal terms. Some evidence collection might involve invasion of privacy or harmful experimentation on human subjects, which would be objectionable on moral and/or legal grounds. But if we abstract from these factors and restrict attention to epistemic considerations, the principle has initial intuitive appeal.

A plausible-seeming corollary, or extension, of S-RTE is a principle governing the practices of a second agent, Y, who is in a position to control the evidence made available to X. This interpersonal principle would say that Y should make available to X all evidence that is subject to his (Y's) control. Of course, like S-RTE itself, the envisaged extension or corollary of S-RTE must be restricted to epistemic contexts or concerns. Thus, we might formulate the 'control' version of RTE roughly as follows:

> (C-RTE)   If agent X is going to make a doxastic decision concerning question Q, and agent Y has control over the evidence that is provided to X, then, from a purely epistemic point of view, Y should make available to X all of the evidence relevant to Q that is (at negligible cost) within Y's control.

The restriction to the epistemic viewpoint is again important. In legal settings, for example, there are many non-epistemic reasons for refusing to provide relevant evidence to jurors. Available evidence may have been illegally obtained. Relevant evidence may be obtainable from the defendant, but the Fifth Amendment forbids his being compelled to testify against himself. Or the defendant may have testified elsewhere under a grant of limited immunity, providing that his testimony would not subsequently be used against him. In these cases, the judge (Y) is obliged not to provide the jurors (X) with all available evidence logically relevant to the question of guilt. These constraints, though, are not of an epistemic nature. Thus, the stated version of C-RTE may still be defensible. Indeed, anyone persuaded by John Stuart Mill's famous thesis, that if we are interested in having truth prevail we should allow all available arguments to be heard, should be attracted to C-RTE (Mill 1956).

I shall argue, nonetheless, that C-RTE is unacceptable. More cautiously, I shall show that existing provisions and practices, both in the law and elsewhere in society, contravene C-RTE. Although I shall not defend each provision and practice in detail, many of them seem to be quite reasonable. This raises some interesting questions for a branch of epistemology that I have elsewhere called *social epistemics*.[3] The aim of this paper is to formulate these questions in a general way and to undertake a preliminary exploration of them.

I

The American legal system has a set of explicitly formulated rules of evidence for the federal courts. These and other trial-related procedures are substantially dedicated to the goal of getting the truth about the issues under litigation (in a criminal trial, the guilt or innocence of the accused). Since the aim of these rules is, accordingly, heavily or predominantly epistemic, they provide excellent examples for our scrutiny.

The Federal Rules of Evidence (1989) resulted from proposals by an Advisory Committee appointed by the Supreme Court, which were passed into law (with some revisions) by Congress in 1975. These rules govern the decisions of judges on the admission or exclusion of evidence. Rule 102 declares their purpose: "These rules shall be construed to secure fairness in administration, elimination of unjustifiable expense and delay, and promotion of growth and development of the law of evidence *to the end that the truth may be ascertained* and proceedings justly determined" (emphasis added). The truth goal is implicit in the declaration (Rule 602) that witnesses may only testify to a matter of which they have "personal" (especially perceptual) knowledge, and in the general exclusion of hearsay evidence (Rule 801). Such rules codify what McCormick calls a "most pervasive manifestation" of the common law, viz., insistence upon "the most reliable sources of information" (Cleary 1984, p. 23). Reliance on reliable sources, clearly, is more likely to produce accurate (i.e., truthful) judgments. The admission of testimony by experts (Rule 702) also exemplifies a dedication to truth, since experts are people presumed to know relevant truths. The requirement of witnesses to make an oath or affirmation before testifying is still another device calculated to secure truthful evidence (Rule 603), as are statutory provisions of penalties for perjury. The entire procedure of cross-examination, which holds an exalted place in the Anglo-American trial system, is similarly rationalizable by reference to the truth goal. Since it is impossible to prevent false evidence from ever being introduced, at least there should be ample opportunity to contravert it, to reduce the likelihood of its being believed by the fact finder and thereby promoting a false verdict.

What is interesting in the present context is that the rules of evidence frequently foster the exclusion of evidence from the jurors, in conflict with principle C-RTE. On the matter of admission or exclusion of evidence, one governing provision is that *relevant* evidence is generally admissible, but *irrelevant* evidence is not admissible (Rule 402).[4] In the matter of hearsay evidence, the basis for exclusion ostensibly falls under a different principle, not irrelevance but unreliability or doubtful veracity. Still other rules promote exclusion even when the evidence is both relevant and presumptively true. Evidence about the character of an accused is not admissible for the purpose of proving that he acted according to character on the occasion in question (Rule 404). In particular, evidence of previous *crimes* by the accused is not admissible to help prove that he committed the present crime. Also evidence that the defendant initially entered a guilty plea on the present charge, and then withdrew it, is inadmissible (Rule 410). Here we have examples of a particularly interesting kind, in which judges are allowed or enjoined to exclude presumptively true and relevant evidence. Can these be rationalized on epistemic grounds?

The general rationale is given in Rule 403, which states in part: "Although relevant, evidence may be excluded if its probative value is substantially outweighed by the danger of unfair prejudice, confusion of the issues, or misleading the jury, ..." The phrase 'misleading the jury' apparently refers to the jury being led into making an incorrect judgment, and the language of 'prejudice' and 'confusion' can also be readily interpreted this way. It appears, then, that the Federal Rules of Evidence provide an *epistemic* rationale for excluding various types of evidence from doxastic decision makers (jurors), contrary to what C-RTE enjoins.

II

A better understanding of the underlying rationale for the relevance rules can be gleaned from a theoretical reconstruction by a legal scholar, Richard Lempert (1977). Lempert offers several reconstructive suggestions, but I shall present just the one employing a Bayesian interpretation. The discussion assumes that the fact finder is a jury and the issue to be resolved is a defendant's guilt.

One form of Bayes's theorem, suitable to the present case, is formulated as follows:

$$O(G/E) = \frac{P(E/G)}{P(E/\text{not-}G)} \cdot O(G)$$

This formula describes the way that a new item of evidence (E) should influence a rational agent's odds (O) that a defendant is guilty (G).[5] It says that the posterior odds of the defendant's guilt is equal to (1) the probability that the evidence would obtain if the defendant is in fact guilty, (2) divided by the probability that that evidence would obtain if the defendant is in fact not guilty, (3) multiplied by the prior odds on the defendant's guilt. The ratio of items (1) and (2) is conventionally called the *likelihood ratio*. On Lempert's reconstruction, a necessary and sufficient condition for evidence to be logically *irrelevant* to the defendant's guilt is that the likelihood ratio be 1 : 1 (or close to 1 : 1). This holds when the evidence in question would be just as likely to arise if the defendant were not guilty as if he were guilty, i.e., if $P(E/G) = P(E/\text{not-}G)$. Evidence of this sort has no "probative" value, that is, warrants no change in the posterior odds of guilt. Such evidence is unhelpful and therefore should not be admitted. Logically *relevant* evidence is evidence whose likelihood ratio departs (substantially) from 1 : 1.

Why should courts declare even relevant evidence inadmissible? Lempert expresses this in terms of the danger that the fact finder will misestimate the probabilities that comprise the likelihood ratio, and hence assign excessive (or insufficient) weight to the evidence. Overestimating the numerator or underestimating the denominator makes the conclusion sought by the proponent of the evidence appear more probable than it actually is; underestimating the numerator or overestimating the denominator has the opposite result. For example, suppose that in an assault case it can be shown that the defendant is a heroin addict, and also that one out of 500 criminal assailants are heroin addicts, whereas of the people who never engage in criminal assault only one in 1,000 are heroin addicts. Then knowledge that the defendant is an addict should result in a doubling of the prior odds that the defendant was the assailant. Suppose further that the fact finder (mistakenly) thinks that the probability that a nonassailant would be a heroin addict was one in 10,000 rather than one in 1,000. This misestimation of the denominator by a factor of ten leads to a twentyfold increase in the odds of guilt rather than a twofold increase. It is precisely this sort of danger that concerns the courts. Rule 403, excluding character evidence, is partly justified on this ground, says Lempert. Jurors are likely to magnify the import of character traits, or past criminal record[6]; and similarly for withdrawn guilty pleas. When courts or the codified rules speak of the problem as one of juror "prejudice", or when they speak of "confusing" or "misleading" the jury, this should be understood, according to Lempert, in terms of the jury being prone to such misestimations.[7]

III

Whether or not Lempert's Bayesian reconstruction is wholly faithful to the intent of the rules, it is apparent that the framers of the rules, and judges themselves, often wish to *protect* jurors in their search for truth. If, in the framers' opinion, jurors are likely to be misled by a certain category of evidence, they are sometimes prepared to require or allow such evidence to be kept from the jurors. This is an example of what I shall call *epistemic paternalism*. The general idea is that the indicated rules of evidence are designed to protect jurors from their own "folly", just as parents might keep dangerous toys or other articles away from children, or might not expose them to certain facts. I do not wish to quibble here over precise definitions of the term 'paternalism'. My usage, however, has much in common with H. L. A. Hart's characterization of paternalism as "the protec- tion of people from themselves" (Hart 1966, p. 31), and with Joel Feinberg's emphasis on the analogy to parental relations with children (Feinberg 1986, pp. 3–8).[8] Jurors may have flaws in their background beliefs, or in their ability to draw apt conclusions from evidence. If so, the courts are prepared to protect them against these information-processing deficiencies in order to get truthful judgments on the issues at hand. Admittedly, in the judicial case the prime objects of "protection" are plausibly the parties to the litigation, or perhaps society at large, not the jurors. So the present use of the term 'paternalism' may extend a bit beyond its standard usage. Howev- er, the indicated parties are protected by getting jurors to make accurate judgments. Protection of the *jurors'* epistemic ends therefore assumes deriv- ative importance.

In any event, I shall construe epistemic paternalism in a broad sense. I shall think of communication controllers as exercising epistemic paternal- ism whenever they interpose their own judgment rather than allow the audience to exercise theirs (all with an eye to the audience's epistemic prospects). Thus, the exclusion of evidence of doubtful veracity (e.g., hear- say evidence) also qualifies as epistemic paternalism. The courts apparently feel that jurors cannot be counted on to discount hearsay testimony adequately. So they substitute their own wisdom for that of the jurors. Similarly, when judges exclude evidence as irrelevant, they must use *their* assessment of whether the evidence affects the probabilities of the propositions in question (the jurors' assessments might have been different). When these categories of exclusion are added, it is clear that courts engage in a substantial amount of epistemic paternalism.

Is such paternalism really warranted? Are these rules *good* rules from an epistemic point of view? This is open to dispute. Lempert contends that evidence should not be excluded when the probative value is substantial, i.e., when the likelihood ratio deviates markedly from 1 : 1. The preferred solution, he says, is to provide the jury with the information needed to assess accurately the probative value of the offered evidence.

There are general problems with this solution, though. For one thing (as Lempert notes), there may not be hard data that indicate just how heavily a piece of evidence should be weighted. There may be no well-researched (base rate) "facts" to give to the jury. Nonetheless, people with judicial experience may have good reasons to suspect that juries would exaggerate the import of that type of evidence. Second, there is a question of whether statistical information, even if it were available, would psychologically displace or override jurors' prior prejudices.[9] Third, there is a question of whether *all* the relevant considerations that bear on the import of the evidence should be given to the jurors. Should they be presented with the Bayesian framework in terms of which the evidence may be interpreted? Should they be informed of theoretical disputes over the correctness of Bayesianism, or the potential for its misapplication? Much of this material would surely confuse most jurors. The dangers of introducing mathematical techniques into the fact-finding process have been emphasized by Laurence Tribe (1971).

I am inclined to think that *some* paternalism is appropriate in this arena, although I shall not take a firm stand on specific policies. What I want to do is identify the questions clearly and put them in the framework of a wider set of questions. What we have here is a set of rules or practices whose adoption has an impact on the truth values of the doxastic decisions that cognizers make. One question is, For each such rule, how good is its impact from a *veritistic* point of view, that is, in terms of the likelihood of getting truth and avoiding error? Would alternative rules or practices have better veritistic properties?

This type of question falls under what I call *social epistemics*. Epistemics generally is my (partly 'reforming') conception of epistemology, with three main divisions: primary individual epistemics, secondary individual epistemics, and social epistemics. All three divisions seek to make evaluations in terms of veritistic ends, i.e., in terms of the effect on people getting truths and avoiding errors. The objects or targets of evaluation, however, differ from division to division. Primary epistemics studies the veritistic properties of basic psychological processes. Secondary epistemics assesses the veritistic properties of learnable problem-solving methods, such as mathematical proof techniques, carbon dating procedures, and the like. Social epistemics studies the veritistic properties of social practices, or institutional rules that directly or indirectly govern communication and doxastic decision. Judicial rules of evidence clearly fall in this last category.[10] The focus of the present paper is the class of institutional rules or practices that have a flavor of epistemic paternalism, e.g., those that weed out some possible communications that might be directed to a cognitive agent, by appeal to that agent's own veritistic ends. Are such rules and practices defensible, and if so, which ones?

Although social epistemics could content itself with the separate evaluation of individual practices, it seems more advisable to address whole classes of practices. What one wants is a general assessment of paternalistic control practices, first in terms of purely epistemic considerations and second on more inclusive grounds. Before turning to general principles, however, let us examine some additional cases of paternalistic practices.

IV

Start with curriculum selection in education, especially in primary and secondary schools. School personnel at various levels—boards of education, principals, and teachers—select curricular materials in the form of textbooks, course syllabi, and so forth. (When teachers do it, they assume something of a dual role: both controller and speaker.) In the nature of this business, some points of view and supporting argumentation are left out. Students are not exposed to all possible ideas on a given subject. Is this objectionable? Set aside highly publicized examples of book banning based on obscenity, profanity, or offensiveness. Think instead of simply ignoring opinions that have (or once had) their exponents, but are regarded by current authorities as palpably false or indefensible. Mathematics classes do not present alternative (crackpot) mathematics. Science classes do not (often) present the flat-earth viewpoint, Ptolemaic astronomy, or astrology. Schools rarely if ever invite Jeane Dixon or her ilk to give guest lectures, or recount as serious alternatives the theories of Velikovsky. Classes in health education do not give 'equal time' to drug pushers to defend the safety of drug use, or to quacks to present and defend their cures. These omissions probably have veritistically good consequences. Of course, it might also be appropriate to have classes sample and compare 'bad' and 'bogus' science along with the good.[11] But this kind of course might be advantageous only for high school students, not for younger pupils, who would only be confused.

The most public controversy surrounds the question of 'equal time' for creationism in biology classes. Here too paternalism seems to be warranted on epistemic grounds. Experts on science should be allowed to decide that creationism is not a scientifically viable or serious contender, and hence should not be taught in the classroom.[12] What about the teaching of creationism in nonscience classes? Is it legitimate for a local community to require this in their schools? Here extra-epistemic issues intrude. Creationism is presumably a religious doctrine, so that Constitutional issues arise about its being taught in public schools. What about the putative right of parents to control their children's education? If such an alleged right is supposed to rest on purely epistemic considerations, it would be very hard to defend. If it is based on non-epistemic considerations of an ethical or sociopolitical nature, it goes beyond the main focus of our discussion, although I shall briefly return to it in section VII.[13]

Turn next to the sphere of commercial advertising, where the Federal Trade Commission has authority to take actions against false or deceptive advertising. This exemplifies epistemic paternalism because it prevents some potential messages from being conveyed to an audience, and it does so with veritistic ends in mind: to keep them from believing untruths about commercial products. The FTC has four types of remedies for inhibiting false and deceptive advertisements, or even requiring truthful disclosures that the "speakers" would not independently make.[14] First, it can issue *cease and desist* orders. Second, it can seek to obtain *affirmative disclosure*, forcing a manufacturer to disclose by mark or label material facts concerning the merchandise. The most familiar such example is the requirement of warning labels on cigarette packages (although this is under the jurisdiction of the Food and Drug Administration, rather than the FTC). A third remedy is *corrective advertising*. When consumer misconceptions about a product have resulted from past advertising, the FTC has sometimes forced the manufacturer to devote 25 percent of its advertising budget for one year to corrections of past inaccuracies. In this arena, then, communication control sometimes takes a stronger form than the one considered thus far: not excluding messages, but mandating messages of a specified kind or content. A fourth remedy is the FTC's advertisement *substantiation* program. This forbids manufacturers to make certain advertising claims unless they have done competent scientific tests that substantiate their claims. This piece of epistemic paternalism has been rationalized by appeal to the relatively poor opportunity of consumers to obtain accurate information themselves.[15]

Another class of examples involves television and radio news. Generally speaking, American network news broadcasts offer a relatively limited variety of interpretations of each news event; nor do they detail the evidence for each of the possible interpretations. This is partly due, no doubt, to severe time constraints. But there is also the deliberate attempt to simplify, to make the news understandable and digestible to a large audience. Certainly this must be included under the rubric of epistemic paternalism. There is room for debate over how acceptable this practice is, and doubtless different programs and newscasters deserve different ratings on this dimension. But it is hard to deny the need for some degree of simplification, especially on technical topics. If this is at all legitimate, some degree of epistemic paternalism again seems inevitable and unobjectionable.

Simplification involves the omission of some truths. So paternalism in this form reduces the number of truths an audience has an opportunity to acquire. Nonetheless, the trade-off of error avoidance, or confusion avoidance, may compensate for this loss (depending partly on how different segments of the audience are affected).

A further element in the trade-off is that simplification can increase the audience size. This may mean that more true beliefs (i.e., belief tokens) are acquired through the simplified set of messages than would otherwise be the case. Although members of the media may care about this chiefly because of Nielsen ratings, and their consequent attractiveness to advertisers, the number of people acquiring true beliefs is a genuinely epistemic value, which I elsewhere call *fecundity* (see chapter 10).

The epistemic consequences of an institutional policy are often difficult to anticipate. The Federal Communication Commission's 'Fairness Doctrine' is a good case in point. Since holders of its broadcast licenses are supposed to operate in the public interest, the FCC has required licensees to devote a reasonable amount of time to issues of public importance. Moreover, if a station presents one side of a controversial issue of public importance, it must afford reasonable opportunity for presentation of contrasting views. This policy (subsequently abandoned under the Reagan administration) was intended to promote veritistic outcomes by exposing the public to a wide diversity of opinion. It has been argued, however, that its actual result was opposite to its intent. The threat of incurring FCC suits allegedly discouraged stations from airing controversial material. This 'chilling' effect tended to guarantee blandness and to retard rather than enhance a free marketplace of ideas. This is a good example of how a policy's epistemic consequences (historical or prospective) can be a complex empirical question. This is why empirical sciences have a role to play in social epistemics.

V

Let us now inquire into the general circumstances in which epistemic paternalism, and other communication control policies, have good or bad epistemic consequences, i.e., good *veritistic* outcomes. A number of variables are relevant, especially: (1) the characteristics of the *controller* (or 'gatekeeper'), (2) the characteristics of the *speakers* who wish to send messages via the communication channel, (3) the controller's *criterion of selection* among speakers or messages, (4) the characteristics of the *audience*, and (5) the availability of *alternate channels* that address the same topic.

Epistemic outcomes obviously depend heavily on the (epistemically) good judgment of the message controller. If the controller accurately distinguishes true and false claims, and/or true and false pieces of evidence for claims (and their relevance), then the choice of included and excluded messages may well promote truth acquisition on the part of the audience. This brings us immediately to variable (3): the criterion of selection. Does the controller select among candidate messages by reference to (A) their specific content, or (B) the characteristics of the speaker (or a combination of the two)? If the messages directly attempt to answer primary questions in the domain, and the controller himself has expertise on these questions, then a selection based on message content may positively contribute to veritistic outcomes. However, the controller may not purport to know answers to the primary questions in the domain. He may only select messages on the basis of prospective speakers' 'credentials'. Was the speaker an eyewitness to the putative events he wants to describe, or does he have some other access to, or authority about, the facts in question? If the controller is to make veritistically good selections, he must at least have expertise on the question of speaker credentials. (We might call this *secondary*, as opposed to *primary*, expertise.) This is what judges or rule-framers claim to have in the field of legal evidence.

Selection criteria do not always involve purely veritistic considerations. A network may shy away from certain political interpretations because of prospective sponsor or audience disapproval. Since this is not a truth-oriented selection rationale, it raises doubts about the epistemic optimality of the control process.

Speaker characteristics are equally critical to (audience) veritistic outcomes. We have already mentioned the 'access' or authority of speakers on the matters whereof they speak. Of almost comparable importance are the speakers' motivational properties. Do prospective speakers have an incentive for accuracy, or do they have incentives for deception and misrepresentation, as in the case of manufacturers, partisan witnesses, and perhaps even research scientists? If there are incentives for deception, does the *controller* know or suspect them, and does he use them in his selection policy?

Turning to audience characteristics, how informed, sophisticated, rational, etc. are the audience members who are likely to receive the channel's messages? How good are they at weighing competing views or complex chains of evidence? How good are they at assessing the reliability of various speakers or sources of evidence? Clearly, all these traits are crucial to veritistic outcomes. Furthermore, to the extent that the controller takes account of audience characteristics in selecting messages, the controller's knowledge (or true belief) about their characteristics is critical. If the controller has an accurate assessment of the audience's cognitive limits or shortcomings, a paternalistic choice of messages to include (or to *mandate*) may avert potential audience error. Or his policy of selection may avert potential *confusion*, which can lead to doxastic indecision or simple incomprehension of the truth (either of which is a comparatively bad veritistic outcome).

Finally, the availability of alternate communication channels can influence veritistic outcomes. If one channel deploys restrictive selection policies, that does not necessarily mean that the audience is confined to those messages. There may be other potential sources of information.

These are some of the salient factors that bear on the epistemic success of various alternative institutions of communication control. They are the sorts of factors to which social epistemics should appeal in evaluating existing or prospective institutions. As the discussion indicates, institutions or policies of these sorts cannot be rated in the *abstract*, apart from the properties of the individuals who occupy, or are likely to occupy, the different institutional roles. The same institution or policy might work well if the controller has considerable expertise, but poorly if he doesn't. In any case, when the cited variables or parameters take on appropriate values, epistemic paternalism will be justified. My previous examples are, quite plausibly, instances of this sort. So C-RTE must be rejected as a universal principle.

VI

I have been equating epistemically valuable outcomes with true belief and error avoidance. Are there additional epistemic values that this ignores? What about Mill's value of a "clearer perception and livelier impression of truth", produced by its collision with error? And what about the skills to be learned from the process of wrestling with competing doctrines? I suspect that the livelier impression of truth, of which Mill speaks, can be cashed out in terms of a grasp of a larger number of related truths. One learns not simply that answer A_1 to question Q is correct, but that certain other answers, A_2, A_3, etc., have been offered to Q, what the arguments for and against these alternative answers are, and why these alternatives are mistaken. Learning these things doubtless has epistemic value, but it is not an additional *kind* of value. Similarly, the value of argumentative skills can be cashed out in terms of their instrumental value for discovering further truths on one's own, when no instructor is available.

Thomas Scanlon (1972) has expressed doubts about epistemic protectionism by appeal to the value of autonomy, which consists in a person seeing himself as sovereign in deciding what to believe and in weighing reasons for action. Is autonomy an epistemic value of which a person is deprived by epistemic paternalism? If sovereignty is a matter of reserving the final doxastic choice to oneself, as some of Scanlon's passages suggest, this is not compromised by epistemic paternalism. The juror who did not hear certain excluded evidence still has to decide whether to believe what was presented. However, perhaps the point is that whenever a cognitive agent is deprived of some doxastic alternative, or some evidence relevant to that alternative, some degree of sovereignty is reduced. This may be granted, but does this reduction constitute a diminution in *epistemic* value (especially *intrinsic* epistemic value)? I doubt it, though the matter is not wholly clear. An analogous case involves 'practical' value, and the range of alternatives actually scanned by a deliberating agent. Suppose agent S wishes to select a plan of action designed to achieve goal G. If an assistant fails to call to S's attention some unnoticed alternative plan which is in fact worthless (it wouldn't achieve G at all, or would be much too costly), S's planning sovereignty has been reduced; he loses an opportunity to deliberate about the unpresented alternative. But is this a loss in "practical" value? Again, I am doubtful.

Even if we concede a measure of (intrinsic) epistemic value to autonomy, a value compromised in epistemic paternalism, it is questionable whether the loss always outweighs the gains. As John Hardwig (1985) has stressed, we live in an epistemically complex world, where each of us cannot reasonably hope to assess all evidence for all theses personally. We often have to depend on the authority of others. Given this situation, it seems likely that epistemic paternalism will frequently be necessary, and sometimes epistemically desirable.

VII

The burden of the preceding sections is that epistemic paternalism can sometimes be warranted on *epistemic* grounds. Extra-epistemic considerations, however, should unquestionably enter into overall assessments of communication control policy. What are these other considerations?

Let me briefly suggest five additional factors that ought to be considered. First is the *practical significance* factor. Some communications induce audience beliefs that are likely to produce immediate actions with serious outcomes, including harms either to themselves or to other agents. (This is similar to the "clear and present danger" idea.) Direct and serious outcomes are salient in a trial, where juror beliefs dictate court sanctions that directly affect the defendant's welfare (and the welfare, one might say, of society).[16] Similarly, consumer beliefs about commercial products standardly lead to consumption choices, which may directly affect health or safety. These are the cases where epistemic paternalism seems most appropriate. Consumers' welfare, for example, seems to outweigh any presumed right of manufacturers to send any message they like.[17]

A second factor is the *power of the controlling agent*. Epistemic paternalism on the part of isolated individuals is quite a different matter from paternalism exercised by the state, or any other powerful organ of society. There are historical reasons for being very cautious about state control of information.

Closely related to this is the third factor: the *scope* of control. The greater the breadth, the greater the dangers of communicational restriction. This was already mentioned in section V, but is worth repeating here. The exclusion of certain viewpoints from school curricula seems more defensible when it is recalled that students have other communication channels available. They can be taught things (e.g., religion) outside of school. In the case of broadcast news, the public is free to select among numerous stations, and to read newspapers, books, and magazines as well. Thus, the extent of control of any single news outlet is *partial* (and small). The chief objection to state censorship, by contrast, is that it is *total*. This is a very different kettle of fish. My condoning of local epistemic paternalisms should not be taken as an endorsement of global state censorship, especially on topics like news, politics, and public affairs.

This brings me to a fourth factor: the *topic* of the messages being controlled. It has been contended—quite plausibly, in my opinion—that an unregulated marketplace of ideas seems essential for political speech but not commercial speech. Thus, policies should differ for different subjects. I mention this here under non-epistemic factors; but actually it *may* be explainable by reference to epistemic ones. Perhaps we feel comfortable with a mathematics or science authority omitting nonstandard treatments from the curriculum because we acknowledge their expertise in their subjects. By contrast, in matters of (normative) politics and religion, we have no analogous conviction—as a society, at any rate—that there are any experts, and certainly no societal consensus on who the experts are (if any).

A fifth factor (or group of factors) concerns the putative *rights* of concerned agents: a speaker's right to freedom of speech, a communication channel owner's right to run his own station or publication, a parent's right or a community's right to predispose their children toward certain values or heritages, and so on. As indicated, some of these (putative) rights may be rationalized by epistemic factors, but others may be independent. In each case, moreover, the right may not be unconditional, but must be balanced by other rights or interests.[18]

How these non-epistemic factors should be balanced along with the (purely) epistemic ones is a complex matter, and I have no formula to offer. However, the variability of situations along these dimensions makes it reasonable to expect epistemic paternalism to be appropriate (all things considered) in some contexts though inappropriate in many others.

VIII

Since expertise is a prime epistemic factor in the defense of epistemic paternalism, more should be said about it. To justify any particular instance of such paternalism, involving a particular controller, we must have grounds for taking that agent to be an expert. But how, it may be asked, are people supposed to *tell* who (if anyone) has expertise? In particular, if (primary) expertise is defined in terms of believing domain-relevant truths, how can people lacking expertise—novices—identify an expert? Furthermore, when different people hold conflicting views and each claims to be an expert, how can the issue be resolved to their mutual satisfaction?

The problem of *expert identifiability* involves large epistemological issues that can only be addressed here partially, not fully. First, let us define an expert as someone who either (1) *has* true answers to core questions in the domain (i.e., believes or assigns high probability to these answers), or (2) has the *capacity* (usually through the possession of learned methods) to acquire true answers to core questions when they arise. Degree of expertise, then, is primarily a function of the candidate's question-answering *power*, i.e., how often he can form a belief in a correct answer as opposed to having either no opinion or an incorrect opinion.[19] Expertise can also be understood in either a *comparative* or an *absolute* sense. Someone is comparatively expert if his question-answering power ranks high compared with others; absolutely expert if his power ranks high in absolute terms.

The crucial requirement for expert identifiability is that, once candidate experts have produced their answers to target questions, there are 'truth-revealing' situations in which novices and rivals can recognize which answers (if any) are correct. With enough such cases, the genuine experts can be identified. In fact, there are many domains in which such truth-revealing situations exist. Let me catalogue four homely domains of this sort: (1) *prediction* domains, (2) *factual record* domains, (3) *repair* domains, and (4) *design* domains.

Prediction domains are ones in which the core questions are questions about future events, e.g., the weather, the economy, the stock market, or an upcoming election. When the events actually occur, the correct answers to the questions are revealed.

Factual record domains can be illustrated with baseball and opera. An expert in these fields can correctly answer (from memory) questions about baseball or opera facts, e.g., who stole the most bases in 1973, which arias are from which operas, and so forth. Here there are undisputed records to which novices and rivals can appeal to verify correctness.

System repair cases are more interesting. Whether a system (e.g., an air conditioner, an automobile, or a human body) is functioning properly or malfunctioning is frequently an uncontested, novice-detectable affair. Suppose system S is malfunctioning, so the question arises: "What techniques, steps, operations, or therapies would be followed by S returning to proper functioning?" A novice will typically have no answer at all. An expert, by contrast, can often answer correctly. The expert electrician, mechanic, or physician commonly proceeds as follows. First, he tries to find a system component that is causing the malfunction, using gauges, instruments, or other diagnostic techniques. Second, having diagnosed the cause, he decides what part replacements, alterations, adjustments, or medications would correct the malfunction. He thereby arrives at an answer to the target question. Can the truth of his answer be checked? Often it can. If and when the prescribed measures are executed, it will be novice-detectable whether the system resumes normal operation.

The fourth category of domains—design domains—is a fairly heterogeneous lot. Here the core question is: "What specific design or performance features would produce a certain desired effect, or meet certain standards or specifications?" This is the sort of question that sundry artists, designers, product engineers, or even mathematicians might be asked. The engineer might be asked for a blueprint of a dam that will meet certain specifications. A mathematician might be asked for a sequence of steps that would comprise a proof of a given theorem (according to understood constraints on the nature of proof).[20] In each of these cases, novices could not answer such questions correctly very often; but an expert could. (At least he could indicate correctly which answers are erroneous.) Is the correctness of an answer novice-detectable? Often the answer is "yes". Unable to produce a proof himself, the novice mathematician may nonetheless be able to verify whether someone else's proposal constitutes a proof. Whereas it may be difficult to design a theater set or choreograph a sequence that produces a desired effect, it may be palpable and uncontroversial that a certain design or sequence *does* (or does not) achieve that effect.

The moral is that in many familiar cases it is relatively easy, even for novices or rivals, to identify expertise. Needless to say, not all cases are straightforward. However, there is no necessary 'paradox', or impossibility in principle, of expert identification. There is no theoretical objection, then, to invoking the notion of expertise, construed veritistically, in the evaluation of communication practices.

IX

Let me return to the theme of epistemic paternalism, first illustrated with the rejection of C-RTE. To the extent that traditional epistemology has been attentive to the existence of multiple agents, it has generally assumed an idealized setting, in which all agents have the same cognitive resources, skills, and opportunities, where there are no time constraints, and so forth. In that sort of setting, a communication control principle like C-RTE might make sense. But in settings marked by different levels of expertise, by different opportunities for information gathering, by different levels of cognitive maturity and training, and by severe time constraints, idealized principles of communication do not plausibly apply. A social epistemology for the real world needs to take these constraints into account.[21]

The very question of communication control policy is relatively neglected in philosophy,[22] perhaps because the topic has been so thoroughly dominated by the Millian dedication to a free market of ideas. Interestingly, though, organized science and scholarship are very far from laissez-faire marketplaces. On the contrary, professional journals rely heavily on (putatively) expert referees and editors to weed out inferior contributions. Only offerings that are judged methodologically sound, well informed, and possibly in the direction of truth are accepted for publication (or, in a related arena, given research funding). Thus, even in the purely intellectual sphere, laissez-faire is not the de facto policy. More precisely, there is a complex layering of institutions. In free societies, governments pursue the laissez-faire policy of allowing private information channels to proliferate. But these information channels may themselves be highly restrictive in the messages they transmit. It could be argued that successful pursuit of epistemic ends depends not only on "deregulation" at the highest level, but on wise regulation at lower levels. This problem needs a more subtle and systematic examination than it has hitherto received. The present paper is intended to help motivate such an examination.

Notes

For valuable comments and advice I am grateful to Holly Smith, Allen Buchanan, Henning Jensen, Joel Feinberg, Richard Lempert, and the members of the 1989 Dubrovnik conference on epistemology and philosophy of mind.
 1. See Carnap 1950, p. 211, and Hempel 1965, pp. 64–67.
 2. See Good 1983 and Horwich 1982, chap. 6. Good's argument for the strong version of RTE appeals to the criterion of maximizing expected utility, so it seems more pragmatic than purely epistemic. Horwich's argument, however, is purely epistemic. He shows that the *expected error* in one's probability judgment vis-à-vis some hypothesis H is minimized by the acquisition of any new evidence E (as long as $0 < \text{prob}(E) < 1$, and $\text{prob}(H/E) \neq \text{prob}(H/-E)$). I shall not discuss these arguments in detail because I am not so much interested in S-RTE as in the two-agent 'control' version of RTE. In fact, I am not even primarily interested in the control version of RTE. I really use it as an

expository heuristic to introduce the topic of epistemic paternalism, and the topic of communication control more generally.

3. See Goldman 1986 (pp. 1, 5–9, 136–138); 1987b; and chapter 10 in this volume.

4. Relevant evidence is characterized as "evidence having any tendency to make the existence of any fact that is of consequence to the determination of the action more probable or less probable than it would be without the evidence" (Rule 401).

5. I do not mean to endorse the Bayesian analysis for all purposes, including legal purposes. I am merely expositing Lempert's reconstruction. The same morals could well be drawn without commitment to Bayesianism. For an alternative account of reasoning principles for the law, see L. J. Cohen 1977 (which I also do not mean to endorse).

6. In defending the rule against character evidence, the Advisory Committee for the Federal Rules of Evidence quotes the California Law Revision Commission with approval: "Character evidence is of slight probative value and may be very prejudicial. It tends to distract the trier of fact from the main question of what actually happened on the particular occasion. It subtly permits the trier of fact to reward the good man and to punish the bad man because of their respective characters despite what the evidence in the case shows actually happened" (Federal Rules 1989, p. 31).

7. In Horwich's (1982) terms we might express the court's fear of jurors being misled by E as an assessment that the result of their getting E would be an *increase* in the probability of their making an error rather than a reduction. The crucial point, of course, is that the court substitutes its *own* expectation of juror error for that of the jurors themselves, who perhaps would welcome information about the accused's character, criminal record, or withdrawn guilty pleas as likely to reduce their probability of error.

8. For other discussions of the definition of paternalism, see Sartorius 1983 and VanDeVeer 1986, pp. 16–24.

9. Studies by Lee Ross and colleagues give evidence of a 'perseveration' phenomenon, in which previously acquired beliefs are not eradicated even by new evidence showing that the original basis of those beliefs was ill-founded (see Nisbett and Ross 1980, chap. 8). I have suggested more generally that beliefs can never be 'erased', but at best only 'overridden'; this allows for *credal residues* (cf. Goldman 1986, pp. 223–226).

10. For further discussion of the divisions of epistemics, and the rationale for them, see chapter 10 and Goldman 1987b. For another treatment of judicial rules of evidence in the context of social epistemics, see Burgess-Jackson 1986. I thank Burgess-Jackson for helping draw my attention to relevance rules.

11. The phraseology is borrowed from the title of Martin Gardner's book, *Science: Good, Bad, and Bogus* (Gardner 1981).

12. This is not to dispute Paul Feyerabend's (1978) point that the expertise of science and scientists must ultimately be judged by laymen. The thesis that laymen can assess the credentials of putative experts is discussed in section VIII.

13. On issues of educational philosophy and the control of educational policy, see Gutmann 1987.

14. On these topics see Gillmor and Barron 1984, chap. 8, and Rohrer 1979, chap. 3.

15. FTC Chairman Miles Kirkpatrick wrote: "The manufacturer has the ability, the know-how, the equipment, the time and the resources to undertake such information by testing or otherwise—the consumer usually does not." (Quoted in Gillmor and Barron 1984, pp. 618–619.)

16. Of course, where the defendant is in fact guilty, his welfare is not served by finding the truth. Presumably, however, society's utility is increased by accurate verdicts.

17. There is ongoing debate, however, over the extent to which commercial speech is protected under First Amendment guarantees of freedom of speech. Not everyone agrees that regulation of advertising is legally defensible, or a good idea (see, for example, Coase 1977).

18. Scanlon (1983) has emphasized that issues in the freedom of expression hinge on the interests of three parties: participants (speakers), audiences, and bystanders. In cases of communication control, however, the interested parties are even more numerous. And in the case of children, some sort of special status (not merely 'bystander') seems appropriate for parents and community.

19. The epistemic importance of question-answering power is emphasized in chapter 9 and in Goldman 1986, chap. 6. A further dimension in the definition of expertise should probably be added: the ability to recognize *wrong* answers as wrong (or assign them a low probability). Even if nobody has a correct answer to question Q, someone who knows (or truly believes) that each of the available answers is wrong is better off, epistemically, than someone who mistakenly believes (or assigns high probability to) wrong answers.

20. Even certain questions of theoretical science might be construed in this fashion, viz., "What is a theory in domain D that meets all the known empirical and conceptual constraints?"

21. I stress a similar theme of psychological realism in Goldman 1986. Issues raised for moral theory by cognitive limits are stressed in H. Smith 1988 and 1989.

22. However, one author who stresses the role of communication in a theory of rationality is Jürgen Habermas (1981).

Chapter 12

An Economic Model of Scientific Activity and Truth Acquisition

with Moshe Shaked

I

Economic forms of analysis have penetrated to many disciplines in the last thirty years: political science, sociology, law, social and political philosophy, and so forth. We wish to extend the economic paradigm to certain problems in epistemology and the philosophy of science. Scientific agents, and scholarly inquirers generally, act in some ways like vendors, trying to "sell" their findings, theories, analyses, or arguments to an audience of prospective "buyers". The analogy with the marketplace is imperfect. The ideas or discoveries that a scientist offers are not private goods in the economist's sense. Nonetheless, there are parallels with the marketplace that are worth exploring.[1]

In this paper we explore the assumption that scientists, scholars, and other inquirers in professional communities engage in activities primarily in the attempt to advance their professional interests. Let us suppose that they choose their actions in accordance with the rule of maximizing expected utility (MEU), and their utility level is determined solely by professional success.[2] We do not claim that professional success *is* the sole motive of scientists (nor do we deny it). However, this thesis is sufficiently attractive to many people that it is worth considering what its ramifications would be for the truth-getting propensities of science.

A widespread view in the "social studies of science" is that a successful descriptive account of science in terms of non-epistemic goals like promoting one's reputation undermines the picture of science as a truth-finding or knowledge-acquiring enterprise. It is commonly assumed (or hinted) that the presence of such a motivational pattern would constitute a refutation or debunking of an objectivist construal of science. We shall argue, to the contrary, that there is no necessary incompatibility between the goal of professional success and the promotion of truth acquisition. Indeed, in some cases, as we shall show, there is a positive connection. On the other hand, we do not claim that the credit-seeking motive is an *ideal* motive for guiding scientific activity. We do not venture as far as David Hull, who speaks of a "coincidence" between the interest of the individual in gaining credit and the institutional aim of science to increase empirical knowledge (Hull 1988, p. 357). A credit-seeking motive may well perturb or deflect scientific activity away from truth acquisition, as compared with the results of a purer, truth-seeking motive. This is a second issue that we address, at least for a limited class of problems.

The model of scientific activity presented here is oversimplified as well as schematic It is usual in model construction, however, to start with simple models, observe their implications, and then proceed to subsequent refinements.

II

In professional communities like science and the academy, personal success consists, in large part, in good reputation. Good reputation often gets translated into other goods: higher salaries, more prestigious appointments, prizes, and so forth. But let us fix our attention on the professional respect or esteem that colleagues accord to an agent. In the case of science and scholarship such respect depends chiefly on the contributions one makes to the field, at least on the community's assessment or reception of these contributions. The emphasis is on original contributions. Credits are earned by the discovery or formulation of new evidence, new hypotheses, or new lines of argumentation and analysis, that bear on the inquiry at hand.

Consider a community, or network, of agents $A_1, A_2, \ldots, A_n$, who are all interested in a certain world-state W. W consists in a set of mutually exclusive and exhaustive possibilities, $w_1, w_2, \ldots, w_k$, which are assumed to be given. We leave open exactly what substitutions can be made for W. The scope of W at least includes such examples as whether it will rain tomorrow, or whether the Earth undergoes continental drift. But we shall not take a firm position on whether "in principle" unobservable states also qualify as world-states for present purposes (though we are inclined to think that they do).

In our model, each agent begins with a prior probability distribution over the possible states. She also starts with other subjective probabilities to be introduced later. To earn scientific or scholarly credits in the community, an agent must make and present a finding, or argument, that changes other agents' subjective probabilities. Actually, we can distinguish *direct*, or *first-order*, respect from *indirect*, or *second-order*, respect. First-order respect is given by specialists in the contributor's own field, who personally change their probabilities as a result of the contributor's work. Second-order respect is conferred by agents outside the field, who ascribe credit only on the testimony of such specialists, not because they personally change their probabilities. We concentrate here on first-order respect.

There are two types of *acts* that agents can perform. First, there are *information seeking*, or *investigative*, acts, in which an agent performs an experiment, samples a population, studies original documents, tries to invent a new hypothesis or refine an old one, or makes funding applications to undertake such research. These activities are what some philosophers of science call *pursuit* (Laudan 1977). Second, there are *speech* acts, in which agents present their findings and/or arguments to the community. We assume that speech acts are published, or "broadcast", to the entire community. A typical speech act cites a newly discovered piece of evidence or argument E in favor of the contention that a particular state w_i of the world actually obtains (did obtain, will obtain). The content of such a speech act is represented as an ordered pair $\langle E, w_i \rangle$. More precisely, such speech acts will be called *primary* speech acts. *Secondary* speech acts are criticisms or rebuttals of primary speech acts. A criticism or rebuttal can take three forms. (i) It can deny that the originally cited evidence E obtains at all. (ii) It can present an argument E' to the effect that E does not really support w_i (or not as strongly as alleged). (iii) It can adduce new evidence E' and argue that E' *defeats* the support that E gives to w_i. In other words, it alleges that the conjunction of E and E' does not support w_i (or not so strongly).

The effect of successful speech acts is to persuade other agents in the community to revise their subjective probabilities vis-à-vis w_i, specifically, to revise them in the direction that the speaker urges. When a hearer A^* makes such a revision in response to the speech act of agent A, then A^* credits A with a "contribution" to the topic. This means she confers added units of (scientific or scholarly) respect to A. This probability-change account of credit is arguably imperfect, but we shall adopt it here as a tolerable *first approximation*.[3]

As indicated earlier, respect of this sort is precisely what we assume that agents value (and it is assumed that they have perfect information about the credits assigned to them). With one qualification, we take it that an agent's utility varies *linearly* with the total credit received from all other agents. The qualification is that an agent may place greater weight on respect received from selected others, e.g., their department head, or prestigious figures in the field. More precisely, then, utility is linear with weighted credit.

Given this source of utility, agents choose both investigative acts and speech acts in terms of expected profit—their expectation of prospective credits minus costs. One measure of the cost of informational activity is time. A protracted research project is costly because it forces one to forego alternate research activities that might be productive of respect.

III

To illustrate these ideas, we construct a hypothetical case and trace it through a cycle of relevant events. The cycle is shown in Table 12.1. There are four agents in this example, A_1, A_2, A_3, and A_4, and three possible world-states, w_1, w_2, and w_3. At time t_0, each agent has a prior probability distribution over these possible states. For example, A_1's subjective probabilities for w_1, w_2, and w_3 are .70, .10, and .20 respectively. At time t_1 primary speech acts are performed, only one in this example. This consists of A_1 presenting evidence e_1 in support of world-state w_1. (This is evidence A_1 obtained prior to t_0.)

In time frame t_2, all agents make probability revisions (possibly null) in response to A_1's speech act. (A_1 makes no revision, since her initial probability distribution was assumed to reflect e_1.) In the most general form of the model, we need not restrict the rules or practices agents use to update their probabilities. Later, however, the assumption of Bayesian conditionalization, or updating, will be invoked.

In the next time frame, agent A_4 engages in information-seeking activity. Let us expand on the nature of such activity. All investigative action consists in engaging or consulting some information *source*. (Even trying to retrieve information from one's own memory, or reflecting on the implications of prior beliefs, might be subsumed under this.) Information sources can be other human agents or Nature herself. In scientific observation or experimentation, which is the central case to be examined here, consultation consists in observing some aspect of the world, perhaps with special instruments or under specially designed experimental arrangements. In the extreme case, one directly observes which of the W states actually obtains. More generally, one observes events that are probabilistically related to the elements of W. The output of an information source will be called an *outcome*. Evidence cited in an experimentally based speech act consists of a specification of the experiment that was performed and the outcome actually observed.

Returning to our imagined cycle of events, in time frame t_3 agent A_4 consults source 7 (the label is arbitrary) and outcome 17 is observed. Let e_2 be the proposition describing the source and outcome. A_4 interprets this outcome as evidence that defeats or rebuts e_1's support for w_1—either total or partial rebuttal. A_4 therefore presents e_2 as a response to A_1's primary speech act. This secondary speech act occurs at time t_4. In the next time frame, agents make another probability revision. The two stages of probability revision determine how many credits are accorded to agents A_1 and A_4.[4]

Suppose agents assign credits as a function of how much they think they have "learned" from a contributor. If someone's contribution makes you

Table 12.1

Time epoch	t_0 Prior probabilities	t_1 Primary speech act	t_2 Revised probabilities	t_3 Investigative act and outcome	t_4 Critical response	t_5 Final probabilities	Credit for A_1	Credit for A_4
A_1	.7, .1, .2	$\langle e_1, w_1 \rangle$	.7, .1, .2			.6, .2, .2		10
A_2	.4, .3, .3		.8, .1, .1			.6, .2, .2	$40 - \frac{1}{2}(20) = 30$	20
A_3	.2, .1, .7		.3, .1, .6			.3, .1, .6	10	0
A_4	.3, .3, .4		.5, .2, .3	Consult source 7 → outcome 17	$\langle e_2; e_2$ defeats $e_1 \rangle$	.3, .3, .4	$20 - \frac{1}{2}(20) = 10$	

revise the plausibility of a certain state obtaining, you feel you have learned something. You may not be wholly confident, of course, that this state obtains; indeed, you might still think it improbable. But if the contribution changes your probability, you assign credits accordingly. However, if the evidence or argument is subsequently rebutted, you no longer accord as much credit to the original contributor. You won't expunge her credits entirely, because she still made a worthwhile contribution. But since the contribution does not (completely) "hold up", you decrement the initial amount of respect it elicited.

Following this line of thought, a pair of credit assignment rules will be adopted. The first rule says that the amount of credit assigned by an agent to an unrebutted contribution in support of w_i equals the magnitude (absolute value) of her probability revision vis-à-vis w_i resulting from that contribution, times 100. (The revision can be upward or downward, as long as it moves in the direction urged by the contributor.) In other words, let α be the agent's prior probability for w_i, α' be her posterior probability, and let C be the credit conferred. Then we have:

Rule 1 $C = 100|\alpha' - \alpha|$.[5]

Where a contribution is judged to be subsequently rebutted, we need a second rule. The rebutting agent gets full credit for the magnitude of probability change that her rebuttal produces. The credit of the original (primary) contributor, however, is decremented by half of the probability reduction that the rebuttal produces. In other words, where α^* is the judge's probability assignment for w_i after the rebuttal, the credit assigned to the primary contributor is given by:

Rule 2 $C = 100(|\alpha' - \alpha| - 1/2|\alpha' - \alpha^*|)$,

where $\alpha \leq \alpha^* \leq \alpha'$, or $\alpha \geq \alpha^* \geq \alpha'$.

Applying Rule 2 to our example, let us trace the credits assigned to A_1. In response to A_1's speech act, A_2 changes her probability assignment for w_1 from .40 at t_0 to .80 at t_2. So A_2's initial change is .40. But after A_4's rebuttal, A_2 reduces her probability assignment to .60. So A_2's post-rebuttal reduction is .20. Using Rule 2, the credit assigned by A_2 to A_1, which will be written $C(A_2, A_1)$, is $100[.40 - 1/2(.20)] = 30$. By similar calculations, $C(A_3, A_1) = 10$ and $C(A_4, A_1) = 10$. Credits assigned to A_4 by the other three agents are determined in the same way, yielding 10, 20, and 0 credits from A_1, A_2, and A_3 respectively.[6]

In gauging a contribution's impact, our model looks only at probability changes concerning a single topic or world-state. Admittedly, some scientific and scholarly contributions, especially theoretical ones, have wide impact, inducing probability changes concerning numerous topics. In any future development of our theme, this dimension ought to be incorporated. In the present paper, however, attention is restricted to a single topic or world-state per example.

IV

Let us now examine the decision processes of selecting actions, both investigative ("pursuit") actions and speech actions. Our paradigm of an information-seeking act is the running of a scientific experiment. In focusing on experiments, we do not, of course, question the importance of activities aimed at developing new hypotheses or theories; nor do we imply that experimental contributions have more impact on probabilities than theoretical ones. We concentrate on experimental activity simply because it is more tractable, because it can be treated analytically and mathematically within a familiar (Bayesian) framework.

The choice of experiment is made by the agent. The choice of experimental *outcome* is made by Nature. Assume that agent A considers three possible experiments: x_1, x_2, and x_3, each with three possible observational outcomes. The outcomes of x_2, for example, are z_{21}, z_{22}, and z_{23}. The probabilities of the outcomes, given a test, depend on the world-state, which can be w_1, w_2, or w_3. Once an outcome occurs, agent A has four speech act alternatives: saying nothing (s_0), presenting the observed result and claiming that it supports w_1 (s_1), presenting the result and claiming that it supports w_2 (s_2), or presenting the result and claiming that it supports w_3 (s_3).[7] Once the speech act is chosen and performed, other agents change their probabilities and assign credits. For present purposes, these reactions of the audience are treated as belonging to Nature. (If they were represented as choices by other agents, we would be drawn into a *game*-theoretic analysis. We want to stick to a *decision*-theoretic analysis in the interest of simplicity.) We shall also henceforth neglect secondary, i.e., "critical", speech acts.

The decision structure is depicted in figure 12.1 by a decision-flow diagram, in which squares represent choice points for the agent and circles represent forks under the control of Nature (or chance). It was previously assumed that all agents assign prior probabilities to the W-states. Now add the assumption that they assign conditional probabilities to the occurrence of the various outcomes given each of the possible world-states. For example, if A performs x_2, she may estimate the conditional probability that z_{23} would occur given w_1 as .45. That is, $pr(z_{23}|x_2 \& w_1) = .45$. We also assume that the agent makes conditional probability estimates of the probability changes (and hence credit assignments) that will ensue if she performs various speech acts, once certain experiment-outcome combinations have

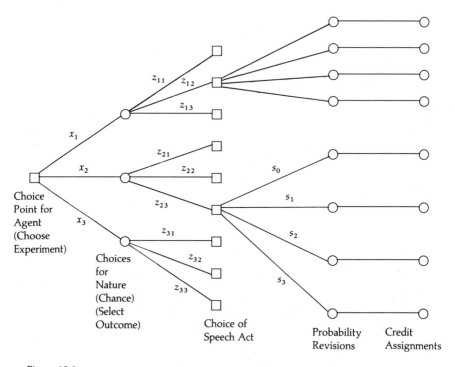

Figure 12.1

transpired. For example, she estimates the credits to be earned if she performs this or that speech act, given that x_2 and z_{23} have already transpired. (These estimates partly depend on her estimates of the prospects of other agents' performing various investigative acts, getting various results, and then performing secondary speech acts. These details are not included in the diagram.)

There is a general algorithm (the folding back algorithm) for selecting a sequence of actions that maximizes expected utility in complex cases of this sort (see Raiffa 1968). We shall not review this technique in detail, nor do we assume that real agents possess such an algorithm. It is reasonable to assume, though, that agents are sensitive to the principal factors that our scheme articulates. They recognize that different possible experiments might yield more or less influential results, and they prefer the (prospectively) more persuasive ones. Similarly, agents are generally sensitive to the threat of critical responses. They prepare their speech acts with an eye to averting or protecting themselves against potentially damaging criticisms. Of course, the expected costs of each of the experiments, measured in utility terms, must also be taken into account, since agents wish to maximize *net* expected utility. We shall not, however, explore details of cost calculations.[8]

V

It is time to turn to the question of truth. Nothing in the discussion thus far bears on the question of whether any agent believes, or assigns a high judgmental probability to, a *true* (or actual) world-state. Nor does it bear on the *objective* probability that scientists will move "closer" to the truth as a result of the motivations and rewards we have described, or the research and speech activities they encourage. Are there circumstances in which truth acquisition would be promoted? If so, what circumstances?

We must first explain more precisely what might be meant by (greater) "acquisition" or "possession" of truth. Possession or acquisition of a truth is most readily understood as *believing* a truth. But here we are dealing with subjective probabilities, not flat-out beliefs. In this context it is natural to think of matters in terms of degrees of truth-possession. *If proposition P is true, then the higher an agent's probability for P, the greater is her "possession" of that truth.* An agent's degree of truth possession for a specified set of possible world-states depends on her probability assignment to the proposition, or possible world-state, that happens to be true (to obtain).[9]

Next we need to separate our general questions into three categories. First, do research findings—e.g., experimental outcomes—tend to promote greater possession of truth? Are there some circumstances, at least, in which truth possession is fostered? Second, does the postulated credit-seeking motive of scientists foster truth acquisition? Third, how does the credit-seeking motive compare with a "purer", truth-seeking motive, in terms of truth acquisition? The first of these questions is addressed in this section, the second and third questions in the following section. In the final section we consider some ancillary topics, e.g., the impact of alternate credit-conferring schemes.

Before proceeding, the further assumption is added that all agents update their subjective probabilities by simple conditionalization.[10] Suppose there are two possibilities for world-state W, w_1 and w_2, and an experiment has been performed that yields outcome z. When z is reported, each agent assigns probability 1.0 to this outcome (the possibility of a false report is ignored). She then determines her posterior probability vis-à-vis w_1, given z, by the Bayesian formula:

$$pr(w_1|z) = \frac{pr(z|w_1)pr(w_1)}{pr(z|w_1)pr(w_1) + pr(z|w_2)pr(w_2)}.$$

Of course, this version of Bayes's theorem is readily generalized to the case of n possible world-states (or hypotheses). It was previously assumed that each agent has a subjective probability assignment for the conditional probability $pr(z|w_1)$, and an assignment for the conditional probability $pr(z|w_2)$. These are commonly called the "likelihoods" (of z). The likelihood ratio (vis-à-vis w_1) is $pr(z|w_1)/pr(z|w_2)$. Conditionalization depends heavily on the likelihood ratio. In particular, in the two-hypothesis case, an agent's probability for w_1 is revised upward if the likelihood ratio is greater than 1, downward if the likelihood ratio is less than 1. Furthermore, the amount of revision increases as the likelihood ratio moves away from 1. The probability remains unchanged if the likelihood ratio = 1, i.e., if the likelihoods are the same.

Clearly, research findings do not necessarily lead to greater possession of truth, even if the agents are Bayesians. If an agent has "crazy" estimates of the relevant likelihoods, newly observed experimental evidence is prone to lead her systematically toward error rather than truth. Let w_1 be the hypothesis that it will rain tomorrow and w_2 the hypothesis that it will not rain. An investigator performs the "experiment" of reading the barometer and reports that it is falling. A listener has a prior probability of .4 for w_1 and .6 for w_2. However, this listener also thinks that a falling barometer (z_f) is more likely to be observed if it is not going to rain than if it is. Let's say, $pr(z_f|w_2) = .6$ and $pr(z_f|w_1) = .3$. These likelihoods will lead the listener to a lower posterior probability for rain, which may in fact lead to greater error.

Now let us suppose that there are *correct* or *objective* likelihoods in these sorts of cases.[11] Then it is plausible to conjecture that if agents update their probabilities in conformity with these likelihoods—if their subjective likelihoods match the objective likelihoods—then their probability revisions will tend to generate greater possession of truth, at least on the average. To put the point in different terminology, if an agent has an accurate "model" (in the stochastic sense) of the phenomenon in question, then her probability revisions conforming to Bayes's theorem will yield an average, or (objectively) expected, improvement in truth possession. This conjecture is correct. Let us mean by an improvement in truth possession a non-negative change in subjective probability vis-à-vis the true hypothesis (or world-state). That is, if w_i is the true hypothesis, α is the agent's subjective prior for w_i, and α' her posterior, then the (objectively) expected change will always be non-negative, that is, $E(\alpha' - \alpha) \geq 0$. Moreover, when $0 < \alpha < 1$, and the likelihood ratio $\neq 1$, then $E(\alpha' - \alpha) > 0$. Of course, there are typically some possible outcomes that would produce a decrease in truth possession. But the average, or expected, change is always non-negative (indeed, positive as long as the indicated conditions hold). A full statement and proof of this appears as Theorem 1 in the appendix.

To get an intuitive feel for the theorem, consider a numerical example. Again let our two hypotheses, w_1 and w_2, be the occurrence and nonoccurrence of rain tomorrow. Let Z be a random observable variable that is probabilistically linked to this (future) world-state. Assume there are three possible values of this variable: z_1, z_2, and z_3. These are meteorological conditions that might obtain today. The table of likelihoods (in statistical terminology, densities) for the present example is given below, The number in each cell represents the probability of the Z-value of the column given the world-state of the row. Thus, the probability .4 in the upper left-most cell represents the probability of z_1 being observed on the assumption that it is going to rain.

	z_1	z_2	z_3
w_1	.4	.1	.5
w_2	.3	.5	.2

Where α is again the prior for w_1 (and $1 - \alpha$ the prior for w_2), the posterior probability α' for w_1 (or $1 - \alpha'$ for w_2) will depend on the Z-value that is observed. Represent the posterior for w_1 that would result from observing z_i as $\alpha'(z_i)$. The value of $\alpha'(z_i)$ is obtained by Bayes's theorem using the relevant agent's subjective likelihoods. (For these purposes, the relevant agent is normally a listener, or prospective creditor.) But since we are now assuming that the subjective likelihoods coincide with the objective ones, we can use the values of the latter throughout.

Consider the case in which $\alpha = .80$. Then if the agent learns of the occurrence of z_1, Bayes's theorem implies that $\alpha' = .84$. This would be an upward revision of $+.04$. Similarly, $\alpha'(z_2) = .47$, a movement of $-.33$; and $\alpha'(z_3) = .91$, an increase of $+.11$.

Now assume first that w_1 is (will be) the *true*, or actual, world-state. Then we calculate the objectively expected change in truth possession associated with observing the value of Z. As implied by the previous paragraph, if z_1 is observed, there will be an increase in truth possession of .04; if z_2, a decrease in truth possession of .33; if z_3, an increase in truth possession of .11. The expected change in truth possession (on the assumption that w_1 is true) is obtained by multiplying each possible change by its objective likelihood (given w_1). This yields $E_1(\alpha' - \alpha) = .4(+.04) + .1(-.33) + .5(+.11) = +.038$. As Theorem 1 implies, this expected value is indeed positive.

Next we calculate the expected change in truth possession on the assumption that w_2 is true. Here an observation of z_1 would generate a probability change for w_2 from .20 to .16; z_2 a change from .20 to .53; and z_3 a change from .20 to .09. These would involve a .04 decrease in truth possession, a .33 increase in truth possession, and a .11 decrease in truth possession, respectively. Multiplying these by their respective objective probabilities (given w_2), we obtain: $E_2[(1 - \alpha') - (1 - \alpha)] = E_2(\alpha - \alpha') = .3(-.04) + .5(+.33) + .2(-.11) = +.131$. This expected value, of course, is also positive. Thus, whichever world-state is the true state, updating as a function of the observed value of Z has an expected increase in truth possession. These calculations were done for $\alpha = .80$. But Theorem 1 ensures an expected improvement in truth possession *for every prior*.

The next plausible conjecture is that experiments with *more extreme* likelihood ratios, i.e., more *discriminating* experiments, produce relatively greater expected increases in truth possession. This is proved in Theorem 2 (see appendix) for the special case of two possible hypotheses (world-states) and two possible values of Z. This theorem will now be illustrated in the text.

Suppose the world-states are w_1 and w_2 as before. Now, however, there are two different meteorological variables, Z and Z^*, whose values can be observed. Z^* is a more "discriminating" observation, or experiment, in roughly the sense that its likelihood ratios are farther from 1 than the corresponding likelihood ratios associated with Z, as shown in the table below. The expected increase in truth possession associated with Z^* is greater than that associated with Z, whichever is the true world-state. This is illustrated for $\alpha = .50$. With that prior, the expected increase from Experiment 1 is .083, and the expected increase from Experiment 2 is .247, whether w_1 or w_2 is true.

Experiment 1

$Z =$	z_1	z_2
w_1	.6	.4
w_2	.2	.8

Experiment 2

$Z^* =$	z_1^*	z_2^*
w_1	.8	.2
w_2	.1	.9

VI

In this section we address the second and third questions posed in section V, viz., Does the credit-seeking motive foster truth acquisition? And how well does this motive perform as compared with a purer, truth-seeking motive, in terms of truth acquisition? Of course, we do not examine these questions in full generality, only for the category of problems to which we have confined our attention.

At this juncture let us change notation slightly and use 'S' for the scientist/decision maker and 'K' for the creditor. Normally, of course, scientific audiences have many members, but for ease of computation and perspicuity of formulation, we consider a single, representative creditor.

Given Theorem 1, it is obvious that there are circumstances in which a credit-seeking agent will perform actions that generate an (objectively expected) increase in truth possession. Suppose that both S and K have accurate likelihoods associated with the possible experiments S might perform. Then if there is any such experiment for which the likelihood ratio $\neq 1$, and for which K's α is neither 0 nor 1, then S will expect that if she performs such an experiment and reports its outcome, she will change K's probability and thereby earn some credit from K. (This assumes that S knows K's α, K's likelihoods, K's Bayesian updating procedure, and K's credit-assignment procedure, which conforms with Rule 1. Notice too that since S's and K's likelihoods coincide, any outcome of an experiment would move K's probability in the same direction as S's.) Then as long as any of S's possible experiments has an expected utility that exceeds its expected cost, S will perform one of these experiments and report its outcome. By Theorem 1, this will generate an average, or objectively expected, increase in K's truth possession.

Now let us see if we can obtain a stronger result about the choice of experiments and the average increase in truth possession, keeping the same assumptions made above. We know from Theorem 2 that for any pair of 2×2 experiments, a more discriminating experiment has a larger average increase in truth possession associated with it than a less discriminating one. So if a credit-seeking agent would always choose the more discriminating experiment from a given pair, it would follow that the credit-seeking agent would always make the optimal choice from the perspective of (average) truth acquisition. Is it the case that a credit-seeking agent would always make this optimal choice (assuming the experiments to be equally costly)?

The answer is: not always, but usually. To see this, we first need to describe how the credit-seeking agent S chooses from a pair of 2×2 experiments. S wants to choose that experiment which maximizes the credit K will confer on her. Since credit is proportional to absolute change in K's probability (whether or not the change is in the direction of truth), S will choose that experiment which maximizes the expected change in K's probability. In some cases, this will depend on the particular value of S's own prior for w_1, which we shall denote by β, as well on as on K's prior, α.

There are two types of cases to be considered. In one type of case, for a given pair of experiments (one more discriminating than the other) and a given value of K's α, the more discriminating experiment generates the greater expected (absolute) change in K's probability *both* under the assumption that w_1 is true *and* under the assumption that w_2 is true. Here the more discriminating experiment *dominates* the less discriminating one, so we call such cases *dominance* cases. In dominance cases the credit-motivated (CM) agent S always chooses the more discriminating experiment, *no matter what her β*.

An example of dominance is the pair of experiments 1 and 2 described at the end of section V, combined with a value of .40 for K's α. To show this, we first calculate the expected change in K's probability that is associated with Experiment 1. If z_1 is observed, K's posterior probability $\alpha' = .67$; and if z_2 is observed, $\alpha' = .25$. This amounts to (absolute) changes of .27 and .15 respectively. Under the assumption that w_1, is true, the expected change $E_1|\alpha' - \alpha| = (.6)(.27) + (.4)(.15) = .216$. Under the assumption that w_2 is true, the expected change $E_2|\alpha' - \alpha| = (.2)(.27) + (.8)(.15) = .174$. Turning to Experiment 2, we find that the outcome z_1^* would yield $\alpha' = .84$, and z_2^* would yield $\alpha' = .13$. This amounts to changes of .44 and .27 respectively. Thus, for this experiment, $E_1|\alpha' - \alpha| = (.8)(.44) + (.2)(.27) = .406$, and $E_2|\alpha' - \alpha| = (.1)(.44) + (.9)(.27) = .287$. Let us now compare the expected changes between the two experiments. If w_1 is true, the expected change for Experiment 1 is .216, for Experiment 2, .406. If w_2 is true, the expected change for Experiment 1 is .174, for Experiment 2, .287. So in either case, the expected change (and hence expected credit) is greater with Experiment 2. So the CM agent will choose Experiment 2.

A second class of cases are pairs of experiments and values of α such that there is no dominance. Under the assumption that one world-state holds, the expected change is greater with the more discriminating experiment, but under the assumption that the other world-state holds, the expected change is greater with the less discriminating experiment. An example of such a *nondominance* case is the following pair of experiments, combined with $\alpha = .90$.

Experiment 3

	z_1	z_2
w_1	.9	.1
w_2	.1	.9

Experiment 4

	z_1^*	z_2^*
w_1	.99	.01
w_2	.01	.99

For this set of assumptions, the expected change in K's probability if w_1 is true is greater for Experiment 3, but the expected change in K's probability if w_2 is true is greater for Experiment 4. (We omit the calculations.) Here S will not necessarily choose the more discriminating experiment (i.e., 4). Her choice will depend on her β, that is, on her own prior probability for the truth of w_1. In general, S's subjectively expected change in K's probability is given by the formula: $EC = \beta \cdot E_1 |\alpha' - \alpha| + (1 - \beta) \cdot E_2 |\alpha' - \alpha|$. Applying the formula to this particular example, S will choose Experiment 3 if $\beta \geq .971$; otherwise she will choose Experiment 4. We have, then, a *counterexample* to the generalization that the CM agent will *always* choose the more discriminating experiment. In this case, for certain (admittedly extreme) values of her prior, S will choose the experiment with the *smaller* expected increase in truth possession.

However, Theorem 3 (see appendix) shows that, for a large number of combinations of α and β, S will choose the experiment with the larger expected increase in truth possession, i.e., the more discriminating experiment. In particular, either of the following two conditions is *sufficient* for the more discriminating experiment to be chosen:

(1) $\alpha \leq \frac{1}{2}$ and $\beta \geq \alpha$, or

(2) $\alpha \geq \frac{1}{2}$ and $\beta \leq \alpha$.

This is depicted in figure 12.2, in which the shaded area corresponds to the combinations of α and β which guarantee that S chooses the more discriminating experiment. These combinations occupy three-quarters of the space of possible (α, β) combinations. Notice, however, that (α, β) combinations lying in the *un*shaded area do *not* guarantee choice of the *less* discriminating experiment. Pairs of experiments associated with these combinations (in particular, with various α's) could still be cases of dominance; indeed, maybe *most* of them are cases of dominance. And dominance, of course, is also a sufficient condition for choice of the "better" experiment. Thus, the fraction of possible cases in which the better experiment would be chosen

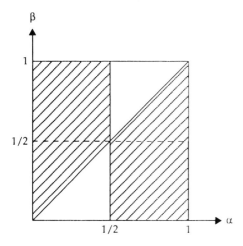

Figure 12.2

is definitely greater than three-quarters (although actual instances may not be evenly distributed over the space of (α, β) combinations).

Finally, we point out that there are no cases in which a less discriminating experiment dominates its more discriminating mate. This follows from Corollary 1, which is presented and proved in the appendix. For any K, either $\alpha \leq .5$ or $(1 - \alpha) \leq .5$. Now if $\alpha \leq .5$, the corollary shows that if w_1 is true, the more discriminating experiment generates a greater expected probability change. On the other hand, if $(1 - \alpha) \leq .5$, the corollary shows that if w_2 is true, the more discriminating experiment generates a greater expected probability change. So there is no case in which the *less* discriminating experiment has a greater expected probability change *both* under the assumption that w_1 is true *and* under the assumption that w_2 is true.

We can sum up this discussion by saying that, *typically*, a CM agent will choose the more discriminating of a pair of (2×2) experiments, either because it is a dominance case, or because it is a nondominance case with appropriate values of α and β. So a CM agent typically chooses the "better" experiment, from the perspective of expected increase in truth possession. However, there are some cases in which the "worse" experiment is chosen.

Let us now turn to the third question posed in section V. How does the performance of a CM agent compare with that of a pure, truth-motivated (TM) agent, whose expected utility is identical to the expected increase in societal truth possession? The TM agent, we suppose, is also an MEUer, only she gets utility from the truth possession of others, not from the credit they confer on her. Obviously, a TM agent who knows the objective likelihoods and can make the requisite calculations always chooses the more discriminating experiment in the choice situations just considered, for (by Theorem 2) that is always the experiment with the larger expected increase in truth possession. Where subjective likelihoods match objective likelihoods, then, there is a coincidence between the TM agent's choice and the optimal choice from a truth possession point of view. Since the CM agent does not always make the optimal choice, the TM agent turns in a superior overall performance. It is not *much* superior, however, since the CM agent makes the worse choice only in atypical cases.

The foregoing results apply where subjective and objective likelihoods coincide. What happens when we drop that assumption? Suppose K's likelihoods are radically inaccurate. What will a CM agent do, who herself has accurate likelihoods but knows (or believes) that K's likelihoods are inaccurate?

At this juncture it is convenient to drop the restriction on credit conferral that restricts such credit to cases in which K revises her probability *in the same direction* as (urged by) S. On further reflection, this requirement is questionable anyway. A hearer may learn something valuable from an experimenter, and credit her for providing this information, even if she thinks that the experimenter draws the wrong conclusion. So let us assume that credit is conferred simply as a function of probability change, even if K is moved by the experimental outcome in a direction opposite from S.

Under this assumption, S will choose the experiment with the greater expected increase in K's probability change, for this experiment will yield the most credit, even though K's direction of change will be opposite to S's own direction of change. However, since the present case assumes that K's likelihoods are radically inaccurate, there will typically be an (objectively) expected *decrease* in K's truth possession. So where S is a *CM* agent operating under these assumptions, she does not choose well from a truth-increase point of view. Under the same assumptions of likelihood accuracy and inaccuracy, a *TM* agent would do better. Because she is only interested in K's (expected) truth possession, and because she believes that any experiment and report would generate an average decrease in K's truth possession, she would presumably decide to perform *no* experiment; or she would not report the outcome of any experiment to K. This would tend to avert an expected decrease in K's truth possession, and would therefore be beneficial from a truth possession point of view.

This case might suggest that when the assumption of likelihood accuracy by *both* agents is dropped, *TM* agents will systematically choose better than *CM* agents (from a truth-acquisition point of view). But this conclusion is too hasty. There is a mirror image of the preceding case, in which S's likelihoods are inaccurate and K's are accurate. In that case, we have the inverse result from the previous one: the *CM* agent serves (objectively expected) truth acquisition better than the *TM* agent! If S is a *CM* agent with inaccurate likelihoods, who wrongly believes K's likelihoods to be inaccurate, S will choose and report one of the experiments (usually the more discriminating one), although she (mistakenly) expects this to decrease K's truth possession. Since K's likelihoods are accurate, the actual result is an average increase in K's truth possession. But if S is a *TM* agent who is misinformed, she will misguidedly refrain from experimenting and/or reporting the outcome, to K's actual detriment!

To summarize: the class of cases we have examined indicate that credit-motivated activity *does* foster truth possession under specified conditions. On balance, however, credit-motivation does not serve truth acquisition *quite* as well as truth motivation; though it compares rather favorably in the range of cases treated here.

VII

In this final section, we sketch some further problems to which the credit-seeking model might be applied and its properties examined. Space limitations dictate a very abbreviated treatment.

The credit-conferring schemes discussed thus far (in the text) have been linear, but many nonlinear schemes are probably at work in scientific and scholarly circles. One such scheme would set a threshold of probability change below which no credit would be assigned. For example, there is the credit function Q such that: (A) if $\Delta P < .10$, then $Q(\Delta P) = 0$; and (B) if $\Delta P \geq .10$, then $Q(\Delta P) = \Delta P$. Another sort of nonlinear scheme would assign "extra credit" to large probability changes, for example: (A) if $\Delta P < .50$, then $Q(\Delta P) = \Delta P$; and (B) if $\Delta P \geq .50$, then $Q(\Delta P) = 10(\Delta P)$. Awards like the Nobel Prize, which restrict themselves to "fundamental breakthroughs", seem to constitute nonlinear credit schemes. Such schemes might provide the added incentive necessary to motivate agents to pursue risky but potentially valuable scientific research programs that would not otherwise be pursued. Plausibly, this promotes the societal increase in truth possession.

Another way in which premiums are conferred for high-impact work (i.e., work that yields large probability changes) is through the communication system, a point that introduces a new wrinkle into the discussion. We have been tacitly assuming that all scientific or scholarly speech acts reach all relevant specialists. Obviously, however, this isn't the case, because nobody reads everything in their field. Works of lesser significance come to fewer practitioners' attention, because they are less frequently cited (both formally and informally) by others. Since total credit received depends partly on the *number* of potential creditors who read or learn of one's work, the communication filter provides extra incentive to produce work with high impact on those it initially reaches.

A further ingredient that should be incorporated into an economic analysis of science is the diversification of efforts. As Philip Kitcher (1990) has shown, the social acquisition of truth may sometimes be fostered by a division of labor, in which different subgroups in a discipline pursue rival research programs rather than all concentrating on the single most promising program. But how, we may ask, is this supposed to arise, if each scientific agent is free to choose her own investigative course? If all have the same evidence, and all evaluate it the same way, won't they all choose to work on the more promising program?

Not necessarily. One diversity-promoting factor (Kitcher discusses others) is variation in cognitive *resources*, stemming from different aptitude, training, or career experience.[12] Even if research program R has greater "intrinsic" probability of yielding breakthroughs than research program R^* (given the current evidence), scientist S may have better prospects of earning credits by working on R^*, because her specific resources mesh better with R^*. In short, her *comparative advantage* may lie with R^*, whereas the comparative advantage of other agents lies with R.

Another factor that influences the research and speech activity of scientific agents is *reputation*. Suppose that agents "take positions" on which world-state is true, and there is a second credit scheme (complementary to our probability-change scheme) in which agents receive credit for being an early defender, or champion, of the true world-state (as judged by the creditor). Then an agent who previously championed world-state w_i will want to avoid doing anything that undermines other agents' acceptance of w_i as correct. This could lead S not to perform certain experiments she would otherwise perform, or not to report the outcome of an experiment she has already performed. Or it might lead her to propound certain arguments in support of w_i despite apparently disconfirming evidence.

Another kind of reputation effect concerns the choice of the world-state, or hypothesis, that S initially decides to endorse (including any new hypothesis she publicly advances). Because her reputation for correctness depends on the acceptability of her chosen hypothesis, this provides an incentive to take a position not too "distant" from popularly accepted positions, just as a supermarket chain will locate a new outlet near potential customers, or a political party will shape its ideology to please some bloc of voters.[13]

In all of these cases, economic paradigms could prove helpful in analyzing the choices of individual scientific agents and their impact on the societal acquisition of truth. This paper gives samples of this form of analysis, but much remains to be done.

Appendix

Let $w_1, \ldots, w_k$ be the possible values of the world-state W (in general k can be infinity). An experiment X is performed and it results in an observation Z. Let $z_1, \ldots, z_m$ be the possible outcomes of Z. (In general m may be ∞. Even more generally the number of possible outcomes of Z may be uncountable, but we do not consider this general case here. See Goldman and Shaked 1991.)

The probability distribution of the random observation Z depends on the "true" value of the world-state W. Let $f_i(z_j)$ denote the probability that $Z = z_j$ when $W = w_i$, We call $f_i(z_j)$ the *likelihood* of z_j under the assumption $W = w_i$.

Let $\alpha_1, \ldots, \alpha_k$ be the subjective probabilities of $w_1, \ldots, w_k$, respectively, as formulated by an agent A. (Of course $\alpha_1 + \cdots + \alpha_k = 1$.) Upon observing the outcome z_j the agent revises (or updates) her subjective probabilities using Bayes's theorem as follows:

$$(1) \quad \alpha_i'(z_j) = \frac{\alpha_i f_i(z_j)}{\alpha_1 f_1(z_j) + \alpha_2 f_2(z_j) + \cdots + \alpha_k f_k(z_j)}, \quad i = 1, 2, \ldots, k.$$

In the sequel it is assumed that the agent has an accurate stochastic "model", that is, that her stipulation of the functions $f_i(\cdot)$ yields the objective probabilities that nature gives to the outcomes of Z under the assumption that $W = w_i$.

Let us identify one of the possible values of the world-state W, say w_1, as the "true" one. Then $\alpha_1'(Z) - \alpha_1$ is called the *change in truth possession*. It may sometimes be negative, viz., when the observed value of Z, z_j say, is such that $\alpha_1'(z_j) < \alpha_1$.

By writing $\alpha_1'(Z) - \alpha_1$ as a function of Z, we emphasize the fact that $\alpha_1'(Z) - \alpha_1$ is random because it is a function of the random observation Z. Thus the mathematical expectation of $\alpha_1'(Z) - \alpha_1$, with respect to the likelihood function $f_1(\cdot)$, can be considered to be its objective average value. This expected value is denoted by and is defined as follows:

(2) $E_1(\alpha_1'(Z) - \alpha_1) = (\alpha_1'(z_1) - \alpha_1)f_1(z_1) + \cdots$

$$+ (\alpha_1'(z_m) - \alpha_1)f_1(z_m).$$

The subscript 1 near the expectation symbol E in (2) denotes the fact that the expectation is computed under the assumption that w_1 is the "true" value of the world-state.

The following result shows mathematically the obvious intuitive fact that, *on the average*, performance of *any* experiment yields a non-negative change (that is, an improvement) in truth possession. To avoid trivialities, the result will be proved under the assumption that $0 < \alpha_1 < 1$ and that $f_1(z_j) > 0$, $j = 1, 2, \ldots, m$. We will also assume that the weighted likelihood ratio $[\alpha_2 f_2(z_j) + \cdots + \alpha_k f_k(z_j)]/[(\alpha_2 + \cdots + \alpha_k)f_1(z_j)]$ is not identically equal to 1 as j varies from 1 through m; otherwise, as can be seen from (1), the experiment has no discriminating power with respect to w_1 and then $\alpha_1'(Z) = \alpha_1$ with probability 1.

THEOREM 1 $E_1(\alpha_1'(Z) - \alpha_1) > 0$.

Proof   First note that

(3) $E_1(\alpha_1'(Z) - \alpha_1)$

$$= \sum_{j=1}^{m} \left[\frac{\alpha_1 f_1(z_j)}{\alpha_1 f_1(z_j) + \alpha_2 f_2(z_j) + \cdots + \alpha_k f_k(z_j)} - \alpha_1 \right] f_1(z_j)$$

$$= \alpha_1 \sum_{j=1}^{m} \frac{f_1(z_j) - \alpha_1 f_1(z_j) - \alpha_2 f_2(z_j) - \cdots - \alpha_k f_k(z_j)}{\alpha_1 f_1(z_j) + \alpha_2 f_2(z_j) + \cdots + \alpha_k f_k(z_j)} f_1(z_j).$$

Observing that $1 - \alpha_1 = \alpha_2 + \cdots + \alpha_m$ it is seen that

$$E_1(\alpha_1'(Z) - \alpha_1)$$

$$= \alpha_1(1 - \alpha_1) \sum_{j=1}^{m} \frac{\alpha_1 f_1(z_j) - \dfrac{\alpha_2 f_2(z_j) + \cdots + \alpha_k f_k(z_j)}{\alpha_2 + \cdots + \alpha_k}}{\alpha_1 f_1(z_j) + \alpha_2 f_2(z_j) + \cdots + \alpha_k f_k(z_j)} f_1(z_j)$$

$$= \alpha_1(1 - \alpha_1) \sum_{j=1}^{m} \frac{1 - \dfrac{\alpha_2 f_2(z_j) + \cdots + \alpha_k f_k(z_j)}{(\alpha_2 + \cdots + \alpha_k) f_1(z_j)}}{\alpha_1 + (1 - \alpha_1) \dfrac{\alpha_2 f_2(z_j) + \cdots + \alpha_k f_k(z_j)}{(\alpha_2 + \cdots + \alpha_k) f_1(z_j)}} f_1(z_j).$$

Define the function h on $[0, 1]$ as follows

$$h(x) = \frac{1 - x}{\alpha_1 + (1 - \alpha_1)x}.$$

It is easy to verify (e.g., by differentiation) that h is a strictly convex function. Now it is seen that

$$E_1(\alpha_1'(Z) - \alpha_1) = \alpha_1(1 - \alpha_1) \sum_{j=1}^{m} h\left(\frac{\alpha_2 f_2(z_j) + \cdots + \alpha_k f_k(z_j)}{(\alpha_2 + \cdots + \alpha_k) f_1(z_j)}\right) f_1(z_j)$$

$$= \alpha_1(1 - \alpha_1) E_1\left[h\left(\frac{\alpha_2 f_2(Z) + \cdots + \alpha_k f_k(Z)}{(\alpha_2 + \cdots + \alpha_k) f_1(Z)}\right)\right]$$

$$> \alpha_1(1 - \alpha_1) h\left(E_1\left[\frac{\alpha_2 f_2(Z) + \cdots + \alpha_k f_k(Z)}{(\alpha_2 + \cdots + \alpha_k) f_1(Z)}\right]\right)$$

where the last inequality follows from the strict convexity of h (using the strict version of Jensen's inequality).[14] But

$$E_1\left[\frac{\alpha_2 f_2(Z) + \cdots + \alpha_k f_k(Z)}{(\alpha_2 + \cdots + \alpha_k) f_1(Z)}\right]$$

$$= \sum_{j=1}^{m} \frac{\alpha_2 f_2(z_j) + \cdots + \alpha_k f_k(z_j)}{(\alpha_2 + \cdots + \alpha_k) f_1(z_j)} f_1(z_j)$$

$$= \frac{\alpha_2}{\alpha_2 + \cdots + \alpha_k} \sum_{j=1}^{m} f_2(z_j) + \cdots + \frac{\alpha_k}{\alpha_2 + \cdots + \alpha_k} \sum_{j=1}^{m} f_k(z_j)$$

$$= \frac{\alpha_2}{\alpha_2 + \cdots + \alpha_k} + \cdots + \frac{\alpha_k}{\alpha_2 + \cdots + \alpha_k} = 1.$$

Therefore

$$E_1(\alpha_1'(Z) - \alpha_1) > \alpha_1(1 - \alpha_1) h(1) = 0. \|$$

We will now consider a comparison of two experiments. Let X and Y be two experiments, each of which results in an observation that can take on only two possible values. Let Z denote the observation associated with X and let its possible values be z_1, and z_2. It can be assumed that also Y results in observation Z with outcomes z_1, z_2. (There is no loss of generality in this assumption because one can arbitrarily assign each outcome of X with an outcome of Y.) Consider, in particular, the case when there are only two possibilities w_1 and w_2 for W. Then each of the two experiments can be described by postulating the two values $f_1(z_1)$ and $f_2(z_2)$. For example, in Experiment 1 in section V $f_1(z_1) = .6$ and $f_2(z_2) = .8$, whereas in Experiment 2 $f_1(z_1) = .8$ and $f_2(z_2) = .9$. In general Experiments X and Y can be described as follows:

Experiment X

	z_1	z_2
w_1	a	$1-a$
w_2	$1-b$	b

Experiment Y

	z_1	z_2
w_1	c	$1-c$
w_2	$1-d$	d

Remark 1   Note that without loss of generality we can assume in Experiment X that $a + b \geq 1$. Because if $a + b < 1$ then $(1 - a) + (1 - b) > 1$. Thus by interchanging the indices of z_1 and z_2 (this amounts to replacing $1 - a$ by a and $1 - b$ by b), one can transform Experiment X into an equivalent experiment in which $a + b \geq 1$.

Denote the expected change in truth possession that arises from Experiment X (respectively, from Experiment Y), under the assumption that $W = w_1$, by $E_1^X(\alpha_1'(Z) - \alpha_1)$ [respectively, $E_1^Y(\alpha_1'(Z) - \alpha_1)$]. The likelihood ratio of Experiment X, with respect to w_1, is $a/(1 - b)$ if $Z = z_1$ and is $(1 - a)/b$ if $Z = z_2$. Since $a + b \geq 1$ (see Remark 1) it follows that both values of the likelihood ratio get farther away from 1 as a and/or b increase. Thus if $a \leq c$ and $b \leq d$ then we may say that Experiment Y has *larger likelihood ratios* (or that it is *more discriminating*) than Experiment X. We already know from Theorem 1 that each of the two experiments causes a non-negative average change in truth possession. One would expect the experiment with the larger likelihood ratios to induce larger average improvement in truth possession. The following theorem shows that this is indeed the case. In the theorem we assume that the indices of z_1 and z_2 have been chosen such that a and b satisfy $a + b \geq 1$ (see Remark 1).

THEOREM 2   If $c \geq a$ and $d \geq b$ then $E_1^X(\alpha_1'(Z) - \alpha_1) \leq E_1^Y(\alpha_1'(Z) - \alpha_1)$.

Proof By specializing (3) to our special case it is seen that

$$E_1^X(\alpha_1'(Z) - \alpha_1)$$

$$= \alpha_1 \left[\frac{a - \alpha_1 a - (1 - \alpha_1)(1 - b)}{\alpha_1 a + (1 - \alpha_1)(1 - b)} a \right.$$

$$+ \left. \frac{(1 - a) - \alpha_1(1 - a) - (1 - \alpha_1)b}{\alpha_1(1 - a) + (1 - \alpha_1)b}(1 - a) \right]$$

$$= \alpha_1(1 - \alpha_1)$$

$$\times \left[\frac{a - 1 + b}{\alpha_1 a + (1 - \alpha_1)(1 - b)} a + \frac{1 - a - b}{\alpha_1(1 - a) + (1 - \alpha_1)b}(1 - a) \right]$$

$$= \alpha_1(1 - \alpha_1)(a + b - 1)$$

$$\times \left[\frac{a}{\alpha_1 a + (1 - \alpha_1)(1 - b)} - \frac{1 - a}{\alpha_1(1 - a) + (1 - \alpha_1)b} \right]$$

$$= \alpha_1(1 - \alpha_1)(a + b - 1)$$

$$\times \left[\frac{1}{\alpha_1 + (1 - \alpha_1)\dfrac{1 - b}{a}} - \frac{1}{\alpha_1 + (1 - \alpha_1)\dfrac{b}{1 - a}} \right]$$

It is easy to verify that the last expression is a monotone nondecreasing function of each of the variables a and b. Thus, replacing a by c and b by d it is seen that

$$E_1^X(\alpha_1'(Z) - \alpha_1)$$

$$\le \alpha_1(1 - \alpha_1)(c + d - 1)$$

$$\times \left[\frac{1}{\alpha_1 + (1 - \alpha_1)\dfrac{1 - d}{c}} - \frac{1}{\alpha_1 + (1 - \alpha_1)\dfrac{d}{1 - c}} \right]$$

$$= E_1^Y(\alpha_1'(Z) - \alpha_1). \|$$

Remark 2 Theorem 2 is stated with expectations under the assumption that $W = w_1$. But under the same restrictions on a, b, c, and d one can show in a similar fashion that also $E_2^X(\alpha_2'(Z) - \alpha_2) \le E_2^Y(\alpha_2'(Z) - \alpha_2)$ where E_2 denotes an expectation under the assumption that $W = w_2$. This means that the experiment with the larger likelihood ratios always yields greater average improvement in truth possession, no matter what is the true world-state.

Remark 3   Extension of Theorem 2 to the case when the number k, of possibilities of the world-state, is larger than 2, is possible (see Goldman and Shaked 1991).

Consider now two experiments X and Y as in Theorem 2. The expected credit from performing experiment X is $\beta E_1^X |\alpha_1'(Z) - \alpha_1| + (1 - \beta) \times E_2^X |\alpha_1'(Z) - \alpha_1|$, and from performing experiment Y is $\beta E_1^Y |\alpha_1'(Z) - \alpha_1| + (1 - \beta) E_2^Y |\alpha_1'(Z) - \alpha_1|$. Again one would expect that the experiment with the larger likelihood ratios would yield larger expected credit. But the example in section VI shows that this is not always true. The next result shows, however, that for a large number of combinations of α and β indeed

$$(4) \quad \beta E_1^X |\alpha_1'(Z) - \alpha_1| + (1 - \beta) E_2^X |\alpha_1'(Z) - \alpha_1|$$

$$\leq \beta E_1^Y |\alpha_1'(Z) - \alpha_1| + (1 - \beta) E_2^Y |\alpha_1'(Z) - \alpha_1|.$$

More explicitly suppose that $b = a$ and $d = c$. The two experiments can then be described as follows:

Experiment X

	z_1	z_2
w_1	a	$1 - a$
w_2	$1 - a$	a

Experiment Y

	z_1	z_2
w_1	c	$1 - c$
w_2	$1 - c$	c

As is explained in Remark 1, by taking $b = a$, it can be assumed, without loss of generality, that $a \geq \frac{1}{2}$. We then have the following result:

THEOREM 3   Suppose $\frac{1}{2} \leq a \leq c < 1$. If

(i) $\alpha_1 \leq \frac{1}{2}, \quad \beta \geq \alpha_1$

or

(ii) $\alpha_1 \geq \frac{1}{2}, \quad \beta \leq \alpha_1,$

then (4) holds.

Proof Consider

(5) $E_1^X|\alpha_1'(Z) - \alpha_1|$

$$= \left[\frac{\alpha_1 a}{\alpha_1 a + (1 - \alpha_1)(1 - a)} - \alpha_1\right] a$$

$$+ \left[\alpha_1 - \frac{\alpha_1(1 - a)}{\alpha_1(1 - a) + (1 - \alpha_1)a}\right](1 - a)$$

$$= \alpha_1 \left[\frac{a - \alpha_1 a - (1 - \alpha_1)(1 - a)}{\alpha_1 a + (1 - \alpha_1)(1 - a)} a\right.$$

$$+ \left.\frac{\alpha_1(1 - a) + (1 - \alpha_1)a - (1 - a)}{\alpha_1(1 - a) + (1 - \alpha_1)a}(1 - a)\right]$$

$$= \alpha_1(1 - \alpha_1)\left[\frac{a - 1 + a}{\alpha_1 a + (1 - \alpha_1)(1 - a)} a\right.$$

$$+ \left.\frac{a - 1 + a}{\alpha_1(1 - a) + (1 - \alpha_1)a}(1 - a)\right]$$

$$= \alpha_1(1 - \alpha_1)(2a - 1)\left[\frac{a}{\alpha_1 a + (1 - \alpha_1)(1 - a)}\right.$$

$$+ \left.\frac{1 - a}{\alpha_1(1 - a) + (1 - \alpha_1)a}\right]$$

$$= \alpha_1(1 - \alpha_1)(2a - 1)$$

$$\times \left[\frac{1}{\alpha_1 + (1 - \alpha_1)\dfrac{1 - a}{a}} + \frac{1}{\alpha_1 + (1 - \alpha_1)\dfrac{a}{1 - a}}\right]$$

Similarly

(6) $E_2^X|\alpha_1'(Z) - \alpha_1| = \alpha_1(1 - \alpha_1)(2a - 1)$

$$\times \left[\frac{1}{\alpha_1 \dfrac{a}{1 - a} + (1 - \alpha_1)} + \frac{1}{\alpha_1 \dfrac{1 - a}{a} + (1 - \alpha_1)}\right]$$

Now let x denote the likelihood ratio, that is, $x = a/(1 - a)$, and define the function g as follows:

$$g(x) = \frac{\beta x + (1 - \beta)}{\alpha_1 x + (1 - \alpha_1)} + \frac{\beta + (1 - \beta)x}{\alpha_1 + (1 - \alpha_1)x}, \quad x > 0.$$

Differentiate g to obtain

$$g'(x) = [\beta(1 - \alpha_1) - \alpha_1(1 - \beta)]$$

$$\times \left[\frac{1}{(\alpha_1 x + (1 - \alpha_1))^2} - \frac{1}{(\alpha_1 + (1 - \alpha_1)x)^2}\right].$$

Since $\beta \geq \alpha_1$, $\alpha_1 \leq \frac{1}{2}$ and $x \geq 1$ (because $x = a/(1 - a)$ and $a \geq \frac{1}{2}$) it follows that $\beta(1 - \alpha_1) \geq \alpha_1(1 - \beta)$ and that $\alpha_1 + (1 - \alpha_1)x \geq \alpha_1 x + (1 - \alpha_1)$. Therefore $g'(x) \geq 0$, that is, $g(x)$ is nondecreasing in x provided $x \geq 1$.

From (5) and (6) it follows that

$$(7) \quad \beta E_1^X |\alpha_1'(Z) - \alpha_1| + (1 - \beta)E_2^X|\alpha_1'(Z) - \alpha_1|$$

$$= \alpha_1(1 - \alpha_1)(2a - 1)g\left(\frac{a}{1 - a}\right).$$

From (7) and the monotonicity of g it is seen that

$$\beta E_1^X |\alpha_1'(Z) - \alpha_1| + (1 - \beta)E_2^X|\alpha_1'(Z) - \alpha_1|$$

$$\leq \alpha_1(1 - \alpha_1)(2c - 1)g\left(\frac{c}{1 - c}\right)$$

$$= \beta E_1^Y |\alpha_1'(Z) - \alpha_1| + (1 - \beta)E_2^Y|\alpha_1'(Z) - \alpha_1|,$$

and the proof of (i) is complete.

In order to prove (ii), note that if $\alpha_1 \geq \frac{1}{2}$ and $\beta \leq \alpha_1$, then $1 - \alpha_1 \leq \frac{1}{2}$ and $1 - \beta \geq 1 - \alpha_1$. The result now follows from (i) with the indices 1 and 2 interchanged.‖

By choosing $\beta = 1$ in (i), or, respectively, $\beta = 0$ in (ii) one obtains the following corollary:

Corollary 1   Suppose $\frac{1}{2} \leq a \leq c < 1$. If $\alpha_1 \leq \frac{1}{2}$, then

$$E_1^X |\alpha_1'(Z) - \alpha_1| \leq E_1^Y |\alpha_1'(Z) - \alpha_1|,$$

and if $\alpha_1 \geq \frac{1}{2}$, then

$$E_2^X |\alpha_1'(Z) - \alpha_1| \leq E_2^Y |\alpha_1'(Z) - \alpha_1|.$$

Note also that (4) holds whenever $\alpha_1 = \beta$ (and of course $\frac{1}{2} \leq a \leq c < 1$).

Notes

We wish to thank the following for helpful comments and discussion: Jim Cox, Hartry Field, David Hull, Mark Isaac, Isaac Levi, Vann McGee, Mike Philips, Holly Smith, Meredith Williams, Michael Williams, and other audience members at Northwestern University and Western Washington University.

1. Among the writers who have viewed science from an economic perspective, or stressed the incentive structure of science, are Robert Merton (1973), Warren Hagstrom (1965), Gordon Tullock (1966), Bruno Latour and Steve Woolgar (1979), David Hull (1988), Nicholas Rescher (1990), and Philip Kitcher (1990).

2. The descriptive adequacy of the MEU model of choice is open to serious question, and in other contexts we would not endorse it. For present purposes, however, its simplicity is convenient.

3. One objection to the probability-change account of credit is that credit can be given for a contribution that confirms, but doesn't change, the antecedent probability assignment. This point can be accommodated by allowing for "higher-order" probabilities, i.e., degrees of confidence in the correctness of lower-order probabilities (see Skyrms 1980). In the type of case imagined, credit is given for something that increases one's confidence in the correctness of the original, first-order assignment. For present purposes, we neglect this refinement.

4. It is important to note that neither probability assignments nor credit assignments are considered to be *actions*. They are not governed by expected-utility maximizing calculations, but rather by other cognitive operations.

5. One alternative to this credit rule is the negative of the log of the absolute difference. We do not have space here to consider this alternative rule, or similar ones, but they could profitably be explored elsewhere.

6. An alternative conceptualization might view credits as *flows* or *streams*, rather than one-time assignments. We shall not explore this alternative.

7. Of course, the choice of what to say in an experiment-based article, or in any article, typically involves many subtleties and complexities. The alternatives we list are greatly oversimplified. Among other things, we ignore the possibility of presenting falsified data.

8. One slightly technical point concerns the choice of speech acts. Under our present assumptions, agents might never choose the null speech act (s_0), because such a choice always has zero expected utility, while some alternative speech act presumably has *some* positive expected utility (however small). To accommodate this, we could introduce the prospect of hearers giving *discredits* for "uninteresting" (positive) speech acts, i.e., acts that generate little or no probability change. This would encourage selection of the null speech act on some occasions.

9. The present model is restricted to sets of exclusive and exhaustive alternatives, so there is always exactly one truth. In a more general context, the approach could be broadened in either of two ways. First, we might introduce degree of "falsehood possession", where this quantity would be a function of the agent's probability assignment to a falsehood. Second, we could entertain the more radical step of associating degree of "*truth* possession" even with a falsehood. Specifically, if P is false, an agent's degree of truth possession vis-à-vis P would be inversely related to her probability assignment for P. These possibilities are not explored, however, in this paper.

10. We do not mean to *endorse* simple conditionalization, as opposed, say, to "Jeffrey conditionalization". We merely examine the truth-getting properties of this inferential procedure. Similarly, although the theorems we shall offer all involve the use of Bayes's theorem, we do not mean to endorse Bayesianism as an account of inferential rationality, especially not as a full account.

11. We shall not pursue here the question of how exactly to interpret these objective probabilities. A more specific worry about this assumption is that, to ensure exhaustiveness of the set of world-states (or hypotheses), there will often be a catchall category, "None of the other world-states (positive hypotheses) holds". Since this can cover a heterogeneous residue of possibilities, it may seem implausible that its asso-

ciated likelihoods have definite objective probabilities. Two points may be made in reply. First, we may simply say that the assumption applies wherever it applies, and we make no guarantee as to its scope of application. Second, as far as the theorems to be presented are concerned, their significance will hold as long as the true hypothesis is among the positive hypotheses, and the latter have objective likelihoods.

12. This factor is stressed by Ronald Giere (1988, chap. 8).

13. The spatial analogy has been explored by economists and economics-inspired thinkers, such as Harold Hotelling (1929) and Anthony Downs (1957).

14. See, for example, exercise 9 on page 80 of Ferguson 1967.

Part IV
Social Power

Chapter 13
Toward a Theory of Social Power

The concept of power has long played a significant role in political thought, and recent decades have witnessed many attempts to analyze power and provide criteria for its measurement.[1] In spite of this impressive literature, however, our understanding of power remains inadequate. Specifically, no fully comprehensive conceptual framework exists within which questions about power can be formulated precisely and dealt with systematically. In the absence of such a framework it is difficult to investigate empirical questions, such as the extent to which a country is dominated by a 'power elite,' and it is hard to discuss normative issues, such as the relationship between power and freedom, or the relationship between equality of power and justice.

In this paper I shall outline a theory of power the ultimate aim of which is to shed light on empirical and normative questions in the political domain. To achieve this aim, however, it is wise to broaden our perspective. The domain of power is not confined to the political realm, narrowly conceived: employers have power over employees and teachers over students. Nor is power purely an interpersonal matter: People have power over nature as well as over other people. Although I am primarily interested in social and political power, I shall construe the notion of power broadly enough to cover all of these areas. There is an even wider sense of 'power' with which I shall not be concerned, the sense in which we speak of the power of an engine or a machine. I shall confine my attention to the sense in which a person or a group of people are said to have power. In this endeavor I shall be in the spirit of Hobbes, who wrote: "The power of a man, to take it universally, is his present means to obtain some future apparent good" (Hobbes 1651, chap. 10).

A theory of power must enable us to account for the fact that George Bush is, on the whole, an extremely powerful person. This does not imply that he has power over every person or every issue. There are many issues over which Bush lacks power completely, e.g., what grade a student receives in my course. Nevertheless, a person's total power is clearly related to his power over particular issues. Thus, in the first section of the paper, I shall explain what it is for an individual to have power with respect to a given issue, for example, who obtains a certain appointment, or whether it rains on Wednesday. Social theory does not restrict its interest to the power of individuals, however; of equal significance is the power of groups. In the second section, therefore, I shall turn to the nature of collective power. An analysis of collective power is needed to appraise the power of a nation, of the Pentagon, or of groups such as automobile manufacturers and ethnic minorities. Moreover, to the extent that a person's power is a function of his membership in groups that have collective power, an understanding of collective power is necessary to complete our account of the power of an individual. The first two sections of the paper primarily concern the conditions in which a person or group has at least *some* power on a given issue. A full-fledged theory, however, must enable us to make comparisons of power. While the secretary of defense has considerable power over military policy, the president has even more power. In the third and fourth sections, then, I shall address the problem of comparisons of power and degrees of power. Finally, in the fifth section, I shall discuss the nature of power over a *person* (as opposed to an *issue*) and to the nature of *overall* power.

Throughout the paper I shall of course try to capture commonsense intuitions and judgments about power (ones that would be shared by people of different political persuasions). My primary concern, however, is not to canvass every use of 'power' in everyday speech, but rather to embark on the construction of a theory. Perhaps it is an inevitable feature of philosophical theorizing that certain intuitions and usages are emphasized while others receive merely passing attention. But the benefits of theory construction can make this price well worth paying.

I. Individual Power

The central idea in the concept of power, I suggest, is connected with *getting what one wants*. An all-powerful being is a being whose every desire becomes reality. An all-powerful dictator is one whose every desire for state policy becomes the policy of the state. One person X has another man Y 'in his power' if what happens to Y is a function of what X wants to happen to him. The central notion, in all of these cases, is that a powerful person is one whose desires are actualized, i.e., a person who gets what he wants.

It would be wrong to conclude that whenever one gets what he wants, one must have power in the matter. A farmer may want rain on a particular occasion and may happen to get what he wants, but it does not follow that he has power or control over the weather. Even a person who *regularly* gets what he wants need not be powerful. The Stoics, and Spinoza as well, recommended that one form one's desires to accord with what can realistically be expected to happen in any case; they regarded freedom as conformity of events with actual desires, or rather, as conformity of desires with events. But as an account of power this is inadequate. To take an extreme example, consider Robert Dahl's case of the 'chameleon' legislator who always correctly predicts beforehand what the legislature is going to decide, and then forms a desire or preference to accord with this outcome.[2] The chameleon always gets what he wants, but he is not one of the more powerful members of the assembly.

What these cases show—and what is probably clear from the outset—is that an analysis of power cannot simply concern itself with what an agent actually wants and actually gets, but must concern itself with what he *would* get on the assumption of various *hypothetical* desires. To say that S is powerful is not to say that he usually gets what he in fact wants, but that whatever he wanted he would get, no matter what he might happen to want. To explicate the concept of power, we must appeal therefore to subjunctive conditionals. Although we shall later discuss what it is for a person to be powerful in general, we begin by asking what it is for a person to have power over, or with respect to, a single issue or event. The following notation will be used. 'E' stands for an issue, e.g., whether or not it rains at a particular time and place; 'e' and 'not-e' stand for possible outcomes of that issue, e.g., the occurrence of rain and the nonoccurrence of rain, respectively. To assess the claim that person S has power with respect to (henceforth to be written: 'w.r.t.') an issue E, let us ask what would happen (a) if S wanted e to occur, (b) if S wanted not-e to occur, and (c) if S were neutral between e and not-e. If E is the issue of whether or not it rains (at a particular time and place), we would consider whether or not it would rain (a) if S wanted rain, (b) if S wanted nonrain, and (c) if S were neutral between rain and non-rain. For any issue E, there are eight (logically) possible situations S might be in w.r.t. E, each represented by a function that maps attitudes of S vis-à-vis E onto outcomes of E. These eight situations are shown in the table below, in which the following notation is used: 'N(S, e)' stands for 'S is neutral between e and not-e,' 'W(S, e)' stands for 'S wants e', and 'W(S, −e)' stands for 'S wants not-e'. The if-thens are subjunctive conditionals. Situation (4), for example, is a situation in which outcome e would occur if S were neutral on the issue, or if S wanted e to occur, but outcome not-e would occur if S wanted not-e to occur.

	If $N(S, e)$, then	If $W(S, e)$, then	If $W(S, -e)$, then
(1)	e	e	e
(2)	e	$-e$	e
(3)	e	$-e$	$-e$
(4)	e	e	$-e$
(5)	$-e$	$-e$	$-e$
(6)	$-e$	$-e$	e
(7)	$-e$	e	e
(8)	$-e$	e	$-e$

In two of these possible cases, viz., (1) and (5), S is impotent w.r.t. the issue. In (1) it would rain no matter how S might feel about it. In other words, S's attitude would make no difference to the outcome, though if he happens to have the 'right' desire, he will get what he wants. In cases (2) and (6) S is even worse off than impotent; he is *counterpotent*. In these possible cases it would rain if S wanted non-rain and it would not rain if S wanted rain. Cases (3) and (7) are rather anomalous, and I have no name for them. But, like the four previous cases, they are not ones in which S has power w.r.t. the rain. Turning finally to (4) and (8), we find cases in which S does have power w.r.t. the rain. In these cases S would get his way on the issue no matter which outcome he might prefer. A desire for rain would lead to rain and a desire for non-rain would lead to non-rain. The difference between (4) and (8) is that in the former, rain would occur if S were neutral on the issue, whereas in the latter, non-rain would occur if S were neutral. In both cases, however, a desire by S for either outcome would lead to the occurrence of that outcome.

The following analysis of power is suggested by the foregoing.

> *S has power w.r.t. issue E if and only if*
> (I) (1) *If S wanted outcome e, then e would occur,* and
>   (2) *If S wanted outcome not-e, then not-e would occur.*

This analysis, I believe, is very much on the right track. But the following difficulty presents itself. Suppose that S is totally paralyzed and incapable of action. Another person, S^*, has the ability to control the weather; but S does not know of S^*'s existence, and even if he did, he would have no idea how to communicate with him. Unbeknownst to S, however, S^* can detect S's desires by ESP (or by appropriate gadgetry attached to his central nervous system), and S^* has freely decided to make the weather conform with whatever desire S has vis-à-vis the weather. In this case S satisfies (I) w.r.t. the weather, but it is doubtful that we would credit S with power w.r.t. the weather. Although S would get what he wants vis-à-vis the weather, this is not because of anything *he* would *do*.

A refinement in our analysis seems to be called for, a refinement that incorporates the element of action. To formulate this refinement, let us introduce the notion of a *basic act-type*. They are certain types of acts, e.g., raising one's hand, taking a step, and uttering certain sounds, which have the following properties: (a) in ordinary circumstances, if a person wanted to perform such an act, he would perform it, and (b) his ability to perform it is independent of knowledge or information concerning other acts that would have to be performed in order to perform it.[3] In sort, a basic act-type is one that a person can do 'at will', an act-type that is 'directly' under his control. Now frequently, in order to achieve a desired outcome, a person has to perform an appropriate sequence of basic acts, and these acts have to be performed at appropriate times. It is necessary, therefore, to attend to temporal matters. First, the issue in question must be clearly specified by indicating its time (i.e., the time of its outcomes). Who will be elected mayor in 1972 is a different issue from who will be elected mayor in 1914; S may have power w.r.t. one of these issues but not the other. Similarly, whether or not it will rain in Ann Arbor on Tuesday is a different issue from whether or not it will rain in Ann Arbor on Wednesday; S's having power w.r.t. one of these issues does not ensure his having power w.r.t. the other. We shall be concerned, then, with the issues that have 'built-in' times.[4] This will be indicated by placing the temporal reference in parentheses. Secondly, we need to specify the time at which a person has power w.r.t. an issue. If, at t_1, there are sequences of acts available to S that would lead to each of the outcomes of E (at t_{10}), then S may have power, at t_1, w.r.t. E (at t_{10}). But if S fails to act appropriately between t_1 and t_5, he may no longer have power, at t_5, w.r.t. E (at t_{10}). With these points in mind, we may propose the following analysis of (individual) power.

> *S has power, at t_1, w.r.t. issue E (at t_n) if and only if*
> (I') (1) *There is a sequence of basic act-types such that*
> (a) *if S wanted e, then he would perform these acts at appropriate times between t_1 and t_n, and*
> (b) *if S performed these acts at these appropriate times, then e would occur (at t_n);*
> (2) *There is a sequence of basic act-types such that*
> (a) *if S wanted not-e, then he would perform these acts at appropriate times between t_1 and t_n, and*
> (b) *if S performed these acts at these appropriate times, then not-e would occur (at t_n).*[5]

Let us see how (I') would apply to the rain example. The issue here is whether or not rain occurs (at t_n). Let us assume that the state of the world (in particular, the meteorological conditions) at t_1 is such that it is going to rain at t_n unless S does certain things between t_1 and t_n. (I assume that the occurrence or nonoccurrence of rain is *determined* by antecedent events, including the acts of S. Determinism will be assumed throughout the paper.) In order to prevent rain, S must disperse the clouds, or evaporate them, and this must be done before t_n. Now there are two possible cases to consider.

Case 1: S is an ordinary fellow who has no way to disperse or evaporate the clouds; in other words, no basic acts of his would lead to the dispersion or evaporation of the clouds prior to t_n. In this case, S does not satisfy (I'). Of course S trivially satisfies the first conjunct of (I'), assuming, at any rate, that he can perform some basic acts. For no matter what sequence of basic acts he performs between t_1 and t_n, it *will* rain at t_n (the rain will not be *caused* by any of his acts, however). But S does not satisfy the second conjunct of (I'), for, *ex hypothesi*, no basic acts S could perform would lead to non-rain at t_n.

Case 2: S possesses a chemical that evaporates rain clouds, and S has an airplane at his disposal that would enable him to spray the chemical onto the clouds (before t_n). Moreover, S knows that the chemical would evaporate the clouds, knows how to fly the plane, and has other requisite pieces of information. In this case, S satisfies the second conjunct of (I') in addition to the first conjuct. There is a sequence of basic acts—viz., acts by which S would place the chemical into the plane, acts by which he would fly the plane into the atmosphere, and acts by which he would spray the chemical onto the clouds—such that (a) if S wanted non-rain he would perform this sequence of acts (at appropriate times), and (b) if S performed them, non-rain would occur (at t_n).

It must be stressed that the conditionals in (I') are subjunctive conditionals, not *causal* subjunctive conditionals. If they were construed as *causal* conditionals, then even in Case 2 S could not be credited with power w.r.t. E. This is because there is no sequence of basic acts S can perform that would *cause* the occurrence of rain at t_n (although there are many sequences of basic acts he can perform such that, if he performed them, rain would occur at t_n).

It might be argued that the use of causal subjunctives could simplify our analysis; instead of requiring that S be able to obtain *both* outcomes of E, we could merely require that S be able to *cause* (at least) *one* outcome of E. (As long as ordinary subjunctives are employed rather than causal subjunctives, the requirement that *two* outcomes be achievable must be retained; otherwise S would qualify for having power w.r.t. the rain even in Case 1. Using causal conditionals, however, it might be sufficient to require that S be able to cause *one* outcome.) Although reliance on causal conditionals probably would simplify the analysis, I believe it would also prove less illuminating. By relying on ordinary subjunctives only, we shall be forced to take a careful look at problems that might be neglected if we allowed ourselves the luxury of the causal idiom. Causal terminology is especially unhelpful in dealing with the kinds of cases of paramount interest to a theory of power, i.e., cases in which an outcome is a function of the actions of numerous agents. In thinking about distributions of power and degrees of power among many persons and many groups, the use of causal terminology is likely to obscure the crucial questions rather than illuminate them. It seems advisable, therefore, to avoid all reliance on the concept of causation from the outset.

A different possible objection to our analysis of power is that it seems to neglect the most important ingredients of power. In most of the literature on power, such things as wealth, authority, status, and similar 'resources' play a crucial role, but they make no appearance whatever in (I'). Is this not a devastating omission? Now although such resources are not explicitly mentioned in our analysis, it should be clear that the satisfaction of (I') in any particular case depends on precisely such factors. Our analysis makes no reference to the existence of certain chemicals or the availability of an airplane, but it is just such things that make it true that S has power w.r.t. the rain (at t_n). Similarly, although our analysans makes no explicit reference to institutional hierarchies or to positions of influence, it is just these sorts of things that determine whether a person has power w.r.t. the granting of a government contract. If S has control over a defense contract, this is not simply because he has a certain basic-act repertoire; it must be because he occupies a position of authority in the governmental structure, or perhaps because he is in a position to influence officials through credible threats or offers. That these are the sorts of resources that give rise to power, however, does not imply that they ought to be mentioned explicitly in the analysis of power. Indeed, it would be foolish to try to construct an analysis that itemizes relevant resources. For even a single issue, the number and variety of potentially relevant resources is endless; and it is surely wholly impossible to say what resources are necessary and sufficient for issues *in general*. What is important, then, is that an analysans imply the *existence* of an appropriate set of resources, without necessarily characterizing these resources 'intrinsically'. This is what we accomplish in our analysans by the use of subjunctive conditionals.

Our analysis of power may be compared to a conditional analysis of disposition terms like 'soluble' or 'fragile'. In analyzing 'X is soluble in water' as 'If X were immersed in water, it would dissolve', we say nothing specific about the internal structure of X, the structure in virtue of which it is true that X would dissolve if immersed in water. Nevertheless, there must *be* some actual structure which makes this conditional true. Moreover, we may construe the hypothetical statement 'If X were immersed in water, it would dissolve' as asserting the existence of such a structure.[6] That is, we may construe it as asserting, 'The structure of X (and the structure of water) is such that if X were immersed in water, it would dissolve'. The case of power is quite analogous. In saying that outcome e would occur if S were to perform certain acts, we do not indicate which facts about the world, which resources possessed by S, make this conditional true. Nevertheless, there must be some such facts or resources. Indeed, we may construe our subjunctive conditionals as asserting their existence. That is, we may construe the force of (1) (b) as follows: 'The state of S's resources (or the state of the world) is such that if S performed the indicated sequence of basic acts at appropriate times, then outcome e would occur (at t_n)'. We may say, therefore, that resources such as wealth, authority, reputation, attractiveness, friendship, and physical location play the same sort of role vis-à-vis power as molecular structure plays vis-à-vis solubility. It is the possession of such resources that confers power, or, if you like, that *is* power.

The preceding remarks give us insight into the kinds of conditions that must obtain in order that certain outcomes would occur if S performed certain sequences of basic acts. In other words, we gain some insight into the conditions underlying clauses (1) (b) and (2) (b) of (I'). But what of (1) (a) and (2) (a)? What conditions must hold in order that S would select an appropriate sequence of basic acts if he wanted outcome e and in order that S would select an appropriate sequence of basic acts if he wanted outcome not-e? The answer is: S must have appropriate items of knowledge or belief. In order that S select appropriate sequences of basic acts—i.e., sequences that would really lead to the desired outcome—it is not sufficient that S simply *want* that outcome. Unless he has knowledge, or belief, concerning *which* acts would lead to the desired outcome, he might select acts that do not lead to it at all. We can imagine cases, indeed, in which there *are* sequences of basic acts that, if performed by S at appropriate times, would lead to whichever outcome he might desire, and yet where S is *counterpotent* w.r.t. the issue! S might be so confused or misinformed that if he wanted e he would perform acts that would lead to not-e, and if he wanted not-e he would perform acts that would lead to e. Under these circumstances, we would hardly say that S has power w.r.t. E. We may conclude, therefore, that the possession of power w.r.t. an issue depends not only on the possession of physical or social resources but also on the possession of informational resources. Hence the maxim 'Knowledge is power'.

It must be acknowledged that there are certain uses of the term 'power'—especially as a count-noun—in which informational resources seem irrelevant. To take an example of Rogers Albritton's, a man who is endowed with a capacity to strike people dead by uttering a magic formula can be said to possess this special *'power'* even though he does know that he has this power, and even though he has no idea what the formula is. Similarly, we may speak of an officer of an organization as having certain powers even if he happens to be ignorant of the fact that he has these powers. In this use of the term 'power', a power simply seems to be a resource of a crucial sort, though not necessarily a resource which is sufficient, by itself, to ensure any particular desired outcome.

Having noted this use, however, I propose henceforth to ignore it. I am interested primarily in the conditions under which a person has power over, or w.r.t., an issue, and the possession of power w.r.t. an issue *does* seem to require informational resources. Suppose S is standing in a large mansion that contains, unknown to S, a hidden button; if this button is pressed, New York City will be destroyed. Suppose, moreover, that there is a sequence of basic acts that, if performed by S, would uncover the button and place him in a position to destroy the city. Does it follow that S has power w.r.t. the destruction of the city (say, in the next ten minutes)? If S has no idea whatever where the button is, and if S has no way of finding out where the button is (in the next ten minutes), then I think it is clear that S does not have power w.r.t. this issue. Thus, the absence of relevant information implies the absence of power.[7]

A precise statement of the required information, however, is difficult to formulate. It is not necessary that S *know*, for each outcome e and not-e, which sequence of basic acts would be appropriate; it is not even necessary that he *believe*—in the sense of *believe it to be more probable than not*—of any sequence that it would lead to the desired outcome. It is sufficient for S to believe, of a certain sequence which happens to be appropriate, that it is *more likely* than any other sequence to lead to the given outcome; this is sufficient even if he thinks that the chances of its leading to that outcome are very small. To introduce some terminology to cover this possibility, we may say that it is sufficient that S *'epistemically* favors' that sequence as a means to that outcome.

Further complications are introduced by temporal considerations. In order for S to have power at t_1 it is not necessary that S be able at t_1 to select an entire sequence of basic acts. If, at t_1, S has a kit for assembling a harpsichord, then he may have power, at t_1, w.r.t. the issue of whether or not there will be a harpsichord in his house at t_n (say, two months later). But there certainly is no entire sequence of basic acts which S epistemically favors, at t_1, as a means to obtaining the outcome of there being a harpsichord in his house at t_n. There are certain basic acts that S epistemically favors as *initial* members of such a sequence, viz., acts that would enable him to read the instruction manual. Moreover, once he performs these initial acts, his reading of the instruction manual will lead him to form beliefs concerning further basic acts to perform. But at no point does he have the entire sequence of appropriate basic acts in mind. Extrapolating from this case, we can say that S would obtain an outcome e, if he wanted it, as long as the following is true:

There is a sequence of basic acts $A_1, \ldots, A_i, \ldots, A_n$ such that

(A)   at t_1 S epistemically favors A_1 as the first act to perform as a means to e,

(B)   for every i ($1 \leqslant i \leqslant n - 1$), if S performed the first i members of the sequence from t_1 through t_i (assuming that each act is performed at a single moment), then S would epistemically favor, at t_{i+1}, act A_{i+1} as the next act to perform as a means to e, and

(C)   if S performed each of the acts A_i at time t_i ($1 \leqslant i \leqslant n$), then e would occur (at t_n).

In the foregoing discussion I have talked as if the only factors that determine which basic acts S performs are, first, his desire for a particular outcome of E, and, second, his beliefs concerning the various means available to him to secure this outcome. In general, however, other desires and aversions come into play as well, not just S's attitude vis-à-vis the outcomes of E. For example, although S wants e to occur, and although he epistemically favors sequence A^* as a means to e, he may choose a different sequence of basic acts because he expects A^* to be very *costly*, that is, because he thinks A^* will have consequences he wants to avoid. In short, an agent's choice of action normally depends on more than one desire, and since more than one desire is involved, the relative strength of these desires is also an important factor. In the present section, however, I am intentionally neglecting these complications. I am assuming that S's desire for e (or for not-e) is the *only* motivating factor in his selection of a course of action. Because it is the only motivating factor, its strength or intensity is of no significance. If S wants e he will perform whatever acts he epistemically favors as a means to e, and if he wants not-e he will perform whatever acts he epistemically favors as a means to not-e. In section IV I shall drop these simplifying assumptions, but they will be retained until then.

Because our analysis makes central use of subjunctive conditionals, several remarks on their interpretation are in order. My approach to subjunctive conditionals follows the general lines of the analysis proposed by Robert Stalnaker (1968). On this analysis, we assess the truth of any conditional 'If A then B' by considering a possible world in which A is true and which otherwise differs minimally from the actual world. A conditional of this form is true if and only if B is true in that possible world. Now if A is true in the actual world, the possible world we select is the actual world;

but if A is contrary to fact, we must select some non-actual possible world. The tricky matter here is to select the respects in which this possible world should resemble the actual world and the respects (other than A itself) in which it may differ. In other words, we must decide what, in addition to A, is to be counterfactualized and what is to be held constant.[8] One constraint is that the possible world must be a nomologically consistent world (using the laws of nature of the actual world); but more must be said about the selection of a possible world.

When we are interested in S's power, at t_1, w.r.t. E (at t_n), we begin by counterfactualizing S's desire vis-à-vis E, more specifically, his desire vis-à-vis E from t_1 through t_n. While counterfactualizing this desire, however, the following three things are held constant: (1) the basic act repertoire of S, (2) the set of beliefs that S has at t_1, and (3) S's resources at t_1. The notion of resources is here construed very broadly, to include not only physical conditions, such as the presence of clouds, but also the acts and inclinations of other persons (at t_1). Thus, to say that we hold constant the resources S has at t_1 is to say, roughly, that we hold constant the state of the entire world at t_1—with the exception, of course, of S's own desire vis-à-vis E and whatever is nomologically implied by that desire (e.g., the state of his brain). Now once we have counterfactualized S's desire vis-à-vis E, other counterfactualizations will have to be made in order to obtain a nomologically consistent world. In particular, if S's desire from t_1 through t_n is different from his desire vis-à-vis E in the actual world, the basic acts he performs from t_1 through t_n will presumably be different (at least many of these acts). Moreover, if these acts are different, various other events that are causally connected with these acts will be different. Thus, once we have been forced to counterfactualize the basic acts S performs, we shall also have to counterfactualize numerous other events, including, perhaps, the acts of other agents and the beliefs S himself forms after t_1 (which in turn influence his subsequent acts). Of paramount importance is a possible change in the outcome of E. Since we are interested in S's power w.r.t. E, the crucial question is whether the counterfactual hypothesis that S desires, say, outcome e nomologically implies the performance of basic acts which nomologically imply the occurrence of outcome e (at t_n).

Our discussion of individual power has heretofore assumed that every issue has exactly two possible outcomes; and, working on this assumption, we have maintained that a person has power w.r.t. an issue only if he can obtain each of these possible outcomes. Both of these assumptions, however, are too restrictive. Most of the interesting issues in the social or political arena admit of more than two possible outcomes, and when this is so, it is not necessary, in order for a person to have power, that he be able to obtain each of the various possible outcomes. Suppose, for example, that money is to be allocated for a certain project, and there are fifty possible amounts that might be allocated: $1 million, $2 million, ... , $49 million, $50 million. Now suppose that although S is not able to ensure *whichever* of these fifty allocations he might desire, he is in a position to ensure any of the first twenty of these allocations. In this case, S clearly has power w.r.t. the issue of how much money is to be allocated for the project. On the other hand, if S is in a position to ensure any of the first forty of these allocations, rather than any of the first twenty, then S has even more power w.r.t. this issue.

To accommodate this sort of case, we proceed as follows. First, instead of *defining* an issue in terms of a partition of outcomes, we think of a *single* issue as subject to a *variety* of different possible partitions. For example, we may take the single issue of *the weather* (at a particular time and place) and partition it into any of the following partitions, where each partition contains outcomes that are mutually exclusive and jointly exhaustive: (1) (a) rain, (b) non-rain; (2) (a) rain, (b) snow, (c) hail, (d) anything else; (3) (a) sunny, (b) cloudy, (c) precipitation; (4) (a) no precipitation, (b) less than an inch of precipitation, (c) an inch or more of precipitation; etc.[9] Once we have the idea of different partitions of the same issue, we can make the following generalizations. If there is any partition of E into two or more mutually exclusive and jointly exhaustive outcomes such that S can obtain the occurrence of *at least two* of the outcomes of this partition, then S has at least *some* power w.r.t. E. Moreover, consider any partition P of E into possible outcomes $e_1, e_2, \ldots, e_n$, where $n \geqslant 2$. (For simplicity, I confine our attention to finite partitions.) Call the set of these n possible outcomes E^*. If we wish to compare S's power w.r.t. E in one possible world (where S possesses certain resources) with S's power w.r.t. E in another possible world (where he possesses different resources), we proceed as follows. We consider subsets E' and E'' of E^*, where E' contains at least two members. Then if the following three conditions are satisfied, S has *more power* w.r.t. E in possible world W_2 than he has w.r.t. E in W_1: (a) in W_1 subset E' is the largest subset of E^* such that S can obtain whichever member he chooses, (b) in W_2 subset E'' is the largest subset of E^* such that S can obtain whichever member he chooses, and (c) E' is a proper subset of E''.[10]

II. Collective Power

I have focused until now on the power of a single person, but this barely touches the more important complexities in the topic of power. Most issues of interest in the social arena are issues in which many persons and many groups have some degree of power. Moreover, we are usually inclined to say, in such cases, that some of these people or groups have more power than others. Nothing I have said thus far, however, sheds light on these matters. I have said nothing concerning the power of groups of people, nor anything about comparisons of power between two or more persons (or groups). An adequate theory of power, obviously, must deal with these matters.

The problems that lurk in these areas can be conveniently introduced by a brief passage from an article in *New York Magazine* entitled "The Ten Most Powerful Men in New York". Having listed his choice for the ten most powerful men in New York, the author (Schaap 1971), writes as follows:

> I offer only one theory in defense of the above list: if all ten men agreed upon the wisdom and necessity of a single, specific act affecting New York City, that act would take place, no matter how the rest of the city's eight million people felt. (Schaap 1971, p. 25)

In passing, we may note two obvious deficiencies in Schaap's suggestion, at least if it is regarded as a criterion for determining the ten most powerful men. First, it is too strong. It is not necessary that the ten most powerful would *always* get their way despite the attitudes of *all* other New Yorkers. Secondly, the test does not ensure uniqueness. A number of different groups of ten might each satisfy the test.

But let us reflect on other features of the test. It is noteworthy that Schaap's test does not require any one of the ten to be able to obtain outcomes *by himself*; that is, it does not require that there be any issue such that at least one of the ten would obtain different outcomes of that issue if he wanted them. The test can be satisfied even if each of the ten is only a *member* of a group whose *joint* preferences would determine the outcomes of issues. This seems perfectly appropriate if we are considering the power of the *group*. But by calling these men "the ten most powerful," Schaap also implies that *each* of them has considerable power. This raises an interesting question for the account of power given in section I. If neither of two persons can *individually* get what he wants, but if the two of them can *jointly* get what they want, can either of them be credited *as a single person* with power w.r.t. the issue? This point requires an investigation both into the nature of group or collective power and into the relationship between collective power and individual power.

Another noteworthy feature of Schaap's 'theory' is the phrase 'no matter how the rest of the city's eight million people felt'. To complete Schaap's test of a proposed list of ten, we must not only hypothesize that all ten agree in supporting a given outcome, but we must also hypothesize that all other New Yorkers oppose that outcome. Only if the ten would achieve their outcome despite everyone else's opposition would it be true that they would achieve it "no matter how the rest of the city's eight million people felt," and only then would they qualify, on Schaap's test, as the ten most powerful. Schaap's requirement is reminiscent of a similar stipulation made by Max Weber, who defined 'power' as "the probability that one actor within a social relationship will be in a position to carry out his own will *despite resistance....*" (Weber 1947, p. 152), and of C. Wright Mills's definition, "By the powerful we mean, of course, those who are able to realize their will, *even if others resist it*" (Mills 1959, p. 9). Our own analysis of power has made no reference to the resistance or opposition, either actual or hypothetical, of other persons. The place of this idea in an account of power must therefore be explored.

In this section, however, we confine our attention to collective power. Suppose that you and I, both healthy and normal people, are standing behind a stalled Buick. If either of us alone pushes at it, the car will not budge; but if we both push simultaneously, it will move. Let E be the issue of the movement of the Buick (in the next several seconds) and let E be partitioned into two outcomes: (e) it moves, and (not-e) it does not move. If both of us want outcome e to occur, then we shall both push at the car and outcome e will take place. If both of us want not-e, neither of us will push and not-e will take place. Thus, if we jointly desire either outcome, that outcome will occur. This is a good reason to conclude that the two of us have *collective power* w.r.t. issue E. It appears, however, that neither of us has individual power w.r.t. E. True enough, if one of us wanted not-e, he would ensure that not-e would occur even if the other wanted e (or was neutral on the issue). But if only one of us wanted outcome e, while the other wanted not-e, the one who preferred e would not succeed in getting his way. It does not seem to be true of either of us, therefore, that for at least *two* outcomes of E, he would get his way on each outcome if he wanted that outcome. Actually, this conclusion is too hasty, as we shall see below. There is no doubt, however, that we must distinguish between collective power and individual power, and that collective power deserves study in its own right.

An analysis of collective power can easily be constructed along the lines of our analysis of individual power. For simplicity we confine our attention to two-outcome partitions.

A group of persons $S_1, \ldots, S_i, \ldots, S_m$ have collective power, at t_1, w.r.t. issue E (at t_n) if and only if

    (II)   (1) *There is a set of sequences of basic act-types, a sequence for each person S_i, such that*
             (a) *if each person S_i wanted outcome e to occur, each would perform his respective sequence of acts at appropriate times between t_1 and t_n, and*
             (b) *if each person S_i performed his sequence at appropriate times, then e would occur (at t_n);*

(2) *There is a set of sequences of basic act-types, a sequence for each*
person S_i, such that
(a) *if each person S_i wanted outcome not-e occur, each would*
perform his respective sequence of acts at appropriate times between
t_1 *and t_n, and*
(b) *if each person S_i performed his sequence at appropriate times,*
then not-e would occur (at t_n).

Paralleling the case of individual power, there are two kinds or classes
of resources that are relevant to the possession of collective power. First,
informational resources are needed to satisfy clauses (1) (a) and (2) (a)
of the analysis. Secondly, non-informational resources of various sorts
are needed to satisfy clauses (1) (b) and (2) (b). Nothing especially distinctive is true of the class of non-informational resources, but some attention
to informational (or epistemic) resources should be instructive.

In collective action toward a common goal, coordination is usually
required in the selection of mutually supportive sequences of acts. For me
to choose an appropriate sequence I may have to know what other members of the group are going to do; and similarly for each of them. Without
information of this sort we may act discordantly despite good intentions.
Often, therefore, acts performed in order to achieve a given outcome are
designed to acquire information about future acts of partners in the undertaking. The nature of coordinative activity is a fascinating subject, which
need not be expanded upon here (see Schelling 1960 and Lewis 1969). It is
(partly) the need for coordination, however, that makes the degree of
organization or structural delineation of a group contribute to its power.
An established pattern of division of labor facilitates the mutual selection
of appropriate courses of action. The political power of lobbies and pressure groups, as opposed to that of random collections of individuals (e.g.,
until recently, consumers), is partly a function of this factor.

Two aspects of the problem of coordination should be distinguished.
First, I may need information about the acts of others to decide *which* acts
would be appropriate for me to perform. Secondly, even if I know which
acts of mine are the ones most likely to lead to the desired outcome, I
may need to know what others are going to do in order to assess *how likely*
it is that the performance of these acts will be followed by the outcome.
In particular, if I believe that others will not 'do their part', and if I
believe that it will be very costly for me to perform my most appropriate
sequence of acts, then even if I know which sequence of acts would be
most appropriate for me to perform (as a means to the desired outcome),
I may choose not to perform them. Admittedly, this consideration introduces the element of cost, which we resolved to abstract from until section
IV. Nevertheless, it is sufficiently important in this context that it should
not be ignored.

Suppose that a small group of bandits are holding up a train containing a large number of passengers. How shall we assess the collective power of the passengers w.r.t. the issue of whether or not they will be robbed? Suppose that the bandits 'have the drop' on the passengers, but that there is a set of sequences of acts, a sequence for each passenger, such that if they performed these sequences of acts, they would disarm the bandits (with no harm to themselves) and foil the robbery. Assume further that each passenger knows which acts would be the most appropriate ones for him to perform as a means to foiling the robbery. This is not enough to ensure that all would perform these acts if all wanted the robbery to be foiled. The rub, of course, is that each passenger has little reason to believe (indeed, has strong reason to disbelieve) that enough other passengers will do their part. Since, for each passenger, it would be very costly if he did his part (e.g., started to disarm the bandit nearest him) while few others did theirs, each passenger would refrain from doing these acts, and the robbery would succeed. A similar problem arises in assessing the power of a large group of slaves over a small group of masters. If all the slaves acted in unison, they would overwhelm their masters. But it does not follow that they have much (or any) collective power over their masters. Like the train passengers, the problem for the slaves is that each is insufficiently confident that rebellious action on his part would be supported by others. There is an important respect, then, in which 'faith is power'. To the extent that members of a group have greater confidence in the reliability of their partners (and hence greater confidence in the efficacy of their own acts as part of the larger group), the group itself has more power, or is more likely to have at least *some* power w.r.t. a selected issue.

With a clearer grasp of the notion of collective power, let us next look more closely at the relationship between collective and individual power. In our discussion of the Buick example it was said that this is a case where you and I have collective power w.r.t. its movement but where neither of us has individual power w.r.t. its movement. Closer examination shows, however, that this is not unconditionally true: it depends on further specification of the example. Suppose, first, that you are not going to push at the Buick in the next few seconds, and that there are no acts I could perform that would induce you to push. In that case, there is no sequence of basic acts I could perform that would lead to the car's moving (in the next few seconds). Hence, it is correct to say that I lack individual power w.r.t. the issue. But suppose now that, as a matter of fact, you *are* going to push at the Buick in the next few seconds (and suppose that you have no inclination *not* to push in case I push). In that case, (I') licenses us to say that I *do* have individual power w.r.t. the issue, for your act of pushing serves as a 'resource' of mine. If I wanted the car to move I would push at it, and, given your pushing as a resource, this would lead to the car's moving.

If I wanted the car not to move, I would not push it, and in this case, despite your pushing, it would not move. Thus, whichever outcome I wanted would occur.

This example brings out the true contrast between collective power and individual power (as we have defined these notions). The difference between them lies in the conditions that we counterfactualize in each case. In making a judgment about the individual power of a person S at t_1, we begin by counterfactualizing his desire (from t_1 through t_n) and his desire only. The only other counterfactualizations that we allow are ones that follow from, or are necessitated by, this initial counterfactualization. In particular, we do not counterfactualize the desires or acts of other persons unless those desires and acts would be affected by the difference in S's desire. In making a judgment about the collective power at t_1 of a *group* of persons, we begin differently. We begin by counterfactualizing *at the outset* the desires of all of the members of the group. We ask what would happen if they *all* wanted outcome e (from t_1 through t_n) and what would happen if they *all* wanted outcome not-e (from t_1 through t_n). Thus, in individual power we consider all persons other than S purely as 'resources' (or liabilities) of his; in collective power we consider all persons outside the *group* purely as resources.

Let us return to the case where you and I have collective power w.r.t. the movement of the Buick but neither of us has individual power (this is the case where neither of us is *in fact* going to push, but where the car would move if we both wanted it to move). According to the analysis of section I it should be concluded that neither of us has any power w.r.t. the issue; for it was implied in section I that a person has power w.r.t. an issue only if he has *individual* power w.r.t. it. This assumption, however, must now be called into question. As noted earlier, Schaap's formula implicitly denies it; for Schaap's formula allows a person to be one of the ten most powerful men in New York simply by being a member of a group that has collective power. What Schaap's formula suggests, then, is some sort of *distributive* principle: if a group of persons has collective power w.r.t. an issue, then every member of the group has power w.r.t. the issue. This formulation, however, is too strong. If group G has collective power w.r.t. E, another group G' can always be formed by adding to G some randomly selected, irrelevant person; and this new group, G', will also have collective power w.r.t. E. But we do not want to say of any randomly selected person that he has power w.r.t. E. A qualification is needed, therefore, to the effect that each member must be *nondispensable* w.r.t. E. This notion can be explained as follows. If there is at least one outcome of E such that (a) if all members of G wanted that outcome it would occur, and (b) if all members of G except S wanted that outcome, whereas S opposed it, it would not occur, then S is a nondispensable member of G w.r.t.

E. In the Buick case, for example, you and I have collective power w.r.t. the issue, and each of us is a nondispensable member of this group (w.r.t. this issue). We can now formulate the following principle:

> *A person S has some power w.r.t. issue E if there is some group G such that S is a nondispensable member of G w.r.t. E and the members of G have collective power w.r.t. E.*

This principle proves useful in a variety of cases. In the Buick case, for example, although neither of us has individual power w.r.t. the issue, it seems plausible to say that each of us has some power, i.e., that neither of us is powerless w.r.t. it. The new principle licenses us to say this.

The principle also permits us to account for the power of each member of a legislature. To illustrate, consider an assembly of 100 legislators, in which 51 votes are required to pass a proposal and 50 to defeat it. Let *E* be the issue of whether a particular bill is passed and let us assume that the actual vote is 75 in favor and 25 opposed. Consider legislator *S* who in fact voted for the bill. Did he have power w.r.t. *E*? Assume that *S* did not have individual power, for the bill would have passed even if he had opposed it. Was *S* a nondispensable member of a group which had collective power w.r.t. *E*? Yes. Let group *G* consist of 25 members of the assembly, including *S*, each of whom actually voted for the bill. Then, holding *constant* the attitudes of the 25 original opponents of the bill and the remaining 50 supporters, we can say that if all members of *G* (including *S*) wanted the bill to be passed, it would have been passed, and if all members of *G* (including *S*) wanted the bill to be defeated, it would have been defeated. Thus, *G* had collective power w.r.t. *E*. But if all members of *G* *except for S* wanted the bill defeated, whereas *S* wanted it passed, then it would *not* have been defeated. Thus, *S* was a nondispensable member of *G* w.r.t. *E*, and hence he had some power w.r.t. *E*.

Consider next a rather different case. Let *E* be the issue of whether Brown will be alive at noon today. At 11:00 a.m. Smith has a loaded gun in his hand, aimed at Brown, and Smith has the requisite beliefs such that he would kill Brown before noon if he wanted Brown dead and he would not kill Brown if he wanted him alive. A third man, Jones, is also in a position to kill Brown by noon. Moreover, Jones is resolved to kill Brown before noon if (and only if) Smith does not kill Brown. Finally, assume that Smith cannot influence Jones's action in this matter. Now in this situation we are surely inclined to say that Smith has some power w.r.t. *E*. According to the account of individual power, though, Smith does not have individual power (at 11:00) w.r.t. *E*.[11] Given the facts concerning Jones, it turns out that there is nothing Smith can do that would lead to Brown's being alive at noon; so Smith is impotent w.r.t. *E*, for Brown will be dead at noon no matter what Smith wants or does about it.

Using the new principle, however, we can account for the intuition that Smith does have at least some power w.r.t. *E*. For Smith is a nondispensable member of a group (viz., Smith and Jones) which has collective power w.r.t. *E*. Smith and Jones have collective power w.r.t. *E* because if they both wanted Brown dead at noon that outcome would ensue, and if they both wanted Brown to be alive at noon they would perform acts leading to that outcome. Smith is a nondispensable member of this group w.r.t. *E* because if Jones wanted Brown to be alive while Smith opposed it, then Brown would not be alive (at noon).

III. Conflict and Comparisons of Power

We turn now to the significance of conflict or opposition in the criteria of power offered by Schaap, Weber, and Mills. Schaap, it will be recalled, characterized the ten most powerful men in New York as the ten that would get their way no matter how the rest of the city's people felt about it. Whether or not this criterion is adequate, its rationale is clear. To determine relative amounts of power between people (or groups), it is appropriate to ask who would 'get his way', i.e., who would get his preferred outcome, in case of conflict. Schaap does not suggest (nor do Weber and Mills) that power is present only in situations of actual conflict or opposition. What is suggested, though, is that comparisons of power can be made by ascertaining what would happen *if* there were conflict or opposition. Since comparisons of power are of central concern, let us reflect on this matter. I shall not try to deal with the relative power of groups, nor with the relative power of three or more individuals. I shall confine my attention to comparisons between two individuals (although third parties will have to be mentioned to clarify the nature of the two-person case).[12]

Let us begin with an example. Jones and I are both standing next to an open door. Jones is a muscular 250-pounder and I a 145-pounder. Let *E* be the issue of whether or not the door remains open. If both Jones and I can rely on raw strength alone, it is pretty clear that he has more power than I do w.r.t. *E*. For there is a sequence of basic acts Jones can perform to ensure, no matter what basic acts I perform, that the door will stay open; and there is a sequence of acts Jones can perform that would ensure that the door will be closed, no matter what basic acts I perform. (Here we rely on the fact that Jones's basic-act repertoire exceeds mine: he can exert a greater amount of pressure on the door than I can.) Thus, assuming Jones has the requisite beliefs, the door would stay open if Jones wanted it open, no matter how I felt about it; and the door would be closed if Jones wanted it closed, no matter how I might feel about it. Should Jones and I have opposing preferences, then, Jones's preferred outcome would be the one to occur.

In this example, Jones can perform a certain sequence of basic acts such that, no matter what basic acts I perform, the door will stay open, and similarly for the door being closed. Is this sort of relationship generally necessary in order that one person have more power than another w.r.t. an issue? Restricting our attention to partitions with two outcomes, this would be generalized as follows: S_1 has more power than S_2 w.r.t. E only if, for each of the two outcomes, there exists a sequence of basic acts S_1 can perform such that, for *any* sequence of basic acts S_2 might perform, the performance of the sequence by S_1 would lead to this outcome. Such a requirement is clearly too strong. It demands the existence of a single course of action for S_1 that would 'win' in the face of all possible responses from S_2. A weaker requirement is therefore needed. The condition that naturally suggests itself next is this: For each of the two outcomes, no matter what basic acts S_2 might perform, there is a sequence of basic acts S_1 could perform that would lead to this outcome. This condition is *too weak*. The statement that for any course of action by S_2 there is a 'winning' course of action for S_1 is compatible with the statement that for any course of action by S_1 there is a 'winning' course of action for S_2.[13] So this requirement would not provide even prima facie grounds for thinking that S_1 has more power than S_2.

The next natural suggestion is to appeal to the game-theoretic notion of a winning strategy. What would be required is that for each outcome, e and not-e, there be a strategy or function F which assigns to S_1 an initial move and which, for every set of possible moves of S_2, assigns to S_1 a succeeding move (or moves), such that if S_1 were to abide by this function, that outcome would occur. In fact, however, even this requirement is too strong. The existence of a winning strategy for S_1 implies that S_1 can win no matter what S_2 does, in other words, even if S_2 adopts the best strategy available to him. But suppose that S_2 does not have information that would lead him to adopt (what is in fact) his best strategy. Then S_1 may be in a position to 'beat' S_2 even if S_1 lacks a *winning* strategy (i.e., a strategy that would win for S_1 against *all* possible strategies of S_2). In fact, S_2 might even have a winning strategy against S_1; yet if S_2 does not know what this strategy is, and has no way to find out, then S_1 may have more power than S_2 in spite of this. His having more power would simply consist in the fact that he would get his preferred outcome (by an appropriate course of action) if the two of them had opposing preferences.

Let us abandon the attempt to specify in detail what combinations of strategy and information would be necessary and sufficient for S_1 to have more power than S_2. Instead, we can give a simple analysis of this notion that parallels our earlier analyses of individual power and collective power.

(III)

> At t_1 S_1 *has more power than S_2 w.r.t. issue E (at t_n) if and only if:*
> (1) *There is a pair of sequences of basic act-types, Σ_1 and Σ_2, such that*
> (a) *if S_1 wanted outcome e and if S_2 wanted outcome not-e, then S_1 would perform Σ_1 at certain times between t_1 and t_n and S_2 would perform Σ_2 at certain times between t_1 and t_n, and*
> (b) *if S_1 were to perform Σ_1 at these times and if S_2 were to perform Σ_2 at these times, then outcome e would occur (at t_n);*
> (2) *There is a pair of sequences of basic act-types, Σ'_2 and Σ'_2, such that*
> (a) *if S_1 wanted outcome not-e and if S_2 wanted outcome e, then S_1 would perform Σ'_2 at certain times between t_1 and t_n and S_2 would perform Σ'_2 at certain times between t_1 and t_n, and*
> (b) *if S_1 were to perform Σ'_1 at these times and if S_2 were to perform Σ'_2 at these times, then outcome not-e would occur (at t_n).*

We might wish to add clauses to the analysis to ensure that S_1 would get his preferred outcome if S_2 were neutral on the issue, but this refinement may be neglected. A far more important refinement concerns the elaboration of the analysis to cover partitions of three or more outcomes.[14] But this complication will also have to be omitted here.

As in the case of collective action, selections of sequences of acts by actors with opposing interests are typically interdependent. If S_1 and S_2 realize that they have conflicting preferences, each will be guided in his choice of action by whatever information he has about the acts his opponent has performed or plans to perform in the future. As before, informational resources are crucial in determining the acts one would select, and therefore important in determining one's relative power.

In our door example we imagined that both Jones and I rely on our own strength alone. In characteristic situations in the political sphere, however, relative power depends on other assets, including positions of influence over other persons that stem from authority, kinship, personal magnetism, or other relationships. In seeking to achieve one's ends in opposition to others, one frequently performs acts designed to call forth aid from other persons. These acts might be orders, commands, or simple requests for help. To illustrate the importance of this, let us revise the door example to include a brawny and faithful companion of mine who is always willing and able to assist me. In this amended case it is no longer true that Jones would get his preferred outcome if his preference were in opposition to mine. If I wanted the door to be closed, for example, I would perform basic acts by which I would ask my friend for help, and then I would perform acts of pushing at the door which, in unison with my friend's pushing, would ensure that the door be closed even if Jones tries to keep it open. Thus, given my brawny and faithful companion, I would get whichever outcome I would prefer on the door issue, no matter how Jones might feel about it.

Is it true, however, that I have more power than Jones w.r.t. *E*? There may be a strong temptation to deny this. It might well be argued that it is only the power of the *two* of us, my companion and me, that exceeds the power of Jones. This view can be defended by pointing out that if we are considering *hypothetical* desires, and *hypothetical* sequences of acts, we should also consider hypothetical desires and acts by the companion. If we do this, we shall quickly see that I do not have the ability, given *any* desires and acts by my companion, to beat Jones at whatever he tries to do. I could be said to have this ability only on the assumption that the companion's desires and acts are wholly contingent on mine. But why should this contingency or dependency be assumed? Admittedly, I introduced the example by saying that the companion is willing to do my bidding, and it would violate this stipulation to hypothesize that I ask him for help but that he does not desire (on the whole) to do what I ask him to do. But why should such a hypothesis not be permitted? In talking about power we are already in the business of making counterfactual assumptions about various people's desires and acts. Why not make counterfactual assumptions about the companion's desires and acts as well? The problem, in short, is this: When making comparisons of power between individuals (or, indeed, in making non-comparative judgments of power), what should be regarded as fixed and what should be regarded as a candidate for counterfactualization?

The answer I propose is that it all depends on what sorts of power comparisons we wish to make. If we wish to compare Jones and myself, then *our* desires and acts are subject to counterfactualization, while the desires and acts of everyone else are to be taken as contingent on ours—at least, if there is anything in the actual world that makes their desires and acts contingent on ours. In other words, in comparing the power of Jones and myself, the *initial* changes we make in constructing different possible worlds concern the desires of Jones and myself; the only other changes that are made are ones nomologically required by these initial changes. On the other hand, if we wish to compare the power of Jones, myself, and my companion, then we would make *initial* counterfactualizations involving my companion's desires as well. Because of these different counterfactuals, of course, different assessments of power are going to be made. There is nothing inconsistent or paradoxical about this, however; it merely reflects the fact that whenever judgments about power are made, certain things are subjected to counterfactualization and others held fixed. A judgment about a person's power that makes certain counterfactualizations cannot be expected to be identical with a judgment that makes different (initial) counterfactualizations. Within certain limits, however, a number of different counterfactual assumptions may legitimately be made.[15]

To illustrate these points consider a departmental secretary who is given substantial responsibility and initiative by the chairman. If we ask about the secretary's power w.r.t. a variety of issues (e.g., assignment of offices, teaching hours, classrooms, etc.) it is not so clear what should be said. On the one hand we may hold fixed, or constant, the chairman's propensity to go along with the secretary's decisions; in other words, we regard the chairman's trust as one of the secretary's *resources*. If so, we would attribute considerable power to the secretary. On the other hand, we may also compare the secretary's power with that of the chairman; we might ask what would happen if the secretary wanted one outcome and the chairman preferred a contrary one. Normally the chairman would win in such cases (let us suppose), and hence the secretary's power is less than the chairman's.

I think we can see from this that a clear, overall picture of someone's power (w.r.t. a given issue) demands a consideration of more than his *individual* power (as defined in section I); it also requires attention to his power *relative to* other persons (and groups of persons). This is a point that is implicit in Weber's and Mills's characterizations of power as the ability to get one's way *despite* (possible) *resistance*. That individual power by itself does not give us the whole story is evident in the following example. Suppose that S^* has a rain-making machine, and this gives him power w.r.t. the noontime weather (since, in the natural course of events, it would not rain at noon). Suppose, in addition, that if S were humbly to beg and plead with S^* to make rain for him (S), then S^* would accede to S's wishes. If so, then according to our analysis of 'individual power', S has individual power w.r.t. the noontime weather. But clearly, if S's only way of affecting the weather is by throwing himself on S^*'s mercy, we would not be inclined to credit S with much power w.r.t. the weather. This can be explained in terms of our theory by appeal to a comparison of power between S and S^*. It is obvious that S^*'s power w.r.t. the weather exceeds that of S. And this must be taken seriously in one's overall appraisal of S's power w.r.t. the weather.

An important problem arises here, however. Suppose that S is able to influence S^* to use his rain-making machine, not by *pleading* with S^*, but by *threatening* him with dire consequences should he (S^*) refuse to employ the machine to make rain. Here we would say that S has quite a lot of power w.r.t. the weather, more, at any rate, than in the previous example. This difference, however, cannot be captured by our account of comparative power, at least not by the account as it stands now. For even in this case our account of comparative power would have us say that S^* has more power than S w.r.t. the weather. This is because *if* S^* wanted non-rain *on the whole*—despite S's threat—then non-rain would occur.[16] What this shows is that our analysis of comparative power must be supplemented or refined in some further way. As our discussion intimates, the needed refinement concerns the element of *cost*. The difference between pleading and threatening is that the latter imposes (prospective) *costs* on S^* which the former does not (at least not such heavy costs). By making use of the notion of cost, we can hope to develop an account of comparative power that will handle the difference we have detected.

IV. Cost and Degrees of Power

The necessity of incorporating the element of cost into our theory was acknowledged early in the paper but postponed until now. Heretofore we have assumed that the only factor motivating the choice of a person's action is his desire or aversion for outcomes of issue E. As noted earlier, though, this assumption is unrealistic. The performance of a sequence of acts often leads to undesired consequences; at a minimum, it typically involves the expenditure of valuable resources or assets. The performance of a sequence of acts, then, involves some *cost*. Now although a person may want outcome *e*, and although he may believe that the performance of sequence Σ is the only way for him to get *e*, he may decide not to perform Σ if the expected cost of performing it exceeds the benefit he would get from *e*. A directly related point we have neglected is the fact that a person can want an outcome to a greater or lesser degree. We have assumed until now that a person either wants *e*, wants not-*e*, or is neutral between them; we have not worried about the strength (actual or hypothetical) of a desire. Once the element of cost is introduced, however, strengths of desire and aversion must be included as well, for the choice of courses of action will depend on whether or not the value of an outcome *exceeds* the (expected) cost of obtaining it.

Introduction of the element of cost has immediate bearing on power. As we have seen, the expected cost of a sequence of action may dissuade a person from performing that sequence even if he wants the outcome to which (he believes) it will lead. It follows, therefore, that the cost of a sequence is a determining factor of whether or not a person *would* get a certain outcome *if* he wanted it (to such-and-such a degree). Hence, it is a determining factor of his power w.r.t. an issue.

The importance of cost in the analysis of power was first stressed by John Harsanyi (1962). He illustrates the idea as follows:

> It is misleading to say that two political candidates have the same power over two comparable constituencies if one needs much more electioneering effort and expenditure to achieve a given majority,

even if in the end both achieve the same majorities; or that one can achieve favorable treatment by city officials only at the price of large donations to party funds, while the other can get the same favorable treatment just for the asking.

Harsanyi stresses how inaccurate an analysis of power can be if it disregards the costs to an agent.

> For instance, suppose that an army commander becomes a prisoner of enemy troops, who try to force him at gun point to give a radio order to his army units to withdraw from a certain area. He may well have the power to give a contrary order, both in the sense of having the physical ability to do so and in the sense of there being a very good chance of his order being actually obeyed by his army units—but he can use this power only at the cost of his life.... [I]t would clearly be very misleading in this situation to call him a powerful individual in the same sense as before his capture.

To generalize this point, we can say that if it is extremely costly for an agent to obtain certain outcomes of an issue—e.g., if it would require the sacrifice of his life, health, or fortune—then he cannot be said to have much power w.r.t. that issue. The amount of power an agent has w.r.t. an issue is thus inversely proportional to the cost of obtaining outcomes of that issue.

The element of cost, then, enters into the analysis of power at the level of individual power. But it is even more important when we turn to comparisons of power, that is, when we consider what would happen in situations of conflict. When two persons have opposing preferences concerning an issue, one of them (or both) frequently tries to get his preferred outcome by the use of threats or sanctions designed to *deter* his opponent from performing certain acts. The intended effect of a threat is not to make the opponent literally *unable* to perform a certain sequence of basic acts; rather it is to make that sequence more *costly* for him to perform. To the extent that the ability to deter people by successful threats is an essential ingredient in the possession of power, it is vital that we incorporate the element of cost into our theory. How, exactly, may this element be incorporated?

The first problem is how to construe the notion of cost and how to measure it. The most promising approach, I think, is suggested by the economist's notion of opportunity cost. To say that the achievement of outcome e would be costly for S is to say that the activity by which S might obtain e would have consequences that are less desirable, or have lower utility, than an alternative course of action open to S. If obtaining outcome e would require an expenditure of money, then the cost of obtaining e is a function of the utility that would have accrued to S from using the money in some alternative way. If e can only be achieved at the cost of imprisonment, then the cost of obtaining e is a function of the difference in utility between going to prison and remaining free. It is evident that in determining the cost of an activity we must refer to the agent's desires, or utility assignments, for various outcomes. In this context, though, we consider the *actual* desires of the agent, not hypothetical desires. True, we continue to regard desires vis-à-vis the outcomes of the issue in question (e and not-e) as subject to counterfactualization. But other desires are held constant (at least so far as this is compatible with whatever counterfactualization is made).[17] Assume that a senator can obtain passage of a certain bill only if he engages in activity that would cost him his reelection. If he is in fact highly averse to losing the election, then the cost would be very high, and we shall say that his power w.r.t. the passage of the bill is correspondingly reduced. But if he in fact cares very little about reelection, then his cost is not so great, and he has more power w.r.t. the passage of the bill.

Problems of cost become complicated when we turn to comparisons of power, and hence to (potential) conflict situations. The complications here are twofold. First, both agents, S_1 and S_2, may be in a position to threaten his opponent with certain penalties, thereby imposing costs on the opponent. Secondly, however, the activity of posing these threats, or of making them credible, may be costly to the threatener himself. In assessing the relative power of S_1 and S_2, therefore, all of the following must be combined: (1) the costs that S_1 can impose on possible courses of action by S_2, (2) the costs *to* S_1 of imposing these costs on S_2, (3) the costs that S_2 can impose on possible courses of action by S_1, and (4) the costs *to* S_2 of imposing these costs on S_1.[18]

To combine these elements and incorporate them into our theory of power, let us make use of matrices resembling those of game theory. In constructing such matrices the following assumptions will be adopted: (1) Issue E is partitioned, as usual, into two outcomes, e and not-e. (2) Two agents, Row and Column, have various sequences of basic acts open to them. For simplicity we depict only three sequences of acts for each agent. (3) It is assumed that interpersonal assignments of utility can be made. (4) A three-by-three matrix, like table 13.1, gives information on three subjects. First, it says what outcome would occur if Row and Column were to choose certain sequence of acts. This outcome is listed in the center of each box of the matrix. Table 13.1 says, for example, that if Row were to choose r_2 and Column were to choose c_3, then outcome e would occur. Secondly, the entry in the lower left-hand corner of each box indicates the cost to Row of the corresponding pair of sequences of acts. Thirdly, the entry in the upper right-hand corner of each box indicates the cost to Column of

Table 13.1

		Column	
	c_1	c_2	c_3
r_1	0 e 0	−10 not-e 0	−30 e 0
Row r_2	0 e −1000	−20 e −1200	−40 e −1000
r_3	0 not-e −600	−10 not-e −500	−30 not-e −600

that pair of courses of action. (5) To ascertain the cost of a pair of activities to a given agent, say Row, we proceed as follows. We begin by *ignoring* all utilities assigned by Row to the outcomes of E. We next consider the (expected) consequences *apart* from e and not-e themselves, of the various alternative sequences of acts open to Row. These consequences might include the expenditure of a certain amount of money and energy, or it might include the commitment of a certain item of patronage, or it might include the undergoing of certain penalties or sanctions.[19] We then select, among all the alternatives open to Row, the sequence(s) of acts that would yield Row the highest utility. This sequence of acts has *zero* (opportunity) cost, and hence the numeral zero is inserted as the entry for Row in each box corresponding to that sequence of action.[20] To determine the cost entry for Row in all other boxes of the matrix, we compare the utility that would accrue to him from each combination of courses of action by Row and Column with the (zero) utility of his best alternative. This *difference* in utility is the cost to Row of that combination of activities, and it is inserted in his corner as a negative quantity. (6) Finally, it is assumed that each agent knows what the outcomes and costs would be (both to himself and to his opponent) of all possible combinations of sequences of acts.

To illustrate this procedure, consider table 13.1. Looking first at the entries in the center of the boxes, it is clear that Row has a sequence of acts available to him—viz., r_2—that would ensure the occurrence of e, and he has a course of action available to him—viz., r_3—that would ensure not-e. It is clear, however, that both r_2 and r_3 would be very costly for Row to perform. Setting aside the potential benefit of outcome e or outcome not-e, the best sequence of acts open to Row—that is, the sequence that would yield the greatest utility (or the least disutility)—is r_1. In comparison with r_1, sequences r_2 and r_3 are very unattractive. But r_1 would neither ensure outcome e nor ensure outcome not-e. Hence although there *are* sequences of acts available to Row that would ensure either of the two outcomes, these sequences of acts are very costly, and it is not clear that Row would perform either of these sequences even if he wanted the outcome it could ensure.

Assuming that Row is a 'rational' agent, what sequence of acts will he perform? That depends on whether he prefers e or prefers not-e, and it depends on how much, or how strongly, he prefers one to the other. It also depends, of course, on what Column is likely to do, which in turn depends on Column's preference as between e and not-e. Since we are interested primarily in comparisons of power, let us suppose that Row and Column have *opposing* preferences. This supposition can be satisfied in two ways: (a) Row prefers e while Column prefers not-e, and (b) Row prefers not-e whereas Column prefers e. Next, some assumption must be made concerning the *degrees* of preference. Let us assume, in each case that the degree of preference for *both* agents is the same, viz., 100 utils. We have, then, two (hypothetical) cases on which to focus: (A) Row prefers e to not-e by 100 utils while Column prefers not-e to e by 100 utils, and (B) Row prefers not-e to e by 100 utils while Column prefers e to not-e by 100 utils. What would happen in each case?

Only a little reflection is needed to see that, in each situation, Row and Column would perform sequences of acts that lead to *Column's* getting his preferred outcome. In each case Row's degree of preference for a given outcome (whether e or not-e) would not suffice to motivate him to perform either r_2 or r_3. The cost of ensuring either outcome would outweigh the benefit from that outcome. Hence, Row would opt for r_1, thereby leaving it up to Column's choice of action to determine whether e or not-e occurs. Now in case (A), where we imagine Column to prefer not-e, he would select sequence c_2. Admittedly, sequence c_2 is more costly, by 10 utils, than sequence c_1. But Column is assumed to prefer not-e to e by 100 utils, and so he would be better off, all things considered, to perform c_2. By selecting c_2, given that Row selects r_1, Column gets his preferred outcome (not-e). By similar reasoning (indeed, even more obviously), Column would get his preferred outcome in case (B); for in this case Row would perform r_1 and Column would perform c_1, a combination that would result in outcome e. Thus, in both hypothetical cases, Column would get his preferred outcome; and this is true despite the fact that Row has 'winning' strategies available to him, and knows that he has these strategies, for both e and not-e.

Let us step back now and take a new look at where our analysis leaves us. According to our initial conception, the idea of power was understood in terms of functional dependencies between the desires of an agent and the outcomes of an issue. We have stressed, however, that the outcomes of an issue are a function, not of desires *simpliciter*, but of *degrees* of desire. If Row's preference for *e* over not-*e* were not of the magnitude 100, but rather of the magnitude 2,000, he would perform a different sequence of acts, and the outcome of the issue would be different. Now in the first three sections of the paper, we have talked about desiring *e* or not-*e* (or of being neutral between them). But the introduction of degrees of desire can help us add further refinements to our theory of power; specifically, it enables us to work toward an account of *degrees* of *power*.[21]

How are degrees of power related to functional dependencies between degrees of desire and outcomes of an issue? The answer is straightforward: *The extent of a person's power w.r.t. an issue is (ceteris paribus) inversely related to the degree of desire required for him to obtain a preferred outcome.* This answer is directly tied to considerations of cost. If obtaining a preferred outcome is very costly for an agent, then it will require a higher degree of desire to motivate him to get that outcome (cf. the captured commander). And the greater the cost of getting an outcome, the less is a man's power w.r.t. that issue.

There is a clear, intuitive idea here that we seek to capture. If a person is in a position vis-à-vis an issue such that even the slightest concern, the merest whim, would suffice for him to get his preferred outcome, then he has great power w.r.t. that issue. But if someone is in a position such that only very great concern would make it worth the trouble, effort, or expenditure of resources to obtain his preferred outcome, then he does not have so much power w.r.t. the issue. If a mere whim on the part of a well-placed corporation executive would suffice to get an appropriate piece of legislation enacted, then he has great power w.r.t. that issue. I might be able to get a similar piece of legislation enacted, but only if I wanted it badly enough to go to a great deal of trouble and effort. This implies that my power w.r.t. this kind of issue is much smaller than the executive's. Similarly, if the executive and I are on opposing sides of some issue, and if it is true that a moderate desire on his part for his most preferred outcome and a large desire on my part for my most preferred outcome would result in a victory for him, then his power exceeds mine. If we apply this idea in the case of table 13.1, it is not at all clear that Row's power exceeds Column's.

It is a consequence of the current suggestion that sometimes a person who has less power w.r.t. an issue will get his preferred outcome over someone who has more power on that issue. This can happen when the degree of preference of the less powerful person far exceeds the degree of preference of the more powerful one. Suppose, for example, that Row prefers outcome *e* to not-*e* by 2,000 utils, while Column prefers not-*e* to *e* by only 100 utils. (Actually, it doesn't matter here what the strength of Column's preference is.) Then Row will choose r_2 and will get his preferred outcome. This does not conclusively falsify the suggestion that Column has more power on the issue than Row. There is no reason to suppose that a more powerful person on a given issue will always get his way over a less powerful one. On the contrary, it seems reasonable to define relative power in such a way that a powerful but relatively uncaring person may lose out to a less powerful but strongly motivated one. What a definition of relative power must ensure is that someone who is powerful w.r.t. a given issue will get his way if the issue is one of considerable importance to him, at least if he is contending against someone whose concern for the issue is comparatively small.

The foregoing discussion suggests that we may conceive of a two-person power relationship as a function that maps pairs of degrees of desire (of the two agents) onto outcomes of the issue in question. This may be illustrated with the aid of simple graphs. Let X and Y be two agents and let e and not-e be two outcomes of an issue. X's preference w.r.t. these outcomes is measured along the X-axis of a coordinate system. A positive number along the X-axis represents a degree of preference by X for e over not-e, and a negative number represents a degree to which X prefers not-e over e. The zero-point signifies indifference between e and not-e. Similarly, Y's preference as between e and not-e is measured along the Y-axis. A point in the coordinate system will then represent a pair of degrees of preference (or desire) by X and Y. The point $(+100, -200)$, for example, represents a preference of 100 utils for e over not-e on the part of X and a preference of 200 utils for not-e over e on the part of Y. Now suppose that the power position of X and Y is such that if X were to want e to degree 100 and Y were to want not-e to degree 200 then e would occur. We shall represent this fact by darkening, or filling in, the point $(+100, -200)$. (Of course we cannot literally darken *points*, but appropriate *areas* can be darkened.) If, on the other hand, such a combination of desires by X and Y would result in not-e, then the point $(+100, -200)$ will be marked by cross-hatching. (Again, it is only areas that can be so marked.) Using these conventions, we can proceed to represent various possible relationships of power of X and Y w.r.t. issue E. Indeed, we can give information concerning both their *collective* power on the issue, and their relative power.

Consider graph 1 of figure 13.1. Looking at the northeast and southwest quadrants, we see that X and Y have the highest degree of *collective* power w.r.t. the issue (at least vis-à-vis this partition). For if X and Y both prefer e to not-e then e will occur—no matter how small their degree of preference, and if they both prefer not-e to e, then not-e will occur—again no matter how small their degree of preference. Looking at the northwest and southeast quadrants, we see what would happen if X and Y had opposing preferences. The graph tells us that, in case of opposing preference, the

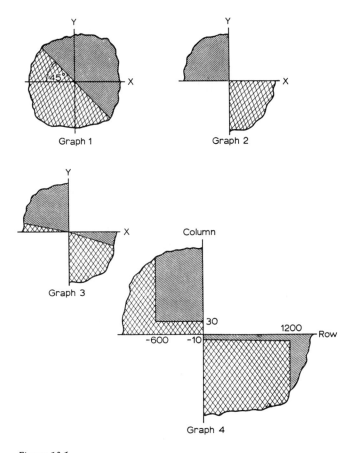

Figure 13.1

agent with the stronger preference gets his way. If Y's preference for e over not-e is greater than X's preference for not-e over e, then e will occur; whereas not-e will occur if the converse holds. Similarly, if Y's preference for not-e over e exceeds S's for e over not-e, then not-e will occur; and e will occur if the converse holds. Here we may conclude that X's power and Y's power w.r.t. E are equal.

Since our primary interest is in comparisons of power, let us restrict our attention to northwest and southeast quadrants. Graphs 2 and 3 depict power-relationships where it is natural to say that Y has more power than X. Graph 2 says that Y gets his way no matter how small his preference and no matter how large X's opposing preference. In other words, graph 2 says that Y is able to ensure either e or not-e at no cost whatever. (This would be true if the courses of action that would ensure e and not-e, respectively, had equal intrinsic attractiveness for Y and were each more attractive, apart from their effect on issue E, than any alternative course of action.) Graph 3 again implies, I believe, that Y has more power than X, but here his excess of power is not as great. According to this graph, there is a wide range of cases in which Y would get his preferred outcome with a smaller degree of preference than X, but there are no cases in which X would get his preferred outcome with a smaller degree of preference than Y. Other cases might also be mentioned in which one agent fairly clearly has more power than another. But I shall not pursue this further in this paper. There will be many cases, of course, in which overall comparisons of power are difficult to make. One such case is that of table 13.1, which is depicted in graphical form in graph 4. Here the pattern of power is complicated, and it is not perfectly evident what conclusion should be drawn. No doubt the judgment we would intuitively make partly depends on the order of magnitude that the numbers in question convey. In any case, we should not expect our theory to yield precise judgments of power comparisons in all cases. Quite obviously, our pre-analytic judgments about power are not so precise to begin with, and we should heed Aristotle's advice not to expect (or impose) more precision than the subject matter allows. What our theory does provide, however, is a framework for expressing in a systematic way the crucial factors that enter into an appraisal of the relative degree of power of two agents w.r.t. an issue.

Before leaving the topic of power and cost, I wish to mention a difficulty confronting our theory that I do not know how to handle. Our use of the notion of opportunity cost has one disadvantage. By measuring cost, and hence power, in terms of the best alternative course of action open to the agent, one makes the degree of cost depend upon actions open to the agent that may have no connection at all with issue E. Suppose, for example, that you can obtain outcome e with an expenditure of \$100. I come along and offer to sell you for \$100 an extremely valuable painting that you would love to own. According to our theory, it would follow that I have reduced your power w.r.t. issue E. If we assume, at any rate, that you only have \$100 to spend (or less than \$200), buying the painting and spending \$100 to get outcome e will be mutually exclusive courses of action. Hence, when I present you with this new opportunity, I thereby increase the cost to you of obtaining outcome e. This consequence of our theory is somewhat counterintuitive (though not entirely counterintuitive, I think), but I do not know how to deal with it without abandoning our theory completely. It seems clear, however, that the notion of cost must play a central role in any adequate theory of power. The approach we have sketched here seems very promising, and it should not lightly be abandoned.

V. Overall Power and Power "Over" People

The foregoing analysis has focused on the power that an agent or group of agents have w.r.t. a single issue. But the concern of most discussions of power in the political arena is not the power of individuals or groups vis-à-vis selected *single* issues, but rather the *overall* power of individuals or groups. We do not merely want to say that George Bush has more power than I do w.r.t. this or that particular issue; we want to say that he has more power than I do *on the whole*. On what basis, however, are such judgments to be made? Is it that Bush has power (or a higher degree of power) w.r.t. a larger *number* of issues than I do? How are we supposed to *count* the number of issues w.r.t. which each of us has power? Issues, it would seem, can be divided up in any way one chooses, and hence both Bush and I could be said to have power w.r.t. indefinitely many issues. A better answer to our question would appeal not to the number of issues over which we have power, but to their *importance*. I may have power w.r.t. what I eat for dinner tonight, what grades my students get, what sentences are written on my blackboard, etc. But Bush has power w.r.t. 'really important' issues. But how is the 'importance' of an issue to be measured? One element that should go into the determination of 'importance' (for present purposes) is the number of people that would be affected by the issue. The fact that I have more power than Bush does w.r.t. what will be written on my blackboard doesn't count for much in assessing my overall power as compared with Bush's. . On the other hand, the fact that Bush has more power than I do w.r.t. U.S. foreign and domestic policies is a very important reason for saying that he has more overall power. One thing that helps account for this is that these policies affect a very large number of people.

But what do we mean when we say that an issue *'affects'* a person? And can one issue 'affect' someone *more* or *less* than another issue? The answer to the first question, I think, is suggested by looking at the second. I am inclined to say that one issue affects a person more than another issue if the outcomes of the first issue would make a larger difference to his *welfare* than the outcomes of the second. An issue whose outcomes would make no difference whatever to his welfare does not affect him at all. In determining a person's overall power, therefore, we must look not only at the number of persons that would be affected by the issues w.r.t. which he has power, but also at *how much* difference in welfare the outcomes of the issue would cause. This principle accords nicely with our intuitions about the 'important' issues of the day. The issue of war or peace, the issue of inflation and unemployment, the issue of pollution and measures for combating it, the issue of poverty and racism, are some of the major issues of contemporary American life. They all have in common the two features we have mentioned: first, they all affect the welfare of a large number of people, and second, the outcomes of these issues make a very large difference in the welfare of these people. It is not surprising, therefore, that individuals or groups who have power w.r.t. these issues, and especially w.r.t. a large number of these issues, are regarded as having a great deal of overall power.

In determining a person's overall power, we shall not simply be interested in the *single* issues w.r.t. which he has power; we shall also be extremely interested in the question of his power w.r.t. *conjunctions* of issues. Suppose there are two independent issues, E and E^*, each partitioned into three outcomes. Issue E has outcomes e_1, e_2 and e_3, and issue E^* has outcomes e_1^*, e_2^*, and e_3^*. Further suppose that Smith is in a position to ensure any of the outcomes of E through a payment of $100 and is in a position to ensure any of the outcomes of E^* through a payment of $100. Then if Smith has exactly $100, he has (individual) power w.r.t. *each* of these issues. Now suppose, however, that we consider the *conjunctive* issue E & E^*. This issue has nine possible outcomes: e_1 & e_1^*, e_1 & e_2^*, ..., e_3 & e_2^*, e_3 & e_3^*. It does not follow from our original supposition that Smith has (individual) power w.r.t. this conjunctive issue. For if he only has $100, he will not be in a position to ensure any of the nine indicated outcomes. If we suppose that Smith has $200, however, it will follow that he not only has power w.r.t. each of the issues, E and E^*, but that he also has power w.r.t. the conjunctive issue, E & E^*. Obviously, in determining the economic and political power of individuals and groups, attention to conjunctions of issues is of crucial importance. If a person has power w.r.t. a conjunction of many issues, each of which significantly affects the welfare of many people, then he is very powerful.

In the foregoing paragraphs the notion of welfare has been taken for granted, and we shall continue to do this in the remainder of the paper. For illustrative purposes, let us associate a person's welfare with the satisfaction or nonsatisfaction of his desires. (It is not clear that welfare should be identified with satisfaction of desires—rather than, say, with the satisfaction of needs or interests—but this is close enough for the moment.) Suppose that the degree of desire (or utility) assigned by Jones to the possible outcomes of E are as follows: $(e_1) + 100$, $(e_2) + 70$, $(e_3) + 20$, $(e_4) - 40$, and $(e_5) - 100$. Further suppose that Jones has no power at all w.r.t. issue E, but that Smith has enough power to ensure any one of the outcomes e_2, e_3, and e_4 (though not e_1 or e_5). We can then say that Smith has the power to make a fairly substantial difference in Jones's welfare—in particular, a difference of 110 utils (the difference between the utility of the best outcome for Jones that Smith can ensure and the utility of the worst outcome that Smith can ensure). Now if Smith had the power to ensure *any* of the five outcomes of E, and not just the middle three, then Smith's power over Jones would be even greater. Of course, our assessment of

Smith's power over Jones is partly a function of the *degree* of power Smith has w.r.t. these outcomes. If it would be quite costly for Smith to secure any of these outcomes, then his power over Jones is less than it would be if the cost to Smith were small. Thus, in determining an agent's overall power, there are several factors to be considered: (1) the issues w.r.t. which the agent has *some* power, (2) the conjunctions of these issues w.r.t. which he has power, (3) the degree of power (in terms of cost) he has w.r.t. these issues, (4) the number of people affected by these issues, and (5) the amounts of the differences in these people's welfare that depend on the outcomes of these issues.

During most of our discussion we have concentrated on the notion of having power 'with respect to' an 'issue'. The term 'power', however, frequently occurs in sentences of the form 'X has power over Y', where 'Y' designates a person or group of people. We still owe an account, therefore, of having power *over a person*. Our remarks in the previous paragraph suggest such an account. Smith has power *over Jones*, we might say, if and only if Smith has power w.r.t. issues that affect Jones—i.e., that make a difference to Jones's welfare.

In addition to the support already given to this approach, the welfare accounts fits neatly with the relation between power and dependence that is often cited by psychologists and sociologists (Thibaut and Kelley 1959, chap. 7; Emerson 1962). If agent X controls certain objects or events which Y desires, or on which he sets a value, then Y is 'dependent' on X for the satisfaction of his desires or interests. Intuitively, this looks like a case in which X has power 'over' Y. This intuition is captured by the welfare approach we have sketched; for if Y is dependent on X for the satisfaction of his desires or interests, then X has power w.r.t. issues that affect the welfare of Y.

The suggested account of having power *over* people is in accord with a number of treatments of power in the literature. But many other writers take a somewhat different approach. Writers such as R. H. Tawney (1931), Robert Dahl (1957), J. C. Harsanyi (1962), and Herbert Simon (1953) conceive of power over people as the ability to affect the *behavior* of those people. Tawney, for example, defines 'power' as "the capacity of an individual, or group of individuals, to modify the conduct of other individuals or groups in the manner which he desires" (Tawney 1931, p. 230). Similarly, Robert Dahl says, "*A* has power over *B* to the extent that he can get *B* to do something that *B* would not otherwise do" (Dahl 1957, pp. 202–203).

Now as a complementary approach to the welfare account, the behavior approach is certainly welcome. But if it is intended to replace the welfare approach, I think it is unsatisfactory. Considered as a replacement, the behavior approach has three problems. First, it is difficult to see how it can throw much light on the determination of the *degrees* of power that person X has over person Y. The main possibility here would be to concentrate on the *number* of acts of Y w.r.t. which X has power.[22] But principles for counting acts or items of behavior are very controversial. On the theory I favor, most cases of changing the behavior of an individual would involve changes in *indefinitely many* acts. Moreover, on any approach to act-individuation one should be able to make temporal divisions any way one pleases, so it will be impossible to decide when one, two, or three acts have been affected. The welfare approach, by contrast, holds greater promise for the measurement of degrees of power.

A second problem for the behavior approach is that behavior control is not clearly a sufficient condition for the exercise of power. Suppose that you are about to sit in a chair. I politely ask you to sit in the next chair instead, and since it is equally comfortable, you oblige. Here I have affected your behavior: I have induced you to do something you would not otherwise have done. But have I exercised *power over* you? This is doubtful. The reason it is doubtful, I think, can be explained by the welfare approach. First of all, there is no difference for your welfare between sitting in the one chair or sitting in the other. Secondly, since my method of inducing the change in behavior did not depend on threats or deprivation of opportunities, there is nothing in the case to suggest that I have any means of (importantly) affecting your welfare. A similar case is that of a skywriter, whose tracks cause many people to perform acts they would not otherwise perform, viz., look up at the sky. There is little temptation to say that the skywriter has exercised power over these people. Although he causes a change in behavior, this change is unaccompanied by any (or very much) change in welfare.

A third problem for the behavior approach is the existence of cases where behavior control fails but where there is inclination to talk of the exercise of power. Suppose I threaten to beat you up unless you do act A. You refuse to comply and so I beat you up. Here I have failed to control your behavior, but isn't my beating you up itself an exercise of power?[23] I am inclined to think that it is. My having power w.r.t. your getting beaten up is a form of power over you, even when unaccompanied by power w.r.t. your doing A. Again, this case is easily accounted for by the welfare approach, since my having power w.r.t. the issue of your getting beaten up is clearly having power w.r.t. an issue that importantly affects your welfare.

It goes without saying, of course, that power w.r.t. behavior and power w.r.t. welfare are in general closely interdependent. (This point is stressed by many authors, including Harsanyi and Thibaut and Kelley to mention just a few.) If X has power w.r.t. issues that affect Y's welfare, and if he knows how they would affect Y's welfare, then he is in a position to make threats or offers to Y in order to affect his behavior.[24] Moreover, certain ways of affecting behavior characteristically result in behavior that is less valuable to the agent affected. If X deters Y by threat from performing an act, or if X prevents Y from performing an act he otherwise would have performed, then there is typically a loss in utility for Y. Even though Y averts the threatened sanction or penalty by complying with X's desires, the substitute course of action is normally less valuable for Y than the act he would have performed had X not intervened. For these reasons, then, there is a close connection between power w.r.t. the *behavior* of Y and power w.r.t. issues affecting the *welfare* of Y.

Nevertheless, it must be admitted that there are cases of power 'over' people that involve only power w.r.t. their behavior, not power w.r.t. their welfare. The most obvious cases of this sort are cases of what Max Weber calls 'imperative control' or 'imperative coordination' (Herrschaft). When the commands of an authority in a corporate group are accepted by the group as 'legitimate', there is a tendency to obey the commands without the need for coercion (or reward). In many such cases, moreover, compliance with these commands have no effect (or very little effect) on the welfare of the compliers. For very often the behavior called for by these imperatives is more-or-less routine behavior of functionaries which is quite inconsequential as far as they themselves are concerned. Needless to say, the possession of imperative control is normally an extremely valuable resource to have in controlling the welfare of people. That is, it normally *enables* its possessor to have significant degrees of power w.r.t. issues that affect people's welfare. The point, however, is that we can abstract from this power w.r.t. welfare and still be left with something important that would ordinarily be called power 'over' people. Thus, it is important to retain the notion of behavior control as a distinct category of power 'over' people, despite its large overlap with the category of welfare control.

A third category of power 'over' people is also called for, though again the overlap with the other categories will be substantial. The third category is power to *persuade*, or more generally, power w.r.t. various psychological states of others, especially *desires*, *beliefs*, and *attitudes*. To the extent that a 'charismatic' leader has power w.r.t. the attitudes of his followers, and to the extent that the controller of communication media has power w.r.t. the desires and beliefs of the public, such people have power 'over' others. To be sure, power of this sort is closely connected with power w.r.t. behavior and power w.r.t. welfare. The difference between true and false belief, for example, will frequently make a difference to one's ability or inability to satisfy one's interests. Nevertheless, there are many cases in which the connection between desires and beliefs, on the one hand, and behavior and welfare, on the other, is at best very indirect and complicated. Many beliefs are never acted upon, and changes in desire are hard to relate to changes in welfare. For these reasons, then, it is worth including the third category as a distinct category of power 'over' others.

A further reason for emphasizing the third category must also be mentioned. Our analysis of power w.r.t. an issue, it should be recalled, makes an essential appeal both to hypothetical desires of an agent and to his actual desires (which determine the *cost* of an activity). It is obvious, therefore, that X's having power w.r.t. Y's desires can have an important bearing on Y's power w.r.t. an issue. In fact, this point raises an important question about our analysis of power w.r.t. issues. According to our analysis, we are interested in whether an outcome of an issue would occur *if* agent Y wanted that outcome. But suppose agent X is in a position to ensure that Y will *not* want this outcome. What does this imply about Y's power w.r.t. that issue? This question must be taken up in a more fully developed theory of power, but this is not the occasion for such a development.

Notes

I am indebted to the Philosophy Department of Harvard University for a George Santayana Fellowship, which supported my work on this paper. Ancestors of the paper were read at the University of Michigan, Harvard University, the University of Pennsylvania, and the Society for Ethical and Legal Philosophy. I have received helpful comments from so many people that it is difficult to acknowledge my debts to them in a short space. Special thanks are owed Holly Smith, who read many versions of the paper and made numerous constructive suggestions.

1. A few of the most prominent works in the field are the following: Dahl 1957, French 1956, Goldhamer and Shils 1939, Harsanyi 1962, Lasswell and Kaplan 1950, March 1955, Russell 1938, and Shapley and Shubik 1954. For a critical review of relevant literature and some reservations about the utility of the power concept for empirical research, see March 1966.

2. See Dahl 1957, pp. 212–213. Actually, Dahl's chameleon just decides to *vote* with the predicted outcome, but I assume that his *desires* change to favor it as well.

3. For further details on the notion of a basic act-type, see Goldman 1970, chap. III, section 4 (and also chap. VII, section 1). In this paper I am ignoring certain complications, such as the existence of 'standard conditions'. I shall also assume, for the most part, that all persons have the same basic act repertoire, though in one of my examples (in section III) I shall drop this assumption.

4. In ordinary language we frequently use the term 'power' without having a particular dated issue in mind. If John has a rain-making machine, for example, we might say that he has power over 'the weather', without specifying the time in question. This loose talk about power can be understood in terms of power w.r.t. dated issues. To say that John has power w.r.t. the weather (in general), is to say that there are dated issues involving the weather w.r.t. which John has power. Having a rain-making machine gives John power over the weather 'in general' because there are particular times at which it would not rain in the normal course of events, and w.r.t. rain *at these times* John has power. To say that John has power over the weather, in this sense, does not imply that John has power w.r.t. *every* dated issue involving the weather. If it is going to rain at time t no matter what John does (and if, in addition, he cannot control how hard it rains), then John has no power w.r.t. the issue of whether or not it rains *at t*. Assuming

that he has no rain-prevention equipment, at any rate, he is impotent w.r.t. the issue of whether or not it rains *at t*.

5. Actually, (I') needs still further refinement. First, it is not enough to require that S would perform the relevant acts; he must perform these acts *in order to* achieve the given outcome (or at least *in the belief* that his performance of them would not prevent the occurrence of that outcome). Second, the analysis still remains open to counterexamples of the sort that beset (I). Suppose that S is not paralyzed and he falsely believes that whenever he snaps his fingers, this causes rain clouds to disperse. It is true of S, then, that if he wanted non-rain he would snap his fingers (moreover, he would snap them in order to obtain non-rain). Further suppose, as in the earlier example, that S^* has the ability to detect S's desires by ESP, and he has resolved to make the weather conform with S's desire. Now although S's snapping his fingers would not be causally relevant to the occurrence of non-rain, there is a sequence of basic acts such that if S wanted non-rain he would perform these acts, and if he performed these acts non-rain would occur. Thus, S satisfies (I') w.r.t. the issue of rain or non-rain. But it is doubtful that we would credit S with power w.r.t. this issue.

What goes wrong here is that S is mistaken about the contribution that his finger-snapping would make to the occurrence of non-rain. He erroneously believes that this act would directly cause the dispersal of the clouds, and he is completely ignorant of the role of S^*. To circumvent such problems we need a provision requiring that the agent's *conception* of the relevance of his action to the outcome must correspond to the relevance his action *would* indeed have. I do not know how to formulate such a provision in adequate detail (similar problems are encountered in the analysis of intentional action and in the analysis of knowing), but I shall suggest a vague formulation for the present.

Each of the conjuncts of (I') should be amended as follows: "There is a sequence of basic act-types such that

(a) if S wanted e [not-e], then, at appropriate times between t_1 and t_n, he would perform these acts, either (i) in order to achieve outcome e [not-e], or (ii) in the belief that they would not preclude the occurrence of e [not-e], and

(b) if S performed these acts at these appropriate times, then they would contribute to the occurrence of e [not-e] in the way S would expect them to contribute, and e [not-e] would occur (at t_n)."

(Notice that my reformulation of clause (b) does not imply that S's action would *cause* the outcome. This is because I want to allow, for one of the outcomes, that it would occur in the 'normal' course of events. This is all right as long as S *realizes*, for the appropriate outcome, that his action would merely 'allow' this outcome to occur, rather than *cause* it to occur.)

The indicated reformulation should be regarded as my 'official' analysis of individual power. I omit it from the text because I want to use (I') as a model for later analyses; to use the more refined analysis, I fear, would obscure the more important structural features of the theory.

6. Cf. Quine 1960, pp. 222–226.

7. Perhaps we should draw a distinction here between an 'epistemic' sense of 'power' and a 'non-epistemic' sense of 'power'. The epistemic sence is captured by (I') as it stands, whereas the non-epistemic sense can be obtained from (I') by deleting clauses (1) (a) and (2) (a). This distinction would parallel the distinction between the epistemic and non-epistemic senses of 'ability' that I draw in Goldman 1970, p. 203. For our purposes, however, the epistemic sense of 'power' seems much more important than the non-epistemic sense.

8. The difficulties here are well known. Cf. Goodman 1955.

9. It is necessary to rule out partitions with 'gimmicky' outcomes. For example, we do not want to partition the weather issue into the three outcomes: (a) it does not rain, (b) it rains with my right hand raised, (c) it rains with my right hand not raised. Unfortunately, I do not know how to formulate a general condition to rule out such a 'gimmicky' partition.

10. Actually, a further condition—condition (d)—must be added. To see the necessity for this, suppose that someone will be chosen from a list of ten candidates, and let E be the issue of who will be chosen. Suppose we consider two partitions of the issue, P and P'. P is the partition whose outcomes are (i) a Democrat is chosen and (ii) a Republican is chosen. P' is the partition whose outcomes are (i') an Eastsider is chosen and (ii') a Westsider is chosen. (Both of these pairs are exhaustive and mutually exclusive.) Further suppose that in W_1 S could ensure either of the outcomes of P but not of P', whereas in W_2 S could ensure either of the outcomes of P' but not of P. Then it follows from (a), (b), and (c) that S has more power w.r.t. E in W_1 than in W_2 *and also* that he has more power w.r.t. E in W_2 than in W_1. To avoid this difficulty, the following condition may be added:

> (d)   There is no other partition P' of E, whose outcomes constitute set E^{**}, for which there are subsets E''' and E'''' such that E'''' contains at least two members, E''' is a proper subset of E'''', in W_1 E'''' is the largest subset of E^{**} any of whose members S can ensure, and in W_2 E''' is the largest subset of E^{**} any of whose members S can ensure.

11. Although Smith does not have individual power w.r.t. the issue of whether or not Brown is alive at noon, he does have individual power w.r.t. the (distinct) issue of whether or not *he* (Smith) *kills* Brown. Thus, even apart from our distributive principle, we have a way of accounting for the intuition that Smith has *some* power here.

12. On the relative power of three or more individuals, see chapter 14.

13. In the game whose matrix is shown below, Column and Row make one move each, simultaneously, with no information about the move of his opponent. We can say here that for any move by Column there is a move available to Row which would 'win' for Row; but similarly, for any move by Row there is a move available to Column which would 'win' for Column.

	c_1	c_2
r_1	$+100$	-100
r_2	-100	$+100$

14. In typical political situations it will be necessary to partition an issue into numerous possible outcomes, e.g., the different possible compromises that might be reached on a piece of legislation, or the different wage increases that might be given to a union. Suppose there is a partition of E into ten outcomes, and suppose that if S_1 and S_2 had diametrically opposite rank orderings then the outcome which is fourth on S_1's list (and seventh on S_2's list) would occur. Does it follow that S_1 has more power than S_2 w.r.t. E? This is not evident (even neglecting other partitions). Further complications arise if S_1 and S_2 have different but not diametrically opposite rank orderings.

15. Reflection on these kinds of cases suggests that statements expressing comparisons of power might be parsed, not in terms of a two-place relation 'x has more power than y', but rather in terms of a three- (or more) place relation such as 'x has more power than

y given *z* as a resource'. This sort of treatment would make explicit which person(s) are being treated as resources. It would also have the virtue of forestalling certain problems of transitivity that might otherwise arise.

16. I assume that the machine can only be operated by S^*; thus, S can only affect the weather *through* S^*, not by operating the machine himself.

17. This point raises difficult problems. If we counterfactualize S's desires vis-à-vis E, it may seem plausible to counterfactualize a variety of other desires of his as well. It would not be plausible to consider the (counterfactual) hypothesis that Bush wants a Democrat to be elected in 1992 without supposing other significant changes in his set of desires. The difficulty here is to decide which changes to make. There is no unique set of changes one is forced to make; numerous counterfactualizations are equally admissible. This is undoubtedly one of the reasons why judgments about power in ordinary life are so ambiguous and difficult to agree about: it is possible to counterfactualize in many different ways, yet these different alternatives are not normally made explicit. For the sake of simplicity, we shall assume in the remainder of the text that *no* additional changes are made in the agent's desires beyond the changes in his desire vis-à-vis E.

18. Strictly speaking, it is not the *actual* costs to be undergone by a person that are relevant to his power; rather, it is his *expected* costs. To avoid any further complications, however, let us assume that both S_1 and S_2 have perfect information about the consequences of their activities, so that expected and actual costs are the same.

19. A question here arises whether to include the (expected) effects of e and of not-e in determining the cost of an activity or whether to include these under the utility assigned to e and not-e themselves (hence omitting them from the determination of cost). This is a tricky question, since the degree to which a given outcome of E is desired commonly depends upon expected consequences of that outcome. What I propose is the following. If C is expected to result from outcome e, then if C would constitute one of the agent's *reasons* for wanting e, then it is included under the value of e (*not* in the category of *cost*). If C would be an *unwelcome* consequence of e (e.g., going to jail), then it is included in the category of cost.

20. For convenience we assume, in this case, that the utility accruing to Row from this course of action is always the same, no matter which sequence of acts is chosen by Column.

21. The introduction of many-outcome partitions also provides a tool for distinguishing degrees of power; but the new approach, making use of degrees of desire, is a more powerful one, I believe.

22. Another possibility, stressed by Dahl and his followers, concerns the amount of change X can make in the *probability* that Y will perform certain acts. This suggestion rests on a problematic appeal to the (objective) probability of an individual event, however, and I do not think it is ultimately satisfactory.

23. Here too Dahl might appeal to a change in the *probability* of an action; he might say that by threatening you, I at least increase the probability that you will do A. But this may simply be false (assuming we can make sense of such statements). If you are extremely averse to doing act A, then there may be no change at all in the probability that you will do A. (The probability that you would do A may have been zero before the threat and zero after it.)

24. For certain purposes one must carefully distinguish between offers and threats (cf. Nozick 1969). But these differences go beyond the purview of this paper.

Chapter 14
On the Measurement of Power

The aim of this paper is to develop a general strategy for measuring the relative power of individuals over any given issue. Three slightly different schemes will be proposed, all of which employ the same basic strategy. Although even the best of these schemes is not finally satisfactory, two important goals will be achieved: (1) the fundamental structure of the approach will be delineated, and (2) the nature of the refinement needed to obtain a fully adequate scheme will be clearly identified.

The underlying conception of power I shall employ is set forth and defended in chapter 13. The present paper combines this conception of power with a modified version of the measurement technique of L. S. Shapley and M. Shubik (1954).

My conception of power is, roughly, that power is *the ability to get what one wants*, or *the ability to realize one's will*.[1] More specifically, it is the ability to realize one's will *despite the* (possible) *resistance or opposition of others*.[2] These formulas conceal a crucial ambiguity, however. They leave it unclear whether 'what one wants' or 'what one wills' refers to one's actual wants only, or to possible desires as well. My conception of power focuses on the latter interpretation. A person's power is not simply a matter of his getting what he actually wants, but of his ability to obtain outcomes that are possible objects of his desire or preference. Furthermore, the possession of power does not require the ability "single-handedly" to obtain a desired outcome. A person has *some* power even if he can only make a "contribution" toward the attainment of a given outcome, that is, if his preference for that outcome would, in combination with similar preferences by others, lead to the attainment of that outcome.

Power is obviously not an all-or-nothing affair. One person's overall power may greatly exceed another's, and yet the latter may not be entirely powerless. In this paper I am not concerned with "overall" power; I restrict my attention to the problem of power over a single issue or a single outcome. Even with this restriction, though, power remains a relative matter, or a matter of degree. Our problem is to devise a method for assessing the relative amounts of power among a number of individuals over a single issue or outcome.

I

The basic conceptual units of the analysis are the concept of an *outcome* and the concept of an *issue*. An outcome is a possible event or state of affairs. An issue is associated with a set of two or more outcomes that are mutually exclusive and jointly exhaustive; different sets of outcomes determine different issues. This conception diverges slightly from the previous paper, but it better serves my current purposes.[3] I shall be concerned (as in the earlier paper) with dated outcomes and issues. One issue, for example, is whether or not it rains in New York City at noon today. The outcomes of this issue are (e) it rains in New-York City at noon today, and (not-e) it does not rain in New York City at noon today. Another issue is associated with the following five outcomes: the federal government's spending for defense in 1974 is (e_1) between \$0 and \$40 billion, (e_2) between \$40 billion and \$60 billion, (e_3) between \$60 billion and \$80 billion, (e_4) between \$80 billion and \$100 billion, and (e_5) more than \$100 billion. Although there may be issues with infinitely many outcomes, attention will be restricted to finite cases.

A fundamental problem in the analysis of power is whether to construe, power as holding over issues or over outcomes. I believe that both of these notions are needed. To keep them distinct, however, a terminological decision must be made. I shall speak of "control" over *issues* and "power" over *outcomes*.[4] Obviously there is a close connection between control over an issue and power over the outcomes of that issue. A person has control over an issue if and only if he has power over one or more of its outcomes. Moreover, the larger the number of outcomes over which he has power, the greater his control over that issue (ceteris paribus).

Under what conditions, then, does person S have power over outcome e? The spirit of my suggestion (though not a precise formulation of it) is that S has power over e just in case S is a nonredundant member of some set of persons such that, if all these persons wanted e to occur, then e would occur. The possession of power, then, depends on the truth of certain subjunctive conditionals, conditionals whose antecedents specify desires or preferences and whose consequents specify corresponding outcomes. Now a person's desires or preferences do not ordinarily influence an outcome directly; rather, his actions influence it—such actions as casting a ballot, making a campaign contribution, threatening reprisals, or requesting a favor. But a person's actions are determined by his desires or preferences. Thus, although in principle we are interested in conjunctions of conditionals of the form "If S wanted e, then S would perform actions $A_1, \ldots, A_n$, and if S performed actions $A_1, \ldots, A_n$, then outcome e would occur," we may for simplicity delete the reference to actions and use conditionals of the form "If S wanted outcome e, then outcome e would occur."

The model I shall present contains an important simplification. In the real world a person's actions are determined not merely by the outcomes that he prefers, but by the *intensity* of his preferences. Thus, there is no reason to think that a conditional of the form "If S wanted e, then S would perform actions $A_1, \ldots, A_n$" has a determinate truth value. Similarly, a conditional of the form "If S wanted e, then e would occur" cannot be expected to have a determinate truth value. Whether outcome e occurs may depend on what S does, and what S does, as we have seen, may depend not only on whether or not he wants e, but on how much he wants it. For the purposes of this paper, however, I make the admittedly unrealistic assumption that all persons' actions are uniquely determined by their preferences (or preference orderings) for the given outcome; in other words, the intensity or strength of their preferences has no significance. Without this simplification I could not articulate the kind of approach I wish to propose. Once this approach has been articulated, it should be possible to relax this assumption and develop a more realistic theory. This final move, however, goes beyond the scope of the present paper.

A further limitation of my analysis is the difficulty it encounters in cases where one person can attain an outcome by influencing the preferences of others vis-à-vis that outcome. The model is not wholly incapable of treating such cases, but, in its present form it cannot deal with them adequately. I shall therefore assume in this paper that a person's preferences, actual or hypothetical, cannot be changed or influenced by the actions (or preferences) of others. The model allows one person to affect the actions of others, for example, by making threats or offers related to those actions. But changing the preferences of others vis-à-vis the issue in question is not to be allowed.

Another assumption of my model is determinism, or the absence of chance. I assume not only (1) that any set of hypothetical preferences of a set of individuals uniquely determines their courses of action, but also (2) that these courses of action—together with the state of the rest of the world—uniquely determine the outcome of the issue. What is precluded is any mere chance relationship between preferences and actions and any mere chance relationship between actions and outcomes. The "state of the rest of the world" is, of course, quite crucial, for it includes "resources" or "enabling conditions" that are relevant to the determination of the outcome. An essential feature of the model is that, whereas preferences (and, derivatively, actions) are counterfactualized, all other features of the actual world (including these resources) are held fixed, at least all features that are nomologically compatible with the hypothetical preferences.[5]

II

The simplest cases of power or control are those in which a person can single-handedly ensure the occurrence of any outcome he prefers. A man who possesses a rain-making and rain-preventing machine, and who can operate it by himself, can single-handedly control the issue of whether or not it rains in New York City at noon today. If he wants rain, it will rain, and if he wants non-rain, it will not rain. But this is not the only kind of situation where one has some degree of control over an issue. Suppose that a rain machine is jointly owned by ten people, who vote on how and when to use it. These ten people hold various amounts of stock in the machine and have a corresponding number of votes. S_1 has five votes, S_2 has two votes, and each of the persons S_3 through S_{10} has one vote each. The machine is used in accordance with a majority of the fifteen votes. Now, although S_1 has more control than any of the others, each of them has *some* degree of control over the issue of rain in New York City at noon today. None of these people (including S_1) can single-handedly obtain whichever outcome he prefers, yet each has some degree of control.

Actually, the question of whether anyone can "single-handedly" obtain a preferred outcome is an ambiguous question. In asking whether S_1 can single-handedly obtain an outcome, we make counterfactual hypotheses, of course, about *his* preferences. But this leaves two possible attitudes to take toward the remaining members of the group: (1) we may hold fixed their actual preferences vis-à-vis the issue, or (2) we may make counterfactual suppositions concerning their preferences as well. There is a significant difference between these two approaches. Suppose we wish to determine whether S_1, with five votes, can "single-handedly" obtain whichever outcome he prefers. If we take the first approach, the preferences of the remaining members are held constant; so some assumption about their preferences in the actual world must be made. Let us assume that these preferences are as follows: S_2, with two votes, and S_3, with one vote, both prefer rain, but the remaining seven members, with one vote each, all prefer non-rain. If we hold these preferences fixed, then S_1 can obtain whichever outcome he prefers. If he wants rain, he casts his five votes for rain, which yields the requisite majority of eight; if he wants non-rain, he casts his five votes for non-rain, yielding a total of twelve votes for non-rain. On approach 1, then, S_1 can "single-handedly" obtain whichever outcome he chooses.[6] On approach (2), however, it is *false* that S_1 can single-handedly obtain whichever outcome he prefers. If we counterfactualize the preferences of all ten persons, there are many suppositions concerning their preferences in which S_1 fails to obtain his preferred outcome.

Now if we wish to compare the control or power of all ten rain-machine owners, I recommend adoption of the second approach, where the preferences of all ten people are subject to (simultaneous) counterfactualization. In other words, I propose that we consider all possible combinations of preference among all ten people.[7]

More generally, suppose that we wish to compare the control of n persons over a selected issue. Clearly we must counterfactualize the preferences of *at least* these n people. The difficult question is whether to counterfactualize the preferences of *exactly* these n people while holding constant all other preferences. This was the principle that was recommended in chapter 13 (though I noted the problems it raises), but it cannot in general be accepted.

To illustrate the difficulties for this principle, consider again the rain-making example, and assume that certain members with a majority of the votes, viz., S_3, S_4, ..., S_{10}, all actually prefer rain. Now suppose that we initially wish to assess the relative control of S_1 and S_2 only. Our principle instructs us to counterfactualize the preferences of S_1 and S_2 only, holding constant all other preferences. Given this counterfactualization, the theory I shall present assigns zero control to both S_1 and S_2. (This is because the preferences of S_3, S_4, ..., S_{10} ensure the occurrence of rain; so the preferences of S_1 and S_2 can make no difference to the outcome.) Suppose next, however, that we wish to compare the control of all ten people, not merely S_1 and S_2. The principle under discussion instructs us to counterfactualize the preferences of all ten people. Given this counterfactualization, our theory will credit S_1 and S_2 with some—i.e., some nonzero—degree of control; and S_1 will be assigned more control than S_2. This second assignment, however, is inconsistent with the first! The first gives S_1 and S_2 an equal amount of control (viz., none), whereas the second gives S_1 more than S_2. Moreover, the first gives zero control to both S_1 and S_2, whereas the second credits both S_1 and S_2 with a positive degree of control.

Of the two assignments, the second is clearly more intuitive. Surely S_1, who has five votes, should be credited with more control than S_2, with only two votes; and surely both of them should be credited with a positive degree of control. Apparently, then, even if we are interested only in the relative control of S_1 and S_2, we ought to counterfactualize the preferences of others as well. Thus, we have two reasons to reject the principle that prescribes counterfactualization of the preferences of exactly those people in whose relative control (or power) we are (currently) interested. First, this principle leads to inconsistencies, and, secondly, it does not ensure the most intuitive assignments.

Having rejected this principle, how shall we choose the set G of persons whose preferences are to be counterfactualized? One possibility is always to let G consist of every person whose preference could, in combination with possible preferences of others, affect the outcome. This counter-factualization would include everyone with any control at all over the issue. The virtue of this suggestion is that it avoids inconsistencies and provides a perfectly general procedure. The drawback is that it seems inadequate as an account of our ordinary procedure for making comparisons of power. In our pre-analytic judgments we often (tacitly) hold fixed the actual preferences of many people whose (hypothetical) preferences could, in principle, affect the outcome. It might be argued that a systematic and theoretically adequate procedure would not do this, that it would counterfactualize everyone's preferences if it counterfactualized anyone's. But this claim requires substantial defense, which I am not prepared to give here.

The problem is difficult, and I propose to sidestep it in this paper. Instead of recommending any general procedure for the selection of G, I shall confine myself to the problem of assigning degrees of power, *given* some group G whose preferences are to be counterfactualized. The only restriction on group G is that it must include *at least* all those persons whose power we seek to compare.

It should be noted that for Gs of any substantial size, actual application of our measurement procedure(s) will be exceedingly difficult. First, the number of conditionals to be considered even for moderate-sized Gs and moderate-sized issues (i.e., issues with a moderate number of outcomes) is enormous. Secondly, it will normally be quite difficult to ascertain the truth value of even one such (counterfactual) conditional, much less the large number of conditionals that will normally be involved. It is apparent, then, that our scheme will be of limited use from an empirical point of view. But this, in any case, is not the intent of the analysis; its intent is to provide a *conceptual elucidation* of the concept of power.

III

In the rain-making example, the power "resources" of the members are the number of votes available to them. Now since the ratio of votes itself indicates the relative amounts of power (approximately, at any rate), one would not expect much difficulty in devising a power-measuring scheme for this kind of case. When a situation offers no obvious quantifiable index of resources, however, the task looks more difficult. But this is precisely our task: to assign numerical values representing amounts of control or power for any sort of issue, whether votes are relevant or not. We want a criterion of measurement that will reflect the significance of all kinds and combinations of resources, including financial assets, positions of authority, physical strength, sociability, and charisma.

By reflecting on weighted voting situations, I think we can discern how to generalize from these situations to situations that do not involve voting at all. How do S_1's five votes make a difference to the amount of power he has in comparison with others? One difference is that if S_1 wants rain, a relatively small number of additional like-minded members are needed to ensure rain. Only three others are needed, in addition to S_1, to ensure the occurrence of rain (only two others if one is S_2), whereas for an ordinary member (S_3 through S_{10}) seven others are needed to ensure the occurrence of rain (unless one of them is S_1 or S_2). Another difference between S_1 and the ordinary members of the group is that there is a larger number of different combinations of members which, combined with him, can ensure the occurrence of rain.

To generalize from these facts, let us borrow some terminology from the study of social welfare functions, to which our model is structurally similar. Let G be the set of individuals whose preferences are to be counter-factualized for a given issue. We shall say that set D ($D \subseteq G$) is a *decisive set for outcome e* if and only if outcome e would occur if all members of D wanted e to occur, no matter what the preferences of the remaining members of G. We shall also say that set M is a *minimal decisive set* (MDS) *for outcome e* if and only if (1) M is a decisive set for e, and (2) no proper subset of M is a decisive set for e. Notice that D's being a decisive set for e does not imply that the members of D *actually prefer* e to other possible outcomes. It just implies that e would occur *if* they all preferred e to the remaining outcomes. In other words, a decisive set is a "potentially" decisive set.

If we reflect on weighted voting situations (or on situations of any sort), we can see that the following three principles should govern our choice of a procedure for measuring power and control. These principles constitute criteria of adequacy for any proposed measurement procedure.

I. Ceteris paribus, the larger the number of minimal decisive sets for e to which S belongs, the greater is S's power over e.

II. Ceteris paribus, the smaller the size of the minimal decisive sets for e to which S belongs, the greater is S's power over e.

III. Ceteris paribus, the larger the number of minimal decisive sets for e to which S does not belong, and the smaller the size of these minimal decisive sets, the less is S's power over e (in comparison with other members of G).

These principles can be defended, in outline, as follows. Clearly, membership in two MDSs for e represents greater power over e than membership in only one of these sets. And, in general, membership in k MDSs represents greater power than membership in only $k - 1$ of these sets. Membership in a larger number of MDSs (for e) implies that one's resources could successfully complement the resources of a wider range of members of G (in attaining outcome e). So principle I is clearly justified. Principle II can be justified as follows. If there is only one MDS for e, and S belongs to it, then its being a two-member set suggests that S has more power over e than if it were a three-member set. For its being a two-member rather than a three-member set implies that there is a larger number of *remaining* members of G whose opposition to e could be overcome.[8] The same reasoning applies to sets of any larger size, and it applies equally when there is more than one MDS. Hence, membership in smaller MDSs represents greater power, ceteris paribus, than membership in larger MDSs. Finally, principle III is justified in light of the fact that we are concerned with the *relative* power of members of G. To the extent that other members of G belong to more and smaller MDSs, their power is greater as compared with the power of S.

The scheme(s) that I shall propose for the measurement of power will satisfy these three principles. Before turning to my scheme(s), however, let us look briefly at the theory of Shapley and Shubik (1954), from which the central idea of my strategy is borrowed.

IV

The scheme proposed by Shapley and Shubik is neatly summarized in the following passage:

> Let us consider the following scheme. There is a group of individuals all willing to vote for some bill. They vote in order. As soon as a majority has voted for it, it is declared passed, and the member who voted last is given credit for having passed it. Let us choose the voting order of the members randomly. Then we may compute the frequency with which an individual belongs to the group whose votes are used and, of more importance, we may compute how often he is *pivotal*. This latter number serves to give us our index. It measures the number of times that the action of an individual actually changes the state of affairs. A simple consequence of this formal scheme is that where all voters have the same number of votes, they will each be credited with $1/n$th of the power, there being n participants. If they have different numbers of votes (as in the case of stockholders of a corporation), the result is more complicated; more votes mean more power, as measured by our index, but not in direct proportion. (Shapley and Shubik 1954, p. 788)

That a given individual is *pivotal* in a certain vote implies that he is a member of a minimal decisive set for the passage of the bill.[9] To show this, we reason as follows. First, the fact that his vote completes a majority implies that he and the previous voters together form a decisive set. Second, the fact that his vote completes a majority implies that the previous voters alone do not constitute a decisive set. Two possibilities therefore remain. Either all the previous voters plus the pivot constitute a minimal decisive set, or a minimal decisive set is constituted by a proper subset of the previous voters plus the pivot. In either case the pivot is a member of some minimal decisive set.

The procedure of Shapley and Shubik is to take all permutations of the members of the committee in question, to assume that they all vote in favor of the bill, and then to compute the number of times each member is a pivot. The relative power of the members is given by the ratio of times each is a pivot. To illustrate this procedure, consider the following allocation of votes in a four-member group.

Member	Number of Votes
A	3
B	4
C	6
D	10

Assuming that a majority of twelve votes ensures a victory, there are the following twenty-four permutations, with the pivot underlined in each case.

1. ABCD	7. BACD	13. CABD	19. DABC
2. ABDC	8. BADC	14. CADB	20. DACB
3. ACBD	9. BCAD	15. CBAD	21. DBAC
4. ACDB	10. BCDA	16. CBDA	22. DBCA
5. ADBC	11. BDAC	17. CDAB	23. DCAB
6. ADCB	12. BDCA	18. CDBA	24. DCBA

The total number of times each member is a pivot is given below.

A: 4   B: 4   C: 4   D: 12

Hence, the ratio of the power of these members is $1 : 1 : 1 : 3$. Initially it may be surprising that the powers of A, B, and C are the same despite the fact that they have unequal numbers of votes. This ceases to be surprising, however, when one notices that each of them can form minimal decisive sets with the same combinations of other members of the group. Specifically, $\{A, B, C\}$ is a MDS, and $\{A, D\}$, $\{B, D\}$, and $\{C, D\}$ are MDSs.

Shapley and Shubik point out that, according to their method, the members of a committee will be credited with the same relative amount of

"blocking power" (or "negative power") as "positive power." That is, they
have the same relative amount of power to block the passage of a bill as
they do to pass a bill. Blocking power is determined by first imagining that
all members vote *against* a bill and then picking out the pivots, i.e., those
whose votes ensure the bill's defeat. This is illustrated in the following
example, where it is assumed that a two-thirds majority of six votes, out of
a total of nine, is required to pass a measure, four votes to defeat it.

Members	Number of Votes	Pivots for Passage		Pivots for Defeat	
A	5	ABC	A: 4	ABC	A: 4
B	2	ACB		ACB	
C	2	BAC	B: 1	BAC	B: 1
		BCA		BCA	
		CAB	C: 1	CAB	C: 1
		CBA		CBA	

   The procedure for measuring power that I wish to propose resembles the
Shapley-Shubik procedure in employing the notion of a pivot in the same
central way. It differs in that it does not simply consider different permutations in which all members vote in favor of an outcome or all vote against
an outcome. Rather, it considers cases in which there are different distributions of preference, some in favor of an outcome and some opposed. My
procedure also differs in that I am concerned with *desires* or *preferences* in
favor or opposed to an outcome, not with *votes* pro or con. On my
procedure the ratio of power attributed to the members is not identical
with that of the Shapley-Shubik index, although it is, I believe, at least as
plausible. Moreover, on my procedure the ratio of "blocking power" is not
necessarily identical with the ratio of "passing power."
   It is worth emphasizing that my procedure will be applicable not only to
voting situations, but to situations in which resources of all sorts may
determine the outcome. Unlike votes, resources in general are not homoge-
neous. Although Jones's resources may make him a valuable member of
one group relative to outcome *e*, the same resources may be relatively
unhelpful to another group relative to the same outcome. Also, the combination of resources of a particular group may be well suited for the attainment of one outcome but not for the attainment of a different outcome.

V

If the outcome of a given issue is not determined by votes, what kind of
information is needed to measure control over this issue? What is required
is a list of the outcomes that would occur given various hypotheses about
the pattern of preferences or desires among the members of the group in

Table 14.1

	If these members preferred *e*, and			if these members preferred not-*e*, then			this outcome would occur.
(1)	A	B	C				*e*
(2)	A	B				C	*e*
(3)	A		C		B		*e*
(4)	A				B	C	not-*e*
(5)		B	C	A			not-*e*
(6)		B		A		C	not-*e*
(7)			C	A	B		not-*e*
(8)				A	B	C	not-*e*

question. In other words, to assign degrees of power to the members of G, we need to know the truth values of a number of counterfactual conditionals (and one factual conditional). Empirically it may be extremely difficult to ascertain the truth values of these conditionals (this is one of the reasons why the application of our scheme will frequently be an empirical impossibility). We are not concerned with empirical applications, however, but only with the conceptual connection between the truth values of these conditionals and degrees of power.

To illustrate our procedure, suppose that group G has three members, A, B, and C, and suppose that the issue in question is a two-outcome issue. Assume, moreover, that table 14.1 represents the outcome of the issue that would occur for each of the possible patterns of desire (or preference) among the three members. In other words, this table specifies their preference-outcome function for this issue. Notice that this function is precisely the one that would obtain in the most recently discussed voting case, where a two-thirds majority was needed to pass the measure, where A had five votes, and B and C had two votes each. The same function could obtain, however, in a situation not involving votes at all (see table 14.1).

Given a function of this sort, it is easy to construct a list of MDSs for each outcome. For example, it is clear from case 1 that {A, B, C} is a decisive set for outcome *e*. But it follows from 2 and 3 that {A, B, C} is not a *minimal* decisive set for *e*. A bit of reflection reveals that the following are the MDSs for the two outcomes:

MDSs for *e*		MDSs for not-*e*	
{A, B}	{A, C}	{A}	{B, C}

Now to obtain the ratio of power between A, B, and C over a given outcome, we proceed as follows. We consider each combination of preferences that would yield that outcome. For each of these combinations, we consider the set of all permutations of which it is susceptible. That is, we consider all the possible *orders* in which the members of the group might be taken. In the present example the group has three members and, hence, six (= 3!) permutations. For each of these permutations, we identify that member who, when taken in the given order, is *pivotal*. Each time a person is a pivot he receives one credit of power vis-à-vis that outcome, The pivotal member in a given permutation is the member (if any) who satisfies the following conditions: (1) the outcome is uniquely determined by his preference together with the preference(s) of the member(s) (if any) who precede him in the permutation; (2) the outcome is not uniquely determined prior to consideration of his preference.

Suppose that we wish to compare the power of A, B, and C over outcome not-*e*, for example. Since the first combination of preferences that yields not-*e* is (4), we begin with combination 4. In this combination, outcome *e* is preferred by A, and outcome not-*e* is preferred by B and by C. In determining pivots, however, we "suspend" our knowledge of this, and pretend that we are given information about the members' preferences one by one.[10] After listing the six permutations of the three members (the same list for each combination of preferences), we start with the first permutation: A-B-C. We imagine first being told that A prefers *e*. Given this information, can it be deduced from the preference-outcome function (or from the list of MDSs) which of the two outcomes will occur? No. Member A's preferring *e* does not uniquely determine the outcome. We therefore proceed to the next member in the order, viz. B, and imagine being told that B prefers not-*e*. Does it follow from this information, together with that about A's preference, which outcome will occur? Again, no. We therefore move to the third member, C. Once we know that C prefers not-*e*, we can deduce from this, and from the preferences of A and B, that not-*e* occurs. Hence, member C is the pivot for this permutation, and receives one "credit" for not-*e*. If we proceed in this fashion for the remaining five permutations, we obtain the following list of credits: a total of three for B, three for C, and none for A (see table 14.2).

Having assigned credits for combination 4, we may then proceed to assign credits for the remaining combinations that yield not-*e* as an outcome. Credits for outcome *e* are assigned in exactly the same way. The resultant list of credits, for both outcomes, is given in table 14.3.

The relative number of total credits, for each outcome, is compatible with the three principles we formulated earlier. Member A belongs to two MDSs for *e*, whereas B and C belong to only one each. This is reflected in the ratio of credits for outcome *e*, viz., 10 : 4 : 4. With respect to not-*e*, all three members belong to one MDS each, but A belongs to a *smaller* MDS. This is reflected in the ratio of credits for not-*e*, viz., 22 : 4 : 4.

Table 14.2
Combination 4
(A prefers *e*; B and C prefer not-*e*)

Permutations	Credits (for not-*e*) A	B	C
AB<u>C</u>			1
AC<u>B</u>		1	
BA<u>C</u>			1
B<u>C</u>A			1
CA<u>B</u>		1	
C<u>B</u>A		1	

Table 14.3

	Preferences for *e*			for not-*e*			Credits *e* A	B	C	not-*e* A	B	C
(1)	A	B	C				4	1	1			
(2)	A	B				C	3	3				
(3)	A		C		B		3		3			
(4)	A				B	C					3	3
(5)		B	C	A						6		
(6)		B		A		C				6		
(7)			C	A	B					6		
(8)				A	B	C				4	1	1
							10	4	4	22	4	4

More generally, the nature of our technique for credit assignment ensures the satisfaction of the three principles. (1) The larger the number of MDSs to which you belong, the more times you will be a pivot, for there will be more permutations in which you are the final member of *some* MDS. (2) The smaller the size of a MDS to which you belong, the more times you will be a pivot, because the smaller its size, the more permutations there are in which you are preceded by its remaining members. For example, for any fixed size of G, the number of permutations in which S_i precedes you is greater than the number of permutations in which *both* S_i and S_j precede you. So, ceteris paribus, you will be a pivot more times if $\{$you, $S_i\}$ is a MDS than if $\{$you, S_i, $S_j\}$ is a MDS. (3) The larger the number of MDSs to which you do *not* belong and the smaller their size, the less often you will be a pivot. This is because the larger the number and the smaller the size of these MDSs, the more permutations there are in which you are preceded by all the members of some MDS to which you do not belong.

It seems fully appropriate, then, to regard the ratios yielded by our technique as specifying the relative amounts of power of the members with respect to each outcome. In addition, it is plausible to add these (raw) figures to obtain their relative control over the issue. In the present example, the ratio of control is $32 : 8 : 8$. According to our procedure—unlike that of Shapley and Shubik—a member may have a different relative amount of power over one outcome than over another. This seems perfectly appropriate, for there are cases in which a person can contribute more toward one outcome than toward another, where his resources are potentially more efficacious in connection with one outcome than another. This is especially clear for multi-outcome issues.

VI

To test the adequacy of our procedure, let us examine its consequences when applied to an unusual preference-outcome function, one that maps *all* combinations of preference into a single outcome, outcome e_i. Intuitively this is a case of *impotence*, a case in which the members of G have no control over the issue, and no power over any of its outcomes. It is a case in which e_i is *bound* to occur: even if all members of G concurred in preferring a different outcome, e_i would nonetheless occur. A simple illustration of this is where human beings are assumed to have no control at all over the weather, and where the issue consists of (e_1) rain in New York City at noon today, (e_2) snow in New York City at noon today, (e_3) hail in New York City at noon today, and (e_4) no precipitation at all in New York City at noon today. Now suppose that the meteorological conditions ensure that outcome e_4 will occur. Then that outcome will occur no matter what the preferences of human beings are with respect to this issue. Even if all people prefer rain, there will still be no precipitation in New York City at noon today. (Notice that there are possible combinations of preference in which the outcome that occurs is the outcome preferred by certain individuals. It does not follow from this, at least it *should* not follow from this, that these individuals have any power over this outcome. Thus, the truth of the conditional "If S wanted no precipitation, then there would be no precipitation" does not entail "S has (some) power over the outcome of there being no precipitation.")

Does our procedure correctly capture the intuition of impotence in this kind of case? Well, what are the MDSs in a case where all combinations of preference yield a single outcome? Clearly there are no MDSs for any outcome *other* than this one. Moreover, for this outcome, e_i, there is exactly one MDS, namely, the *null set*. To show this, we note first that the null set is a decisive set. This is so because, if each member of the null set—i.e., nobody—prefers outcome e_i, then e_i occurs, no matter what the remaining members of G—i.e., all members of G—may prefer. Next we note that the null set is a *minimal* decisive set. This follows from the fact that it has no proper subset. Now, since the null set is the only MDS for any outcome of the issue, no member of G belongs to any MDS for any of the issue's outcomes. This strongly suggests that no member of G has any control or power (over the issue or its outcomes). This conclusion does not quite follow, because, as we shall see in section VII, our criterion for pivot selection does not entail that a pivot is a member of a MDS. Nevertheless, our conclusion does hold, as an examination of the pivot-selection procedure reveals. In our example *nobody* is chosen as a pivot in any of the combinations and permutations. This is because the outcome is uniquely determined in each permutation before consideration of even the first member's preference, and this violates condition (2) of our pivot selection criterion. Since no one is ever a pivot in this example, no one receives any power credits. Hence our theory yields the desired consequence that none of the members of G has any control over the issue.

VII

I wish now to look more closely at our procedure for pivot selection. I shall raise doubts about our current procedure by discussing cases with two-outcome issues. The major significance of the discussion, though, is its bearing on multi-outcome issues.

Our current pivot-selection procedure stipulates that the pivot (if there is one) is the first member in a permutation whose preference, together with the preference(s) of preceding member(s), suffices to determine the outcome uniquely. This procedure becomes dubious when we consider the possibility of "counterpotent" agents. It is theoretically possible for someone to have a tendency to contribute toward outcome e if he prefers not-e and to contribute toward not-e if he prefers e. This might happen, for example, if he has radically mistaken beliefs about the appropriate actions to perform in order to contribute toward these outcomes. Or it might happen if other power holders have a very strong desire to keep him from getting his preferred outcome (whatever that might be). This might motivate them to act against whatever outcome he prefers, even if it happens to be the outcome that they too prefer.[11] Suppose that S_j is such a counterpotent person vis-à-vis outcome e. Specifically, suppose that the set $\{S_1, \ldots, S_i\}$ is not a decisive set for e, but that if all members of this coalition preferred e, and if, in addition, S_j preferred not-e, then outcome e would be (somehow) ensured. According to our current procedure for pivot selection, S_j will be considered a pivot in some permutations. (This is despite the fact that he may not be a member of any MDS for e. We see, then, that being a pivot does not imply membership in any MDS.) The question arises, however, whether this result accords with our fundamental conception of power as the ability to *get what one wants*. I suggest it does not, and I therefore propose to amend our procedure for pivot selection.

Let us call the member selected by our original pivot-selection procedure the "virtual pivot." Our new procedure selects the pivot as follows:

1. In a given combination and permutation the virtual pivot is the pivot if and only if (in this combination) he prefers the outcome that results from this combination.
2. If the virtual pivot is not the pivot, then the pivot is the last member before the virtual pivot who satisfies the following conditions:
a. the outcome that results from the combination is the outcome he prefers, and
b. if he were deleted from the permutation, then the outcome would not be uniquely determined by the preferences of the virtual pivot and all (other) members who precede the virtual pivot.
3. If there is no virtual pivot, then there is no pivot.

The new procedure is especially relevant to multi-outcome issues, since there are presumably many cases of multi-outcome issues analogous to counterpotency cases, viz., cases in which a member's preferring outcome e_i would help ensure the occurrence of a *different* outcome, e_j. If we have an issue with fifteen outcomes, ordered in terms of some natural ordering, it is quite possible that S_j's preferring outcome e_{12} would, given a preference for outcome e_{11} on the part of other members, ensure the occurrence of e_{11}. For the action S_j would take in order to secure e_{12} might well contribute toward the occurrence of a "neighboring" outcome. In this sort of case our old pivot-selection procedure would assign S_j some power credits over outcome e_{11} even in combinations where he preferred e_{12}. Our new procedure would assign these credits to someone else.

Let us illustrate the application of our new procedure to a multi-outcome issue. Consider a three-outcome issue and a set of three persons, A, B, and C, whose preference-outcome function for this issue is presented on the left-hand side of table 14.4. Using our new procedure, we obtain the credit assignments listed on the right-hand side of the table. The general pattern of power in this case is not seriously affected by the choice of our new pivot-selection procedure. (What gives A so much power over outcome e_2, for example, is that he constitutes *by himself* a MDS for e_2.) There are six combinations, however, in which our new procedure yields different assignments from the old procedure, i.e., (7), (8), (9), (24), (26), and (27). In each of these cases there is no MDS for any outcome whose members all prefer that outcome. For example, in combination 7 only members B and C prefer e_3, but $\{B, C\}$ is not a MDS for outcome e_3. Given that B and C prefer e_3, the outcome still depends on A's preference: if A prefers e_3 (combination 19) or e_1 (combination 7), then e_3 occurs, whereas if A prefers e_2 (combination 16), then e_2 occurs. Now in case 7 A prefers e_1, and so e_3 occurs. On our old procedure, A would be a pivot in some of the permutations of this combination. Under the new procedure, however, only B and C are pivots in this combination.

VIII

It will be noted that our new pivot procedure, like the original, makes use of *topmost* preferences only, rather than entire preference orderings. The avoidance of complete preference orderings has a distinct practical advantage: the introduction of preference orderings (even if indifferences continue to be ignored) would vastly increase the number of combinations. In the simple case of three persons and three outcomes, there are 216 combinations of preference orderings and hence 1,296 permutations. From a practical point of view, our neglect of preference orderings is understandable. From a conceptual point of view, however, this neglect faces two serious objections.

First, although it may be granted that a person should receive no power credits for *total* counterpotency, i.e., for cases in which he would contribute toward the occurrence of a *least* preferred outcome, surely there is good reason to give him *some* credit for having the ability to contribute toward the occurrence of a second or third most preferred outcome. This point assumes special importance when we recognize that, in cases involving numerous outcomes, the outcome that would result from a given combination of preference orderings may not coincide with *anyone's most* preferred outcome. This is what occurs, for example, in the case of "compromises":

Table 14.4

	Preferences for e_1	Preferences for e_2	Preferences for e_3	Outcome	e_1 A	e_1 B	e_1 C	e_2 A	e_2 B	e_2 C	e_3 A	e_3 B	e_3 C
(1)	A B C			e_1	4	1	1						
(2)	A B	C		e_1	3	3							
(3)	A B		C	e_1	3	3							
(4)	A C	B		e_1	3		3						
(5)	A C		B	e_1	3		3						
(6)	A	B C		e_2					3	3			
(7)	A		B C	e_3								3	3
(8)	A	B	C	e_1	6								
(9)	A	C B		e_1	6								
(10)		A B C		e_2				4	1	1			
(11)	C	A B		e_2				6					
(12)		A B	C	e_2				6					
(13)	B	A	C	e_2				6					
(14)		A C	B	e_2				6					
(15)	B C	A		e_2				6					
(16)		A	B C	e_2				6					
(17)	B	A	C	e_2				6					
(18)	C	A	B	e_2				6					
(19)			A B C	e_3							4	1	1
(20)	C		A B	e_3							3	3	
(21)		C	A B	e_3							3	3	
(22)	B		A C	e_3							3		3
(23)		B	A C	e_3							3		3
(24)	B C	A		e_1		3	3						
(25)		B C	A	e_2					3	3			
(26)	B		C A	e_1		6							
(27)	C	B	A	e_2					6				
					28	16	10	52	13	7	16	10	10

the outcome that occurs is nobody's most preferred outcome. Do we not wish to assign credits of power to members in virtue of their ability to obtain a *second* or *third* most preferred outcome, especially if the outcome that would occur "in the natural course of events" (e.g., if all the members of G were indifferent among all the outcomes) is quite different?

The second objection is even more serious. Our procedure has assumed that a hypothesis about the topmost preferences of members of G uniquely determines the outcome of the issue in question. But is this assumption justified? The outcome of the issue is presumably determined by the actions that would be performed by the members of G if they had the hypothetical preferences. But does a hypothesis about their topmost preferences uniquely determine their actions? Quite clearly not. In most cases a person's choice of action depends not only on his topmost preference, but on the rest of his preference ordering as well. Consequently, a procedure that incorporates complete preference orderings is required.

To formulate such a procedure, the third and last we shall consider, let us return to our original criterion for the selection of pivots. Now, however, instead of assigning one credit of power to each pivot, let us assign different *weights* for being a pivot, weights that reflect the ranking of the resultant outcome in the pivot's (hypothetical) preference ordering. If a person ensures the occurrence of his least preferred outcome, he receives no credit at all. If he ensures the occurrence of his most preferred outcome, he receives maximum credit. And if he ensures the occurrence of an intermediately ranked outcome, he receives an intermediate amount of credit. More precisely: if member S is the pivot in permutation P of combination C and if the outcome that results from combination C is the ith item from the bottom of S's preference ordering in C, then S is assigned $i - 1$ credits in permutation P. For example, suppose that S is the pivot in permutation P of combination C in which S's preference ordering over the five outcomes of the issue is as follows: $e_5 \succ e_4 \succ e_3 \succ e_2 \succ e_1$. Then, if the outcome of combination C is e_5, S receives four credits; if the outcome is e_4, S receives three credits; ... ; if the outcome is e_1, S receives no credits.[12]

Although the theory is substantially improved by the introduction of preference orderings, the difficulty posed by the "second objection" is still unresolved. A hypothesis about a person's preference ordering on a given issue still does not uniquely determine his action and, hence, does not determine the nature of his influence on the issue. In deciding how to act, an agent compares alternative courses of action in terms of their total benefits and total costs. Assuming we hold fixed his valuation of various other (expected) consequences of a given course of action, his decision to engage or not to engage in that course of action depends upon whether the *intensity* of his preference for his most preferred (or other preferred) outcome *exceeds* the (expected) costs of that course of action. Thus, only hypotheses about the utilities assigned by the agent to the outcome(s) uniquely determine his course of action.

The point I am making, of course, only restates the earlier point about the "unrealism" of our model. To reformulate the theory to make it more "realistic," we need to consider conditionals whose antecedents describe not patterns of preference orderings but patterns of utility assignments by the members of G. Two problems confront this move, however. First, there are infinitely many patterns of possible utility assignments to consider; so the treatment of these would require a different apparatus from the one we have been using. Second, it remains to be explained exactly what the relationship is between degrees of power and the ability to obtain a given outcome with higher or lower assignments of utility (degrees of intensity). In chapter 13 I have dealt with this problem for the case of two persons and two-outcome issues. There is reason to believe that the same general approach might be applied to many persons and many-outcome issues. Nonetheless, serious complications would be involved in extending this approach to many persons and many-outcome issues. In any case, this task is beyond the scope of the present paper.

Notes

I have received helpful comments from Nuel D. Belnap, Jr., John G. Bennett, Arthur Burks, Fred Feldman, and Jaegwon Kim.

1. This conception of power is familiar. For example, James S. Coleman writes: "the power of an actor in a system is his ability to realize his interests" (Coleman 1969, p. 431).

2. This sort of definition is favored by Max Weber and C. Wright Mills. Weber writes, "'Power' [Macht] is the probability that one actor within a social relationship will be in a position to carry out his own will despite resistance" (Weber 1947, p. 152). Mills says, "By the powerful we mean, of course, those who are able to realize their will, even if others resist it" (Mills 1959, p. 9).

3. In chapter 13 I allowed the same issue to be partitioned in different ways. In the present paper issues are individuated by partitions of outcomes; different partitions determine different issues.

4. In the earlier paper only issues were regarded as the domain of power; so here too my analysis diverges from the earlier one.

5. For more details on the treatment of counterfactuals in the analysis, see chapter 13, section I.

6. S_1 need not be the only member of the group who (on interpretation I) can "single-handedly" obtain whichever outcome he chooses. Suppose that S_1's actual preference (and vote) is for rain. Then S_2 is in the same position as S_1; he too can "single-handedly" obtain either outcome. For if we hold constant the actual preferences (and votes) of everyone other than S_2, there are six votes for rain (five from S_1 and one from S_3) and seven votes for nonrain. But then S_2's two votes can determine the outcome in either direction. (I assume here, as throughout, that all members vote simultaneously and independently.)

7. Strictly speaking, not all possible combinations of preference will be considered. In particular, cases of indifference between pairs of outcomes will be ignored. The effect of indifference *can* provide useful information and should be included in a fully compre-

hensive theory; but our present model will be so complicated that it behooves us to omit this further complication. Notice that the omission of indifferences is admissible despite the fact that actual preference orderings frequently include indifferences. Our analysis of power and control is not tied to actual preference orderings at all, but only to the connection between possible preferences and resultant outcomes.

8. It might be suggested that perhaps the *other* member of the MDS is the "really" powerful member, that S is only a minor adjunct. If this is so, however, then that other member ought to be able to combine with members with whom S cannot combine to form MDSs. Thus, this other member would belong to *more* MDSs than S and would be counted as more powerful, by principle I.

9. This statement is not quite accurate, for reasons that need not concern us at this juncture. We shall see in section VII that being a member of a minimal decisive set is not, in general, a necessary condition for being a pivot. Being a member of a minimal decisive set is a sufficient condition for being a pivot, however.

10. We do not suppose that their preferences *occur* in different temporal orders; we just suppose that *we* are *informed* of their preferences in different temporal orders.

11. Strictly speaking, this kind of case cannot be handled without introducing intensity of preference, or utilities, which our model is not constructed to accommodate. But I mention it here for the sake of completeness.

12. In the last case (where e_1 occurs) no credits at all are awarded for this permutation. If this seems unsatisfactory, we can introduce an alternative procedure that would assign credits not only to the pivot, but also to members that precede the pivot, until a total of four credits are awarded.

References

Adams, R. 1979. "Primitive Thisness and Primitive Identity." *Journal of Philosophy* 76, 5–26.

Alston, W. 1971. "Varieties of Privileged Access." *American Philosophical Quarterly* 8, 223–241.

Alston, W. 1985. "Concepts of Epistemic Justification." *The Monist* 68, 57–89.

Alston, W. 1986. "Internalism and Externalism in Epistemology." *Philosophical Topics* 14, 179–221.

Alston, W. 1988. "An Internalist Externalism." *Synthese* 74, 265–283.

Anderson, J. 1985. *Cognitive Psychology and Its Implications*, 2nd ed. New York: W. H. Freeman.

Armstrong, D. M. 1968. *A Materialist Theory of the Mind*. New York: Humanities.

Armstrong, D. M. 1973. *Belief, Truth and Knowledge*. Cambridge: Cambridge University Press.

Austin, J. L. 1961. "Other Minds." In *Philosophical Papers*. Oxford: Clarendon Press.

Averill, E. W. 1985. "Color and the Anthropocentric Problem." *Journal of Philosophy* 82, 281–303.

Bacharach, M. 1989. "The Role of 'Verstehen' in Economic Theory." *Ricerche Economiche* 43, 129–150.

Barnes, B. 1977. *Interests and the Growth of Knowledge*. London: Routledge and Kegan Paul.

Barnes, B., and D. Bloor. 1982. "Relativism, Rationalism and the Sociology of Knowledge." In M. Hollis and S. Lukes, eds., *Rationality and Relativism*. Cambridge, MA: MIT Press.

Baron-Cohen, S., A. Leslie, and U. Frith. 1985. "Does the Autistic Child Have a 'Theory of Mind'?" *Cognition* 21, 37–46.

Berlin, B., and P. Kay. 1969. *Basic Color Terms*. Berkeley: University of California Press.

Berwick, R. 1986. "Learning From Positive-Only Examples: The Subset Principle and Three Case Studies." In R. S. Michalski, J. G. Carbonell, and T. M. Mitchell, eds., *Machine Learning: An Artificial Intelligence Approach*, vol. 2. Los Altos, CA: Morgan Kaufmann.

Biederman, I. 1987. "Recognition-By-Components: A Theory of Human Image Understanding." *Psychological Review* 94, 115–147.

Biederman, I. 1990. "Higher-Level Vision." In D. Osherson, S. M. Kosslyn, and J. M. Hollerbach, eds., *Visual Cognition and Action: An Invitation to Cognitive Science*. Cambridge, MA: MIT Press.

Black, M. 1952. "The Identity of Indiscernibles." *Mind* 61, 153–164.

Block, N. 1980. "Troubles with Functionalism." In N. Block, ed., *Readings in Philosophy of Psychology*, vol. I. Cambridge, MA: Harvard University Press.

Bloor, D. 1973. "Wittgenstein and Mannheim on the Sociology of Mathematics." *Studies in History and Philosophy of Science* 4, 173–191.

Bloor, D. 1976. *Knowledge and Social Imagery*. London: Routledge and Kegan Paul.

Boghossian, P., and J. D. Velleman. 1991. "Physicalist Theories of Color." *Philosophical Review* 100, 67–106.

BonJour, L. 1980. "Externalist Theories of Empirical Knowledge." In P. French, T. Uehling, and H. Wettstein, eds., *Midwest Studies in Philosophy*, vol. 5, *Studies in Epistemology*. Minneapolis: University of Minnesota Press.

BonJour, L. 1985. *The Structure of Empirical Knowledge*. Cambridge, MA: Harvard University Press.

Boyd, R., and P. Richerson. 1985. *Culture and the Evolutionary Process*. Chicago: University of Chicago Press.

Burgess-Jackson, K. 1986. "An Epistemic Approach to Legal Relevance." *St. Mary's Law Journal* 18, 463–480.

Campbell, D. 1986. "Science's Social System of Validity-Enhancing Collective Belief Change and the Problems of the Social Sciences." In D. Fiske and R. Shweder, eds., *Metatheory in Social Science*. Chicago: University of Chicago Press.

Cantor, G. N. 1975. "A Critique of Shapin's Social Interpretation of the Edinburgh Phrenology Debate." *Annals of Science* 33, 245–256.

Carnap, R. 1950. *Logical Foundations of Probability*. Chicago: University of Chicago Press.

Cavalli-Sforza, L. L., and M. W. Feldman. 1981. *Cultural Transmission and Evolution*. Princeton: Princeton University Press.

Chandler, H. 1975. "Rigid Designation." *Journal of Philosophy* 72, 362–369.

Cherniak, C. 1986. *Minimal Rationality*. Cambridge, MA: MIT Press. A Bradford Book.

Chisholm, R. 1966. *Theory of Knowledge*. Englewood Cliffs, NJ: Prentice-Hall.

Chisholm, R. 1967. "Identity Through Possible Worlds: Some Questions." *Nous* 1, 1–8.

Chisholm, R. 1977. *Theory of Knowledge*, 2nd ed. Englewood Cliffs, NJ: Prentice-Hall.

Chisholm, R. 1982. *The Foundations of Knowing*. Minneapolis: University of Minnesota Press.

Churchland, P. 1981. "Eliminative Materialism and the Propositional Attitudes." *Journal of Philosophy* 78, 67–90.

Churchland, P. 1989. "Folk Psychology and the Explanation of Human Behavior." In *The Neurocomputational Perspective*. Cambridge, MA: MIT Press. A Bradford Book.

Clark, M. 1963. "Knowledge and Grounds: A Comment on Mr. Gettier's Paper." *Analysis* 24, 46–48.

Cleary, E., ed. 1984. *McCormick on Evidence*, 3rd ed. St. Paul, MN: West Publishing Co.

Coase, R. H. 1977. "Advertising and Free Speech." *Journal of Legal Studies* 6, 1–34.

Code, L. 1987. *Epistemic Responsibility*. Hanover, NH: University Press of New England.

Cohen, L. J. 1977. *The Probable and the Provable*. Oxford: Oxford University Press.

Cohen, L. J. 1981. "Can Human Irrationality Be Experimentally Demonstrated?" *Behavioral and Brain Sciences* 4, 317–331.

Cohen, S. 1984. "Justification and Truth." *Philosophical Studies* 46, 279–295.

Cohen, S. 1986. "Knowledge and Context." *Journal of Philosophy* 83, 574–583.

Cohen, S. 1987. "Knowledge, Context, and Social Standards." *Synthese* 73, 3–26.

Cohen, S. 1988. "How to Be a Fallibilist." In J. Tomberlin, ed., *Philosophical Perspectives*, vol. 2. Atascadero, CA: Ridgeview.

Coleman, J. S. 1969. "Beyond Pareto Optimality." In S. Morgenbesser, P. Suppes, and M. White, eds., *Philosophy, Science, and Method*. New York: St. Martin's Press.

Collingwood, R. 1946. *The Idea of History*. Oxford: Clarendon Press.

Dahl, R. A. 1957. "The Concept of Power." *Behavioral Science* 2, 201–215.

Davidson, D. 1970. "Mental Events." In L. Foster and J. Swanson, eds., *Experience and Theory*. Amherst, MA: University of Massachusetts Press.

Davidson, D. 1980. *Essays on Actions and Events*. Oxford: Oxford University Press.

Davidson, D. 1984. *Inquiries Into Truth and Interpretation*. Oxford: Oxford University Press.

Davidson, D. 1986. "A Coherence Theory of Truth and Knowledge." In E. LePore, ed., *Truth and Interpretation*. Oxford: Basil Blackwell.

Dennett, D. 1971. "Intentional Systems." *Journal of Philosophy* 68, 87–106.

Dennett, D. 1987a. "True Believers." In *The Intentional Stance*. Cambridge, MA: MIT Press.

Dennett, D. 1987b. "Making Sense of Ourselves." In *The Intentional Stance*. Cambridge, MA: MIT Press.

Dennett, D. 1987c. "Evolution, Error, and Intentionality." In *The Intentional Stance*. Cambridge, MA: MIT Press.

Downs, A. 1957. *An Economic Theory of Democracy*. New York: Harper.

Dretske, F. 1970. "Epistemic Operators." *Journal of Philosophy* 67, 1007–1023.

Dretske, F. 1971. "Conclusive Reasons." *Australasian Journal of Philosophy* 49, 1–22.

Dretske, F. 1981a. *Knowledge and the Flow of Information*. Cambridge, MA: MIT Press. A Bradford Book.

Dretske, F. 1981b. "The Pragmatic Dimension of Knowledge." *Philosophical Studies* 40, 363–378.

Dretske, F. 1988. *Explaining Behavior*. Cambridge, MA: MIT Press. A Bradford Book.

Emerson, R. M. 1962. "Power-Dependence Relations." *American Sociological Review* 27, 31–41.

Federal Rules of Evidence for United States Courts and Magistrates. 1989. St. Paul, MN: West Publishing Co.

Feinberg, J. 1986. *Harm to Self*. New York: Oxford University Press.

Feldman, R. 1988. "Having Evidence." In D. Austin, ed., *Philosophical Analysis*. Dordrecht: Kluwer.

Ferguson, T. 1967. *Mathematical Statistics*. New York: Academic Press.

Feyerabend, P. 1975. *Against Method*. London: New Loft Books.

Feyerabend, P. 1978. *Science in a Free Society*. London: Verso.

Field, H. 1977. "Logic, Meaning, and Conceptual Role." *Journal of Philosophy* 74, 379–409.

Fillmore, C. 1982a. "Towards a Descriptive Frameword for Spatial Deixis." In R. J. Jarvella and W. Klein, eds., *Speech, Place, and Action*. London: Wiley.

Fillmore, C. 1982b. "Frame Semantics." In The Linguistic Society of Korea, ed., *Linguistics in the Morning Calm*. Seoul: Hanshin.

Firth, R. 1978. "Are Epistemic Concepts Reducible to Ethical Concepts?" In A. Goldman and J. Kim, eds., *Values and Morals*. Dordrecht: D. Reidel.

Firth, R. 1981. "Epistemic Merit, Intrinsic and Instrumental." In *Proceedings and Addresses of the American Philosophical Association* 55, 5–23.

Fodor, J. 1983. *The Modularity of Mind*. Cambridge, Mass: MIT Press. A Bradford Book.

Fodor, J. 1987. *Psychosemantics*. Cambridge, Mass.: MIT Press. A Bradford Book.

Fodor, J. 1990. *A Theory of Content and Other Essays*. Cambridge, MA: MIT Press. A Bradford Book.

Foley, R. 1985. "What's Wrong with Reliabilism?" *The Monist* 68, 188–202.

Forman, P. 1971. "Weimar Culture, Causality and Quantum Theory, 1918–1927: Adaptation by German Physicists and Mathematicians to a Hostile Intellectual Environment." In R. McCormach, ed., *Historical Studies in the Physical Sciences*, no. 3. Philadelphia: University of Pennsylvania Press.

French, J., Jr. 1956. "A Formal Theory of Social Power." *Psychological Review* 63, 181–194.

Gärdenfors, P., and N. E. Sahlin, eds. 1988. *Decision, Probability, and Utility*. Cambridge: Cambridge University Press.

Gardner, M. 1981. *Science: Good, Bad, and Bogus*. Buffalo: Prometheus Books.

Gettier, E. 1963. "Is Justified True Belief Knowledge?" *Analysis* 23, 121–123.

Giere, R. 1988. *Explaining Science: A Cognitive Approach*. Chicago: University of Chicago Press.

Gillmor, D., and J. Barron. 1984. *Mass Communication Law*, 4th ed. St. Paul, MN: West Publishing Co.

Ginet, C. 1985. "*Contra* Reliabilism." *The Monist* 68, 175–187.

Gleb, G. 1988. "Two Conceptions of Knowledge." Unpublished ms. Rutgers University.

Gleitman, H. 1981. *Psychology.* New York: W. W. Norton.

Gold, E. M. 1967. "Language Identification in the Limit." *Information and Control* 10, 447–474.

Goldhamer, H., and E. Shils. 1939. "Types of Power and Status." *American Journal of Sociology* 45, 171–182.

Goldman, A. I. 1970. *A Theory of Human Action.* Englewood Cliffs, NJ: Prentice-Hall.

Goldman, A: I. 1975. "Innate Knowledge." In S. Stich, ed., *Innate Ideas.* Berkeley: University of California Press.

Goldman, A. I. 1977. "Perceptual Objects." *Synthese* 35, 257–284.

Goldman, A. I. 1980. "The Internalist Conception of Justification." In P. French, T. Uehling, and H. Wettstein, eds., *Midwest Studies in Philosophy V.* Minneapolis: University of Minnesota Press.

Goldman, A. I. 1986. *Epistemology and Cognition.* Cambridge, MA: Harvard University Press.

Goldman, A. I. 1987a. "Cognitive Science and Metaphysics." *Journal of Philosophy* 84, 537–544.

Goldman, A. I. 1987b. "The Cognitive and Social Sides of Epistemology." In A. Fine and P. Machamer, eds., *PSA 1986,* vol. 2. East Lansing, MI: Philosophy of Science Association.

Goldman, A. I. 1991. "Review of S. Stich, *The Fragmentation of Reason.*" *Philosophy and Phenomenological Research* 51, 189–193.

Goldman, A. I., and M. Shaked. 1991. "Results on Inquiry and Truth Possession." *Statistics and Probability Letters* 14.

Good, I. J. 1983. "On the Principle of Total Evidence." *Good Thinking.* Minneapolis: University of Minnesota Press.

Goodman, N. 1955. *Fact, Fiction, and Forecast.* Cambridge, MA: Harvard University Press.

Gordon, R. 1986. "Folk Psychology as Simulation." *Mind and Language* 1, 158–171.

Gordon, R. 1987. *The Structure of Emotions.* Cambridge: Cambridge University Press.

Grandy, R. 1973. "Reference, Meaning, and Belief." *Journal of Philosophy* 70, 439–452.

Grice, H. P. 1961. "The Causal Theory of Perception." *Proceedings of the Aristotelian Society,* supplementary vol. 35.

Gutmann, A. 1987. *Democratic Education.* Princeton: Princeton University Press.

Habermas, J. 1981. *The Theory of Communicative Action,* vol. 1, *Reasons and the Rationalization of Society.* Boston: Beacon Press.

Hagstrom, W. 1965. *The Scientific Community.* New York: Basic Books.

Harman, G. 1973. *Thought.* Princeton: Princeton University Press.

Harman, G. 1977. *The Nature of Morality.* New York: Oxford University Press.

Hardin, C. L. 1988. *Color for Philosophers.* Indianapolis: Hackett Publishing Co.

Hardwig, J. 1985. "Epistemic Dependence." *Journal of Philosophy* 82, 335–349.

Harris, P. 1989. *Children and Emotion.* Oxford: Basil Blackwell.

Harsanyi, J. C. 1962. "Measurement of Social Power, Opportunity Costs, and the Theory of Two-Person Bargaining Games." *Behavioral Science* 7, 67–80.

Hart, H. L: A. 1966. *Law, Liberty, and Morality.* New York: Vintage Books.

Heal, J. 1986. "Replication and Functionalism." In J. Butterfield, ed., *Language, Mind, and Logic.* Cambridge: Cambridge University Press.

Hempel, C. G. 1965. "Inductive Inconsistencies." *Aspects of Scientific Explanation.* New York: The Free Press.

Hendry, J. 1980. "Weimar Culture and Quantum Causality." *History of Science* 18, 155–80.

Hilbert, D. 1987. *Color and Color Perception.* Stanford: Center for the Study of Language and Information.

Hintikka, J. 1969. "On the Logic of Perception." In N. S. Care and R. H. Grimm, eds., *Perception and Personal Identity.* Cleveland, OH: Case Western Reserve.

Hintzman, D. 1986. "'Schema Abstraction' in a Multiple-Trace Memory Model." *Psychological Review* 93, 411–428.

Hirsch, E. 1982. *The Concept of Identity*. New York: Oxford University Press.

Hirsch, E. 1988. "Rules for a Good Language." *Journal of Philosophy* 85, 694–717.

Hobbes, T. 1651. *Leviathan*.

Horwich, P. 1982. *Probability and Evidence*. Cambridge, MA: MIT Press.

Horwich, P. 1987. *Asymmetries in Time*. Cambridge, Mass.: MIT Press. A Bradford Book.

Hotelling, H. 1929. "Stability in Competition." *Economic Journal* 39, 41–57.

Hull, D. 1988. *Science as a Process*. Chicago: University of Chicago Press.

Husserl, E. 1928. *The Phenomenology of Internal Time-Consciousness*. Translated by J. S. Churchill. Bloomington: Indiana University Press.

Jackendoff, R. 1983. *Semantics and Cognition*. Cambridge, MA: MIT Press.

Johnson, C. N. 1988. "Theory of Mind and the Structure of Conscious Experience." In J. Astington, P. Harris, and D. Olson, eds., *Developing Theories of Mind*. Cambridge: Cambridge University Press.

Kahneman, D., and D. Miller. 1986. "Norm Theory: Comparing Reality to Its Alternatives." *Psychological Review* 93, 136–153.

Kahneman, D., and A. Tversky. 1982. "The Simulation Heuristic." In D. Kahneman, P. Slovic, and A. Tversky, eds., *Judgment under Uncertainty*. Cambridge: Cambridge University Press.

Kamp, H. 1985. "Context, Thought and Communication." *Proceedings of the Aristotelian Society* 85, 239–261.

Kitcher, P. 1990. "The Division of Cognitive Labor." *Journal of Philosophy* 87, 5–22.

Klein, P. D. 1971. "A Proposed Definition of Propositional Knowledge." *Journal of Philosophy* 68, 471–482.

Knorr-Cetina, K. 1981. *The Manufacture of Knowledge*. Oxford: Pergamon Press.

Kornblith, H. 1983. "Justified Belief and Epistemically Responsible Action." *Philosophical Review* 92, 33–48.

Kosslyn, S. 1980. *Image and Mind*. Cambridge, MA: Harvard University Press.

Kratzer, A. 1977. "What 'Must' and 'Can' Must and Can Mean." *Linguistics and Philosophy* 1, 337–335.

Kripke, S. 1971. "Identity and Necessity." In M. Munitz, ed., *Identity and Individuation*. New York: New York University Press.

Kripke, S. 1980. *Naming and Necessity*. Cambridge, MA: Harvard University Press.

Kripke, S. 1982. *Wittgenstein on Rules and Private Language*. Cambridge, MA: Harvard University Press.

Kuhn, T. 1970. *The Structure of Scientific Revolutions*, 2nd ed. Chicago: University of Chicago Press.

Lakatos, I. 1976. *Proofs and Refutations*. Cambridge: Cambridge University Press.

Lakoff, G. 1987. *Women, Fire, and Dangerous Things*. Chicago: University of Chicago Press.

Lasswell, H. D., and A. Kaplan. 1950. *Power and Society*. New Haven, CT: Yale University Press.

Latour, B., and S. Woolgar. 1979. *Laboratory Life: The Social Construction of Scientific Facts*. Beverly Hills: Sage Publications.

Laudan, L. 1977. *Progress and Its Problems*. Berkeley: University of California Press.

Laudan, L. 1984. "The Pseudo-Science of Science?" In J. Brown, ed., *Scientific Rationality: The Sociological Turn*. Dordrecht: D. Reidel.

Lehrer, K. 1965. "Knowledge, Truth, and Evidence." *Analysis* 25, 168–175.

Lehrer, K. 1974. *Knowledge*. Oxford: Oxford University Press.

Lehrer, K. 1981. "A Self Profile." In R. Bogdan, ed., *Keith Lehrer*. Dordrecht: D. Reidel.

Lehrer, K., and S. Cohen. 1983. "Justification, Truth, and Coherence." *Synthese* 55, 191–207.

Lehrer, K., and T. Paxson, Jr. 1969. "Knowledge: Undefeated Justified True Belief." *Journal of Philosophy* 66, 225–237.

Lehrer, K., and C. Wagner. 1981. *Rational Consensus in Science and Society*. Dordrecht: D. Reidel.

Leith, E. N., and J. Upatnieks. 1965. "Photography by Laser." *Scientific American* 212, 6, 24.

Lempert, R. 1977. "Modeling Relevance." *Michigan Law Review* 75, 1021–1057.

Lerdahl, F., and R. Jackendoff. 1982. *A Generative Theory of Tonal Music*. Cambridge, MA: MIT Press.

Leslie, A. 1987. "Pretense and Representation: The Origins of 'Theory of Mind'." *Psychological Review* 94, 412–426.

Levi, I. 1985. "Illusions About Uncertainty." *British Journal for the Philosophy of Science* 36, 331–340.

Lewis, D. 1969. *Convention*. Cambridge, MA: Harvard University Press.

Lewis, D. 1972. "Psychophysical and Theoretical Identifications." *Australasian Journal of Philosophy* 61, 249–250.

Lewis, D. 1983a. "Radical Interpretation." In *Philosophical Papers*, vol. 1. New York: Oxford University Press.

Lewis, D. 1983b. "How to Define Theoretical Terms." In *Philosophical Papers*, vol. 1. New York: Oxford University Press.

Lewis, D. 1983c. "New Work for a Theory of Universals." In *Philosophical Papers*, vol. 1. New York: Oxford University Press.

Lewis, D. 1983d. "Scorekeeping in a Language Game." In *Philosophical Papers*, vol. 1. New York: Oxford University Press.

Lewis, D. 1983e. "Counterpart Theory and Quantified Modal Logic." In *Philosophical Papers*, vol. 1. New York: Oxford University Press.

Lewis, D. 1986. *On the Plurality of Worlds*. Oxford: Basil Blackwell.

Loar, B. 1987. "Subjective Intentionality." *Philosophical Topics* 15, 89–124.

Loar, B. 1990. "Phenomenal States." In J. Tomberlin, ed., *Philosophical Perspectives, 4, Action Theory and Philosophy of Mind*. Atascadero, CA: Ridgeview.

Luper-Foy, S. 1985. "The Reliabilist Theory of Rational Belief." *The Monist* 68, 203–225.

Mackie, J. L. 1974. "*De* What *Re* Is *De Re* Modality?" *Journal of Philosophy* 71, 551–561.

March, J. G. 1955. "An Introduction to the Theory and Measurement of Influence." *American Political Science Review* 49, 431–451.

March, J. G. 1966. "The Power of Power." In D. Easton, ed., *Varieties of Political Theory*. Englewood Cliffs, NJ: Prentice-Hall.

McGinn, C. 1977. "Charity, Interpretation, and Belief." *Journal of Philosophy* 74, 521–535.

McGinn, C. 1983. *The Subjective View*. Oxford: Oxford University Press.

McGinn, C. 1986. "Radical Interpretation and Epistemology." In E. LePore, ed., *Truth and Interpretation*. Oxford: Basil Blackwell.

McTaggart, J. M. E. 1908. "The Unreality of Time." *Mind* 17, 457–474.

Medin, D. L., and M. M. Schaffer. 1978. "A Context Theory of Classification Learning." *Psychological Review* 85, 207–238.

Merton, R. 1973. *The Sociology of Science*. Chicago: University of Chicago Press.

Mill, J. S. 1956. *On Liberty*. Indianapolis: Bobbs-Merrill.

Miller, G., and P. Johnson-Laird. 1976. *Language and Perception*. Cambridge, MA: Harvard University Press.

Miller, I. 1984. *Husserl, Perception, and the Awareness of Time*. Cambridge, MA: MIT Press. A Bradford Book.

Millikan, R. 1984. *Language, Thought, and Other Biological Categories*. Cambridge, MA: MIT Press. A Bradford Book.

Mills, C. W. 1959. *The Power Elite*. New York: Oxford University Press.

Montgomery, R. 1987. "Psychologism, Folk Psychology and One's Own Case." *Journal for the Theory of Social Behavior* 17, 195–218.

Morton, A. 1980. *Frames of Mind*. Oxford: Oxford University Press.

Murphy, G., and D. Medin. 1985. "The Role of Theories in Conceptual Coherence." *Psychological Review* 92, 289–316.

Nagel, T. 1979. "Moral Luck." In *Mortal Questions*. Cambridge: Cambridge University Press.

Nagel, T. 1986. *The View from Nowhere*. New York: Oxford University Press.

Newton-Smith, W. H. 1981. *The Rationality of Science*. London: Routledge and Kegan Paul.

Nisbett, R., and L. Ross. 1980. *Human Inference: Strategies and Shortcomings of Social Judgment*. Englewood Cliffs, NJ: Prentice-Hall.

Nozick, R. 1969. "Coercion." In S. Morgenbesser, P. Suppes, and M. White, eds., *Philosophy, Science, and Method*. New York: St. Martin's Press.

Nozick, R. 1981. *Philosophical Explanations*. Cambridge, MA: Harvard University Press.

Osherson, D., M. Stob, and S. Weinstein. 1985. *Systems That Learn*. Cambridge, MA: MIT Press. A Bradford Book.

Parfit, D. 1984. *Reasons and Persons*. Oxford: Oxford University Press.

Pinker, S. 1990. "Language Acquisition." In D. N. Osherson and H. Lasnik, eds., *Language: An Invitation to Cognitive Science*. Cambridge, MA: MIT Press. A Bradford Book.

Plantinga, A. 1986. "Epistemic Justification." *Nous* 20, 1–18.

Plantinga, A. 1988. "Positive Epistemic Status and Proper Function." In J. Tomberlin, ed., *Philosophical Perspectives*, Vol. 2. Atascadero, CA: Ridgeview.

Pollock, J. 1979. "A Plethora of Epistemological Theories." In G. Pappas, ed., *Justification and Knowledge*. Dordrecht: D. Reidel.

Pollock, J. 1984. "Reliability and Justified Belief." *Canadian Journal of Philosophy* 14, 103–114.

Pollock, J. 1986. *Contemporary Theories of Knowledge*. Totowa, NJ: Rowman and Littlefield.

Popper, K. 1972. "Epistemology Without a Knowing Subject." In *Objective Knowledge*. Oxford: Oxford University Press.

Posner, M. I. 1973. *Cognition: An Introduction*. Glenview, IL: Scott, Foresman.

Potter, M. 1990. "Remembering." In D. N. Osherson and E. E. Smith, eds., *Thinking: An Invitation to Cognitive Science*. Cambridge, MA: MIT Press. A Bradford Book.

Putnam, H. 1975. "The Meaning of 'Meaning'." In *Mind, Language and Reality*. Cambridge: Cambridge University Press.

Putnam, H. 1978. *Meaning and the Moral Sciences*. London: Routledge and Kegan Paul.

Putnam, H. 1983. "Why Reason Can't Be Naturalized." In *Realism and Reason*. Cambridge: Cambridge University Press.

Putnam, H. 1988. *Representation and Reality*. Cambridge, MA: MIT Press.

Quine, W. V. 1960. *Word and Object*. Cambridge, MA: MIT Press.

Quine, W. V. 1969a. "Natural Kinds." In *Ontological Relativity and Other Essays*. New York: Columbia University Press.

Quine, W. V. 1969b. "Epistemology Naturalized." In *Ontological Relativity and Other Essays*. New York: Columbia University Press.

Quine, W. V. 1969c. "Propositional Objects." In *Ontological Relativity and Other Essays*. New York: Columbia University Press.

Quine, W. V. 1974. *The Roots of Reference*. La Salle, IL: Open Court.

Quine, W. V. 1981. "Worlds Away." In *Theories and Things*. Cambridge, MA: Harvard University Press.

Quine, W. V., and J. Ullian. 1970. *The Web of Belief*. New York: Random House.

Quinton, A. 1973. *The Nature of Things*. London: Routledge and Kegan Paul.

Raiffa, H. 1968. *Decision Analysis*. Reading, MA: Addison-Wesley.

Rescher, N. 1990. *Cognitive Economy: The Economic Dimension of the Theory of Knowledge.* Pittsburgh: University of Pittsburgh Press.

Riding, A. 1989. *Distant Neighbors: A Portrait of the Mexicans.* New York: Vintage Books.

Ripstein, A. 1987. "Explanation and Empathy." *Review of Metaphysics* 40, 465–482.

Rohrer, D. 1979. *Mass Media, Free Speech, and Advertising.* Dubuque, IO: Kendall/Hunt Publishing Co.

Rorty, R. 1979. *Philosophy and the Mirror of Nature.* Princeton: Princeton University Press.

Rosch, E. 1975. "Cognitive Representations of Semantic Categories." *Journal of Experimental Psychology: General* 104, 192–233

Rosch, E. 1978. "Principles of Categorization." In E. Rosch and B. Lloyd, eds., *Cognition and Categorization.* Hillsdale, NJ: Lawrence Erlbaum.

Roth, E., and E. Shoben. 1983. "The Effect of Context on the Structure of Categories." *Cognitive Psychology* 15, 346–378.

Rudwick, M. 1985. *The Great Devonian Controversy.* Chicago: University of Chicago Press.

Rumelhart, D., P. Smolensky, J. McClelland, and G. Hinton. 1986. "Schemata and Sequential Thought Processes in PDP Models." In J. McClelland, D. Rumelhart, and the PDP Research Group, *Parallel Distributed Processing,* vol. 2. Cambridge, MA: MIT Press. A Bradford Book.

Russell, B. 1921. *The Analysis of Mind.* London: Allen & Unwin.

Russell, B. 1938. *Power: A New Social Analysis.* New York: W. W. Norton.

Salmon, N. 1982. *Reference and Essence.* Princeton: Princeton University Press.

Sarkar, H. 1983. *A Theory of Method.* Berkeley: University of California Press.

Sartorius, R., ed. 1983. *Paternalism.* Minneapolis: University of Minnesota Press.

Saunders, J. T., and N. Champawat. 1964. "Mr. Clark's Definition of 'Knowledge'." *Analysis* 25, 8–9.

Scanlon, T. 1972. "A Theory of Freedom of Expression." *Philosophy and Public Affairs* 1, 204–226.

Scanlon, T. 1983. "Freedom of Expression and Categories of Expression." In D. Copp and S. Wendell, eds., *Pornography and Censorship.* Buffalo: Prometheus Books.

Schaap, D. 1971. "The Ten Most Powerful Men in New York." *New York Magazine* 4, 1, 24–31.

Schelling, T. 1960. *The Strategy of Conflict.* Cambridge, MA: Harvard University Press.

Schiffer, S. 1987. *Remnants of Meaning.* Cambridge, MA: MIT Press. A Bradford Book.

Sellars, W. 1963. "Philosophy and the Scientific Image of Man." In *Science, Perception and Reality.* London: Routledge and Kegan Paul.

Shapin, S. 1975. "Phrenological Knowledge and the Social Structure of Early Nineteenth-Century Edinburgh." *Annals of Science* 32, 219–243.

Shapin, S. 1982. "History of Science and Its Sociological Reconstructions." *History of Science* 20, 157–211.

Shapley, L. S., and B. Grofman. 1984. "Optimizing Group Judgmental Accuracy in the Presence of Interdependence." *Public Choice* 43, 329–343.

Shapley, L. S., and M. Shubik. 1954. "A Method for Evaluating the Distribution of Power in a Committee System." *American Political Science Review* 48, 787–792.

Shepard, R., and L. Cooper. 1982. *Mental Images and Their Transformations.* Cambridge, MA: MIT Press. A Bradford Book.

Shoemaker, S. 1979. "Identity, Properties, and Causality." In P. French, T. Uehling, and H. Wettstein, eds., *Midwest Studies in Philosophy,* vol. 4. Minneapolis: University of Minnesota Press.

Sidelle, A. 1989. *Necessity, Essence, and Individuation.* Ithaca, NY: Cornell University Press.

Simon, H. 1953. "Notes on the Observation and Measurement of Political Power." *Journal of Politics* 15, 500–516.

Skyrms, B. 1967. "The Explication of 'X knows that p'." *Journal of Philosophy* 64, 373–389.

Skyrms, B. 1980. "Higher Order Degrees of Belief." In D. Mellor, ed., *Prospects for Pragmatism*. Cambridge: Cambridge University Press.

Slovic, P. 1985. "Violations of Dominance in Rated Attractiveness of Playing Bets." *Decision Research Report*, Eugene, OR.

Smart, J. J. C. 1975. "On Some Criticisms of a Physicalist Theory of Colors." In C. Cheng, ed., *Philosophical Aspects of the Mind-Body Problem*. Honolulu: University Press of Hawaii.

Smith, E. E. 1988. "Concepts and Thought." In R. Sternberg and E. E. Smith, eds., *The Psychology of Human Thought*. Cambridge: Cambridge University Press.

Smith, E. E. 1990. "Categorization." In D. Osherson and E. Smith, eds., *Thinking: An Invitation to Cognitive Science*. Cambridge, MA: MIT Press. A Bradford Book.

Smith, E. E., and M. Medin. 1981. *Categories and Concepts*. Cambridge, MA: Harvard University Press.

Smith, H. 1983. "Culpable Ignorance." *Philosophical Review* 92, 543–572.

Smith, H. 1988. "Making Moral Decisions." *Nous* 21, 89–108.

Smith, H. 1989. "Two-Tier Moral Codes." *Social Philosophy and Policy* 7, 112–132.

Sosa, E. 1964. "The Analysis of 'Knowledge that p'." *Analysis* 25, 1–3.

Sosa, E. 1974. "How Do You Know?" *American Philosophical Quarterly* 11, 113–122.

Sosa, E. 1985. "Knowledge and Intellectual Virtue." *The Monist* 68, 226–263.

Sosa, E. 1986. "On Knowledge and Context." *Journal of Philosophy* 83, 584–585.

Sosa, E. 1988. "Beyond Scepticism, to the Best of our Knowledge." *Mind* 97, 153–188.

Sosa, E. 1991. "Reliabilism and Intellectual Virtue." In *Knowledge in Perspective*. Cambridge: Cambridge University Press.

Spelke, E. 1985. "Perception of Unity, Persistence, and Identity: Thoughts on Infants' Conception of Objects." In J. Mehler, ed., *Neonate Cognition*. Hillsdale, NJ: Lawrence Erlbaum.

Sperber, D., and D. Wilson. 1986. *Relevance*. Oxford: Basil Blackwell.

Stalnaker, R. 1968. "A Theory of Conditionals." In N. Rescher, ed., *Studies in Logical Theory*. American Philosophical Quarterly Monograph Series. Oxford: Basil Blackwell.

Stalnaker, R. 1972. "Pragmatics." In D. Davidson and G. Harman, eds., *Semantics of Natural Language*. Boston: D. Reidel.

Steward, H. 1990. "Identity Statements and the Necessary A Posteriori." *Journal of Philosophy* 87, 385–398.

Stich, S. 1983. *From Folk Psychology to Cognitive Science*. Cambridge, MA: MIT Press. A Bradford Book.

Stich, S. 1985. "Could Man Be an Irrational Animal?" In H. Kornblith, ed., *Naturalizing Epistemology*. Cambridge, MA: MIT Press. A Bradford Book.

Stich, S. 1990. *The Fragmentation of Reason*. Cambridge, MA: MIT Press. A Bradford Book.

Stich, S., and R. Nisbett. 1980. "Justification and the Psychology of Human Reasoning." *Philosophy of Science* 47, 188–202.

Stine, G. 1976. "Skepticism, Relevant Alternatives and Deductive Closure." *Philosophical Studies* 29, 249–260.

Strawson, P. F. 1959. *Individuals*. London: Methuen.

Sturgeon, N. 1985. "Moral Explanations." In D. Copp and D. Zimmerman, eds., *Morality, Reason and Truth*. Totowa, NJ: Rowman and Allanheld.

Swain, M. 1974. "Epistemic Defeasibility." *American Philosophical Quarterly* 11, 15–25.

Talbott, W. 1990. *The Reliability of the Cognitive Mechanism: A Mechanist Account of Empirical Justification*. New York: Garland Publishing.

Tawney, R. H. 1931. *Equality*. New York: Harcourt, Brace.

Thagard, P., and R. Nisbett. 1983. "Rationality and Charity." *Philosophy of Science* 50, 250–267

Thaler, R. 1980. "Towards a Positive Theory of Consumer Choice." *Journal of Economic Behavior and Organization* 1, 39–60.

Thibaut, J. W., and H. H. Kelley. 1959. *The Social Psychology of Groups*. New York: Wiley and Sons.

Tribe, L. 1971. "Trial by Mathematics: Precision and Ritual in the Legal Process." *Harvard Law Review* 84, 1329–1393.

Tullock, G. 1966. *The Organization of Inquiry*. Durham, NC: Duke University Press.

Tversky, A. 1977. "Features of Similarity." *Psychological Review* 84, 327–352.

Tversky, A., and D. Kahneman. 1973. "Availability: A Heuristic for Judging Frequency and Probability." *Cognitive Psychology* 5, 207–232.

Tversky, A., and D. Kahneman. 1981. "The Framing of Decisions and the Psychology of Choice." *Science* 211, 453–458.

Tversky, A., and D. Kahneman. 1983. "Extensional Versus Intuitive Reasoning: The Conjunction Fallacy in Probability Judgment." *Psychological Review* 90, 293–315.

Unger, P. 1968. "An Analysis of Factual Knowledge." *Journal of Philosophy* 65, 157–170.

VanDeVeer, D. 1986. *Paternalistic Intervention*. Princeton: Princeton University Press.

Van Fraassen, B. 1980. *The Scientific Image*. Oxford: Oxford University Press.

Weber, M. 1947. *The Theory of Social and Economic Organization*. New York: Oxford University Press.

Welbourne, M. 1981. "The Community of Knowledge." *Philosophical Quarterly* 31, 302–314.

Wertheimer, M. 1938. "Laws of Organization in Perceptual Forms." In W. Ellis, ed., *A Source Book of Gestalt Psychology*. London: Routledge and Kegan Paul.

Whitley, R. 1984. *The Intellectual and Social Organization of the Sciences*. Oxford: Oxford University Press.

Wiggins, D. 1980. *Sameness and Substance*. Cambridge, MA: Harvard University Press.

Williams, B. 1973. "The Self and the Future." In *Problems of the Self*. Cambridge: Cambridge University Press.

Williams, B. 1976. "Moral Luck." *Proceedings of the Aristotelian Society*, supplementary vol. 1.

Wimmer, H., and J. Perner. 1983. "Beliefs About Beliefs: Representation and Constraining Function of Wrong Beliefs in Young Children's Understanding of Deception." *Cognition* 13, 103–128.

Ziff, P. 1960. *Semantic Analysis*. Ithaca, NY: Cornell University Press.

Ziman, J. 1978. *Reliable Knowledge*. Cambridge: Cambridge University Press.

Index

Action, 18, 261
Adams, Robert, 60–61
AI. *See* Artificial intelligence
Albritton, Rogers, 264
Alston, William, 164
Analogy, argument from, 29–30
Analysis, philosophical, 143–153
Anti-universalism, 185–186, 200–201
Appeal to authority. *See* Expertism
Applicability, problem of, 203–205
Arationality assumption, 180
Armstrong, David, 91
Artificial intelligence, 2. *See also*
  Connectionism; PDP
Autism, 23
Availability heuristic, 173–174

Bacharach, Michael, 5
Barnes, Barry, 180, 185, 200
Baron-Cohen, Simon, 22–23
Basic level of categories, 27
Bayes's theorem, 212–214, 230, 233,
  235–237, 245
Behaviorism, 3
Berkeley, George, 42
Berlin, Brent, 45
Berwick, Robert, 169
Biederman, Irving, 166–168
Black, Max, 60
Block, Ned, 31
Bloor, David, 180, 182, 185, 200
BonJour, Laurence, 158–159, 161
Boyd, Robert, 199
Bush, George, 257, 289

Campbell, Donald, 193
Cantor, G. N., 182
Cartesian
  demon, 88–89, 134–138, 152, 158, 163

epistemology, 2, 101–102, 105, 117–118
Categorial conservatism, 160–161
Causal theory
  of inference, 73
  of justified belief, 112–113
  of knowing, 65, 69–83, 85, 118
  of memory, 71–72
  of perception, 70–71
Causation, 46, 69–82, 85, 87. *See also*
  Causal theory of knowing; Perception,
  and causation
Champawat, Narayan, 77–78
Chandler, Hugh, 41
Charity theory, 3, 10–14, 16, 20, 30 (*see*
  also Rationality theory of interpretation)
Cherniak, Christopher, 13
Children, interpretational ability of, 22–23
Chisholm, Roderick, 56, 60, 108–109,
  118, 130
Chomsky, Noam, 26, 46
Churchland, Paul, 24–25, 30
Clark, Michael, 69, 74–75, 77–78
Cleary, E., 211
Closure principle. *See* Knowledge, and
  closure
Code, L., 169
Cognitive
  architecture, 29, 36–37, 46
  haecceitism (*see* Haecceitism)
  virtues (*see* Virtues, intellectual)
Cognitive science and philosophy, 2–4
Cohen, L. J., 13
Cohen, Stewart, 145
Coherence, probabilistic, 12–13
Coherence theory, 117–118, 186–187
Color, 43–45, 49–52, 61, 63, 161
Commercial advertising, 216, 221
Concepts, psychology of, 150–153,
  157–158